Points of View

Readings in American Government and Politics

SEVENTH EDITION

Edited by

Robert E. DiClerico
West Virginia University

Allan S. Hammock
West Virginia University

Boston, Massachusetts   Burr Ridge, Illinois
Dubuque, Iowa   Madison, Wisconsin   New York, New York
San Francisco, California   St. Louis, Missouri

McGraw-Hill

A Division of The **McGraw·Hill** *Companies*

POINTS OF VIEW:
Readings in American Government and Politics, Seventh Edition

This book is printed on acid-free paper.

1 2 3 4 5 6 7 8 9 0   DOC/DOC   9 0 9 8 7

ISBN 0-07-016870-9

Editorial director: *Jane Vaicunas*
Sponsoring editor: *Lyn Uhl*
Developmental editor: *Monica Freedman*
Marketing manager: *Annie Mitchell*
Project manager: *Amy Hill*
Production supervisor: *Melonie Salvati*
Designer: *Larry J. Cope*
Compositor: *Shepherd Inc.*
Typeface: *10/12 Times Roman*
Printer: *R. R. Donnelley & Sons Company*

Library of Congress Cataloging-in-Publication Data

Points of view : readings in American government and politics /
    [edited by] Robert E. DiClerico, Allan S. Hammock.—7th ed.
        p.   cm.
    Includes bibliographical references.
    ISBN   0-07-016870-9 (acid-free paper)
    I. United States—Politics and government.   I. DiClerico, Robert
E. II. Hammock, Allan S., 1938–
JK21.P59   1998
320.973—dc21   97-30864

http://www.mhhe.com

About the Editors

ROBERT E. DICLERICO is Eberly Professor of Political Science at West Virginia University. An Indiana University (Bloomington, Ind.) Ph.D. and a Danforth fellow, he is author of *The American President,* 4th edition (1995); co-author, *Few Are Chosen: Problems in Presidential Selection* (1984); and editor, *Analyzing the Presidency* (1985).

ALLAN S. HAMMOCK is an Associate Professor and Chairman of the Department of Political Science at West Virginia University. He received his Ph.D. from the University of Virginia and is the co-author of *West Virginia Politics and Government* (1996). He currently serves as chairman of the West Virginia Election Commission.

Contents

PREFACE   *viii*

A NOTE TO THE INSTRUCTOR   *ix*

Chapter 1   Democracy   1

Howard Zinn: *How Democratic Is America?*   2

Sidney Hook: *How Democratic Is America? A Response
to Howard Zinn*   14

Chapter 2   The Constitution   27

Charles A. Beard: *An Economic Interpretation of the Constitution
of the United States*   28

Robert E. Brown: *Charles Beard and the Constitution:
A Critical Analysis*   33

Chapter 3   Federalism   39

U.S. Senator Spencer Abraham (R–Michigan): *Unfunded Mandates:
The Negative Effects*   40

U.S. Representative George Miller (D–California): *Unfunded Mandates:
Laws that Bind Us Together*   43

Chapter 4   Public Opinion   47

Duane Elgin: *Revitalizing Democracy through Electronic
Town Meetings*   48

Norman Ornstein and Amy Schenkenberg: *The Promise and Perils
of Cyberdemocracy*   54

Chapter 5   Voting   59

    Curtis B. Gans: *So Much at Stake. So Many Voters. Why Didn't They Turn Out?*   60

    Austin Ranney: *Nonvoting Is Not a Social Disease*   64

Chapter 6   Campaigns and the Media   71

    Darrell M. West: *Advertising and Democratic Elections: What Can Be Done?*   72

    Stephen Bates and Edwin Diamond: *Damned Spots: A Defense of Thirty-Second Campaign Ads*   79

Chapter 7   Elections   83

  Campaign Finance   83

    Milton S. Gwirtzman: *The Supreme Problem*   84

    Larry J. Sabato and Glenn R. Simpson: *Campaign Finance Reform: Phony Cures versus a Workable Solution*   87

  The Electoral College   92

    Lawrence D. Longley: *The Electoral College Should Be Abolished*   93

    Robert Weissberg: *In Defense of the Electoral College*   100

Chapter 8   Political Parties   105

    Theodore J. Lowi: *The Party Crasher: The Need for a Third Party*   106

    Paul S. Herrnson: *Fizzle or Crash and Burn? Ross Perot's Challenge to the Two-Party System*   110

Chapter 9   Interest Groups   117

    Philip M. Stern: *Still the Best Congress Money Can Buy: A PAC Primer*   118

    Larry J. Sabato: *The Misplaced Obsession with PACs*   127

Chapter 10   Congress   135

  Representation   135

    General Assembly of Virginia: *The Legislator as Delegate*   136

John F. Kennedy: *The Legislator as Trustee*   140

George B. Galloway: *The Legislator as Politico*   143

Congressional Reform: Term Limitation   147

George F. Will: *Congress, Term Limits and the Recovery of Deliberative Democracy*   148

Norman Ornstein: *Term Limits Would Just Make Things Worse*   153

Chapter 11   The Presidency   157

Michael Lind: *The Out-of-Control Presidency*   158

R. Gordon Hoxie: *The Not-So-Imperial Presidency*   166

Chapter 12   The President and Congress   173

James L. Sundquist: *A Government Divided against Itself*   174

David R. Mayhew: *Divided Party Control: Does It Make a Difference?*   178

David S. Broder: *Gridlock Begins at Home: How We Build Political Failure into the System*   183

Chapter 13   Bureaucracy   187

Edward Meadows: *The Government Is the Worst-Run Enterprise in America*   188

Steven Kelman: *How Much Waste in Government? An Alternate View*   196

Chapter 14   The Judiciary   207

The Supreme Court   207

Edwin Meese III: *A Jurisprudence of Original Intention*   208

Irving R. Kaufman: *What Did the Founding Fathers Intend?*   214

Crime and the Courts   220

Bernard Gavzer: *"We're in the Fight of Our Lives"*   221

John C. Kilwein: *Just Make It a Fair Fight*   225

Chapter 15   Civil Liberties   235

  Free Speech   235

     Chester E. Finn Jr.: *The Campus: "An Island of Repression in a Sea
     of Freedom"*   236

     Charles R. Lawrence III: *The Justification for Curbing Racist Speech
     on Campus*   241

  Pornography   245

     Ernest van den Haag: *Pornography and Censorship*   246

     Geoffrey R. Stone: *Repeating Past Mistakes: The Commission
     on Obscenity and Pornography*   252

Chapter 16   Civil Rights   257

  Affirmative Action   257

     Terry Eastland: *Ending Affirmative Action: The Case for
     Colorblind Justice*   258

     Barbara R. Bergmann: *In Defense of Affirmative Action*   266

  Abortion   276

     Susan R. Estrich and Kathleen M. Sullivan: *Abortion Politics:
     The Case for the Right to Privacy*   277

     James Bopp Jr. and Richard E. Coleson: *Abortion on Demand Has No
     Constitutional or Moral Justification*   288

Preface

Reflecting both the press of events and editorial judgments, the changes made for the seventh edition of *Points of View* have been extensive. We have added two new topics. Under the general topic of Elections, in Chapter 7, we have included a new topic on "Campaign Finance," and to Chapter 14 on the Judiciary we have added a topic on "Crime and the Courts." In addition to these changes, the chapters on Federalism, Public Opinion, the Presidency, and the Civil Rights subtopic "Affirmative Action" now contain completely new selections. Finally, of the articles we have retained from the previous edition, some have been updated, including Howard Zinn's essay on the meaning of democracy, Robert Weissberg's defense of the Electoral College, and Paul Herrnson's analysis of third parties in the American context.

The basic goals of the book remain the same—namely, to provide students with a manageable number of selections that present readable, succinct, thoughtful, and diverse perspectives across a broad range of issues related to American government.

We would like to extend our thanks to a number of individuals who made valuable contributions to this project. A special debt of gratitude is owed to Amy Hill who had primary editorial responsibility for this latest edition and whose keen eye for detail was instrumental in improving the style and content of the final manuscript.

We would also like to express our appreciation to the sponsoring editor Lyn Uhl, to the developmental editor Monica Freedman, who had overall responsibility for coordinating this latest revision, and to Elizabeth Neimann and assistant editor Katrina Redmond, all of whom greatly facilitated the timely completion of this project.

In the course of revising and updating this manuscript, we repeatedly called upon the typing skills of administrative associate Lee Ann Musick, who cheerfully reproduced manuscripts with unfailing accuracy and under the pressure of very tight deadlines.

Finally, we would like to express our deep appreciation to the following academicians who carefully read the previous edition of *Points of View* and offered very constructive recommendations for this, the seventh edition: Professor John Clark, University of Georgia; Professor Jeanne Jensen, Augusta State University; and Professor John Gilmour, College of William and Mary.

Robert E. DiClerico
Allan S. Hammock
Morgantown, West Virginia
June 1997

A Note to the Instructor

For some years now, both of us have jointly taught the introductory course to American government. Each year we perused the crop of existing readers, and while we adopted several different readers over this period, we were not wholly satisfied with any of them. It is our feeling that many of the readers currently on the market suffer from one or more of the following deficiencies: (1) Some contain selections which are difficult for students to comprehend because of the sophistication of the argument, the manner of expression, or both. (2) In many instances, readers do not cover all of the topics typically treated in an introductory American government course. (3) In choosing selections for a given topic, editors do not always show sufficient concern for how—or whether—one article under a topic relates to other articles under the same topic. (4) Most readers contain too many selections for each topic—indeed, in several cases the number of selections for some topics exceeds ten. Readers are nearly always used in conjunction with a textbook. Thus, to ask a student to read a lengthy chapter—jammed with facts—from a textbook and then to read anywhere from five to ten selections on the same topic from a reader is to demand that students read more than they can reasonably absorb in a meaningful way. Of course, an instructor need not assign all the selections under a given topic. At the same time, however, this approach justifiably disgruntles students who, after purchasing a reader, discover that they may only be asked to read one-half or two-thirds of it.

Instead of continuing to complain about what we considered to be the limitations of existing American government readers, we decided to try our own hand at putting one together. In doing so, we were guided by the following considerations:

Readability

Quite obviously, students will not read dull, difficult articles. As well as having something important to say, we feel that each of the articles in *Points of View* is clearly written, well organized, and free of needless jargon.

Comprehensiveness

The sixteen topics included in *Points of View* constitute all the major areas of concern that are typically treated in the standard introductory course to American government.

Economy of Selections

We decided, in most instances, to limit the number of selections to two per topic, although we did include four selections for some topics that we deemed especially important. The limitation on selections will maximize the possibility that students will read them. It has been our experience that when students are assigned four, five, or more selections under a given topic, they simply do not read them all. In addition, by limiting the selections for each topic, there is a greater likelihood that students will be able to associate an argument with the author who made it.

Juxtaposition

The two selections for each topic will take *opposing* or *different* points of view on some aspect of a given topic. This approach was chosen for three reasons. First, we believe that student interest will be enhanced by playing one article off against the other. Thus, the "interest" quality of a given article will derive not only from its own content, but also from its juxtaposition with the other article. Second, we think it is important to sensitize students to the fact that one's perspective on an issue will depend upon the values that he or she brings to it. Third, by having both selections focus on a particular issue related to a given topic, the student will have a greater depth of understanding about that issue. We think this is preferable to having five or six selections under a topic, with each selection focusing on a different aspect, and with the result that the student ultimately is exposed to "a little of this and a little of that"—that is, if the student even bothers to read all five or six selections.

    While the readers currently available take into account one or, in some instances, several of the considerations identified above, we believe that the uniqueness of *Points of View* lies in the fact that it has sought to incorporate *all* of them.

Robert E. DiClerico
Allan S. Hammock

1
DEMOCRACY

Any assessment of a society's democratic character will be fundamentally determined by what the observer chooses to use as a definition of democracy. While the concept of democracy has commanded the attention of political thinkers for centuries, the following selections by Howard Zinn and Sidney Hook serve to demonstrate that there continues to be considerable disagreement over its meaning. Each of them has scanned the American scene and reached different conclusions regarding the democratic character of our society. This difference of opinion is explained primarily by the fact that each approaches his evaluation with a different conception of what democracy is.

For Zinn, the definition of democracy includes not only criteria which bear upon how decisions get made, but also upon what results *from such decisions. Specifically, he argues that such results must lead to a certain level of human welfare within a society. In applying these criteria of human welfare to the United States, he concludes that we fall short of the mark in several areas.*

Although Sidney Hook is willing to acknowledge that democracy may indeed function more smoothly in societies where the conditions of human welfare are high, he insists that these conditions do not themselves constitute the definition of democracy. Rather, he maintains that democracy is a process—a way of making decisions. Whether such decisions lead to the conditions of human welfare that Zinn prescribes is irrelevant. The crucial test, according to Hook, is whether or not the people have the right, by majority rule, to make choices about the quality of their lives—whatever those choices may be.

How Democratic Is America?

Howard Zinn

To give a sensible answer to the question "How democratic is America?" I find it necessary to make three clarifying preliminary statements. First, I want to define "democracy," not conclusively, but operationally, so we can know what we are arguing about or at least what I am talking about. Second, I want to state what my criteria are for measuring the "how" in the question. And third, I think it necessary to issue a warning about how a certain source of bias (although not the only source) is likely to distort our judgments.

Our definition is crucial. This becomes clear if we note how relatively easy is the answer to our question when we define democracy as a set of formal institutions and let it go at that. If we describe as "democratic" a country that has a representative system of government, with universal suffrage, a bill of rights, and party competition for office, it becomes easy to answer the question "how" with the enthusiastic reply, "Very!" . . .

I propose a set of criteria for the description "democratic" which goes beyond formal political institutions, to the quality of life in the society (economic, social, psychological), beyond majority rule to a concern for minorities, and beyond national boundaries to a global view of what is meant by "the people," in that rough, but essentially correct view of democracy as "government of, by, and for the people."

Let me list these criteria quickly, because I will go on to discuss them in some detail later:

1. To what extent can various people in the society participate in those decisions which affect their lives: decisions in the political process and decisions in the economic structure?
2. As a corollary of the above: do people have equal access to the information which they need to make important decisions?
3. Are the members of the society equally protected on matters of life and death—in the most literal sense of that phrase?
4. Is there equality before the law: police, courts, the judicial process—as well as equality *with* the law-enforcing institutions, so as to safeguard equally everyone's person, and his freedom from interference by others, and by the government?
5. Is there equality in the distribution of available resources: those economic goods necessary for health, life, recreation, leisure, growth?
6. Is there equal access to education, to knowledge and training, so as to enable persons in the society to live their lives as fully as possible, to enlarge their range of possibilities?

Howard Zinn is professor emeritus of political science at Boston University. This essay was originally published in Robert A. Goldwin, ed., How Democratic Is America? *pp. 39–60 (Chicago, Rand McNally, 1971). The author revised and updated the original for* Points of View *in 1985 and again in 1997.*

7. Is there freedom of expression on all matters, and equally for all, to communicate with other members of the society?
8. Is there freedom for individuality in private life, in sexual relations, family relations, the right of privacy?
9. To minimize regulation: do education and the culture in general foster a spirit of cooperation and amity to sustain the above conditions?
10. As a final safety feature: is there opportunity to protest, to disobey the laws, when the foregoing objectives are being lost—as a way of restoring them? . . .

Two historical facts support my enlarged definition of democracy. One is that the industrialized Western societies have outgrown the original notions which accompanied their early development: that constitutional and procedural tests sufficed for the "democracy" that overthrew the old order; that democracy was quite adequately fulfilled by the Bill of Rights in England at the time of the Glorious Revolution, the Constitution of the United States, and the declaration of the Rights of Man in France. It came to be acknowledged that the rhetoric of these revolutions was not matched by their real achievements. In other words, the limitations of that "democracy" led to the reformist and radical movements that grew up in the West in the middle and late nineteenth century. The other historical note is that the new revolutions in our century, in Africa, Asia, Latin America, while rejecting either in whole or in part the earlier revolutions, profess a similar democratic aim, but with an even broader rhetoric. . . .

My second preliminary point is on standards. By this I mean that we can judge in several ways the fulfillment of these ten criteria I have listed. We can measure the present against the past, so that if we find that in 1997 we are doing better in these matters than we were doing in 1860 or 1910, the society will get a good grade for its "democracy." I would adjure such an approach because it supports complacency. With such a standard, Russians in 1910 could point with pride to how much progress they had made toward parliamentary democracy; as Russians in 1985 could point to their post-Stalin progress away from the gulag; as Americans could point in 1939 to how far they had come toward solving the problem of economic equality; as Americans in the South could point in 1950 to the progress of the southern African-American. Indeed, the American government has given military aid to brutal regimes in Latin America on the ground that a decrease in the murders by semiofficial death squads is a sign of progress.

Or, we could measure our democracy against other places in the world. Given the high incidence of tyranny in the world, polarization of wealth, and lack of freedom of expression, the United States, even with very serious defects, could declare itself successful. Again, the result is to let us all off easily; some of our most enthusiastic self-congratulation is based on such a standard.

On the other hand, we could measure our democracy against an ideal (even if admittedly unachievable) standard. I would argue for such an approach, because, in what may seem to some a paradox, the ideal standard is the pragmatic one; it affects what we *do*. To grade a student on the basis of an improvement over past performance is justifiable if the intention is to encourage someone discouraged about his ability. But if he is rather pompous about his superiority in relation to other students (and I suggest this is frequently true of Americans evaluating American "democracy"), and if in addition he is a medical student about to graduate into a world ridden with disease, it would be best to judge him by an ideal standard. That might spur him to an improvement fast enough to save lives. . . .

My third preliminary point is a caution based on the obvious fact that we make our appraisals through the prism of our own status in society. This is particularly important in assessing democracy, because if "democracy" refers to the condition of masses of people, and if we as the assessors belong to a number of elites, we will tend (and I am not declaring an inevitability, just warning of a tendency) to see the present situation in America more benignly than it deserves. To be more specific, if democracy requires a keen awareness of the condition of black people, of poor people, of young people, of that majority of the world who are not American—and we are white, prosperous, beyond draft age, and American—then we have a number of pressures tending to dull our sense of inequity. We are, if not doomed to err, likely to err on the side of complacency—and we should try to take this into account in making our judgments.

1. PARTICIPATION IN DECISIONS

We need to recognize first, that whatever decisions are made politically are made by representatives of one sort or another: state legislators, congressmen, senators, and other elected officials, governors and presidents; also by those appointed by elected officials, like Supreme Court justices. These are important decisions, affecting our lives, liberties, and ability to pursue happiness. Congress and the president decide on the tax structure, which affects the distribution of resources. They decide how to spend the monies received; whether or not we go to war; who serves in the armed forces; what behavior is considered a crime; which crimes are prosecuted and which are not. They decide what limitations there should be on our travel, or on our right to speak freely. They decide on the availability of education and health services.

If representation by its very nature is undemocratic, as I would argue, this is an important fact for our evaluation. Representative government is *closer* to democracy than monarchy, and for this reason it has been hailed as one of the great political advances of modern times; yet, it is only a step in the direction of democracy, at its best. It has certain inherent flaws—pointed out by Rousseau in the eighteenth century, Victor Considerant in the nineteenth century, Robert Michels in the beginning of the twentieth century, Hannah Arendt in our own time. No representative can adequately represent another's needs; the representative tends to become a member of a special elite; he has privileges which weaken his sense of concern at others' grievances; the passions of the troubled lose force (as Madison noted in *The Federalist 10*) as they are filtered through the representative system; the elected official develops an expertise which tends toward its own perpetuation. Leaders develop what Michels called "a mutual insurance contract" against the rest of society. . . .

If only radicals pointed to the inadequacy of the political processes in the United States, we might be suspicious. But established political scientists of a moderate bent talk quite bluntly of the limitations of the voting system in the United States. Robert Dahl, in *A Preface to Democratic Theory,* drawing on the voting studies of American political scientists, concludes that "political activity, at least in the United States, is positively associated to a significant extent with such variables as income, socio-economic status, and education." He says:

> By their propensity for political passivity the poor and uneducated disfranchise themselves . . . . Since they also have less access than the wealthy to the organizational, financial, and propaganda resources that weigh so heavily in campaigns, elections, legislative, and executive decisions, anything like equal control over government policy is triply barred to the members of Madison's unpropertied masses. They are barred by their relatively greater inactivity, by their relatively limited access to resources, and by Madison's nicely contrived system of constitutional checks.[1]

Dahl thinks that our society is essentially democratic, but this is because he expects very little. (His book was written in the 1950s, when lack of commotion in the society might well have persuaded him that no one else expected much more than he did.) Even if democracy were to be superficially defined as "majority rule," the United States would not fulfill that, according to Dahl, who says that "on matters of specific policy, the majority rarely rules."[2] After noting that "the election is the critical technique for insuring that governmental leaders will be relatively responsive to nonleaders," he goes on to say that "it is important to notice how little a national election tells us about the preferences of majorities. Strictly speaking, all an election reveals is the first preferences of some citizens among the candidates standing for office."[3] About 45 percent of the potential voters in national elections, and about 60 percent of the voters in local elections do not vote, and this cannot be attributed, Dahl says, simply to indifference. And if, as Dahl points out, "in no large nation state can elections tell us much about the preferences of majorities and minorities," this is "even more true of the interelection period." . . .

Dahl goes on to assert that the election process and interelection activity "are crucial processes for insuring that political leaders will be *somewhat* responsive to the preferences of *some* ordinary citizens."[4] I submit (the emphasized words are mine) that if an admirer of democracy in America can say no more than this, democracy is not doing very well.

Dahl tells us the election process is one of "two fundamental methods of social control which, operating together, make governmental leaders so responsive to nonleaders that the distinction between democracy and dictatorship still makes sense." Since his description of the election process leaves that dubious, let's look at his second requirement for distinguishing democracy: "The other method of social control is continuous political competition among individuals, parties, or both." What it comes down to is "not minority rule but minorities rule."[5]

If it turns out that this—like the election process—also has little democratic content, we will not be left with very much difference—by Dahl's own admission—between "dictatorship" and the "democracy" practiced in the United States. Indeed, there is much evidence on this: the lack of democracy within the major political parties, the vastly disproportionate influence of wealthy groups over poorer ones. What anti-smoking consumer group in the election year of 1996 could match the five million dollars donated to the Republican Party by the tobacco interests? What ordinary citizen could have the access to President Bill Clinton that a group of bankers had in May of that election year when they were invited to the White House?[6] All of this, and more, supports the idea of a "decline of American pluralism" that Henry Kariel has written about. What Dahl's democracy comes down to is "the steady appeasement of relatively small groups."[7] If these relatively small groups turn out to be the aircraft industry far more than the aged, the space industry far more than the poor, the Pentagon far more than the college youth—what is left of democracy?

Sometimes the elitism of decision-making is defended (by Dahl and by others) on the ground that the elite is enacting decisions passively supported by the mass, whose tolerance is proof of an underlying consensus in society. But Murray Levin's studies in *The Alienated Voter* indicate how much nonparticipation in elections is a result of hopelessness rather than approval. And Robert Wiebe, a historian at Northwestern University, talks of "consensus" becoming a "new stereotype." He approaches the question historically.

> Industrialization arrived so peacefully not because all Americans secretly shared the same values or implicitly willed its success but because its millions of bitter enemies lacked the mentality and the means to organize an effective counterattack.[8]

Wiebe's point is that the passivity of most Americans in the face of elitist decision-making has not been due to acquiescence but to the lack of resources for effective combat, as well as a gulf so wide between the haves and have-nots that there was no ground on which to dispute. Americans neither revolted violently nor reacted at the polls; instead they were subservient, or else worked out their hostilities in personal ways. . . .

Presidential nominations and elections are more democratic than monarchical rule or the procedures of totalitarian states, but they are far from some reasonable expectation of democracy. The two major parties have a monopoly of presidential power, taking turns in the White House. The candidates of minority parties don't have a chance. They do not have access to the financial backing of the major parties, and there is not the semblance of equal attention in the mass media; it is only the two major candidates who have free access to prime time on national television.

More important, both parties almost always agree on the fundamentals of domestic and foreign policy, despite the election-year rhetoric which attempts to find important differences. Both parties arranged for United States intervention in Vietnam in the 1950s and 1960s, and both, when public opinion changed, promised to get out (note the Humphrey-Nixon contest of 1968). In 1984, Democratic candidate Walter Mondale agreed with Republican candidate Ronald Reagan that the United States (which had ten thousand thermonuclear warheads) needed to continue increasing its arms budget, although he asked for a smaller increase than the Republicans. Such a position left Mondale unable to promise representatives of the black community (where unemployment was over 20 percent) that he would spend even a few billion dollars for a jobs program. Meanwhile, Democrats and Republicans in Congress were agreeing on a $297 billion arms bill for the 1985 fiscal year.[9]

I have been talking so far about democracy in the political process. But there is another serious weakness that I will only mention here, although it is of enormous importance: the powerlessness of the American to participate in economic decision-making, which affects his life at every moment. As a consumer, that is, as the person whom the economy is presumably intended to serve, he has virtually nothing to say about what is produced for him. The corporations make what is profitable; the advertising industry persuades him to buy what the corporations produce. He becomes the passive victim of the misallocation of resources, the production of dangerous commodities, the spoiling of his air, water, forests, beaches, cities.

2. ACCESS TO INFORMATION

Adequate information for the electorate is a precondition for any kind of action (whether electoral or demonstrative) to affect national policy. As for the voting process, Berelson, Lazarsfeld, and McPhee tell us (in their book, *Voting*) after extensive empirical research: "One persistent conclusion is that the public is not particularly well informed about the specific issues of the day." . . .

Furthermore, there are certain issues which never even reach the public because they are decided behind the scenes. . . .

Consider the information available to voters on two major kinds of issues. One of them is the tax structure, so bewilderingly complex that the corporation, with its corps of accountants and financial experts, can prime itself for lobbying activities, while the average voter, hardly able to comprehend his own income tax, stands by helplessly as the president, the Office of Management and Budget, and the Congress decide the tax laws. The dominant influences are those of big business, which has the resources both to understand and to act.

Then there is foreign policy. The government leads the citizenry to believe it has special expertise which, if it could only be revealed, would support its position against critics. At the same time, it hides the very information which would reveal its position to be indefensible. The mendacity of the government on the Bay of Pigs operation and the withholding of vital information about the Tonkin Gulf events are only two examples of the way the average person becomes a victim of government deception.

In 1990, historian Warren Cohen resigned as adviser to the State Department in its publication of the series *Foreign Relations of the United States,* pointing out that the government was refusing to cover events less than thirty years old. And even what it did publish was not trustworthy. "The United States government is publishing blatantly fraudulent accounts of its activities in Guatemala, Iran, and Southeast Asia in the 1950s" (*World Monitor Magazine,* 1990).

When the United States invaded the tiny island of Grenada in the fall of 1983, no reporters were allowed to observe the invasion, and the American public had little opportunity to get independent verification of the reasons given by the government for the invasion. As a result, President Reagan could glibly tell the nation what even one of his own supporters, journalist George Will, admitted was a lie: that he was invading Grenada to protect the lives of American medical students on the island. He could also claim that documents found on the island indicated plans for a Cuban-Soviet takeover of Grenada; the documents showed no such thing.[10]

Furthermore, the distribution of information to the public is a function of power and wealth. The government itself can color the citizens' understanding of events by its control of news at the source: the presidential press conference, the "leak to the press," the White Papers, the teams of "truth experts" going around the country at the taxpayers' expense. As for private media, the large networks and mass-circulation magazines have the greatest access to the public mind. There is no "equal time" for critics of public policy. . . .

3. EQUAL PROTECTION

Let us go now from the procedural to the substantive, indeed to the *most* substantive of questions: the right of all people to life itself. Here we find democracy in America tragically inadequate. Not only Locke, one of the leading theorists of the democratic tradition, declared the ultimate right of any person to safeguard his own life when threatened by the government; Hobbes, often looked on as the foe of democratic thought, agreed. Yet, in matters of foreign policy, where the decisions involve life or death for large numbers of Americans, power rests in the hands of the president and a small group of advisers. Despite the constitutional provision that war must be declared by Congress, in reality the President can create situations (as in the Mexican War, as in both world wars) which make inevitable congressional votes for war. And in all post–World War II conflicts (Korea, Vietnam, Iraq) there was no declaration of war by Congress.

It is in connection with this most basic of rights—life itself, the first and most important of those substantive ends which democratic participation is designed to safeguard—that I would assert the need for a global view of democracy. One can at least conceive of a democratic decision for martial sacrifice by those ready to make the sacrifice; a "democratic" war is thus a theoretical possibility. But that presumption of democracy becomes obviously false at the first shot because then *others* are affected who did not decide. . . . Nations making decisions to slaughter their own sons are at least theoretically subject to internal check. The victims on the other side fall without any such chance. For the United States today, this failure of democracy is total; we have the capacity to destroy the world without giving it a chance to murmur a dissent; we did, in fact, destroy a part of southeast Asia on the basis of a unilateral decision made in Washington. There is no more pernicious manifestation of the lack of democracy in America than this single fact.

4. EQUALITY BEFORE THE LAW

Is there equality before the law? At every stage of the judicial process—facing the policeman, appearing in court, being freed on bond, being sentenced by the judge—the poor person is treated worse than the rich, the black treated worse than the white, the politically or personally odd character is treated worse than the orthodox. A defendant's poverty affects his preliminary hearing, his right to bail, the quality of his counsel. The evidence is plentiful in the daily newspapers, which inform us that an African-American boy fleeing the scene of a two-dollar theft may be shot and killed by a pursuing police-man, while a wealthy man who goes to South America after a million-dollar swindle, even if apprehended, need never fear a scratch. The wealthy price-fixer for General Motors, who costs consumers millions, will get ninety days in jail, the burglar of a liquor store will get five years. An African-American youth, or a bearded white youth poorly dressed, has much more chance of being clubbed by a policeman on the street than a well-dressed white man, given the fact that both respond with equal tartness to a question. . . .

Aside from inequality among citizens, there is inequality between the citizen and his government, when they face one another in a court of law. Take the matter of coun-sel: the well-trained government prosecutor faces the indigent's court-appointed coun-sel. Four of my students did a study of the City Court of Boston several years ago. They sat in the court for weeks, taking notes, and found that the average time spent by court-appointed counsel with his client, before arguing the case at the bench, was seven minutes.

5. DISTRIBUTION OF RESOURCES

Democracy is devoid of meaning if it does not include equal access to the available resources of the society. In India, democracy might still mean poverty; in the United States, with a Gross National Product of more than $3 trillion a year, democracy should mean that every American, working a short work-week, has adequate food, clothing, shelter, health care, education for himself and his family—in short, the material resources necessary to enjoy life and freedom. Even if only 20 percent of the American population is desperately poor . . . in a country so rich, that is an inexcusable breach of the democratic principle. Even if there is a large, prosperous middle class, there is something grossly unfair in the fact that in 1995 the richest 1 percent of the population owned over 40 percent of the total wealth, a figure that, throughout our history, has rarely been under 33 percent.

Whether you are poor or rich determines the most fundamental facts about your life: whether you are cold in the winter while trying to sleep, whether you suffocate in the summer; whether you live among vermin or rats; whether the smells around you all day are sweet or foul; whether you have adequate medical care; whether you have good teeth; whether you can send your children to college; whether you can go on vacation or have to take an extra job at night; whether you can afford a divorce, or an abortion, or a wife, or another child. . . .

6. ACCESS TO EDUCATION

In a highly industrialized society, education is a crucial determinant of wealth, political power, social status, leisure, and the ability to work in one's chosen field. Educational resources in our society are not equitably distributed. Among high-school graduates of the same IQ levels, a far higher percentage of the well-to-do go on to college than the poor.[11] A mediocre student with money can always go to college. A mediocre student without money may not be able to go, even to a state college, because he may have to work to support his family. Furthermore, the educational resources in the schools—equipment, teachers, etc.—are far superior in the wealthy suburbs than in the poor sections of the city, whether white or black.

7. FREEDOM OF EXPRESSION

Like money, freedom of expression is available to all in America, but in widely varying quantities. The First Amendment formally guarantees freedom of speech, press, assembly, and petition to all—but certain realities of wealth, power, and status stand in the way of the equal distribution of these rights. Anyone can stand on a street corner and talk to ten or a hundred people. But someone with the resources to buy loudspeaker equipment, go through the necessary red tape, and post a bond with the city may hold a meeting downtown and reach a thousand or five thousand people. A person or a corporation with $100,000 can buy time on television and reach 10 million people. A rich person simply has much more freedom of speech than a poor person. The government has much more freedom of expression than a private individual, because the president can command the airwaves when he wishes, and reach 60 million people in one night.

Freedom of the press also is guaranteed to all. But the student selling an underground newspaper on the street with a nude woman on the cover may be arrested by a policeman, while the airport newsstand selling *Playboy* and ten magazines like it will remain safe. Anyone with $10,000 can put out a newspaper to reach a few thousand people. Anyone with $10 million can buy a few newspapers that will reach a few million people. Anyone who is penniless had better have a loud voice; and then he might be arrested for disturbing the peace.

8. FREEDOM FOR INDIVIDUALITY

The right to live one's life, in privacy and freedom, in whatever way one wants, so long as others are not harmed, should be a sacred principle in a democracy. But there are hundreds of laws, varying from state to state, and sometimes joined by federal laws, which regulate the personal lives of people in this country: their marriages, their divorces, their sexual relations. Furthermore, both laws and court decisions protect policemen and the FBI in their use of secret devices which listen in on private conversations, or peer in on private conduct.

9. THE SPIRIT OF COOPERATION

The maintenance of those substantive elements of democracy which I have just sketched, if dependent on a pervasive network of coercion, would cancel out much of the benefit of that democracy. Democracy needs rather to be sustained by a spirit in society, the tone and the values of the culture. I am speaking of something as elusive as a mood, alongside something as hard as law, both of which would have to substitute cooperation tinged with friendly competition for the fierce combat of our business culture. I am speaking of the underlying drive that keeps people going in the society. So long as that drive is for money and power, with no ceiling on either, so long as ruthlessness is built into the rules of the game, democracy does not have a chance. If there is one crucial cause in the failure of American democracy—not the only one, of course, but a fundamental one—it is the drive for corporate profit, and the overwhelming influence of money in every aspect of our daily lives. That is the uncontrolled libido of our society from which the rape of democratic values necessarily follows.

The manifestations are diverse and endless: the drug industry's drive for profit has led to incredible overpricing of drugs for consumers (700 percent markup, for instance, for tablets to arthritic patients). It was disclosed in 1979 that Johns-Manville, the nation's largest asbestos manufacturer, had deliberately withheld from its workers X-ray results that showed they were developing cancer. In 1984, a company making an intrauterine birth control device—the Dalkon Shield—was found by a Minnesota court to have allowed tens of thousands of women to wear this device despite knowing that it was dangerous to their health (*Minneapolis Star and Tribune,* May 18, 1984). In the mid-1990s, it was revealed that tobacco companies had concealed information showing the narcotic nature of cigarettes. All in the interest of maximizing profit.

If these were isolated cases, reported and then eliminated, they could be dismissed as unfortunate blemishes on an otherwise healthy social body. But the major allocations of resources in our society are made on the basis of money profit rather than social use. . . .

. . . News items buttress what I have said. The oil that polluted California's beautiful beaches in the 1960s . . . was produced by a system in which the oil companies' hunger for profit has far more weight than the ordinary person's need to swim in clean water. This is not to be attributed to Republicanism overriding the concern for the little fellow of the Democratic Party. Profit is master whichever party is in power; it was the liberal Secretary of the Interior Stewart Udall who allowed the dangerous drilling to go on. . . .

In 1984, the suit of several thousand veterans against the Dow Chemical Company, claiming that they and their families had suffered terrible illnesses as a result of exposure in Vietnam to the poisonous chemical Agent Orange, was settled. The Dow corporation avoided the disclosures of thousands of documents in open court by agreeing to pay $180 million to the veterans. One thing seemed clear: the company had known that the defoliant used in Vietnam might be dangerous, but it held back the news, and blamed the government for ordering use of the chemical. The government itself, apparently wanting to shift blame to the corporation, declared publicly that Dow Chemical had been motivated in its actions by greed for profit.

10. OPPORTUNITY TO PROTEST

The first two elements in my list for democracy—decision-making and information to help make them—are procedural. The next six are substantive, dealing with the consequences of such procedures on life, liberty, and the pursuit of happiness. My ninth point, the one I have just discussed, shows how the money motive of our society corrupts both procedures and their consequences by its existence and suggests we need a different motive as a fundamental requisite of a democratic society. The point I am about to discuss is an ultimate requisite for democracy, a safety feature if nothing else— neither procedures nor consequences nor motivation—works. It is the right of citizens to break through the impasse of a legal and cultural structure, which sustains inequality, greed, and murder, to initiate processes for change. I am speaking of civil disobedience, which is an essential safeguard even in a successful society, and which is an absolute necessity in a society which is not going well.

If the institutional structure itself bars any change but the most picayune and grievances are serious, it is silly to insist that change must be mediated through the processes of that legal structure. In such a situation, dramatic expressions of protest and challenge are necessary to help change ways of thinking, to build up political power for drastic change. A society that calls itself democratic (whether accurately or not) must, as its ultimate safeguard, allow such acts of disobedience. If the government prohibits them (as we must expect from a government committed to the existent) then the members of a society concerned with democracy must not only defend such acts, but encourage them. Somewhere near the root of democratic thought is the theory of popular sovereignty, declaring that government and laws are instruments for certain ends, and are not to be deified with absolute obedience; they must constantly be checked by the citizenry, and challenged, opposed, even overthrown, if they become threats to fundamental rights.

Any abstract assessment of *when* disobedience is justified is pointless. Proper conclusions depend on empirical evidence about how bad things are at the moment, and how adequate are the institutional mechanisms for correcting them. . . .

One of these is the matter of race. The intolerable position of the African-American, in both North and South, has traditionally been handled with a few muttered apologies and tokens of reform. Then the civil disobedience of militants in the South forced our attention on the most dramatic (southern) manifestations of racism in America. The massive African-American urban uprisings of 1967 and 1968 showed that nothing less than civil disobedience (for riots and uprisings go beyond that) could make the nation see that the race problem is an American—not a southern—problem and that it needs bold, revolutionary action.

As for poverty: it seems clear that the normal mechanisms of congressional pretense and presidential rhetoric are not going to change things very much. Acts of civil disobedience by the poor will be required, at the least, to make middle-class America take notice, to bring national decisions that begin to reallocate wealth.

The war in Vietnam showed that we could not depend on the normal processes of "law and order," of the election process, of letters to the *Times,* to stop a series of especially brutal acts against the Vietnamese and against our own sons. It took a nationwide storm of protest, including thousands of acts of civil disobedience (14,000 people were arrested in one day in 1971 in Washington, D.C.), to help bring the war to an end. The role of draft resistance in affecting Lyndon Johnson's 1968 decision not to escalate the war further is told in the Defense Department secret documents of that period. In the 1980s and 1990s civil disobedience continued, with religious pacifists and others risking prison in order to protest the arms race and the plans for nuclear war.

The great danger for American democracy is not from the protesters. That democracy is too poorly realized for us to consider critics—even rebels—as the chief problem. Its fulfillment requires us all, living in an ossified system which sustains too much killing and too much selfishness, to join the protest.

NOTES

1. Robert A. Dahl, *A Preface to Democratic Theory* (Chicago: University of Chicago Press, 1963), p. 81.
2. *Ibid.,* p. 124.
3. *Ibid.,* p. 125.
4. *Ibid.,* p. 131.
5. *Ibid.,* pp. 131–32.
6. *New York Times,* January 25, 27, 1997.
7. Dahl, *A Preface to Democratic Theory,* p. 146.
8. Robert Wiebe, "The Confinements of Consensus," *TriQuarterly,* 1966, Copyright by TriQuarterly 1966. All rights reserved.
9. *New York Times,* September 25, 1984.
10. The *New York Times* reported, November 5, 1983: "There is nothing in the documents, however, that specifically indicates that Cuba and the Soviet Union were on the verge of taking over Grenada, as Administration officials have suggested."
11. See the Carnegie Council on Children study, *Small Futures,* by Richard deLore, 1979.

How Democratic Is America?
A Response to Howard Zinn

Sidney Hook

Charles Peirce, the great American philosopher, once observed that there was such a thing as the "ethics of words." The "ethics of words" are violated whenever ordinary terms are used in an unusual context or arbitrarily identified with another concept for which other terms are in common use. Mr. Zinn is guilty of a systematic violation of the "ethics of words." In consequence, his discussion of "democracy" results in a great many methodological errors as well as inconsistencies. To conserve space, I shall focus on three.

I

First of all, he confuses democracy as a political *process* with democracy as a political *product* or state of welfare; democracy as a *"free* society" with democracy as a *"good* society," where good is defined in terms of equality or justice (or both) or some other constellation of values. One of the reasons for choosing to live under a democratic political system rather than a nondemocratic system is our belief that it makes possible a better society. That is something that must be empirically established, something denied by critics of democracy from Plato to Santayana. The equality which is relevant to democracy as a *political process* is, in the first instance, political equality with respect to the rights of citizenship. Theoretically, a politically democratic community could vote, wisely or unwisely, to abolish, retain, or establish certain economic inequalities. Theoretically, a benevolent despotism could institute certain kinds of social and even juridical equalities. Historically, the Bismarckian political dictatorship introduced social welfare legislation for the masses at a time when such legislation would have been repudiated by the existing British and American political democracies. Some of Mr. Zinn's proposed reforms could be introduced under a dictatorship or benevolent despotism. Therefore, they are not logically or organically related to democracy.

The second error in Mr. Zinn's approach to democracy is "to measure our democracy against an ideal (even if admittedly unachievable) standard . . . even if utopian . . ." without *defining* the standard. His criteria admittedly are neither necessary nor sufficient for determining the presence of democracy since he himself admits that they are applicable to societies that are not democratic. Further, even if we were to take his criteria as severally defining the presence of democracy—as we might take certain

Sidney Hook (1902–1989) was head of the department of philosophy at New York University from 1934 to 1969 and was a senior research fellow at the Hoover Institution on War, Revolution, and Peace at Stanford University from 1973 to 1989. This essay was originally published in How Democratic Is America? *ed. Robert A. Goldwin, pp. 62–75 (Chicago, Rand McNally, 1971). The author revised and updated the original for* Points of View *in 1985.*

physical and mental traits as constituting a definition of health—he gives no operational test for determining whether or not they have been fulfilled. For example, among the criteria he lists for determining whether a society is democratic is this: "Are the members of the society equally protected on matters of life and death—in the most literal sense of that phrase?" A moment's reflection will show that here—as well as in other cases where Zinn speaks of equality—it is impossible for all members to be equally protected on matters of life and death—certainly not in a world in which men do the fighting and women give birth to children, where children need *more* protection than adults, and where some risk-seeking adults require and deserve less protection (since resources are not infinite) than others. As Karl Marx realized, "in the most literal sense of that phrase," there cannot be absolute equality even in a classless society. . . .

The only sensible procedure in determining the absence or presence of equality from a democratic perspective is comparative. We must ask whether a culture is more or less democratic in comparison to the past with respect to some *desirable* feature of equality (Zinn ignores the fact that not all equalities are desirable). It is better for some people to be more intelligent and more knowledgeable than others than for all to be unintelligent and ignorant. There never is literally equal access to education, to knowledge and training in any society. The question is: Is there more access today for more people than yesterday, and how can we increase the access tomorrow?

Mr. Zinn refuses to take this approach because, he asserts, "it supports complacency." It does nothing of the sort! On the contrary, it shows that progress is possible, and encourages us to exert our efforts in the same direction if we regard the direction as desirable.

It will be instructive to look at the passage in which Mr. Zinn objects to this sensible comparative approach because it reveals the bias in his approach:

"With such a standard," he writes, "Russia in 1910 could point with pride to how much progress they had made toward parliamentary democracy; as Russians in 1985 could point to their post-Stalin progress away from the gulag; as Americans could point in 1939 to how far they had come in solving the problem of economic equality; as Americans in the South could point in 1950 to the progress of the southern African-American."

a. In 1910 the Russians were indeed moving toward greater progress in local parliamentary institutions. Far from making them complacent, they moved towards more inclusive representative institutions which culminated in elections to the Constituent Assembly in 1918, which was bayoneted out of existence by Lenin and the Communist Party, with a minority party dictatorship established.

b. Only Mr. Zinn would regard the slight diminution in terror from the days of Stalin to the regime of Chernenko as progress toward democracy. Those who observe the ethics of words would normally say that the screws of repression had been slightly relaxed. Mr. Zinn seems unaware that as bad as the terror was under Lenin, it was not as pervasive as it is today.* But no one with any respect for the

---

* These words and subsequent references to the Soviet Union preceded the reforms initiated under Mikhail Gorbachev and continued with greater intensity under Boris Yeltsin—*Editors.*

ethics of words would speak of "the progress of democracy" in the Soviet Union from Lenin to Stalin to Khrushchev to Chernenko. Their regimes were varying degrees of dictatorship and terror.

c. Americans could justifiably say that in 1939 progress had been made in giving workers a greater role, not as Mr. Zinn says in "solving the problem of economic equality" (a meaningless phrase), but in determining the conditions and rewards of work that prevailed in 1929 or previously because the existence of the Wagner Labor Relations Act made collective bargaining the law of the land. They could say this *not* to rest in complacency, but to use the organized force of their trade unions to influence further the political life of the country. And indeed, it was the organized labor movement in 1984 which in effect chose the candidate of the Democratic Party.

d. Americans in the South in 1950 could rightfully speak of the progress of the southern African-American over the days of unrestricted Jim Crow and lynching bees of the past, *not* to rest in complacency, but to agitate for further progress through the Supreme Court decision of *Brown* v. *Board of Education in Topeka* and through the Civil Rights Act of Congress. This has not made them complacent, but more resolved to press further to eliminate remaining practices of invidious discrimination.

Even Mr. Zinn should admit that with respect to some of his other criteria this is the only sensible approach. Otherwise we get unhistorical answers, the hallmark of the doctrinaire. He asks—criterion 1—"To what extent can various people in the society participate in those decisions which affect their lives?" and—criterion 7—"Is there freedom of expression on all matters, and equally for all, to communicate with other members of the society?" Why doesn't Mr. Zinn adopt this sensible comparative approach? Because it would lead him to inquire into the extent to which people are free to participate in decisions that affect their lives *today,* free to express themselves, free to organize, free to protest and dissent today, *in comparison with the past.* It would lead him to the judgment *which he wishes to avoid at all costs,* to wit, that despite the grave problems, gaps, and tasks before us, the United States is *more* democratic today than it was a hundred years ago, fifty years ago, twenty years ago, five years ago with respect to every one of the criteria he has listed. To recognize this is *not* an invitation to complacency. On the contrary, it indicates the possibility of broadening, deepening, and using the democratic political process to improve the quality of human life, to modify and redirect social institutions in order to realize on a wider scale the moral commitment of democracy to an equality of concern for all its citizens to achieve their fullest growth as persons. This commitment is to a process, not to a transcendent goal or a fixed, ideal standard.

In a halting, imperfect manner, set back by periods of violence, vigilantism, and xenophobia, the political democratic process in the United States has been used to modify the operation of the economic system. The improvements and reforms won from time to time make the still-existing problems and evils more acute in that people become more aware of them. The more the democratic process extends human freedoms, and the more it introduces justice in social relations and the distribution of wealth, the greater grows the desire for *more* freedom and justice. Historically and psychologically, it is false to assume that reforms breed a spirit of complacency. . . .

The third and perhaps most serious weakness in Mr. Zinn's view is his conception of the nature of the formal political democratic process. It suffers from several related defects. First, it overlooks the central importance of majority rule in the democratic process. Second, it denies in effect that majority rule is possible by defining democracy in such a way that it becomes impossible. . . .

"Representation by its very nature," claims Mr. Zinn, "is undemocratic." This is Rousseauistic nonsense. For it would mean that no democracy—including all societies that Mr. Zinn ever claimed at any time to be democratic—could possibly exist, not even the direct democracies or assemblies of Athens or the New England town meetings. For all such assemblies must elect officials to carry out their will. If no representative (and an official is a representative, too) can adequately represent another's needs, there is no assurance that in the actual details of governance, the selectmen, road commissioners, or other town or assembly officials will, in fact, carry out their directives. No assembly or meeting can sit in continuous session or collectively carry out the common decision. In the nature of the case, officials, like representatives, constitute an elite and their actions *may* reflect their interests more than the interests of the governed. This makes crucial the questions whether and how an elite can be removed, whether the consent on which the rule of the officials or representatives rests is free or coerced, whether a minority can peacefully use these mechanisms, by which freely given consent is registered, to win over or become a majority. The existence of representative assemblies makes democracy difficult, not impossible.

Since Mr. Zinn believes that a majority never has any authority to bind a minority as well as itself by decisions taken after free discussion and debate, he is logically committed to anarchy. Failing to see this, he confuses two fundamentally different things—the meaning or definition of democracy, and its justification.

1. A democratic government is one in which the general direction of policy rests directly or indirectly upon the freely given consent of a majority of the adults governed. Ambiguities and niceties aside, that is what democracy means. It is not anarchy. The absence of a unanimous consensus does not entail the absence of democracy.

2. One may reject on moral or religious or personal grounds a democratic society. Plato, as well as modern totalitarians, contends that a majority of mankind is either too stupid or vicious to be entrusted with self-government, or to be given the power to accept or reject their ruling elites, and that the only viable alternative to democracy is the self-selecting and self-perpetuating elite of "the wise," or "the efficient," or "the holy," or "the strong," depending upon the particular ideology of the totalitarian apologist. The only thing they have in common with democrats is their rejection of anarchy.

3. No intelligent and moral person can make an *absolute* of democracy in the sense that he believes it is always, everywhere, under any conditions, and no matter what its consequences, ethically legitimate. Democracy is obviously not desirable in a head-hunting or cannibalistic society or in an institution of the feeble-minded. But wherever and whenever a principled democrat accepts the political system of democracy, he must accept the binding authority of legislative decisions, reached after the free give-and-take of debate and discussion, as binding upon him whether

he is a member of the majority or minority. Otherwise the consequence is incipient or overt anarchy or civil war, the usual preface to despotism or tyranny. Accepting the decision of the majority as binding does not mean that it is final or irreversible. The processes of freely given consent must make it possible for a minority to urge amendment or repeal of any decision of the majority. Under carefully guarded provisions, a democrat may resort to civil disobedience of a properly enacted law in order to bear witness to the depths of his commitment in an effort *to reeducate* his fellow citizens. But in that case he must voluntarily accept punishment for his civil disobedience, and so long as he remains a democrat, voluntarily abandon his violation or noncompliance with law at the point where its consequences threaten to destroy the democratic process and open the floodgates either to the violent disorders of anarchy or to the dictatorship of a despot or a minority political party.

4. That Mr. Zinn is not a democrat but an anarchist in his views is apparent in his contention that not only must a democracy allow or tolerate civil disobedience within limits, but that "members of a society concerned with democracy must not only defend such acts, but encourage them." On this view, if southern segregationists resort to civil disobedience to negate the long-delayed but eminently just measures adopted by the government to implement the amendments that outlaw slavery, they should be encouraged to do so. On this view, any group that defies any law that violates its conscience—with respect to marriage, taxation, vaccination, abortion, education—should be encouraged to do so. Mr. Zinn, like most anarchists, refuses to generalize the principles behind his action. He fails to see that if all fanatics of causes deemed by them to be morally just were encouraged to resort to civil disobedience, even our imperfect existing political democracy would dissolve in chaos, and that civil disobedience would soon become quite uncivil. He fails to see that *in a democracy the processes of intelligence, not individual conscience, must be supreme.*

II

I turn now to some of the issues that Mr. Zinn declares are substantive. Before doing so I wish to make clear my belief that the most substantive issue of all is the procedural one by which the inescapable differences of interests among men, once a certain moral level of civilization has been reached, are to be negotiated. The belief in the validity of democratic procedures rests upon the conviction that where adult human beings have freedom of access to relevant information, they are, by and large, better judges of their own interests than are those who set themselves up as their betters and rulers, that, to use the homely maxim, those who wear the shoes know best where they pinch and therefore have the right to change their political shoes in the light of their experience. . . .

Looking at the question "How democratic is America?" with respect to the problems of poverty, race, education, etc., we must say "Not democratic enough!", but not for the reasons Mr. Zinn gives. For he seems to believe that the failure to adopt *his* solutions and proposals with respect to foreign policy, slum clearance, pollution, etc., is evidence of the failure of the democratic process itself. He overlooks the crucial difference between the procedural process and the substantive issues. When he writes that democracy is devoid of meaning if it does not include "equal access to the available resources of the society," he is simply abusing language. Assuming such equal access is desirable (which some might question who believe that access to *some* of society's resources—for example, to specialized training or to scarce supplies—should go not equally to all but to the most needful or sometimes to the most qualified), a democracy may or may not legislate such equal access. The crucial question is whether the electorate has the power to make the choice, or to elect those who would carry out the mandate chosen. . . .

When Mr. Zinn goes on to say that "in the United States . . . democracy should mean that every American, working a short work-week, has adequate food, clothing, shelter, health care, . . ." he is not only abusing language, he is revealing the fact that the procedural processes that are essential to the meaning of democracy, in ordinary usage, are not essential to his conception. He is violating the basic ethics of discourse. If democracy "should mean" what Zinn says it should, then were Huey Long or any other dictator to seize power and introduce a "short work-week" and distribute "adequate food, clothing, shelter, health care" to the masses, Mr. Zinn would have to regard his regime as democratic.

After all, when Hitler came to power and abolished free elections in Germany, he at the same time reduced unemployment, increased the real wages of the German worker, and provided more adequate food, clothing, shelter, and health care than was available under the Weimar Republic. On Zinn's view of what democracy "should mean," this made Hitler's rule more democratic than that of Weimar. . . .

Not surprisingly, Mr. Zinn is a very unreliable guide even in his account of the procedural features of the American political system. In one breath he maintains that not enough information is available to voters to make intelligent choices on major political issues like tax laws. (The voter, of course, does not vote on such laws but for representatives who have taken stands on a number of complex issues.) "The dominant influences are those of big business, which has the resources both to understand and to act." In another breath, he complains that the electorate is at the mercy of the propagandist. "The propagandist does not need to lie; he overwhelms the public with so much information as to lead it to believe that it is all too complicated for anyone but the experts."

Mr. Zinn is certainly hard to please! The American political process is not democratic because the electorate hasn't got enough information. It is also undemocratic because it receives too much information. What would Zinn have us do so that the public gets just the right amount of information and propaganda? Have the government control the press? Restrict freedom of propaganda? But these are precisely the devices of totalitarian societies. The evils of the press, even when it is free of government control, are many indeed. The great problem is to keep the press free and responsible. And as defective as the press and other public media are today, surely it is an exaggeration to say that with respect to tax laws "the dominant influences are those of big business." If they were, how can we account for the existence of the income tax laws? If the influence of big business on the press is so dominant and the press is so biased, how can we account for the fact that although 92 percent of the press opposed Truman's candidacy in 1948, he was reelected? How can we account for the profound dissatisfaction of Vice

President Agnew with the press and other mass media?* And since Mr. Zinn believes that big business dominates our educational system, especially our universities, how can we account for the fact that the universities are the centers of the strongest dissent in the nation to public and national policy, that the National Association of Manufacturers bitterly complained a few years ago that the economics of the free enterprise system was derided, and often not even taught, in most Departments of Economics in the colleges and universities of the nation?

Mr. Zinn's exaggerations are really caricatures of complex realities. Far from being controlled by the monolithic American corporate economy, American public opinion is today marked by a greater scope and depth of dissent than at any time in its history, except for the days preceding the Civil War. The voice and the votes of Main Street still count for more in a democratic polity than those of Wall Street. Congress has limited, and can still further limit, the influence of money on the electoral process by federal subsidy and regulations. There are always abuses needing reforms. By failing to take a comparative approach and instead focusing on some absolute utopian standard of perfection, Mr. Zinn gives an exaggerated, tendentious, and fundamentally false picture of the United States. There is hardly a sentence in his essay that is free of some serious flaw in perspective, accuracy, or emphasis. Sometimes they have a comic effect, as when Mr. Zinn talks about the lack of "equal distribution of the right of freedom of expression." What kind of "equal distribution" is he talking about? Of course, a person with more money can talk to more people than one with less, although this does not mean that more persons will listen to him, agree with him, or be influenced by him. But a person with a more eloquent voice or a better brain can reach more people than you or I. What shall we do to insure equal distribution of the right of freedom of expression? Insist on equality of voice volume or pattern, and equality of brain power? More money gives not only greater opportunity to talk to people than less money but the ability to do thousands of things barred to those who have less money. Shall we then decree that all people have the same amount of money all the time and forbid anyone from depriving anyone else of any of his money even by fair means? "The government," writes Mr. Zinn, "has much more freedom of expression than a private individual because the president can command the airwaves when he wishes, and reach 60 million people in one night."

Alas! Mr. Zinn is not joking. Either he wants to bar the president or any public official from using the airwaves or he wants all of us to take turns. One wonders what country Mr. Zinn is living in. Nixon spoke to 60 million people several times, and so did Jimmy Carter. What was the result? More significant than the fact that 60 million people hear the president is that 60 million or more can hear his critics, sometimes right after he speaks, and that no one is compelled to listen.

Mr. Zinn does not understand the basic meaning of equality in a free, open democratic society. Its philosophy does not presuppose that all citizens are physically or intellectually equal or that all are equally gifted in every or any respect. It holds that all enjoy a *moral* equality, and that therefore, as far as is practicable, given finite resources,

---

* Spiro Agnew, former governor of Maryland and vice president before being forced from office during the first term of Richard Nixon (1968–1972), was a frequent and vociferous critic of the "liberal" press—*Editors.*

the institutions of a democratic society should seek to provide an equal opportunity to all its citizens to develop themselves to their full desirable potential.

Of course, we cannot ever provide complete equal opportunity. More and more is enough. For one thing, so long as children have different parents and home environments, they cannot enjoy the same or equal opportunities. Nonetheless, the family has compensating advantages for all that. Let us hope that Mr. Zinn does not wish to wipe out the family to avoid differences in opportunity. Plato believed that the family, as we know it, should be abolished because it did not provide equality of opportunity, and that all children should be brought up by the state.

Belief in the moral equality of men and women does not require that all individuals be treated identically or that equal treatment must be measured or determined by equality of outcome or result. Every citizen should have an equal right to an education, but that does not mean that, regardless of capacity and interest, he or she should have the same amount of schooling beyond the adolescent years, and at the same schools, and take the same course of study. With the increase in national wealth, a good case can be made for an equal right of all citizens to health care or medical treatment. But only a quack or ideological fanatic would insist that therefore all individuals should have the same medical regimen no matter what ails them. This would truly be putting all human beings in the bed of Procrustes.

This conception of moral equality as distinct from Mr. Zinn's notions of equality is perfectly compatible with intelligent recognition of human inequalities and relevant ways of treating their inequalities to further both the individual and common good. Intelligent and loving parents are equally concerned with the welfare of all their children. But precisely because they are, they may provide different specific strategies in health care, education, psychological motivation, and intellectual stimulation to develop the best in all of them. The logic of Mr. Zinn's position—although he seems blissfully unaware of it—leads to the most degrading kind of egalitarian socialism, the kind which Marx and Engels in their early years denounced as "barracks socialism."

It is demonstrable that democracy is healthier and more effective where human beings do not suffer from poverty, unemployment, and disease. It is also demonstrable that to the extent that property gives power, private property in the means of social production gives power over the lives of those who must live by its use, and, therefore, that such property, whether public or private, should be responsible to those who are affected by its operation. Consequently one can argue that political democracy depends not only on the extension of the franchise to all adults, not only on its active exercise, but on programs of social welfare that provide for collective bargaining by free trade unions of workers and employees, unemployment insurance, minimum wages, guaranteed health care, and other social services that are integral to the welfare state. It is demonstrable that although the existing American welfare state provides far more welfare than was ever provided in the past—my own lifetime furnishes graphic evidence of the vast changes—it is still very far from being a genuine welfare state. Political democracy can exist without a welfare state, but it is stronger and better with it.

The basic issue that divides Mr. Zinn from others no less concerned about human welfare, but less fanatical than he, is how a genuine welfare state is to be brought about. My contention is that this can be achieved by the vigorous exercise of the existing democratic process, and that by the same coalition politics through which great gains have been achieved in the past, even greater gains can be won in the future.

For purposes of economy, I focus on the problem of poverty, or since this is a relative term, hunger. If the presence of hunger entails the absence of the democratic political process, then democracy has never existed in the past—which would be an arbitrary use of words. Nonetheless, the existence of hunger is always a *threat* to the continued existence of the democratic process because of the standing temptation of those who hunger to exchange freedom for the promise of bread. This, of course, is an additional ground to the even weightier moral reasons for gratifying basic human needs.

That fewer people go hungry today in the United States than ever before may show that our democracy is better than it used to be but not that it is as good as it can be. Even the existence of one hungry person is one too many. How then can hunger or the extremes of poverty be abolished? Certainly not by the method Mr. Zinn advises: "Acts of civil disobedience by the poor will be required, at the least, to make middle-class America take notice, to bring national decisions that begin to reallocate wealth."

This is not only a piece of foolish advice, it is dangerously foolish advice. Many national decisions to reallocate wealth have been made through the political process— what else is the system of taxation if not a method of reallocating wealth?—without resort to civil disobedience. Indeed, resort to civil disobedience on this issue is very likely to produce a backlash among those active and influential political groups in the community who are aware that normal political means are available for social and economic reform. The refusal to engage in such normal political processes could easily be exploited by demagogues to portray the movement towards the abolition of hunger and extreme poverty as a movement towards the confiscation and equalization of all wealth.

The simplest and most effective way of abolishing hunger is to act on the truly revolutionary principle, enunciated by the federal government, that it is responsible for maintaining a standard of relief as a minimum beneath which a family will not be permitted to sink. . . .

For reasons that need no elaboration here, the greatest of the problems faced by American democracy today is the race problem. Although tied to the problems of poverty and urban reconstruction, it has independent aspects exacerbated by the legacy of the Civil War and the Reconstruction period.

Next to the American Indians, African-Americans have suffered most from the failure of the democratic political process to extend the rights and privileges of citizenship to those whose labor and suffering have contributed so much to the conquest of the continent. The remarkable gains that have been made by African-Americans in the last twenty years have been made primarily through the political process. If the same rate of improvement continues, the year 2000 may see a rough equality established. The growth of African-American suffrage, especially in the South, the increasing sense of responsibility by the white community, despite periodic setbacks resulting from outbursts of violence, opens up a perspective of continuous and cumulative reform. The man and the organization he headed chiefly responsible for the great gains made by African-Americans, Roy Wilkins and the NAACP, were convinced that the democratic political process can be more effectively used to further the integration of African-Americans into our national life than by reliance on any other method. . . .

The only statement in Mr. Zinn's essay that I can wholeheartedly endorse is his assertion that the great danger to American democracy does not come from the phenomena of protest as such. Dissent and protest are integral to the democratic process. The danger comes from certain modes of dissent, from the substitution of violence and threats of violence for the mechanisms of the political process, from the escalation of that violence as the best hope of those who still have grievances against our imperfect American democracy, and from views such as those expressed by Mr. Zinn which downgrade the possibility of peaceful social reform and encourage rebellion. It is safe to predict that large-scale violence by impatient minorities will fail. It is almost as certain that attempts at violence will backfire, that they will create a climate of repression that may reverse the course of social progress and expanded civil liberties of the last generation. . . .

It is when Mr. Zinn is discussing racial problems that his writing ceases to be comic and silly and becomes irresponsible and mischievous. He writes:

> The massive African-American urban uprisings of 1967 and 1968 showed that nothing less than civil disobedience (for riots and uprisings go beyond that) could make the nation see that the race problem is an American—not a southern—problem and that it needs bold, revolutionary action.

First of all, every literate person knows that the race problem is an American problem, not exclusively a southern one. It needs no civil disobedience or "black uprisings" to remind us of that. Second, the massive uprisings of 1967 and 1968 were violent and uncivil, and resulted in needless loss of life and suffering. The Civil Rights Acts, according to Roy Wilkins, then head of the NAACP, were imperiled by them. They were adopted despite, not because, of them. Third, what kind of "revolutionary" action is Mr. Zinn calling for? And by whom? He seems to lack the courage of his confusions. Massive civil disobedience when sustained becomes a form of civil war.

Despite Mr. Zinn and others, violence is more likely to produce reaction than reform. In 1827 a resolution to manumit slaves by purchase (later, Lincoln's preferred solution) was defeated by three votes in the House of Burgesses of the State of Virginia. It was slated to be reintroduced in a subsequent session with excellent prospects of being adopted. Had Virginia adopted it, North Carolina would shortly have followed suit. But before it could be reintroduced, Nat Turner's rebellion broke out. Its violent excesses frightened the South into a complete rejection of a possibility that might have prevented the American Civil War—the fiercest and bloodiest war in human history up to that time, from whose consequences American society is still suffering. Mr. Zinn's intentions are as innocent as those of a child playing with matches.

III

One final word about "the global" dimension of democracy of which Mr. Zinn speaks. Here, too, he speaks sympathetically of actions that would undermine the willingness and capacity of a free society to resist totalitarian aggression.

The principles that should guide a free democratic society in a world where dictatorial regimes seek to impose their rule on other nations were formulated by John

Stuart Mill, the great defender of liberty and representative government, more than a century ago:

> To go to war for an idea, if the war is aggressive not defensive, is as criminal as to go to war for territory or revenue, for it is as little justifiable to force our ideas on other people, as to compel them to submit to our will in any other aspect. . . . *The doctrine of non-intervention, to be a legitimate principle of morality, must be accepted by all governments.* The despots must consent to be bound by it as well as the free states. Unless they do, the profession of it by free countries comes but to this miserable issue, that the wrong side may help the wrong side but the right may not help the right side. Intervention to enforce non-intervention is always right, always moral *if not always prudent.* Though it may be a mistake to give freedom (or independence—S.H.) to a people who do not value the boon, it cannot be right to insist that if they do value it, they shall not be hindered from the pursuit of it by foreign coercion (*Fraser's Magazine,* 1859, emphasis mine).

Unfortunately, these principles were disregarded by the United States in 1936 when Hitler and Mussolini sent troops to Spain to help Franco overthrow the legally elected democratic Loyalist regime. The U.S. Congress, at the behest of the administration, adopted a Neutrality Resolution which prevented the democratic government of Spain from purchasing arms here. This compelled the Spanish government to make a deal with Stalin, who not only demanded its entire gold supply but the acceptance of the dread Soviet secret police, the NKVD, to supervise the operations. The main operation of the NKVD in Spain was to engage in a murderous purge of the democratic ranks of anti-Communists which led to the victory of Franco. The story is told in George Orwell's *Homage to Catalonia.* He was on the scene.

The prudence of American intervention in Vietnam may be debatable but there is little doubt that [UN ambassador] Adlai Stevenson, sometimes referred to as the liberal conscience of the nation, correctly stated the American motivation when he said at the UN on the very day of his death: "My hope in Vietnam is that resistance there may establish the fact that changes in Asia are not to be precipitated by outside force. This was the point of the Korean War. This is the point of the conflict in Vietnam."

. . . Mr. Zinn's remarks about Grenada show he is opposed to the liberal principles expressed by J. S. Mill in the passage cited above. His report of the facts about Grenada is as distorted as his account of present-day American democracy. On tiny Grenada, whose government was seized by Communist terrorists, were representatives of every Communist regime in the Kremlin's orbit, Cuban troops, and a Soviet general. I have read the documents captured by the American troops. They conclusively establish that the Communists were preparing the island as part of the Communist strategy of expansion.[1]

It is sad but significant that Mr. Zinn, whose heart bleeds for the poor Asians who suffered in the struggle to prevent the Communist takeover in Southeast Asia, has not a word of protest, not a tear of compassion for the hundreds of thousands of tortured, imprisoned, and drowned in flight after the victory of the North Vietnamese "liberators," not to mention the even greater number of victims of the Cambodian and Cuban Communists.

One summary question may be asked whose answer bears on the issue of how democratic America is. Suppose all the iron and bamboo and passport curtains of the world were lifted today, in what direction would freedom loving and democratic people move? Anyone is free to leave the United States today, except someone fleeing from the law, but in [some of] the countries arrayed against the United States people are penned in like animals and cannot cross a boundary without risking death. Has this no significance for the "global" aspect of our question?

NOTE

1. *The Grenada Papers: The Inside Story of the Grenadian Revolution—and the Making of a Totalitarian State as Told in Captured Documents* (San Francisco: Institute of Contemporary Studies, 1984).

2

THE CONSTITUTION

Of the many books that have been written about the circumstances surrounding the creation of our Constitution, none generated more controversy than Charles Beard's An Economic Interpretation of the Constitution of the United States *(1913). An historian by profession, Beard challenged the belief that our Constitution was fashioned by men of democratic spirit. On the contrary, in what appeared to be a systematic marshaling of evidence, Beard sought to demonstrate (1) that the impetus for a new constitution came from individuals who saw their own economic interests threatened by a growing trend in the population toward greater democracy; (2) that the Founding Fathers themselves were men of considerable "personalty" (i.e., holdings other than real estate), who were concerned not so much with fashioning a democratic constitution as they were with protecting their own financial interests against the more democratically oriented farming and debtor interests within the society; and, finally, (3) that the individuals charged with ratifying the new Constitution also represented primarily the larger economic interests within the society. While space limitations prevent a full development of Beard's argument, the portions of his book that follow should provide some feel for both the substance of his argument and his method of investigation.*

Beard's analysis has been subject to repeated scrutiny over the years. The most systematic effort in this regard came in 1956 with the publication of Robert Brown's Charles Beard and the Constitution: A Critical Analysis of "An Economic Interpretation of the Constitution." *Arguing that the rigor of Beard's examination was more apparent than real, Brown accuses him of citing only the facts that supported his case while ignoring those that did not. Moreover, he contends that even the evidence Beard provided did not warrant the interpretation he gave to it. Brown concludes that the best evidence now available does not support the view that "the Constitution was put over undemocratically in an undemocratic society by personal property."*

An Economic Interpretation of the Constitution of the United States

Charles A. Beard

Suppose it could be shown from the classification of the men who supported and opposed the Constitution that there was no line of property division at all; that is, that men owning substantially the same amounts of the same kinds of property were equally divided on the matter of adoption or rejection—it would then become apparent that the Constitution had no ascertainable relation to economic groups or classes, but was the product of some abstract causes remote from the chief business of life—gaining a livelihood.

Suppose, on the other hand, that substantially all of the merchants, money lenders, security holders, manufacturers, shippers, capitalists, and financiers and their professional associates are to be found on one side in support of the Constitution and that substantially all or the major portion of the opposition came from the nonslaveholding farmers and the debtors—would it not be pretty conclusively demonstrated that our fundamental law was not the product of an abstraction known as "the whole people," but of a group of economic interests which must have expected beneficial results from its adoption? Obviously all the facts here desired cannot be discovered, but the data presented in the following chapters bear out the latter hypothesis, and thus a reasonable presumption in favor of the theory is created.

Of course, it may be shown (and perhaps can be shown) that the farmers and debtors who opposed the Constitution were, in fact, benefited by the general improvement which resulted from its adoption. It may likewise be shown, to take an extreme case, that the English nation derived immense advantages from the Norman Conquest and the orderly administrative processes which were introduced, as it undoubtedly did; nevertheless, it does not follow that the vague thing known as "the advancement of general welfare" or some abstraction known as "justice" was the immediate, guiding purpose of the leaders in either of these great historic changes. The point is, that the direct, impelling motive in both cases was the economic advantages which the beneficiaries expected would accrue to themselves first, from their action. Further than this, economic interpretation cannot go. It may be that some larger world process is working through each series of historical events: but ultimate causes lie beyond our horizon. . . .

Charles A. Beard (1874–1948) was professor of history and political science at Columbia University and former president of the American Political Science Association. From Charles A. Beard, pp. 16–18, 149–151, 268–270, 288–289, 324–325. Reprinted with the permission of Simon & Schuster from An Economic Interpretation of the Constitution of the United States *by Charles A. Beard. Copyright 1935 by Macmillan Publishing Company, copyright renewed © 1963 by William Beard and Miriam Beard Vagts.*

THE FOUNDING FATHERS: AN ECONOMIC PROFILE

A survey of the economic interests of the members of the Convention presents certain conclusions:

A majority of the members were lawyers by profession.

Most of the members came from towns, on or near the coast, that is, from the regions in which personalty was largely concentrated.

Not one member represented in his immediate personal economic interests the small farming or mechanic classes.

The overwhelming majority of members, at least five-sixths, were immediately, directly, and personally interested in the outcome of their labors at Philadelphia, and were to a greater or less extent economic beneficiaries from the adoption of the Constitution.

1. Public security interests were extensively represented in the Convention. Of the fifty-five members who attended no less than forty appear on the Records of the Treasury Department for sums varying from a few dollars up to more than one hundred thousand dollars. . . .

   It is interesting to note that, with the exception of New York, and possibly Delaware, each state had one or more prominent representatives in the Convention who held more than a negligible amount of securities, and who could therefore speak with feeling and authority on the question of providing in the new Constitution for the full discharge of the public debt. . . .

2. Personalty invested in lands for speculation was represented by at least fourteen members. . . .

3. Personalty in the form of money loaned at interest was represented by at least twenty-four members. . . .

4. Personalty in mercantile, manufacturing, and shipping lines was represented by at least eleven members. . . .

5. Personalty in slaves was represented by at least fifteen members. . . .

It cannot be said, therefore, that the members of the Convention were "disinterested." On the contrary, we are forced to accept the profoundly significant conclusion that they knew through their personal experiences in economic affairs the precise results which the new government that they were setting up was designed to attain. As a group of doctrinaires, like the Frankfort assembly of 1848, they would have failed miserably; but as practical men they were able to build the new government upon the only foundations which could be stable: fundamental economic interests.[1] . . .

RATIFICATION

New York

There can be no question about the predominance of personalty in the contest over the ratification in New York. That state, says Libby, "presents the problem in its simplest form. The entire mass of interior counties . . . were solidly Anti-federal, comprising the agricultural portion of the state, the last settled and the most thinly populated. There were however in this region two Federal cities (not represented in the convention [as such]), Albany in Albany county and Hudson in Columbia county. . . . The Federal area centred about New York city and county: to the southwest lay Richmond county (Staten Island); to the southeast Kings county, and the northeast Westchester county; while still further extending this area, at the northeast lay the divided county of Dutchess, with a vote in the convention of 4 to 2 in favor of the Constitution, and at the southeast were the divided counties of Queens and Suffolk. . . . These radiating strips of territory with New York city as a centre form a unit, in general favorable to the new Constitution; and it is significant of this unity that Dutchess, Queens, and Suffolk counties, broke away from the anti-Federal phalanx and joined the Federalists, securing thereby the adoption of the Constitution."[2]

Unfortunately the exact distribution of personalty in New York and particularly in the wavering districts which went over to the Federalist party cannot be ascertained, for the system of taxation in vogue in New York at the period of the adoption of the Constitution did not require a state record of property.[3] The data which proved so fruitful in Massachusetts are not forthcoming, therefore, in the case of New York; but it seems hardly necessary to demonstrate the fact that New York City was the centre of personalty for the state and stood next to Philadelphia as the great centre of operations in public stock.

This somewhat obvious conclusion is reinforced by the evidence relative to the vote on the legal tender bill which the paper money party pushed through in 1786. Libby's analysis of this vote shows that "no vote was cast against the bill by members of counties north of the county of New York. In the city and county of New York and in Long Island and Staten Island, the combined vote was 9 to 5 against the measure. Comparing this vote with the vote on the ratification in 1788, it will be seen that of the Federal counties 3 voted against paper money and 1 for it; of the divided counties 1 (Suffolk) voted against paper money and 2 (Queens and Dutchess) voted for it. Of the anti-Federal counties none had members voting against paper money. The merchants as a body were opposed to the issue of paper money and the Chamber of Commerce adopted a memorial against the issue."[4]

Public security interests were identified with the sound money party. There were thirty members of the New York constitutional convention who voted in favor of the ratification of the Constitution and of these no less than sixteen were holders of public securities. . . .

South Carolina

South Carolina presents the economic elements in the ratification with the utmost simplicity. There we find two rather sharply marked districts in antagonism over the Constitution. "The rival sections," says Libby, "were the coast or lower district and the upper, or more properly, the middle and upper country. The coast region was the first settled and contained a larger portion of the wealth of the state; its mercantile and commercial interests were important; its church was the Episcopal, supported by the state."

This region, it is scarcely necessary to remark, was overwhelmingly in favor of the Constitution. The upper area, against the Constitution, "was a frontier section, the last to receive settlement; its lands were fertile and its mixed population was largely small farmers. . . . There was no established church, each community supported its own church and there was a great variety in the district."[5]

A contemporary writer, R. G. Harper, calls attention to the fact that the lower country, Charleston, Beaufort, and Georgetown, which had 28,694 white inhabitants, and about seven-twelfths of the representation in the state convention, paid £28,081:5:10 taxes in 1794, while the upper country, with 120,902 inhabitants, and five-twelfths of the representation in the convention, paid only £8390:13:3 taxes.[6] The lower districts in favor of the Constitution therefore possessed the wealth of the state and a disproportionate share in the convention—on the basis of the popular distribution of representation.

These divisions of economic interest are indicated by the abstracts of the tax returns for the state in 1794 which show that of £127,337 worth of stock in trade, faculties, etc. listed for taxation in the state, £109,800 worth was in Charleston, city and county—the stronghold of Federalism. Of the valuation of lots in towns and villages to the amount of £656,272 in the state, £549,909 was located in that city and county.[7]

The records of the South Carolina loan office preserved in the Treasury Department at Washington show that the public securities of that state were more largely in the hands of inhabitants than was the case in North Carolina. They also show a heavy concentration in the Charleston district.

At least fourteen of the thirty-one members of the state-ratifying convention from the parishes of St. Philip and Saint Michael, Charleston (all of whom favored ratification) held over $75,000 worth of public securities. . . .

Conclusions

At the close of this long and arid survey—partaking of the nature of catalogue—it seems worthwhile to bring together the important conclusions for political science which the data presented appear to warrant.

The movement for the Constitution of the United States was originated and carried through principally by four groups of personalty interests which had been adversely affected under the Articles of Confederation: money, public securities, manufactures, and trade and shipping.

The first firm steps toward the formation of the Constitution were taken by a small and active group of men immediately interested through their personal possessions in the outcome of their labors.

No popular vote was taken directly or indirectly on the proposition to call the Convention which drafted the Constitution.

A large propertyless mass was, under the prevailing suffrage qualifications, excluded at the outset from participation (through representatives) in the work of framing the Constitution.

The members of the Philadelphia Convention which drafted the Constitution were, with a few exceptions, immediately, directly, and personally interested in, and derived economic advantages from, the establishment of the new system.

The Constitution was essentially an economic document based upon the concept that the fundamental private rights of property are anterior to government and morally beyond the reach of popular majorities.

The major portion of the members of the Convention are on record as recognizing the claim of property to a special and defensive position in the Constitution.

In the ratification of the Constitution, about three-fourths of the adult males failed to vote on the question, having abstained from the elections at which delegates to the state conventions were chosen, either on account of their indifference or their disfranchisement by property qualifications.

The Constitution was ratified by a vote of probably not more than one-sixth of the adult males.

It is questionable whether a majority of the voters participating in the elections for the state conventions in New York, Massachusetts, New Hampshire, Virginia, and South Carolina, actually approved the ratification of the Constitution.

The leaders who supported the Constitution in the ratifying conventions represented the same economic groups as the members of the Philadelphia Convention; and in a large number of instances they were also directly and personally interested in the outcome of their efforts.

In the ratification, it became manifest that the line of cleavage for and against the Constitution was between substantial personalty interests on the one hand and the small farming and debtor interests on the other.

The Constitution was not created by "the whole people" as the jurists have said; neither was it created by "the states" as southern nullifiers long contended; but it was the work of a consolidated group whose interests knew no state boundaries and were truly national in their scope.

NOTES

1. The fact that a few members of the Convention, who had considerable economic interests at stake, refused to support the Constitution does not invalidate the general conclusions here presented. In the cases of Yates, Lansing, Luther Martin, and Mason, definite economic reasons for their action are forthcoming; but this is a minor detail.
2. O. G. Libby, *Geographical Distribution of the Vote of the Thirteen States on the Federal Constitution*, p. 18. Libby here takes the vote in the New York convention, but that did not precisely represent the popular vote.
3. *State Papers: Finance*, vol. 1, p. 425.
4. Libby, *Geographical Distribution*, p. 59.
5. *Ibid.*, pp. 42–43.
6. "Appius," *To the Citizens of South Carolina* (1794), Library of Congress, Duane Pamphlets, vol. 83.
7. *State Papers: Finance*, vol. 1, p. 462. In 1783 an attempt to establish a bank with $100,000 capital was made in Charleston, S.C., but it failed. "Soon after the adoption of the funding system, three banks were established in Charleston whose capitals in the whole amounted to twenty times the sum proposed in 1783." D. Ramsey, *History of South Carolina* (1858 ed.), vol. 2, p. 106.

Charles Beard and the Constitution:
A Critical Analysis

Robert E. Brown

At the end of Chapter XI [of *An Economic Interpretation of the Constitution of the United States*], Beard summarized his findings in fourteen paragraphs under the heading of "Conclusions." Actually, these fourteen conclusions merely add up to the two halves of the Beard thesis. One half, that the Constitution originated with and was carried through by personalty interests—money, public securities, manufactures, and commerce—is to be found in paragraphs two, three, six, seven, eight, twelve, thirteen, and fourteen. The other half—that the Constitution was put over undemocratically in an undemocratic society—is expressed in paragraphs four, five, nine, ten, eleven, and fourteen. The lumping of these conclusions under two general headings makes it easier for the reader to see the broad outlines of the Beard thesis.

Before we examine these two major divisions of the thesis, however, some comment is relevant on the implications contained in the first paragraph. In it Beard characterized his book as a long and arid survey, something in the nature of a catalogue. Whether this characterization was designed to give his book the appearance of a coldly objective study based on the facts we do not know. If so, nothing could be further from reality. As reviewers pointed out in 1913, and as subsequent developments have demonstrated, the book is anything but an arid catalogue of facts. Its pages are replete with interpretation, sometimes stated, sometimes implied. Our task has been to examine Beard's evidence to see whether it justifies the interpretation which Beard gave it. We have tried to discover whether he used the historical method properly in arriving at his thesis.

If historical method means the gathering of data from primary sources, the critical evaluation of the evidence thus gathered, and the drawing of conclusions consistent with this evidence, then we must conclude that Beard has done great violation to such method in this book. He admitted that the evidence had not been collected which, given the proper use of historical method, should have precluded the writing of the book. Yet he nevertheless proceeded on the assumption that a valid interpretation could be built on secondary writings whose authors had likewise failed to collect the evidence. If we accept Beard's own maxim, "no evidence, no history," and his own admission that the data had never been collected, the answer to whether he used historical method properly is self-evident.

Neither was Beard critical of the evidence which he did use. He was accused in 1913, and one might still suspect him, of using only that evidence which appeared to support his thesis. The amount of realty in the country compared with the personalty,

Robert E. Brown is professor emeritus of history at Michigan State University. From Brown, Robert E., Charles Beard and the Constitution: A Critical Analysis. *Copyright © 1956, renewed 1984 by Princeton University Press. Reprinted by permission of Princeton University Press.*

the vote in New York, and the omission of the part of *The Federalist,* No. 10, which did not fit his thesis are only a few examples of the uncritical use of evidence to be found in the book. Sometimes he accepted secondary accounts at face value without checking them with the sources; at other times he allowed unfounded rumors and traditions to color his work.

Finally, the conclusions which he drew were not justified even by the kind of evidence which he used. If we accepted his evidence strictly at face value, it would still not add up to the fact that the Constitution was put over undemocratically in an undemocratic society by personalty. The citing of property qualifications does not prove that a mass of men were disfranchised. And if we accept his figures on property holdings, either we do not know what most of the delegates had in realty and personalty, or we know that realty outnumbered personalty three to one (eighteen to six). Simply showing that a man held public securities is not sufficient to prove that he acted only in terms of his public securities. If we ignore Beard's own generalizations and accept only his evidence, we have to conclude that most of the country, and that even the men who were directly concerned with the Constitution, and especially Washington, were large holders of realty.

Perhaps we can never be completely objective in history, but certainly we can be more objective than Beard was in this book. Naturally, the historian must always be aware of the biases, the subjectivity, the pitfalls that confront him, but this does not mean that he should not make an effort to overcome these obstacles. Whether Beard had his thesis before he had his evidence, as some have said, is a question that each reader must answer for himself. Certain it is that the evidence does not justify the thesis.

So instead of the Beard interpretation that the Constitution was put over undemocratically in an undemocratic society by personal property, the following fourteen paragraphs are offered as a possible interpretation of the Constitution and as suggestions for future research on that document.

1. The movement for the Constitution was originated and carried through by men who had long been important in both economic and political affairs in their respective states. Some of them owned personalty, more of them owned realty, and if their property was adversely affected by conditions under the Articles of Confederation, so also was the property of the bulk of the people in the country, middle-class farmers as well as town artisans.

2. The movement for the Constitution, like most important movements, was undoubtedly started by a small group of men. They were probably interested personally in the outcome of their labors, but the benefits which they expected were not confined to personal property or, for that matter, strictly to things economic. And if their own interests would be enhanced by a new government, similar interests of other men, whether agricultural or commercial, would also be enhanced.

3. Naturally there was no popular vote on the calling of the convention which drafted the Constitution. Election of delegates by state legislatures was the constitutional method under the Articles of Confederation, and had been the method long established in this country. Delegates to the Albany Congress, the Stamp Act Congress, the First

Continental Congress, the Second Continental Congress, and subsequent congresses under the Articles were all elected by state legislatures, not by the people. Even the Articles of Confederation had been sanctioned by state legislatures, not by popular vote. This is not to say that the Constitutional Convention should not have been elected directly by the people, but only that such a procedure would have been unusual at the time. Some of the opponents of the Constitution later stressed, without avail, the fact that the Convention had not been directly elected. But at the time the Convention met, the people in general seemed to be about as much concerned over the fact that they had not elected the delegates as the people of this country are now concerned over the fact that they do not elect our delegates to the United Nations.

4. Present evidence seems to indicate that there were no "propertyless masses" who were excluded from the suffrage at the time. Most men were middle-class farmers who owned realty and were qualified voters, and, as the men in the Convention said, mechanics had always voted in the cities. Until credible evidence proves otherwise, we can assume that state legislatures were fairly representative at the time. We cannot condone the fact that a few men were probably disfranchised by prevailing property qualifications, but it makes a great deal of difference to an interpretation of the Constitution whether the disfranchised comprised 95 percent of the adult men or only 5 percent. Figures which give percentages of voters in terms of the entire population are misleading, since less than 20 percent of the people were adult men. And finally, the voting qualifications favored realty, not personalty.

5. If the members of the Convention were directly interested in the outcome of their work and expected to derive benefits from the establishment of the new system, so also did most of the people of the country. We have many statements to the effect that the people in general expected substantial benefits from the labors of the Convention.

6. The Constitution was not just an economic document, although economic factors were undoubtedly important. Since most of the people were middle class and had private property, practically everybody was interested in the protection of property. A constitution which did not protect property would have been rejected without any question, for the American people had fought the Revolution for the preservation of life, liberty, and property. Many people believed that the Constitution did not go far enough to protect property, and they wrote these views into the amendments to the Constitution. But property was not the only concern of those who wrote and ratified the Constitution, and we would be doing a grave injustice to the political sagacity of the Founding Fathers if we assumed that property or personal gain was their only motive.

7. Naturally the delegates recognized that protection of property was important under government, but they also recognized that personal rights were equally important. In fact, persons and property were usually bracketed together as the chief objects of government protection.

8. If three-fourths of the adult males failed to vote on the election of delegates to ratifying conventions, this fact signified indifference, not disfranchisement. We must not confuse those who could *not* vote with those who *could* vote but failed to exercise their right. Many men at the time bewailed the fact that only a small portion of the voters ever exercised their prerogative. But this in itself should stand as evidence that the conflict over the Constitution was not very bitter, for if these people had felt strongly one way or the other, more of them would have voted.

Even if we deny the evidence which I have presented and insist that American society was undemocratic in 1787, we must still accept the fact that the men who wrote the Constitution believed that they were writing it for a democratic society. They did not hide behind an iron curtain of secrecy and devise the kind of conservative government that they wanted without regard to the views and interests of "the people." More than anything else, they were aware that "the people" would have to ratify what they proposed, and that therefore any government which would be acceptable to the people must of necessity incorporate much of what was customary at the time. The men at Philadelphia were practical politicians, not political theorists. They recognized the multitude of different ideas and interests that had to be reconciled and compromised before a constitution would be acceptable. They were far too practical, and represented far too many clashing interests themselves, to fashion a government weighted in favor of personalty or to believe that the people would adopt such a government.

9. If the Constitution was ratified by a vote of only one-sixth of the adult men, that again demonstrates indifference and not disfranchisement. Of the one-fourth of the adult males who voted, nearly two-thirds favored the Constitution. Present evidence does not permit us to say what the popular vote was except as it was measured by the votes of the ratifying conventions.

10. Until we know what the popular vote was, we cannot say that it is questionable whether a majority of the voters in several states favored the Constitution. Too many delegates were sent uninstructed. Neither can we count the towns which did not send delegates on the side of those opposed to the Constitution. Both items would signify indifference rather than sharp conflict over ratification.

11. The ratifying conventions were elected for the specific purpose of adopting or rejecting the Constitution. The people in general had anywhere from several weeks to several months to decide the question. If they did not like the new government, or if they did not know whether they liked it, they could have voted *no* and there would have been no Constitution. Naturally the leaders in the ratifying conventions represented the same interests as the members of the Constitutional Convention—mainly realty and some personalty. But they also represented their constituents in these same interests, especially realty.

12. If the conflict over ratification had been between substantial personalty interests on the one hand and small farmers and debtors on the other, there would not have been a constitution. The small farmers comprised such an overwhelming percentage of the voters that they could have rejected the new government without any trouble. Farmers and debtors are not synonymous terms and should not be confused as such. A town-by-town or county-by-county record of the vote would show clearly how the farmers voted.

13. The Constitution was created about as much by the whole people as any government could be which embraced a large area and depended on representation rather than on direct participation. It was also created in part by the states, for as the *Records* show, there was strong state sentiment at the time which had to be appeased by compromise. And it was created by compromising a whole host of interests throughout the country, without which compromises it could never have been adopted.

14. If the intellectual historians are correct, we cannot explain the Constitution without considering the psychological factors also. Men are motivated by what they believe as well as by what they have. Sometimes their actions can be explained on the basis of what they hope to have or hope that their children will have. Madison understood this fact when he said that the universal hope of acquiring property tended to dispose people to look favorably upon property. It is even possible that some men support a given economic system when they themselves have nothing to gain by it. So we would want to know what the people in 1787 thought of their class status. Did workers and small farmers believe that they were lower class, or did they, as many workers do now, consider themselves middle class? Were the common people trying to eliminate the Washingtons, Adamses, Hamiltons, and Pinckneys, or were they trying to join them?

As did Beard's fourteen conclusions, these fourteen suggestions really add up to two major propositions: the Constitution was adopted in a society which was fundamentally democratic, not undemocratic; and it was adopted by a people who were primarily middle-class property owners, especially farmers who owned realty, not just by the owners of personalty. At present these points seem to be justified by the evidence, but if better evidence in the future disproves or modifies them, we must accept that evidence and change our interpretation accordingly.

After this critical analysis, we should at least not begin future research on this period of American history with the illusion that the Beard thesis of the Constitution is valid. If historians insist on accepting the Beard thesis in spite of this analysis, however, they must do so with the full knowledge that their acceptance is founded on "an act of faith," not an analysis of historical method, and that they were indulging in a "noble dream," not history.

3

FEDERALISM

The Tenth Amendment to the U.S. Constitution states: "The powers not delegated to the United States by the Constitution, nor prohibited by it to the States, are reserved to the States respectively, or to the people." Although this brief amendment, containing just slightly more than 25 words, seems simple and uncomplicated, it has, in fact, constituted the basis for one of the more protracted debates in U.S. history—namely, the extent of the national government's powers in relation to those of the states.

A modern manifestation of this debate is to be found in the controversy over "unfunded federal mandates." Unfunded mandates are those laws passed by Congress that require states to carry out national regulations without federal government funding. *Examples are the Clean Water Act of 1972, the Americans with Disabilities Act of 1990, and the National Voter Registration Act of 1993. While noble in purpose, these acts have frequently been criticized as interfering with the powers and financial responsibilities of the states in violation of the spirit, if not the letter, of the constitutional division of powers between the national government and the states.*

In the selections that follow, unfunded mandates are debated by two members of Congress. In the first selection, U.S. Senator Spencer Abraham (R-Mich.) develops the case for limiting the number of federal mandates and requiring Congress to conduct a full review of the costs of any mandate. Senator Abraham's arguments against unfunded mandates are grounded in the belief that the national government should not impose on the states financial burdens for programs to which the states have not agreed; nor should Congress seek to bypass its own responsibility in fiscal matters by passing along to the states the costs of federal programs.

In the second selection, U.S. Representative George Miller (D-Cal.) makes the case for keeping the system of federal mandates, both funded and unfunded. Representative Miller rests his case both on the good that has come from such mandates and also on the continuing unwillingness or inability of the states to solve pressing social, economic, and environmental problems on their own.

Unfunded Mandates:
The Negative Effects

U.S. Senator Spencer Abraham (R-Mich.)

Mr. President, I rise in support of S.1, which, of course, addresses the problem of unfunded Federal mandates. S.1 would significantly limit the Federal Government's ability to require State or local governments to undertake affirmative activities or comply with Federal standards unless the Federal Government was also prepared to reimburse the costs of such activities or compliance. As with direct Federal expenditures, the financial burdens of such mandates fall squarely upon the middle-class taxpayer. . . .

Perhaps nothing better reflects contemporary trends in government than the enormous growth in the level of unfunded Federal mandates over the past two decades. An unfunded mandate arises when the Federal Government imposes some responsibility or obligation upon a State or local government to implement a program or carry out an action without, at the same time, providing the State or local government with the necessary funding. Several recent illustrations of unfunded mandates include obligations imposed on States and localities to establish minimum voter registration procedures in the Motor Vehicle Voter Registration Act; obligations imposed on States and localities to conduct automobile emissions testing programs under the Clean Air Act; and obligations imposed on States and localities to monitor water systems for contaminants under the Safe Drinking Water Act. These examples, however, are only the smallest tip of the iceberg.

While there is virtually no area of public activity in which Federal mandates are absent, such mandates are most visible in the area of environmental legislation. Of the 12 most costly mandates identified by the National Association of Counties in a 1993 survey, 7 of them involve environmental programs such as the Resource Conservation and Recovery Act, the Endangered Species Act, the Safe Drinking Water Act, and the Superfund Act.

The negative effect of unfunded Federal mandates are at least fivefold: First, such mandates camouflage the full extent of Federal Government spending by placing an increasingly significant share of that spending off-budget, in the form of costs imposed upon other levels of government. While it is extraordinarily difficult to assess the dollar costs of unfunded mandates, a sense of their magnitude is evidenced by a 3-month study done earlier this year by the State of Maryland, in which they concluded that approximately 24 percent of their total budget was committed to meeting legal requirements mandated by Congress. Assuming the rough accuracy of this estimation, and assuming that Maryland is not subject to extraordinary levels of mandates, this would amount to approximately $80 to $85 billion imposed nationally upon all State

Spencer Abraham is a Republican U.S. Senator from the state of Michigan. Excerpted from a speech delivered in the U.S. Senate, Congressional Record, *Proceedings and Debates of the 104ᵗʰ Congress, 1ˢᵗ Session, Senate, January 19, 1995, vol. 141, No. 11, S1183–S1184.*

governments. This figure does not include mandates imposed upon local governments. To calculate the true burden of Federal spending, the costs of these mandates must be added to an already bloated Federal budget. The Federal government consumes the limited resources of the people every bit as much when it compels State or local governments to do something as when it directly does something itself.

Second, the impact of the unfunded Federal mandate is to distort the cost-benefit analysis that Congress undertakes in assessing individual pieces of legislation. The costs imposed by the Congress upon States and localities are rarely considered, much less estimated with any accuracy. As a result, the presumed benefits of legislative measures are not viewed in the full context of their costs. Legislative benefits tend consistently to be overestimated and legislative costs tend consistently to be underestimated.

Third, unfunded Federal mandates burden State and local governments with spending obligations for programs which they have never chosen to incur while requiring them to reduce spending obligation for programs which they have chosen to incur. For the options are clear when mandates are imposed by Washington: Either State and local governments must raise taxes—since they do not have the same access to deficit spending as the Federal Government—or they must reorder their budget by reducing or terminating programs which had already been determined to merit public resources. With State balanced budget requirements and with taxpayers already burdened to the hilt by government demands for a share of their income, State and local governments are forced into a zero-sum analysis by unfunded mandates; every new Federal mandate must be compensated for directly by a reduction in another area of State or local spending. Further, every Federal mandate must effectively be treated as the number one spending priority by State and local governments, notwithstanding the sense of their community and the judgment of their elected officials. Such governments must first budget whatever is necessary to pay for the mandates and only afterwards evaluate the level of resources remaining for other spending measures.

Which leads to the fourth impact of the unfunded Federal mandate. An increasing proportion of State and local budgets is devoted to spending measures deemed to be important not by the elected representatives in those jurisdictions, but rather by decisionmakers in Washington. In 1993, for example, compliance with Federal Medicaid mandates cost the State of Michigan $95.3 million, which exceeded by $7 million the combined expenses of the Michigan Departments of State, Civil Rights, Civil Services, Attorney General, and Agriculture. Although the Supreme Court in recent years has reduced the 10th Amendment to effective insignificance, I believe nevertheless that there are constitutional implications to this trend. It is lamentable enough that the Federal budget has grown at the pace that we have witnessed over the past generation; for Washington additionally to be determining the budgetary priorities of Michigan and Texas and Pennsylvania is for it to trespass upon the proper constitutional prerogatives of the States. To the extent that the States are straitjacketed in their ability to determine the composition of their own budgets, their sovereignty has been undermined.

Indeed, the Constitution aside, it is difficult to understand how a reasoned assessment of the efficacy of Federal Government programs over the past several decades would encourage anyone in the notion that Washington had any business instructing other governments how best to carry out their responsibilities.

Finally, unfunded Federal mandates erode the accountability of government generally. The average citizen now finds that his State and local representatives disavow
responsibility for spending measures resulting from Federal mandates, while his Washington representatives also claim not to be responsible. Lines of accountability are simply too indirect and too convoluted where Federal mandates are involved. The result is
that the citizenry come to feel that no one is clearly responsible for what government is
doing, and that they have little ability to influence its course.

I am particularly supportive of S.1 because I believe that it will result in governments at all levels thinking more seriously about the proper scope of government. In
truth, unfunded mandates are but one symptom of the more fundamental problem that
the Federal Government has lost sight of the proper scope of its functions. While there
are some mandates that are reasonable, Congress should be prepared to reimburse the
States for the costs attendant to such mandates. In cases where the wisdom of mandates
is more dubious, S.1 would force upon Congress a more balanced and a sober decision-
making process. Instead of neglecting the hidden pass-the-buck costs entailed in
unfunded mandates, Congress instead would be forced to make hard-headed decisions
about the costs and benefits of new programs. In at least some of these cases, I am confident that the legislative balance will be drawn differently than that we have consistently seen over recent decades. I am confident that the virtues of federalism will be recognized more readily when new programs are no longer free but must be explicitly
accounted for in the Federal budget. The one-size-fits-all mentality which tends to
underlie most Federal mandates may also be reconsidered in the process.

At the same time, State and local officials will also have to make difficult decisions.
With Congress likely to curtail or terminate altogether some mandates when confronted
with the requirement that they have to pay for them, State and local governments will
have to determine whether they are willing to support such programs on their own. No
longer will they be able to enjoy the benefits of such programs while being able to
divert responsibility for their costs to the Federal Government. Rather, they will have to
make equally hard decisions as those that will have to be make by Washington lawmakers about the relative merits of public programs.

Perhaps the greatest long-term benefit of the present legislation is that it will force
more open and honest decision making and budgeting upon all levels of government.
When greater governmental accountability is achieved, the public will be better posi-
tioned to punish and reward public officials for actions. As a result, government will be
more responsive to the electorate in its spending decisions. Government, in short, will
be made more representative by this legislation. . . .

Unfunded Mandates:
Laws That Bind Us Together

U.S. Representative George Miller (D-Cal.)

Mr. Chairman, this legislation strikes at the very heart of the body of laws that bind us together as a progressive society, and with the highest standard of living in the world, the body of law that ensures that no matter where you live in this country, you can enjoy clean water: that no matter where you live in this country, local government and the private sector are working every day to improve the air that you breathe, so we no longer have to send our children indoors because it is too smoggy out. We no longer have to tell our senior citizens they cannot go out for a walk because the air quality is too bad, or we cannot drive to work because they do not want the automobiles on the road.

These are the laws that accomplished those successes. These are laws that said "Yes, if you take money from the Federal Government, we are going to put onto you an obligation to educate the handicapped children of this Nation," because before that was the law, the handicapped children of this Nation could not get an education in the public school systems run by the States and localities that we now say are so ready to do the job.

But for that law, tens of thousands of handicapped children, because they have cerebral palsy, because they have Downs syndrome, would not be allowed in our public schools, but that is a Federal mandate. Yes, we pay part of the freight, but this law would say "Unless the Federal Government presents 100 percent of it, no school district would be required to educate that handicapped child. Unless the Federal Government spends 100 percent of the money to clean up the local water supply, the local sewage treatment, the city would have no obligation."

What happens along the Mississippi River in Indiana or Minnesota if they choose, or in Ohio, if they choose not to clean up the municipal sewage because the Federal Government will not pay 100 percent? That means the people in Mississippi and Louisiana have to inherit that sewage.

An unfunded mandate upstream is untreated sewage downstream. What does that mean to the fishermen, to the commercial enterprises, and to the tourist industry in those States? It means they suffer. That is why we have national laws.

When I was a young man you could smell San Francisco Bay before you could see it, but now we require all of the cities, not just the town that I live in, not just the oil industry, not just the chemical industry, but the cities upstream and downstream [to clean up]. Some of them, we had to take them to court to tell them to clean it up. Today San Francisco Bay is a tourist attraction. Commercial fishing is back. People can use it for recreation.

George Miller is a Democratic U.S. Representative from the state of California. Excerpted from a speech delivered in the U.S. House of Representatives, Congressional Record, *Proceedings and Debates of the 104th Congress, 1st Session, House of Representatives, January 19, 1996, vol. 141, No. 11, H355–H356.*

That is what these mandates have done. Yes, we have not paid 100 percent, but we have put billions and billions and billions of dollars into helping local communities make airports safe so they could become international airports, so people would have confidence in going to those cities. We have cleaned up their water and air. We have made it safe to drink. That is what this legislation is an assault on.

Mr. Chairman, the proponents of this legislation would have us believe this is a simple and straightforward initiative: Congress should mandate the States and local governments to do nothing that Congress is not willing to pay for in its entirety.

In fact, this legislation strikes at the very heart of the entire concept on which our Government is based. Government does not have the responsibility to require that those in our societies—private individuals, businesses, and State and local governments—meet certain responsibilities.

Even the drafters of this legislation recognize that some mandates need not be paid for. They are ideologues of convenience. They do not require we pay for compliance with civil rights and disability laws. But they would compel funding for actions relating to public health and safety, protection of the environment, education of children, medical services to our elderly, safeguards to our workers.

And they would require that we pay only when that burden is imposed on entities of government. Private industry, many of which compete with State and local government in the provision of services, is accorded no relief. And those who work for Government, performing exactly the same services as those in the private sector, are potentially denied such basic protections as minimum wages, worker right to know about hazardous substances, and OSHA protections.

Never mind that the same State and local governments to whose aid we are rushing impose precisely the same unfunded mandates on lower levels of government.

So, I think this clearly demonstrates what is going on here: this is not about unfunded mandates: It is about undermining this Nation's environmental, education, health and labor laws, and wrapping the attack in the flag of unfunded mandates.

The last time we tried this deceptive tactic—cutting away at the basic role of Government in the name of cost savings—we tripled the national debt in 8 years.

But let me take issue with the very name of this concept—unfunded mandates.

Unfunded? Really?

We have spent tens of billions of dollars helping States and local communities meet these mandates by improving water systems, upgrading drinking water supplies, building and improving transportation systems, improving education programs, and on and on.

Have we funded every mandate fully? No. Should the Federal Government have to pay States and local communities to protect their employees, their environment and their public health and safety? Because let's remember: A lot of them were not protecting those people and those resources before the Federal mandates came along.

No, we haven't funded every dollar. But have we covered 50, 75, 90 percent of the cost of many of these projects? Time and time again.

And have we provided these same State and local governments with hundreds of billions of dollars to build, expand and improve highways, rapid transit and harbors and to respond to disasters—even when there was no Federal responsibility to provide a dollar? Have we provided money to assure that communities are safe from nuclear power plants and hazardous waste sites? Have we provided money to educate the handicapped, to train the jobless, and to house tens of millions of Americans?

I have little doubt that those who champion this legislation fully expect that its passage would have no effect on our willingness to fund their future actions in these areas. They are very wrong. Every State and community should be aware that the appetite of the Congress for funding local projects and programs that fail to meet a Federal standard of quality and protection and performance is going to be very minimal, particularly in light of the coming effort for a balanced budget amendment that would slash Federal spending radically.

So I think we should proceed with some caution here. If the States and local communities don't want the mandates, don't expect the Federal dollars either.

I find it somewhat ironic that in my own State of California, for example, the Governor has failed to come up with his promise of matching funds for the $5 billion in Federal disaster aid following last year's Northridge earthquake. Now he wants more Federal money for earthquake assistance; and he will want more still for the flooding, and he'll probably throw in a few billion dollars' worth of dams and other infrastructure from Federal taxpayers.

Yet he is one of the biggest proponents of this unfunded mandates legislation—and at the same time that he forces unfunded mandates down the throat of every county and city in California.

We see that kind of hypocrisy in the legislation before us today.

In case you didn't read the fine print, this mandate ban neglects to include the dozens of new unfunded Federal mandates contained in the Republicans' Contract With America. Just the mandates in the welfare bill alone could bring the States to their knees. But all those new mandates are exempted, even though none of them have yet been enacted into law. So much for being honest with the American people.

Let's be very clear what this legislation is going to do to some of the most important laws this Congress has passed and has spent billions of dollars helping States and local communities implement.

Safe drinking water. We have upgraded the water supply across this Nation, virtually eliminating disease, contamination and danger. Much of that has been paid for by Federal dollars. Which local community would like to have taken on that task without Federal assistance? Which Americans want to put the future and the consistency of our safe drinking water at risk through this legislation?

Clean water. You used to be able to smell San Francisco Bay before you could see it. You used to need a battery of shots if you stuck your toe in the Potomac River. The sewage and waste water of 80 million Americans from a score of States flows out of the mouth of the Mississippi River, and for years contaminated the commercial fishing areas. A few years before the Clean Water Act was passed, the Cuyohoga River in Cleveland was burning. Want to go back to those days? You tell me which financially strapped city and State will take on that burden without Federal assistance?

Nuclear safety. Should nuclear power plants and generators of radioactive wastes—which exist in every large city and many small ones—be able to ignore Federal safety standards for operations and waste disposal?

Deadbeat parents. We are collecting hundreds of millions of dollars a year from parents who have ignored their financial responsibilities to their children, thanks to Federal law. Should we just abandon that program?

The list of inequities goes on and on. What happens to reauthorizations of existing laws? What if those reauthorizations are delayed for years by obstructive tactics in Congress? The answer is: We don't know. And the reason we are legislating in the dark here is because this complex bill, which would fundamentally alter the entire nature of Federal-State relations, was drafted in haste, denied public comment and public hearings, and marked up in a haphazard and manipulated process that made thoughtful review all but impossible.

Of course we should examine whether Federal funding of mandates has been adequate. In fact, that process was begun last year. . . .

But let us not rush to pass a deeply flawed, confusing, and deceptive bill, . . . a bill that misrepresents not only the need for mandates, but ignores the billions of dollars we have given to States and communities to help meet those mandates.

4

PUBLIC OPINION

At a time when a substantial number of Americans see government as increasingly remote and suffocated by special interests, it is not altogether surprising that some scholars and commentators are calling for new ways to give citizens a greater voice and influence in the decisions of government. Foremost among the proposals to "reconnect" the American people with their government is a proposal to use interactive television in "Electronic Town Meetings" (ETMs) as a means to record public opinion on the issues of the day. Those who advocate linking technology to citizen involvement and government decision making see hundreds, if not thousands of communities, utilizing interactive television to communicate citizen concerns to their representatives.

In the two selections that follow, contrasting arguments are presented on the potential for using the new technology to improve the public discourse and government decision making. In the first, Duane Elgin, a proponent of ETMs, argues that interactive TV has the potential to reduce the feeling of powerlessness among the American people and to once again give citizens a feeling of being "engaged and responsible for society and its future." In the second selection, two Washington, D.C. commentators, Norman Ornstein and Amy Schenkenberg, raise very serious questions about the new TV technology and the role that the public should play in our representative system of government. Ornstein and Schenkenberg ask: Who's going to control such a system and determine the questions that are asked of the public? What's to assure that all citizens will, at a minimum, be interested in, and have access to such a system? And, most importantly, do we really want the sometime disinterested and ill-informed public to exert control over policymaking?

Revitalizing Democracy through Electronic Town Meetings

Duane Elgin

Each generation must renew its contract with democracy in ways that respond to the changing needs of the times. In his inaugural speech, President Clinton rightly recognized the need for "bold and persistent experimentation" to revitalize democracy as we confront unprecedented challenges.

The United States confronts an enormous deficit, crumbling infrastructure, a failing education system, chronic drug abuse, violent crime, a health crisis and many other major problems. Compounding matters, many state and local governments are in gridlock. The nation seems to be adrift without a sense of purpose. Not surprisingly, many citizens feel powerless and disconnected from politics.

Global problems that threaten the domestic society and economy include climate change, ozone depletion, rain forest devastation, dwindling oil reserves, mounting population, the extinction of plant and animal species and many more. Economic progress is turned into ecological devastation as the biosphere is wounded by humanity's actions. . . .

THE OPPORTUNITY TO REVITALIZE DEMOCRACY

Abraham Lincoln said, "With public sentiment, nothing can fail; without it, nothing can succeed." To respond to current challenges, we need a communicating democracy where public sentiments are mobilized on behalf of constructive action. We need an informed democracy where citizens regularly engage in dialogues among themselves and with elected leaders.

A strong democracy is impossible with weak citizen participation. Because communication is the lifeblood of democracy, a whole new level of citizen communication is needed to revitalize governance. Until recently, this would have been impossible. No longer. A communications revolution is providing citizens and governments with the tools to build a new level of understanding and consensus. The most prominent technology in this revolution is television (which is evolving rapidly into a multimedia system that is integrated with computers, telephones, satellites and other technologies).

In the United States, 98 percent of all homes have a television set (more than have stoves, refrigerators or indoor toilets); the average person watches more than four hours per day, and a majority of people get most of their news about their community and world from this medium. If important issues or choices do not appear on television then, for all practical purposes, they do not exist in our mass social consciousness.

Duane Elgin is director of Choosing Our Future, a nonpartisan and nonprofit organization promoting electronic town meetings, located in Larkspur, California. From Duane Elgin, "Revitalizing Democracy through Electronic Town Meetings," Spectrum: The Journal of State Government *66 (Spring 1993), pp. 6–13. Reprinted with permission from The Council of State Governments, copyright 1993.*

Television has become the "social brain" or "central nervous system" of our society and democracy. With the speed of light, television can extend our involvement to the entire planet. Through the eyes of television, we can see urban decay in New York, violent crime in California, homelessness in Florida, starving villagers in Africa and the destruction of rain forests in Brazil. Given the power and pervasiveness of television, we can build a more conscious democracy. . . .

Power in democracy is the power to build and mobilize a working consensus to support policy initiatives. Without a strong and sustained consensus, political support for creative and innovative policies will wither and collapse. The ability to build a working consensus in the new world of unprecedented challenges depends upon the ability to continuously communicate with the public. No longer can a single election provide a mandate for governance. We have entered an era where change is so dramatic and so rapid that we need a continuous campaign, engaging the public in an ongoing process at dialogue and consensus building.

Lech Walesa of Poland was once asked what caused the democratic revolution that swept through Eastern Europe. He pointed to a TV set and remarked, "It all came from there." Although many government officials recognize mass media's power to impact the political consciousness of citizens, historically there has been little enthusiasm among public officials for encouraging citizens to use television to engage more fully in the governing process. Now that citizens need to get more directly involved, the time is ripe to reconsider the roles of the public, the mass media and governments. We require a new partnership between citizens, governments and the mass media if we are to revitalize democracy with a more effective process of communication and consensus building. Adjustments are required from everyone involved:

- First, government officials at every level will need to accept new voices. In addition to media professionals, public officials will increasingly hear the engaged and passionate voices of concerned citizens and communities.
- Second, media professionals will need to accept citizens as participants in the policy process as they play a larger role in defining the agenda and participating in televised discussions.
- Third, the public will need to move beyond passivity and take charge of its own dialogue and feedback processes.

These new relationships will require patience and flexibility as the creative process of designing a more conscious democracy unfolds.

Three ingredients are vital for revitalizing democracy: an informed citizenry that talks to itself and knows its own mind and engages in regular dialogue with its leaders. Although I want to emphasize the latter and the potential for interactive communication to revitalize democracy, the foundation for success is an informed and knowledgeable public. . . .

If we are to revitalize democracy, . . . a first requirement is for a hearty and robust diet of socially relevant programming that educates citizens about the critical issues and choices that we face—as communities, states and a nation. We require far more documentaries and investigative reports. We need programs that show us the tradeoffs and choices between different ways to allocate scarce resources. We need vivid scenarios of the future that show what life could be like depending upon our course of action.

Power in a democracy depends on the ability of citizens and leaders to coalesce and maintain a working consensus on policy initiatives and directions. If the public's understanding of choices and tradeoffs is weak, then the consensus that emerges from electronic dialogues will be weak. The first ingredient in a strong democracy is a well-informed public. Elected leaders at every level of government need to call for television programming (as well as coverage by newspapers, magazines and radio) that supports an informed debate among citizens about issues critical to our future. . . .

ELECTRONIC TOWN MEETINGS

Democracy has been called "the art of the possible." However, when a society enters an era of change and people don't know what their fellow citizens think and feel about critical choices, then neither the public nor the politicians know what is possible. Instead, the democratic process drifts aimlessly and is unable to mobilize citizens into constructive action. To revitalize democracy, citizens must have an ongoing way to "know their own minds" as an entire community. The most direct way to discover our collective sentiments is through electronic town meetings or ETMs.

The concept of ETMs means different things to different people. For some, it conjures up images of a televised program where viewers call to ask questions of elected leaders. For others, it suggests a live debate, such as at a city-council meeting, where members of the public ask questions or make comments. For others, it implies a public affairs TV show with telephone numbers flashed on the TV screen to allow viewers to voice their reactions to the issue under discussion. While there are valid forms of electronic dialogue, they do not use the full potential of our powerful communication technologies.

There are two basic requirements for revitalizing democracy via ETMs. First, citizens and decision-makers must be able to obtain accurate feedback regarding public sentiments. Second, feedback must be fast enough to enable citizens to give more than a single knee-jerk response to an issue raised during a televised town meeting.

Interactive processes need to enable a representative group of citizens to answer questions that explore the direction, texture, depth and intensity of public sentiments on critical policy issues. These requirements can be met. With existing technologies, we can obtain rapid and representative feedback from a preselected scientific sample of citizens who use their home telephones for dialed-in "voting."

Just as a doctor can take a small sample of blood and use it to acquire an accurate picture of the total condition of one's body, we can use feedback from a randomly selected sample of citizens to get a highly accurate sense of community (or state or national) views. By drawing upon a scientific sample of citizens who are watching the ETM and dialing in their "votes," the number of respondents is kept small enough to avoid overloading the phone lines. With a random sample, feedback can be obtained within one or two minutes, making it possible to poll on multiple questions during a single ETM.

A practical example of this design was developed in the San Francisco Bay Area in 1987 with a prime-time ETM on broadcast television. This pioneering experiment was developed through the cooperative efforts of Choosing Our Future, a nonprofit and nonpartisan media organization, and the local ABC-TV station. Prior to ETM, a cross section of the public in the metropolitan region was identified with the assistance of a university-based survey research center. Two weeks before the ETM, citizens were invited to participate. Those who agreed were sent a list of phone numbers that corresponded to various options. Although the only options for the pilot were yes/no, technology exists to register multiple choice responses and intensity of feeling responses.

The San Francisco ETM pilot began with an informative minidocumentary to place the issue in context, then moved to an in-studio dialogue with experts and a diverse studio audience. As key questions arose in the studio discussion, they were presented to the scientific sample viewing the ETM. The dialed-in "votes" were obtained in the TV studio within minutes and were displayed to participants in the studio and viewers at home. Six votes were easily taken during the prime-time, hour-long ETM. This program was viewed by more than 300,000 persons in the Bay Area and just begins to demonstrate the potential for achieving a dramatic increase in the scope of public dialogue and consensus building.

KEY ISSUES INVOLVING ELECTRONIC TOWN MEETINGS

The power of ETMs raises many issues concerning their possible misuse. These technologies are neither inherently good nor bad—their impact depends upon their design and use. Given their potential for manipulation, it seems natural that interest groups will seek to exploit these technologies. With our eyes open to dangers of abuse, we must design systems that minimize their risks and amplify our opportunities. Key issues include:

- Trust in the Public's Judgment: Historically, public knowledge about nitty-gritty aspects of policy choices often has been fragmentary. Some question the wisdom of bringing an ill-informed public into the decision-making process through ETMs. Yet, it is not the task of citizens to micromanage government; rather, it is the job of the public to be clear about overall priorities that guide the governing process.

  Research indicates that when the public is reasonably well informed about broad public policy issues, its judgment can be trusted. George Gallup Jr.[1] reviewed his organization's experience in polling American public opinion over a half a century and found the collective judgment of citizens to be "extraordinarily sound." Indeed, Gallup discovered that citizens were often ahead of their elected leaders in accepting innovations. Therefore, with the mature use of the mass media as a vehicle of social learning, there is good reason to welcome the citizenry into the governing process.

- Direct Versus Representative Democracy: If the public is more involved in governance through electronically enhanced dialogues, then how direct a role should citizens play? Again, it is not the role of ETMs to enable citizens to inject themselves into the details of policy decisions; instead, it is to enable citizens to build an ongoing consensus regarding the overall direction of public policy. For example, as we run out of cheap oil, we need to know public sentiments on solar power, wind generation, conservation and nuclear power. As citizens redefine their views through electronically supported dialogues, their elected representatives can develop appropriate public policy. Assuming public feedback is advisory, ETMs respect the responsibility of elected leaders to make decisions and the responsibility of citizens to communicate with those who govern.

- Who Sponsors the ETMs: Perhaps no factor will have a greater impact on the design, character and implementation of ETMs than who sponsors them. Consider three major possibilities. First, ETMs that are initiated by commercial TV stations will tend to be designed to sell consumers and entertain an audience—not to inform citizens and involve the public in choosing its future. Second, if ETMs are sponsored by a local, state or national government, there will be a natural tendency to use ETMs as a public relations tool rather than as an authentic forum for open dialogue by the community. Third, if ETMs are sponsored by an issue-oriented organization or by an institution representing a particular ethnic, racial or gender group, then there will be a tendency to focus narrowly on the concerns of this group. The conclusion seems inescapable that a new social institution is needed to act on behalf of all citizens as the nonpartisan sponsor of Electronic Town Meetings.

   Metropolitan areas need to develop nonpartisan and nonprofit "community voice" organizations that perform two key functions: (1) conduct research to determine critical community concerns, and (2) work with television stations to broadcast ETMs. The ETM organization would not promote or advocate any outcome; rather, its goal would be to support community learning, dialogue and consensus building, and let the chips fall where they may. . . .

- Safeguarding Against Manipulation: Given the power and reach of televised dialogues, there is the danger that a charismatic leader or influential interest group will monopolize the conversation of democracy and steer public policy in an unfortunate direction. There are various ways to safeguard against such an outcome. ETMs can be designed to insure a continuing variety of voices and views so no one person or group dominates. In addition, the range of issues considered can be so broad that no one person or organization can have an overpowering influence. Views and voices can be deliberately invited in from other metropolitan regions or states so as to provide a moderating influence. Finally, assuming George Gallup Jr. was correct in asserting that the public's judgment can be trusted, then with accurate feedback from a scientific sample of the public, there will be another corrective force. Overall, with foresight, checks and balances can be designed into the ETM process to minimize manipulation.

- Multiple Forms of Feedback: So that no one is shut out of the dialogue, responses from the scientific sample need to be supplemented with other types of feedback. First, the random sample can be supplemented with feedback that draws selectively from different age and ethnic groups, geographic areas and so forth. Second, other forms of telephone-based feedback can be included, for example, dial-ins where anyone can call an 800 number and register views that range from simple yes/no answers to sophisticated choices like those used by telemarketing organizations. Third, newspapers can participate by publishing ballots for the public to clip and mail in for tabulation. Fourth, computer-based electronic bulletin boards offer another approach for obtaining the views of the community. Fifth, community organizations that represent various causes or ethnic, gender or racial groups can be invited to give feedback and provide perspective.

- Cable TV Versus Broadcast TV: The scale of the electronically supported dialogues needs to match the scale of the issues being addressed. Otherwise, citizens will feel the dialogues are a meaningless exercise and tune out. Many of the larger metropolitan areas are served by a number of unconnected cable systems. Therefore, it is impractical to use cable TV to support metropolitan-wide dialogues. This is why many current ETM experiments should be developed in cooperation with broadcast TV stations that reach an entire metropolitan area.

CONCLUSION

With non-partisan "community voice" organizations sponsoring ETMs in major metropolitan areas around the country, a whole new level of citizen dialogue could soon be realized. The conversation of democracy could then be expanded to statewide and nationwide dialogues as changing coalitions of metropolitan organizations call for ETMs on particular issues. The opportunity to revitalize our democracy is genuine, immediate and breathtaking.

A healthy democracy requires the active consent of the governed, not simply their passive acquiescence. Involving citizens through ETMs will not guarantee the right choices will be made, but it will guarantee that citizens feel involved and invested in those choices. Rather than feeling cynical and powerless, citizens will feel engaged and responsible for society and its future. With an involved citizenry, democracy can, in President Clinton's words, become the "engine of our renewal."

NOTE

1. George Gallup, Jr. "50 Years of American Opinion," *San Francisco Chronicle,* Oct. 21, 1985.

The Promise and Perils of Cyberdemocracy

Norman Ornstein and Amy Schenkenberg

In 1992, Ross Perot promised that if elected president he would use electronic town hall meetings to guide national decisions. Perot lost the election (and never made clear how those meetings would operate), but the idea of "cyberdemocracy" aroused much interest and is spreading quickly as technology advances. Every U.S. senator and 190 representatives currently have World Wide Web pages, as do all eight major Republican presidential contenders. In 1995, the Library of Congress, under the leadership of Newt Gingrich, established an on-line system offering all legislation considered and passed by Congress.

On the local level, the city government of Colorado Springs has a non-commercial electronic bulletin board called Citylink. Established in 1990 to allow citizens to communicate with city managers and city council members, it's available free of charge. In 1994, the Minnesota Electronic Democracy Project conducted on-line debates among candidates in the gubernatorial and senate races.

States have begun fashioning their governmental processes around this direct-democracy ideal. Twenty-four states permit citizen initiatives that place legislation or constitutional amendments on the ballot. Oregon has held local vote-by-mail elections since 1981, and in 1995 initiated its first state-wide mail ballot to replace Senator Bob Packwood. North Dakota's 1996 presidential primary will be by mail ballot.

All this may be just the beginning. As new technologies emerge, many futurists paint rosy scenarios of more direct roles for individuals in law-making. Some prophesy that legislators will vote and debate from their home state through computers and televisions, eliminating the need for the actual houses of Congress in Washington. Lawrence Grossman, former president of PBS and NBC, imagines Congress evolving into a body that discusses issues and disseminates information, but only makes decisions after being instructed by the public. Futurist Christine Slaton questions the need for elected legislators at all. She envisions using technology to create a participatory democracy where representatives are selected by lot and rotated regularly. Alvin and Heidi Toffler of "third wave" fame predict that today's political parties will disappear, replaced by fluid coalitions that vary according to changing legislative interests. The Tofflers also envision representatives chosen by lot, or at a minimum, elected officials casting 50 percent of a vote and a random sampling of the public casting the other 50 percent. In this scenario, individuals will not only vote on more things than they do now,

Norman Ornstein is a resident scholar and Amy Schenkenberg is a research associate at the American Enterprise Institute, a government and public policy research organization in Washington, D.C. Reprinted from Norman Ornstein and Amy Schenkenberg, "The Promise & Perils of Cyberdemocracy," American Enterprise, *March/April 1996, pp. 53–54. Reprinted with the permission of The American Enterprise Institute for Public Policy Research, Washington D.C.*

they'll vote on more complex questions, as simple yes/no votes are replaced by if-then referenda. Nor will voters have to inconvenience themselves by traveling to the local polling station. They probably won't even have to lick a stamp. Instead, voters will simply punch in their vote from their TV remote control, never leaving the house, never having to speak with another individual, not even having to spend more than a few seconds thinking about their choice.

Enchanting as these innovations may sound to Americans grown weary of Washington ways, several questions arise: Would cyberdemocracy in fact be more representative? Would voters take seriously their new responsibilities? Would they even be interested? Who will determine the exact questions the public will decide? And most importantly, what sort of deliberation, if any, will exist under this new regime?

A cyberdemocracy based on personal computers and upscale television systems will not be equally open to all citizens. Twenty-two percent of college graduates go on line at least weekly, while only 1 percent of those with a high school diploma do, a recent Times Mirror survey reports. Men are twice as likely as women to be daily on-line users. Twenty-seven percent of families with incomes of $50,000 or greater have gone on line, but only 6 percent of those with incomes under $20,000 have. Indeed, the Colorado Springs information systems manager reported that in 1995 there were only 250 active Citylink users in a city of over 300,000. No doubt the popularity of comparable information systems will increase substantially over time, and costs will come down, but a skew toward the highly educated and well-to-do is inevitable.

Even if the technology were made available to everyone equally, how would interest be sustained? Lloyd Morrisett, president of the Markle Foundation, recently wrote that he envisions the early fascination with cyberdemocracy ebbing until cybervoting falls into the same predicament as current voting rights: treasured but not necessarily used. Studying California's experience with referenda, Morrisett found that "the ballot has become so loaded with complex initiatives that it seems to discourage people from going to the polls, rather than motivating them to express their judgment." If the average voter tuned out complex items flashing across his screen, "voting" would be much less representative than it is today.

Cyberdemocracy's greatest danger lies in the way it would diminish deliberation in government. Everyone applauds technology's capacity to inform voters and to improve communications between them and their representatives. But we must also recall that the Founders expressly rejected "pure" democracies where citizens "assemble and administer the government in person," because they usually end in the tyranny of the majority. The Constitution instead establishes a republic where voters select representatives to make and execute the laws. The Founders designed this process to produce a public *judgment,* enlarging upon and refining popular opinions. That judgment, as opposed to public emotions, can only arise through deliberation. In the slow process of debate, give-and-take, and face-to-face contact among representatives, all perspectives and interests can be considered. The need to persuade an informed group of representatives with diverse concerns should, the Founders thought, result in decisions that are more just and more likely to meet the test of time with citizens.

Deliberation even figures in our political campaigns. Over weeks and months, campaigns provide a larger deliberative canvas, an opportunity for voters to consider issues, governing philosophies, and questions of leadership, resulting in a great appreciation of the choices that will face Congress and the President. Of course, our governing system does not always live up to the challenges of serious deliberation, but it still remains our foundation.

What happens to deliberation with the ascent of cyberdemocracy? Consider elections. For all the understandable criticism of never-ending campaigns, negative advertising, and demagoguery, campaigns still work, at least sometimes, as deliberative processes. Voters' initial inclination, not to mention their priorities on issues, often change as they receive more information. Early polls rarely reflect the actual voting. Citizens striving for informed judgments usually make them in the final, most intense days of a campaign. Instantaneous electronic voting would destroy whatever is left of this deliberative process. In Oregon most voters return their mail ballots within five days, casting their votes well before the final days (or even weeks) of intense campaigning.

Mail or electronic balloting also removes the symbolic quality of voting as an act where voters make a private judgment in a public place, surrounded by their fellow citizens, acknowledging simultaneously our individuality and our collective responsibility and common purpose. Compare standing in line at a polling place, going into a private booth, and making individual choices with the alternative of vote-by-mail—the political equivalent of filling out a Publishers Clearing House ballot—or electronic voting, where elections would resemble the Home Shopping Network.

Voting by mail or electronically is only one challenge cyberpolitics presents to deliberative democracy. Consider the difference between laws passed by referenda and laws passed in legislatures. Legislative deliberation encourages informed debate among somewhat-informed individuals with different interests. It allows a proposal to change, often dramatically, as it goes through the gantlet of hearings, floor debate, and amendment in both houses of Congress.

To be sure, some debate can occur during a state referendum campaign, through ads and media analysis, but that is no substitute for face-to-face debate involving not just two sides, but sometimes dozens or hundreds, reflected in representatives from various areas and constituencies. Mail or electronic balloting would short-circuit campaigns even further. And referenda have no amendment process, no matter how complex the issue. Their outcome relies on voters who have many other things to do besides study the issues, much less read the bills or provisions.

Could electronic town meetings provide a popular equivalent to traditional legislating? Theoretically, a broad mass of voters could be part of a different deliberative process. That's the thesis of political scientist James Fishkin, whose "deliberative poll" brought a random sample of 600 citizens together in late January at considerable expense for three days of expert-guided discussion in Austin, Texas. Even if the Fishkin experiment were scrupulously fair, such enterprises generally seem susceptible to undemocratic manipulation by "experts" and agenda-setters. And "deliberative polls" are unlikely to win out over the allure of a quick, trigger-like vote on the TV or computer. Cyberdemocratic meetings would likely turn into fancier versions of "Talk Back Live." And most deliberation would be reduced—as now in California and other initiative-prone states—to high-tech public relations campaigns by powerful interests with the resources to put their issues on the ballot—making for more special interest influence, not more democracy.

Cyberspace offers wonderful possibilities for citizens to discuss issues. New electronic alliances based on similar interests can be enjoyed. And every day, citizens and legislators can download more information. But the combination of cynical distrust of political institutions, a rising tide of populism glorifying "pure" democracy, and the increased speed of information technology, is a highly dangerous one. While Newt Gingrich has benefited from the political cynicism and populism that drove voters in 1994, he knows the dangers facing deliberative democracy. As he told one of his college classes, "Direct democracy says, Okay, how do we feel this week? We all raise our hand. Let's rush off and do it. The concept of republican representation, which is very clear in the Founding Fathers, is you hire somebody who you send to a central place. . . . They, by definition, learn things you don't learn, because you don't want to—you want to be able to live your life. They are supposed to use their judgment to represent you. . . . [The Founders] feared the passion of the moment."

Newt is right. But preserving the Founders' vision as the "third wave" of cybertechnology approaches won't be easy.

5

VOTING

Despite the fact that our population is better educated and faces fewer procedural impediments to voting than ever before, a significant portion of the American electorate does not participate in elections. Indeed, from 1960 through 1996 voting turnout declined some 14 percentage points, and the turnout figure of just over 49 percent in 1996 was the lowest in 72 years.

Is nonvoting in the United States a source of concern? The two selections in this chapter address this question. In the first selection, the director of the Committee for the Study of the American Electorate, Curtis Gans, argues that we should be quite worried about both the causes and consequences of low turnout. According to Gans, the causes of low voter turnout, *in themselves disturbing, are the cynicism of the American people caused by an assortment of "shocks" to the political system, the fragmentation of society caused by television and the new computer technology, and the decay of some of our integrating institutions, including political parties and labor unions. Even more troublesome to Gans, however, are the* consequences of low turnout. *Among these are an increase in the influence of "special interests," a general decline in civil life and participation, and a bleak future for the young people of America.*

The author of the second article, political scientist Austin Ranney, argues that we need not fear the fact that many persons choose not to vote. Ranney bases his argument on two main propositions: first, he contends that since voters and nonvoters do not differ significantly in policy and candidate preferences, no great harm is done to our system of representation if a sizable percentage of people does not vote; and second, nonvoting does not offend any basic democratic principle, for the right not *to vote is every bit as precious as the right to vote.*

So Much at Stake. So Many Voters. Why Didn't They Turn Out?

Curtis B. Gans

Consider the following facts about the 1996 election:

- A likely net increase since 1992 of five million in the number of citizens able to vote thanks to the new motor-voter law.
- An unprecedented amount of money being spent by candidates, parties, and independent expenditure groups.
- An equally unprecedented level of voter mobilization activities by labor, business, environmentalists, Christian fundamentalists, women's groups, youth organizations, and minorities, among others.
- A set of four presidential and vice-presidential candidates whose stature, ability, and plausibility has not been equaled by both major parties since 1960.
- An important, if often obfuscated, underlying issue—the role of government, in general, and the federal government, in particular.
- A burgeoning journalistic industry attempting to connect the public with the political process and mitigate the corrosive effects of the campaign, including, but not limited to, debates, debate watches, free airtime, ad watches, the Democracy Project of PBS, and the growing field of civic journalism.
- Large-scale engagement efforts by nonpartisan institutions, including the First Vote project of People for the American Way and Rock the Vote, both aimed at registering the young; Kids Voting, targeted at getting families to vote together; the Minnesota Compact, aimed at voluntary promotion of political civility; and the continuing educational efforts of the League of Women Voters.

Add to this mix the demographic factors of an older, better-educated, and less-mobile electorate—the key indicators all pointing to greater participation—and one should have a recipe for a high-turnout election.

But the press and the polls told another story. Interest in this election was a full 15 percentage points below what it was in 1992. The viewership of the presidential debates was sharply down. Both interest in and desire to participate in politics among the young was, according to at least two separate polls, at an all-time low. Turnout for the congressional races was five or six points lower than for the presidential race, as it has been in past elections.

And that always reliable commercial barometer—the amount of time network news devotes to the coverage of politics in attempting to provide a satisfactory viewership return on its advertisers' dollars—fell by 40 percent compared with four years ago.

Curtis B. Gans is director of the Committee for the Study of the American Electorate, Washington, D.C. Reprinted by permission from Roll Call.

There seemed little question that turnout would be down in the 1996 election, perhaps sharply, mitigated from dropping to truly historic levels only by the additions to the voter rolls produced by the motor-voter law.

The 1996 election . . . heralded the resumption of a declining pattern of voter participation, which saw voter turnout drop between 1960 and 1968 (and between 1966 and 1990 in midterm elections) by 20 percent nationally and 30 percent outside the South. . . .

The questions occur: [W]hy, in the face of all the factors that should argue for greater voter participation, should turnout continue to decline? And why should this question be something anybody cares about?

Some of the answers to the first question have been building over time:

- In events. Shocks to our political system—Vietnam, Watergate, Iran-Contra; prevarication from the Johnsonian and Nixonian bully pulpit; scandals magnified by television; broken political promises; the abuse of limited mandates by President Clinton in his first two years and the Republican Congress of 1995—have conspired to produce an abiding cynicism among citizens and an even greater cynicism among journalists.

- In the declining quality of education, particularly urban public education; the lack of commitment to citizenship education in favor of education for jobs; and in shifting values away from civic responsibility and engagement with government and toward self-seeking and antigovernment demagoguery. This produced, in turn, a 12 percent participation rate of 18- and 19-year-olds in the 1994 election and the first coming-of-political-age generation in the last half-century, a majority of whose parents are nonvoters.

- In the fragmentation caused by television, which may bring the world community into an individual's living room on some channels, but whose real force is to bring an individual into his or her living room. The medium atomizes our society, making citizens passive spectators and consumers of politics rather than participants and stockholders.

- In the further fragmentation of a societally shared body of information across an ever growing spectrum of channels and computer terminals, the majority of which give no information whatsoever on politics and public affairs; and in the amount of time wasted on this medium (*TV Guide* says seven hours a day for the average citizen)—leaving us with the least engaged and civically literate society ever.

- In the decay of our major integrating and mobilizing institutions: the political parties, which have become little more than funnels for fundraising and consultant services; the labor unions, which have been a geriatric shell of their former power and vigor; and the churches, whose civic role (with the exception of conservative Christian fundamentalists), moral force, and parishioners' allegiance have been atrophying.

There are, in addition, three major problems evident in the 1996 election:

1.   Civility and Savagery.   Praise has rightly been heaped on the presidential candidates for their civility in debate. But what the public witnesses—far more than the biennial four and a half hours of civilized debate—is the savagery of attack ads for one to two hours every day on every television outlet for two months every election season.

These ads effectively give the voters a choice between bad and awful, casting a pall over the entire political process and dampening the will to participate.

These ads also oversimplify and distort the stakes, undermine real and vigorous debate, and raise the cost of and limit access to the political process. They destroy public trust, virtually eliminate grassroots engagement, restrict public policy options, undermine accountability, and put the future of American politics in the hands of non-responsible and increasingly irresponsible political consultants.

2. Party Alignment.   It is hardly a secret that the cause of Bob Dole's inability to emerge from a double-digit deficit in the polls . . . was the conduct of the 1995 Congress—a Congress that was willing to shut down government, not on the issue of a balanced budget upon which there was general national consensus, but rather on issues of dismantling government with respect to popular services ranging from environmental protection to occupational safety.

This, in turn, stems from a gross misalignment of the two major political parties. Since 1964 the core of the Republican party has moved so far right of the American political center that Barry Goldwater, the perceived 1964 right-wing extremist, is seen by the present GOP grassroots as a raving liberal.

And the Democratic party, which has not durably redefined its message in 30 years and was seen as a cacophony of special pleading in the 1970s, is now a party without a believable message more constant than the most proximate public opinion poll, which currently has them reciting the mantra "middle class" in every paragraph of every speech.

This misalignment has two important consequences: It leaves out of the process what used to be the core of the Republican party, moderates and classical liberals, as well as citizens at the bottom of the income scale. It also produces elections like the last three (including this one) in which the outcome is being decided as a reaction to the foibles of one party or another, but without real hope on the part of large numbers of citizens that anything will change substantially for the better.

3. Debt.   It may seem that the growing national debt and the increasing share of the federal budget allocated to debt service have a tangential relationship to civic decay. But what was missing from the political debate in 1996 was any broad vision of what a good society in the next century could look like and the steps needed to get from here to there.

Why that is missing is that even if such a vision were available, debt service constrains the ability to propose the steps that would move America in that direction. So, because of debt, Dole proposed tax cuts to free the private sector to pursue its private vision and President Clinton proposed exceedingly modest, mostly technological fixes that cost minimal amounts of money.

And the resulting dialogue felt as substantial as a Chinese meal at one hour's remove.

Why should we care about all of this? Because voting is, by and large, a lowest common denominator political act. People who don't vote tend not to participate in any other aspect of civic life. Which means that as voting rates decline, the reservoir of volunteers for socially useful tasks also declines.

And, conversely, as participation atrophies, our politics and policies become dominated by the intensely interested at the expense of the general interest.

We should care because when young people (18–24) vote at the rate of slightly more than 15 percent as they did in the last midterm, we are looking at a bleak future for both participation and leadership.

And we should care about the precipitous decline in the participation rates of those at the bottom of the income scale (a 21 percent decline for those whose incomes are below $15,000 in 1994) as indicative not only of the growing income gap between rich and poor but also of a politics and government that represents only some of the people.

And we should care because a healthy democracy depends on the positive engagement of its citizens, something we do not now have.

It is said by some that 1996's lack of interest was fostered by a one-sided, largely negative race in which distrust and dislike for President Clinton's character was the motivation for Republicans and fear of Republican extremism united Democrats.

But in 1964, the nation held a similar election that produced the third highest turnout since women were given the right to vote.

It is said by others—mostly intellectual charlatans—that 1996's low turnout was fostered by general public contentment. Yet, were that true, why are people on the bottom of the income scale least likely to turn out?

Perhaps more pertinently, while it is true that profound and shared unhappiness— such as the recession of 1982 and 1992—can boost turnout on a one-time basis out of fear and anger, sustaining high turnout requires precisely the opposite. Turnout rates rose, by and large, and were sustained at comparatively high levels between 1932 and the late 1960s during a period governed by strong civic values, positive feelings of engagement with government, and relatively strong political and societal institutions. In a word, hope.

Restoring that hope will not be accomplished by panacea and pabulum—by quick fixes like mail voting and early voting, by public service announcements and rock-star-generated registration campaigns, by educational television efforts viewed by a minuscule fraction of the nation. Rather, it will take the fulsome address of the all-too-evident problems underlying our civic decay.

We cannot replay the events that helped produce voter cynicism; our lives are not going to get less stressful anytime soon, and the institutions of television and the computer will continue to be with us. But we can improve the quality of education and civic education within it; we can promote a more community and civic-oriented set of values; we can realign our political parties to more nearly encompass the polity; we can wean the young off television; we can strengthen our political and civic institutions; we can reduce our debt and debt service; and we can cease being the only democracy in the world that does not by time or format, regulate political advertising on television.

In the 1996 election, 91.5 million eligible Americans did not vote. It is a problem too large to ignore or about which to think small.

Nonvoting Is Not a Social Disease

Austin Ranney

In 1980 only 53 percent of the voting-age population in the United States voted for president, and in 1982 only 38 percent for members of the House [The 1996 presidential election turnout was 49 percent; the 1994 congressional election turnout was 37 percent—*Editors*]. As the statistics are usually presented, this rate is, on the average, from 10 to 40 points lower than in the democratic nations of Western Europe, Scandinavia, and the British Commonwealth—although such numbers involve major technical problems of which we should be aware.[1] We also know that the level of voter participation has [declined] since the early 1960s.

All forms of *in*voluntary nonvoting—caused by either legal or extralegal impediments—are violations of the most basic principles of democracy and fairness. Clearly it is a bad thing if citizens who want to vote are prevented from doing so by law or intimidation. But what about *voluntary* nonvoters—the 30 percent or so of our adult citizens who *could* vote if they were willing to make the (usually minimal) effort, but who rarely or never do so? What does it matter if millions of Americans who could vote choose not to?

We should begin by acknowledging that suffrage and voting laws, extralegal force, and intimidation account for almost none of the nonvoting. A number of constitutional amendments, acts of Congress, and court decisions since the 1870s—particularly since the mid-1960s—have outlawed all legal and extralegal denial of the franchise to African-Americans, women, Hispanics, people over the age of 18, and other groups formerly excluded. Moreover, since the mid-1960s most states have changed their registration and voting laws to make casting ballots a good deal easier. Many states, to be sure, still demand a somewhat greater effort to register than is required by other democratic countries. But the best estimates are that even if we made our voting procedures as undemanding as those in other democracies, we would raise our average turnouts by only nine or so percentage points. That would still leave our voter participation level well below that of all but a handful of the world's democracies, and far below what many people think is the proper level for a healthy democracy.

Throughout our history, but especially in recent years, many American scholars, public officials, journalists, civic reformers, and other people of good will have pondered our low level of voting participation and have produced a multitude of studies, articles, books, pamphlets, manifestoes, and speeches stating their conclusions. On one point they agree: All start from the premise that voluntary, as well as involuntary, nonvoting is a bad thing for the country and seek ways to discourage it. Yet, despite the critical importance of the question, few ask *why* voluntary nonvoting is a bad thing.

Austin Ranney is professor emeritus of political science at the University of California–Berkeley and a former president of the American Political Science Association. This selection was adapted from a paper delivered to the ABC/Harvard Symposium on Voter Participation on October 1, 1983. From Austin Ranney, "Nonvoting Is Not a Social Disease," Public Opinion, October/November 1983, pp. 16–19. Reprinted with permission of American Enterprise Institute for Public Policy Research, Washington, D.C.

Voluntary nonvoting's bad name stems from one or a combination of three types of arguments or assumptions. Let us consider these arguments in turn.

WHAT HARM DOES IT DO?

One of the most often-heard charges against nonvoting is that it produces unrepresentative bodies of public officials. After all, the argument runs, if most of the middle-class WASPs vote and most of the African-Americans, Hispanics, and poor people do not, then there will be significantly lower proportions of African-Americans, Hispanics, and poor people in public office than in the general population. Why is that bad? For two reasons. First, it makes the public officials, in political theorist Hanna Pitkin's term, "descriptively unrepresentative." And while not everyone would argue that the interests of African-Americans are best represented by African-American officials, the interests of women by women officials, and so on, many people believe that the policy preferences of the underrepresented groups will get short shrift from the government. Second, this not only harms the underrepresented groups but weakens the whole polity, for the underrepresented are likely to feel that the government cares nothing for them and they owe no loyalty to it. Hence it contributes greatly to the underclasses' feelings of alienation from the system and to the lawlessness that grows from such alienation.

This argument seems plausible enough, but a number of empirical studies comparing voters with nonvoters do not support it. They find that the distributions of policy preferences among nonvoters are approximately the same as those among voters, and therefore the pressures on public officials by constituents for certain policies and against others are about the same as they would be if everyone, WASPs and minorities, voted at the same rate.

Moreover, other studies have shown that the level of cynicism about the government's honesty, competence, and responsiveness is about the same among nonvoters as among voters, and an increased level of nonvoting does not signify an increased level of alienation or lawlessness. We can carry the argument a step further by asking if levels of civic virtue are clearly higher and levels of lawlessness lower in Venezuela (94 percent average voting turnout), Austria (94 percent), and Italy (93 percent) than in the United States (58 percent), Switzerland (64 percent), and Canada (76 percent). If the answer is no, as surely it is, then at least we have to conclude that there is no clear or strong relationship between high levels of voting turnout and high levels of civic virtue.

Another argument concerns future danger rather than present harm to the Republic. Journalist Arthur Hadley asserts that our great and growing number of "refrainers" (his term for voluntary nonvoters) constitutes a major threat to the future stability of our political system. In his words:

> These growing numbers of refrainers hang over the democratic process like a bomb, ready to explode and change the course of our history as they have twice in our past. . . . Both times in our history when there have been large numbers of refrainers, sudden radical shifts of power have occurred. As long as the present gigantic mass of refrainers sits outside of our political system, neither we nor our allies can be certain of even the

normally uncertain future. This is why creating voters, bringing the refrainers to the booth, is important.

Hadley's argument assumes that if millions of the present nonvoters suddenly voted in some future election, they would vote for persons, parties, and policies radically different from those chosen by the regular voters. He asserts that that is what happened in 1828 and again in 1932, and it could happen again any time. Of course, some might feel that a sudden rush to the polls that produces another Andrew Jackson or Franklin Roosevelt is something to be longed for, not feared, but in any case his assumption is highly dubious. We have already noted that the policy preferences of nonvoters do not differ greatly from those of voters, and much the same is true of their candidate preferences. For example, a leading study of the 1980 presidential election found that the five lowest voting groups were African-Americans, Hispanics, whites with family incomes below $5,000 a year, whites with less than high school educations, and working-class white Catholics. The study concluded that if all five groups had voted at the same rate as the electorate as a whole, they would have added only about one-and-a-half percentage points to Carter's share of the vote, and Reagan would still have been elected with a considerable margin. So Hadley's fear seems, at the least, highly exaggerated.

WHAT SOCIAL SICKNESS DOES NONVOTING MANIFEST?

Some writers take the position that, while a high level of voluntary nonvoting may not in itself do harm to the nation's well-being, it is certainly a symptom of poor civic health. Perhaps they take their inspiration from Pericles, who, in his great funeral oration on the dead of Marathon, said:

> . . . Our ordinary citizens, though occupied with the pursuits of industry, are still fair judges of public matters; for, unlike any other nation, regarding him who takes no part in these duties not as unambitious but as useless. . . .

One who holds a 20th-century version of that view is likely to believe that our present level of voluntary nonvoting is a clear sign that millions of Americans are civically useless—that they are too lazy, too obsessed with their own selfish affairs and interests, and too indifferent to the welfare of their country and the quality of their government to make even the minimum effort required to vote. A modern Pericles might ask, How can such a nation hope to defend itself in war and advance the public welfare in peace? Are not the lassitude and indifference manifested by our high level of nonvoting the root cause of our country's declining military strength and economic productivity as well as the growing corruption and bungling of our government?

Perhaps so, perhaps not. Yet the recent studies of nonvoters have shown that they do not differ significantly from voters in the proportions who believe that citizens have a civic duty to vote or in the proportions who believe that ordinary people have a real say in what government does. It may be that nonvoters are significantly less patriotic citizens, poorer soldiers, and less productive workers than voters, but there is no evidence to support such charges. And do we accept the proposition that the much higher turnout rates for the Austrians, the French, and the Irish show that they are significantly better on any or all of these counts than the Americans? If not, then clearly there is no compelling reason to believe that a high level of nonvoting is, by itself, a symptom of sickness in American society.

WHAT BASIC PRINCIPLES DOES IT OFFEND?

I have asked friends and colleagues whether they think that the high level of voluntary nonvoting in America really matters. Almost all of them believe that it does, and when I ask them why they usually reply not so much in terms of some harm it does or some social illness it manifests but rather in terms of their conviction that the United States of America is or should be a democracy, and that a high level of voluntary nonvoting offends some basic principles of democracy.

Their reasoning goes something like this: The essential principle of democratic government is government by the people, government that derives its "just powers from the consent of the governed." The basic institution for ensuring truly democratic government is the regular holding of free elections at which the legitimate authority of public officials to govern is renewed or terminated by the sovereign people. Accordingly, the right to vote is the basic right of every citizen in a democracy, and the exercise of that right is the most basic duty of every democratic citizen.

Many have made this argument. For example, in 1963 President John F. Kennedy appointed an 11-member Commission on Registration and Voting Participation. Its report, delivered after his death, began:

> Voting in the United States is the fundamental act of self-government. It provides the citizen in our free society the right to make a judgment, to state a choice, to participate in the running of his government. . . . The ballot box is the medium for the expression of the consent of the governed.

In the same vein the British political philosopher Sir Isaiah Berlin declares, "Participation in self-government is, like justice, a basic human requirement, *an end in itself.*"

If these views are correct, then any nominal citizen of a democracy who does not exercise this basic right and fulfill this basic duty is not a full citizen, and the larger the proportion of such less-than-full citizens in a polity that aspires to democracy, the greater the gap between the polity's low realities and democracy's high ideals.

Not everyone feels this way, of course. Former Senator Sam Ervin, for example, argues:

> I'm not going to shed any real or political or crocodile tears if people don't care enough to vote. I don't believe in making it easy for apathetic, lazy people. I'd be extremely happy if nobody in the United States voted except for the people who thought about the issues and made up their own minds and wanted to vote. No one else who votes is going to contribute anything but statistics, and I don't care that much for statistics.

The issues between these two positions are posed most starkly when we consider proposals for compulsory voting. After all, if we are truly convinced that voluntary nonvoting is a violation of basic democratic principles, and a major social ill, then why not follow the lead of Australia, Belgium, Italy, and Venezuela and enact laws *requiring* people to vote and penalizing them if they do not?

The logic seems faultless, and yet most people I know, including me, are against compulsory voting laws for the United States. All of us want to eradicate all vestiges of *in*voluntary nonvoting, and many are disturbed by the high level of voluntary nonvoting. Yet many of us also feel that the right to abstain is just as precious as the right to vote, and the idea of legally compelling all citizens to vote whether they want to or not is at least as disturbing as the large numbers of Americans who now and in the future probably will not vote without some compulsion.

THE BRIGHT SIDE

In the light of the foregoing considerations, then, how much should we worry about the high level of voluntary nonvoting in our country? At the end of his magisterial survey of voting turnout in different democratic nations, Ivor Crewe asks this question and answers, "There are . . . reason[s] for *not* worrying—too much."

I agree. While we Americans can and probably should liberalize our registration and voting laws and mount register-and-vote drives sponsored by political parties, civic organizations, schools of government, and broadcasting companies, the most we can realistically hope for from such efforts is a modest increase of 10 or so percentage points in our average turnouts. As a college professor and political activist for 40 years, I can testify that even the best reasoned and most attractively presented exhortations to people to behave like good democratic citizens can have only limited effects on their behavior, and most get-out-the-vote drives by well-intentioned civic groups in the past have had disappointingly modest results.

An even more powerful reason not to worry, in my judgment, is that we are likely to see a major increase in our voting turnouts to, say, the 70 or 80 percent levels, only if most of the people in our major nonvoting groups—African-Americans, Hispanics, and poor people—come to believe that voting is a powerful instrument for getting the government to do what they want it to do. The . . . register-and-vote drives by the NAACP and other African-American-mobilization organizations have already had significant success in getting formerly inactive African-American citizens to the polls. . . . Organizations like the Southern Voter Registration Education Project have had some success with Hispanic nonvoters in Texas and New Mexico and may have more. Jesse Helms and Jerry Falwell may also have success in their . . . efforts to urge more conservatives to register and vote. But hard evidence that voting brings real benefits, not exhortations to be good citizens, will be the basis of whatever success any of these groups enjoy.

If we Americans stamp out the last vestiges of institutions and practices that produce *in*voluntary nonvoting, and if we liberalize our registration and voting laws and procedures to make voting here as easy as it is in other democracies, and if the group-mobilization movements succeed, then perhaps our level of voting participation may become much more like that of Canada or Great Britain. (It is unlikely ever to match the levels in the countries with compulsory voting or even those in West Germany or the Scandinavian countries.)

But even if that does not happen, we need not fear that our low voting turnouts are doing any serious harm to our politics or our country, or that they deprive us of the right to call ourselves a democracy.

NOTE

1. European and American measures of voting and nonvoting differ significantly. In all countries the numerator for the formula is the total number of votes cast in national elections. In most countries the denominator is the total number of persons on the electoral rolls—that is, people we would call "registered voters"—which includes almost all people legally eligible to vote. In the United States, on the other hand, the denominator is the "voting-age population," which is the estimate by the Bureau of the Census of the number of people in the country who are 18 or older at the time of the election. That figure, unlike its European counterpart, includes aliens and inmates of prisons and mental hospitals as well as persons not registered to vote. One eminent election analyst, Richard M. Scammon, estimates that if voting turnout in the United States were computed by the same formula as that used for European countries, our average figures would rise by 8 to 10 percentage points, a level that would exceed Switzerland's and closely approach those of Canada, Ireland, Japan, and the United Kingdom.

6
CAMPAIGNS AND THE MEDIA

Probably nothing has so revolutionized American politics as the emergence of television as the principal means of communicating with the voters. What used to be the experience of only a few people—hearing and seeing a candidate at a campaign rally, for example—is now an experience shared by many millions of Americans. Since television enables political candidates to be seen and heard in every living room in the country, it is no wonder that politicians devote so much time and resources to producing television advertisements and other political programming.

The advent of TV advertising also has led to shorter and shorter campaign spots, in which candidates in 30-second or shorter sound and picture bites "bash" their opponents or attempt to communicate key word messages to the sometimes uninformed, unsuspecting, and undecided voters. These political advertisements are most often referred to as "negative ads," but they need not be.

The 30-second campaign TV spot has prompted a great deal of attention from both political scientists and the popular press. One of the more serious and thoughtful critics of the current mode of TV political advertising is political scientist Darrell M. West, a professor at Brown University and the author of Air Wars, *an important book on campaign advertising. Portions of Professor West's book are reprinted as the first selection in this chapter. West argues that today's TV ads are harmful not only because they frequently misrepresent candidates' views but also because they tend to be divisive, often emphasizing issues that pit one social group (racial, gender, economic) against another. Although West does not believe that we should do away with such ads, he argues that the mass media ought to serve as the "watchdog" of campaign ads, holding the sponsors of such ads to ever-stricter standards of truth and honesty.*

Still, there are those who defend TV spots and argue that political ads actually are highly useful. Such a point of view is presented by the authors of our second selection—Stephen Bates and Edwin Diamond. Bates and Diamond, while recognizing that TV spots have their negative aspects, are not convinced that such spots are as bad as the critics allege. Indeed, they see such ads as contributing greatly to political "discourse," leaving the voter better informed than would otherwise be the case. To Bates and Diamond, then, reforming TV campaigns spots is like trying to remove politics from campaigns. TV is the modern medium of politics; it cannot and should not be "turned off" for the sake of satisfying the critics.

Advertising and Democratic Elections:
What Can Be Done?

Darrell M. West

DIFFERENT ARENAS, DIFFERENT THREATS

The susceptibility of voters to advertising appeals has long generated despair from political observers. McGinniss's book, *The Selling of the President,* and Spero's volume, *The Duping of the American Voter,* express common fears about the dangers of advertisements.[1] But these authors failed to recognize that not all electoral arenas are subject to the same threat. The visibility of the setting makes a big difference.

The major threat in highly visible arenas, such as presidential general election campaigns, is substantive manipulation. The 1988 general election gave a textbook illustration of this danger, as the relatively unknown Dukakis saw his entire campaign shattered by Bush's successful efforts to move the campaign from past performance to flags, furloughs, and patriotism. Bush used advertising on tax and spending matters as well as crime that year to fill in the public profile of the relatively unknown Dukakis. The vice president was able to dominate the campaign because few voters knew much about the Massachusetts governor, 1988 was a year with a fluid policy agenda, and Dukakis did not successfully defend himself. Bush painted a portrait of the Massachusetts governor that many observers considered grossly exaggerated; Bush pictured an unrepentant liberal who was soft on crime and out of touch with the American people. Combined with uncritical coverage for the media, Bush's ads in this election had consequences that were both substantial and quite disturbing.

Less visible electoral arenas, such as presidential nomination campaigns, are more vulnerable to strategic manipulation. Because they are less visible contests that are heavily influenced by campaign dynamics, they contain fewer of the countervailing forces than are present in presidential general elections. Democrats compete against Democrats and Republicans against Republicans in a sequential nominating process.[2] In this situation, party identification is not central to vote choice. The setting limits the power of long-term forces and makes it possible for short-term factors, such as advertising and media coverage, to dominate.

Senate races share some features with nominating races. These contests are susceptible to ad appeals because relatively unknown candidates compete in races that resemble roller-coaster rides. There often are wild swings in electoral fortunes during the course of the campaign. The absence of prior beliefs about the candidates makes adver-

Darrell M. West is professor of political science at Brown University. From Darrell M. West, "Advertising and Democratic Elections," Air Wars: Television Advertising in Election Campaigns, 1952–1992, *pp. 154–60. Reprinted with the permission of Congressional Quarterly, Inc. Notes have been renumbered to correspond with edited text—Editors.*

tising influential.[3] It is easier to create a new political profile (for yourself or the opponent) than to alter a well-defined image. Candidates who are the least known are the most able to use advertisements to influence the public. But they also are the most susceptible to having an opponent create an unfair image of themselves through television.

SLICING AND DICING THE ELECTORATE

Campaign advertisements also pose problems for democratic elections on the systemic level. Even if ads influence voting behavior only in certain circumstances, they have consequences for the way in which the campaign is viewed. Advertisements are one of the primary means of communication, and much of how people feel about the electoral system is a product of how campaign battles are contested.

In contemporary elections it is common for political consultants to divide voters into advertising segments based on public opinion polls and focus groups: the committed (those who are for you), the hopeless (those who are against you and about whom little can be done), and the undecided (those who could vote either way). The last group, of course, is the central target of campaign tactics.

Ads are developed to stir the hopes and fears of the 20 to 30 percent of the electorate that is undecided, not the 70 to 80 percent that is committed or hopeless. Narrow pockets of support are identified and targeted appeals are made. Many Americans complain that campaign discussions do not reflect their concerns. Their complaints are legitimate. With advertising appeals designed for the small group of voters who are undecided, it is little wonder many voters feel left out.

In this system of segmentation and targeted appeals, candidates have clear incentives to identify pockets of potential support and find issues that will move these voters. Whether it is the backlash against affirmative action among white rural dwellers in North Carolina (one of the winning issues for Helms in 1990) or Bush's attacks on Clinton for his 1969 antiwar demonstrations (which did not save the election for Bush), the current electoral system encourages candidates to find divisive issues that pit social group against social group.

It is not surprising in this situation that Americans feel bad at the end of election campaigns. Candidates engage in an electronic form of civil war not unlike what happens in divided societies. The battleground issues often touch on race, lifestyle, and gender, which are among the most contentious topics in America. Ads and sound bites are the weapons of choice in these confrontations.

The long-run dangers from the electronic air wars are ill feelings and loss of a sense of community. Bill Clinton addressed these fears in his nomination acceptance speech. Long before his patriotism had been challenged, Clinton warned about the danger of divisiveness and the importance of community: "The New Covenant is about more than opportunities and responsibilities for you and your families. It's also about our common community. Tonight every one of you knows deep in your heart that we are too divided. It is time to heal America. . . . Look beyond the stereotypes that blind us. We need each other . . . this is America. There is no them. There is only us."[4]

WHAT CAN BE DONE?

The controversies that have arisen concerning television commercials have generated heartfelt pleas for fundamental changes in U.S. campaigns. Following the example of Australia, and until recently West Germany, some have called for an outright ban on televised campaign ads in the United States. Others have suggested the application of the rule followed in France, where ads are banned during the closing weeks of the campaign.[5] These calls undoubtedly reflect deep frustration over the uses of advertisements in the United States.[6] But it is far too simple to blame ads for electoral deficiencies. The problem of political commercials is as much a function of campaign structure and voters' reactions as of candidates' behavior. Structural and attitudinal changes have loosened the forces that used to restrain elite strategies. The rise of a mass-based campaign system at a time when candidates have powerful means of influencing viewers rewards media-centered campaigns.

At the same time, voters are vulnerable to candidates' messages because the forces that used to provide social integration have lost their influence. Intermediary organizations no longer organize political reality. Consensus has broken down on key domestic and foreign policy questions. Voters are bombarded with spot ads precisely because of their proven short-term effectiveness, as has been evident in recent races.

Recent court rulings make an outright ban on campaign commercials unlikely. Most court decisions have treated candidates' expenditures on advertisements as tantamount to free speech.[7] Since ads are a form of expression, they are subject to constitutional protection and are thereby quite difficult to restrict. Most attempts at direct regulation have been resisted as unconstitutional encroachments upon free speech.[8] Self-monitoring efforts, such as those proposed by the National Association of Political Consultants, are of limited value.

However, there is an informal mechanism in the advertising area which when combined with regulatory reform, promises more success: the media. In the case of candidates' advertising, government regulation clearly would be inadequate without direct and effective media oversight. Reporters have the power to make or break the regulation of advertising by how they cover spot commercials.

For example, follow-up reporting by the news media would enable viewers to link ad sponsorship to responsibility. Journalists who aggressively focused on negative commercials would help the public hold candidates accountable for ads that crossed the threshold of acceptability. This attention would alter the strategic environment of campaigns and create clear disincentives for the excessive or unfair use of attack ads.

Currently, advertising coverage falls far short of what would be needed to uphold democratic elections. Reporters devote plenty of attention to candidates' ads, but not necessarily in a way that furthers citizens' knowledge. They are more likely, for example, to use ads to discuss the horse race than the policy views of the candidates.

But with a different approach to ad coverage, television could become an enlightening force in American elections. Journalists in the United States have an unusually high credibility with the public. American reporters are seen as being more fair and trustworthy than in other countries. A recent comparative study of five countries illustrates this point. Whereas 69 percent of the Americans surveyed had great confidence in the media, only 41 percent of Germans and 38 percent of the British gave high ratings to journalists.[9]

What is needed in the United States is a "truth in political advertising" code which would feature a prominent oversight role for the media. Both [Kathleen Hall] Jamieson and David Broder have suggested that journalists should exercise their historic function of safeguarding the integrity of the election process.[10] The media could use their high public credibility to improve the functioning of the political system.

There are several tenets to this code that would improve the quality of electoral discourse. Reporters must use Ad Watches to evaluate the accuracy of candidates' claims. Candidates periodically make exaggerated claims in their efforts to win votes. Journalists need to look into their claims and report to voters on their accuracy. The 1992 race was notable because journalists made detailed assessments of candidates' claims. Newspapers routinely printed the text of commercials in Ad Watches, with sentence-by-sentence evaluations of their honesty. In addition, television reporters reviewed videos of commercials with an eye toward false claims, exaggerated promises, or unrealistic commitments.[11]

These efforts are valuable, but journalists must go beyond fact checking to true oversight. Commercials have become the major strategic tool for the contesting of American elections. Candidates devote the largest portion of their overall campaign budgets to advertising. Their ads feature their own appeals as well as comments about their opposition. Arbitrators are needed to ensure that ads are not misused and that the electronic battle is fought fairly. Almost every election now features claims and counter claims regarding the fairness of television ads. Voters are not usually in a position to assess these claims, and the Federal Election Commission has chosen not to adjudicate them.

The media are left with the responsibility to expose manipulation, distortion, and deception, not just inaccurate use of facts. Candidates who exceed the boundaries of fair play should be brought to task by reporters. Unfair tactics or misleading editing needs to be publicized. Commercials that engage in obvious appeals to racism, for example, should be condemned. Media pressure could protect the airwaves, as happened when the "Daisy" ad was condemned in 1964. [The "Daisy" ad showed a nuclear bomb explosion superimposed on a young girl holding a daisy. The ad was directed at the so-called reckless policy statements on nuclear weapons by the Republican candidate for president, Barry Goldwater. The ad was withdrawn after severe criticism.—*Editors*]

Television has a special obligation because it is the medium through which most Americans receive their political news. The Cable News Network pioneered the Ad Watch technique of broadcasting the spot in a smaller square on the side of the screen so that the ad would not overpower the analysis. This valuable innovation should become a model for the rest of the electronic media.

Aggressive Ad Watches are especially important in spots involving race, lifestyle issues, gender, or other topics with emotional overtones.[12] The danger in focusing on such commercials is that viewers will remember the candidate's message, not the critique. Since ads on "hot button" issues using well-recognized codewords are becoming quite common, reporters need to check candidates' messages to limit manipulatory appeals.

These actions will help protect the integrity of the electoral process. Reporters are the only major group with the credibility vis-à-vis the American public to arbitrate electoral advertising. In fact, a 1985 Gallup poll revealed that citizens would like the media to undertake an aggressive watchdog role.[13] Government regulators at the Federal Communications Commission or the Federal Election Commission would not be as effective in such a role. Nor would political elites be seen as credible because they are associated with partisan politics.

There is some danger for the media in openly assuming this role. Many Americans already are concerned about what they believe is excessive influence and bias on the part of the news media.[14] If journalists aggressively challenge candidates' statements, they may be viewed as part of the problem rather than the solution. There are increasing signs of a backlash against the media, and reporters could become subject to more stringent criticism regarding their overall influence and objectivity.

In 1991, for example, Louisiana gubernatorial candidate [David] Duke tried to foster antipathy to the media through a last-minute ad directly criticizing coverage of his campaign: "Have you ever heard such weeping and gnashing of teeth? The news media have given up any pretense of fair play. The liberals have gone ballistic. The special interests have gone mad. The politicians who play up to them are lining up on cue. Principles lie abandoned and hypocrisy rules the day. I raise issues that must be discussed, and get back venom instead. Try a little experiment. Next time you hear them accuse me of intolerance and hatred, notice who is doing the shouting."[15] Bush also attempted to build support for his 1992 reelection in his slogan: "Annoy the media: re-elect Bush."

Local surveys conducted in Los Angeles during the fall 1992 race revealed that 44 percent rated the media as having done a fair or poor job of covering the presidential campaign while 54 percent thought the media had done an excellent or good job. In the fall campaign, 43 percent felt reporters had been biased against particular candidates and 49 percent said they had not been. When asked to identify which campaigner had received the most biased coverage, 43 percent named Bush, 32 percent named Clinton, 21 percent named Perot, and 4 percent cited other candidates. Content analysis from the Center for Media and Public Affairs reveals that Bush earned the highest percentage of negative comments (71 percent) from network evening newscasts, compared with Clinton (48 percent) and Perot (55 percent). The content analysis also fits with evidence that reporters were more likely to report Democratic leanings in 1992 than in earlier years.[16]

Despite the drawbacks, oversight by the media is vital enough to the political system to warrant the risk of backlash. The quality of information presented during elections is important enough to outweigh the practical difficulties facing the fourth estate. Nothing is more central to democratic elections than electoral discourse. Without informative material, voters have little means of holding leaders accountable or engaging in popular consent.[17] By encouraging candidates to address the substantive concerns of the electorate, media watchdogs will raise the caliber of the political process and help voters make meaningful choices.

NOTES

1. Joe McGinniss, *The Selling of the President* (New York: Simon and Schuster, 1969); and Robert Spero, *The Duping of the American Voter* (New York: Lippincott and Crowell, 1980).

2. J. Gregory Payne, John Marlier, and Robert Baukus, "Polispots in the 1988 Presidential Primaries," *American Behavioral Scientist* 32 (1989): 375.

3. Where strong prior beliefs are present, the danger of advertising goes down dramatically. But, of course, in a rapidly changing world where traditional moorings are disappearing—witness the collapse of communism on the world scene—even prior assumptions are being challenged. For a discussion of constraints on ad influence, see Elizabeth Kolbert, "Ad Effect on Vote Slipping," *New York Times,* March 22, 1992, "Week in Review," 4.

4. The Clinton quote comes from the text of his acceptance speech as printed in *Congressional Quarterly Weekly Report,* July 18, 1992, 2130.

5. Klaus Schoenbach, "The Role of Mass Media in West German Election Campaigns," *Legislative Studies Quarterly* 12 (1987): 373–94. For a review of the experience of other countries, see Howard Penniman and Austin Ranney, "The Regulation of Televised Political Advertising in Six Selected Democracies" (Paper prepared for the Committee for the Study of the American Electorate, Washington, D.C., undated).

6. Critics have also complained about the effectiveness of ad targeting on underage youths by tobacco companies. Research reported in the December 11, 1991, issue of the *Journal of the American Medical Association* has shown that the cartoon figure Old Joe Camel, used to advertise Camel cigarettes, has been a huge hit among youths aged twelve to nineteen years. Compared with adults in general, students were much more likely to indicate that they recognized Old Joe, liked him as a friend, and thought the ads looked cool. See Walecia Konrad, "I'd Toddle a Mile for a Camel," *Business Week,* December 23, 1991, 34.

7. The classic Supreme Court ruling in the campaign area was *Buckley v. Valeo* in 1976. This case struck down a number of finance regulations as unconstitutional encroachments. See Clarke Caywood and Ivan Preston, "The Continuing Debate on Political Advertising: Toward a Jeopardy Theory of Political Advertising as Regulated Speech," *Journal of Public Policy and Marketing* 8 (1989): 204–26. For other reviews of newly emerging technologies, see Jeffrey Abramson, Christopher Arterton, and Gary Orren, *The Electronic Commonwealth* (New York: Basic Books, 1988), and Erwin Krasnow, Lawrence Longley, and Herbert Terry, *The Politics of Broadcast Regulation,* 3d ed. (New York: St. Martin's, 1982).

8. A more extended discussion of reform proposals can be found in Darrell West, "Reforming Campaign Ads," *PS: Political Science and Politics* 24 (1992): 74–77.

9. Laurence Parisot, "Attitudes about the Media: A Five-Country Comparison," *Public Opinion* 10 (1988): 18–19, 60. However, viewers do see differences in the helpfulness of television and newspapers. A May 1992 survey of Los Angeles residents revealed that those who followed Ad Watches in newspapers were much more likely (35 percent) to see them as being very helpful than those who relied on television (16 percent).

10. Kathleen Hall Jamieson, "For Televised Mendacity, This Year Is the Worst Ever," *Washington Post,* October 30, 1988, C1; and David Broder, "Five Ways to Put Some Sanity Back in Elections," *Washington Post,* January 14, 1990, B1.

11. Media scholar Jamieson has been instrumental in encouraging these Ad Watch efforts. According to personal correspondence from her, 42 campaigns in 1990 were subjected to detailed critiques. For example, television stations airing discussions of particular ads included WFAA in Dallas, KVUE in Austin, WCVB in Boston, KRON in San Francisco, WBBM in Chicago, and WCCO in Minneapolis. Newspapers that followed ad campaigns closely were the *New York Times, Washington Post, Los Angeles Times, Chicago Sun-Times, Dallas Morning News, Houston Chronicle, Cleveland Plain-Dealer, Akron Beacon-Journal,* and *Louisville Courier-Journal.*

12. Race, of course, has been a controversial subject in many areas of American life. For a discussion of controversial rapper Ice Cube, see Craig McCoy, "Korean-American Merchants Claim Victory against Rapper Ice Cube," *Boston Globe,* November 28, 1991, A35. Also see Edward Carmines and James Stimson, *Issue Evolution: Race and the Transformation of American Politics* (Princeton: Princeton University Press, 1989).

13. Quoted by Kathleen Jamieson and Karlyn Kohrs Campbell in *The Interplay of Influence,* 2d ed. (Belmont, Calif.: Wadsworth, 1988), 55.

14. For an example of this thinking, see L. Brent Bozell and Brent Baker, eds., *And That's the Way It Isn't* (Alexandria, Va.: Media Research Center, 1990). Also see Lynda Lee Kaid, Rob Gobetz, Jane Garner, Chris Leland, and David Scott, "Television News and Presidential Campaigns: The Legitimization of Televised Political Advertising," *Social Science Quarterly* 74 (June 1993), 274–85, and Elizabeth Kolbert, "As Political Campaigns Turn Negative, the Press Is Given a Negative Rating," *New York Times,* May 1, 1992, A18.

15. Text is quoted from Robert Suro, "In Louisiana, Both Edwards and Duke Are Sending a Message of Fear," *New York Times,* November 15, 1991, A20.

16. The media rating was in response to an October 1992 question in our Los Angeles County survey: "So far this year, would you say the news media have done an excellent, good, fair, or poor job of covering this presidential campaign?" The press bias question also was asked in the October survey: "In your opinion, has news coverage of this year's fall presidential campaign been biased against any individual candidate? If so, which candidate received the most biased coverage?" The figures on television coverage come from Howard Kurtz, "Networks Stressed the Negative in Comments about Bush, Study Finds," *Washington Post,* November 15, 1992, A7. The longitudinal evidence on the party leanings of reporters is discussed by William Glaberson in "More Reporters Leaning Democratic, Study Says," *New York Times,* November 18, 1992, A20. Also see Elizabeth Kolbert, "Maybe the Media Did Treat Bush a Bit Harshly," *New York Times,* November 22, 1992, "Week in Review," 3.

17. Jeffrey Tulis, *The Rhetorical Presidency* (Princeton: Princeton University Press, 1987).

Damned Spots:
A Defense of Thirty-Second Campaign Ads
Stephen Bates and Edwin Diamond

. . . [E]veryone denounc[es] 30-second spots as demeaning, manipulative, and responsible for all that's wrong with American politics. David Broder, the mandarin of the op-ed page, admits he's "a crank on the subject." Otherwise staunch First Amendment champions, including *Washington Monthly* and, yes, *The New Republic,* want Congress to restrict the content of political ads. In fact, such commercials are good for the campaign, the voter, and the republic.

To cite the most common complaints:

1. TV Spots Make Campaigns Too Expensive.   The problem is nearly as old as television itself. William Benton, an ad-agency founder and a U.S. senator from Connecticut, talked of the "terrifying" cost of TV back in 1952. Campaign spending has risen sharply since then, and television advertising has contributed disproportionately. Whereas total political spending, adjusted for inflation, has tripled since 1952, the amount spent on television has increased at least fivefold. In some races, nine out of ten campaign dollars go to TV.

The important question is what candidates get in return. Quite a lot: a dollar spent on TV advertising may reach as many voters as $3 worth of newspaper ads or $50 worth of direct mail. Banning spots would probably *increase* campaign spending, by diverting candidates to less efficient forms of communication. In addition, spots reach supporters, opponents, and fence-sitters alike. This mass auditing imposes a measure of accountability that other media, particularly direct mail, lack.

2. A Candidate Can't Say Anything Substantive in 30 Seconds.   Referring to sound bites as well as spots, Michael Dukakis [1988 Democratic candidate for president] sourly concluded that the 1988 campaign was about "phraseology," not ideology. But a lot can be said in thirty seconds. John Lindsay's 1972 presidential campaign broadcast a 30-second spot in Florida that gave the candidate's positions on, among other issues, gun control (for), abortion rights (for), and school prayer (against). Lindsay's media manager, David Garth, later joked that the spot "probably lost the entire population of Florida."

A candidate can even make his point in 10 seconds. In California's recent [1992] Republican primary for U.S. Senate, one spot said simply: "I'm Bruce Herschensohn.

Stephen Bates is a Senior Fellow with the Annenberg Washington Program in Communication Policy Studies, Washington, D.C. Edwin Diamond is professor of journalism at New York University and a media columnist for the New Yorker *magazine. From "Damned Spots,"* New Republic, *September 7 and 14, 1992, pp. 14–18. Reprinted by permission of the* New Republic, © *1992, The New Republic, Inc.*

My opponent, Tom Campbell, was the only Republican congressman opposing the 1990 anti-crime bill. He's liberal and wrong." Campbell replied in kind: "Bruce Herschensohn is lying, Tom Campbell voted to extend the death penalty to twenty-seven crimes, and was named Legislator of the Year by the California Fraternal Order of Police."

Though hardly encyclopedic, these spots reveal something about the candidates' priorities. They assert facts that can be checked and conclusions that can be challenged. If nothing else, they improve on what may have been the first ten-second spot, broadcast in 1954: "Minnesota needs a wide-awake governor! Vote for Orville Freeman and bring wide-awake action to Minnesota's problems!"

Brief ads do have one shortcoming. In 30 seconds, a candidate cannot hope to answer a half-true attack spot. In Bush's [Wille Horton] "revolving door" prison ad of 1988, for instance, the voice-over says that Dukakis "gave weekend furloughs to first-degree murderers not eligible for parole," while the text on the screen tells viewers that "268 escaped" and "many are still at large." But as reporters discovered, only 4 of the 268 escapees were first-degree murderers, and only three escapees—none of them a murderer—were still at large. The Willie Horton example was an aberration.

This point might have been hard for the Dukakis team to convey in 30 seconds. What kept them from responding to Hortonism, however, was not the constraints of brevity; it was their decision to try to get public attention off the furlough program—a subject that, even without the Bush campaign's factual finagling, was bound to cost them votes. No sensible candidate will defend himself by saying he's only half as bad as his opponent charges.

Just as short spots aren't invariably shallow, long telecasts aren't invariably thoughtful. The 1960 John F. Kennedy campaign aired a two-minute spot with a bouncy jingle; it conveyed youth and vitality, but scarcely any information (except for a musical reference to Kennedy's Catholicism: "Can you deny to any man/The right he's guaranteed/To be elected president/No matter what his creed?"). As Ross Perot demonstrated, a candidate determined to be evasive can do so in a 30-second spot or in a two-hour live Q&A session.

3. *Political Ads Are Responsible for the Low-Down-and-Dirty State of Political Discourse.*   According to Arthur Schlesinger Jr., television is "draining content out of campaigns." But that assertion romanticizes the past. In the 1890s James Bryce, a Briton, decried American political campaigns in 1990s terms. Campaigns devote less attention to issues, he fretted, than to "questions of personal fitness," such as any "irregularity" in the candidate's relations with women. These issueless campaigns diminish the "confidence of the country in the honor of its public men."

Sleazy ads hardly raise the level of political discourse, but they aren't the super-weapon that critics claim. "When a client of ours is attacked," boasts Democratic consultant Bob Squier, "the people of that state are going to get some kind of response the next day." These responses are invariably revealing. In a 1988 Dukakis ad, the candidate watches a TV set showing a Bush ad. "I'm fed up with it," Dukakis says. "Never seen anything like it in twenty-five years of public life—George Bush's negative television ads, distorting my record. . . ." But instead of presenting a sharp reply, Dukakis only turns off the set—a metaphor for his entire campaign.

4. TV Ads Keep the Potatoes on the Couch.   Barely half of eligible citizens voted in 1988, the lowest turnout in 40 years [Turnout in 1996 was even lower—49 percent.—*Editors*]. In fact, turnout has declined steadily since 1960, during the same period campaign-TV expenditures have tripled in constant dollars. Many of the TV dollars have been diverted from doorbell pushing, rallies, and other activities that involve citizens in politics. And, according to critics, simplistic, unfair spots discourage people from voting.

It is nearly impossible to untangle the factors that influence voter turnout. Some consultants, like Republican Eddie Mahe, argue that the decline in voting is a passing consequence of demographics. In the 1960s and 1970s the baby-boom generation reached voting age and lowered voting figures (so did the 26th Amendment, which changed the voting age from 21 to 18). No surprises there: turnout is traditionally lower among the young. So, as the boomer generation ages, turnout will increase.

As for how spots affect turnout in particular elections, the evidence goes both ways. In the 1990 race for U.S. Senate in North Carolina, early polls showed blue-collar whites inclined to stay home. But many of them turned out to vote for Jesse Helms after his anti-quotas spot received heavy air play and news coverage.

Are spots, then, blameless for the parlous state of voter participation? Well, no. Even if they don't cloud the mind, they may in some sense sap the political will. To the extent that spots resemble lifestyle commercials—It's Miller Time, It's Morning in America—they may be taken no more seriously than other TV advertising. This is especially so when no other campaign is visible to the viewer. Today's political rally, as Democratic consultant Robert Shrum has said, consists of three people around the TV set.

But the doomsayers' solution—to try to divorce politics from TV—won't work. Since the 1950s the voting classes have increasingly stayed home to be entertained, a trend encouraged by demographics (the suburban migration), by new at-home options (cable, VCRs), and at least partly by fear (crime in the streets). Banning political spots, as some cranks in the press and Congress would do, wouldn't bring voters outdoors. It would deprive the couch-potato/citizen of a sometimes abused but ultimately unmatched source of electoral information. As Dukakis discovered, melodramatically turning off the TV resolves nothing.

7

ELECTIONS

Campaign Finance

It was the magnitude of money scandals in the 1972 presidential election that spurred Congress to action, producing by 1974 the most comprehensive campaign finance reforms enacted in our nation's history. These included contribution limits, spending limits, public financing, more rigorous disclosure requirements, and a Federal Election Commission to oversee the campaign finance process. The 1996 presidential election, however, brought with it renewed concern about campaign financing. Indeed, never before had so much money been contributed and spent on a presidential election—much of it legal and some of it not—thereby prompting many to conclude that the 1974 reforms had turned into a dismal failure.

While most political observers believe that further reform is necessary, there is considerable disagreement over what direction it should take. The two selections which follow are reflective of this fact. In the first, Milton Gwirtzman contends that there was nothing wrong with the campaign finance reform laws passed back in 1974. Rather, the problem lies with subsequent rulings by the United States Supreme Court—rulings that served to gut some of the most important provisions in these laws, thereby making it possible for huge sums of money to be funneled into the 1996 presidential election campaign. Gwirtzman further contends that the reasoning behind the Court's decisions was not only faulty but also seriously out of touch with public sentiment in the country. Hopeful that the Court will see the error of its ways and reverse itself, as it has done on other occasions, Gwirtzman calls upon Congress to reenact the spending limits declared unconstitutional by the Court.

Larry Sabato and Glenn Simpson, on the other hand, reject both spending limits and public financing, arguing that they are neither desirable nor feasible correctives to the problems associated with money in elections. Instead, they argue for what they call Deregulation Plus—a reform that they say takes into account the realities of campaign fundraising and runs little risk of being overturned by the courts.

The Supreme Problem

Milton S. Gwirtzman

The most formidable obstacle to campaign finance reform is not the politicians who depend upon the present sleazy system to get elected. It is the U.S. Supreme Court, whose members hold office for life. Unless the court is willing to change its view that campaign spending is the equivalent of free speech, any effective reform law is sure to be struck down as unconstitutional. . . .

The first and last time Congress passed comprehensive campaign finance reform was in 1974, after large contributions to the Nixon campaign from corporate executives were used to sabotage opposition candidates and were found in the bank accounts of the Watergate burglars. The law limited contributions to $1,000 per person, per election. It set realistic ceilings on what candidates could spend from their own pockets and what others could spend on their behalf. It would have worked. But key parts of it were never allowed to go into effect.

In a series of decisions flowing from *Buckley v. Valeo* in 1976, the Supreme Court used the free speech guarantee of the First Amendment to dismantle the law, piece by piece, until, as the last election showed, there are no effective restraints left on the amount of money that can be poured into campaigns. The *Buckley* case was an unusual one in that the court was being asked to render an advisory opinion on a law before it had a chance to work. The decision reads like the pronouncement of Plato's philosopher king on campaigns in an ideal world. But, as Justice Byron White warned in his dissent, the politicians who wrote the law knew much more about campaign reality than the court did.

The result has been a fundamental disconnect between the way Americans want campaigns to be conducted and the way they are actually run under what the court calls its "campaign finance jurisprudence." The court claims limits on campaign spending violate the First Amendment's free speech clause because they "reduce the number of issues discussed, the depth of their exploration and the size of the audience reached." But most campaigns do nothing of the sort. Candidates and their strategists spend most of their money on television ads attacking the record of opponents and distorting their positions. Far from offering a thorough airing of the issues, the expensive ads concentrate on a few "hot button" ones presented in the shallowest and most simplistic way: "The Republicans are going to cut your Medicare!" "Bill Clinton gave us the largest tax increase in history!"

The court showed the same naivete when it gave the green light to the unlimited "independent expenditures" that were the source of such embarrassment in the 1996 presidential election. The court, having in mind the lone activist who prints fliers to hand out in the street, said this kind of spending "may well provide little assistance to

Milton S. Gwirtzman is a member of the Senior Advisory Board of the Institute of Politics at Harvard University and a practicing attorney in Washington, D.C. Reprinted from Milton S. Gwirtzman, "The Supreme Problem: Why the Court's Previous Rulings Prevent Real Change," The Washington Post, *Jan. 12, 1997, p. C3.*

the candidate's campaign." The court did not anticipate that interest groups and political parties would raise hundreds of millions of dollars outside the contribution limits and spend it to promote specific candidates.

The court has also been clueless about who controls modern campaigns. "In the free society ordained by our Constitution," it said in *Buckley,* "it is not the government but the people—individually as citizens and candidates and collectively as associations and political committees—who must retain control over the quantity and range" of political debate.

But the voters have little say in the matter. Campaign debate is controlled by the candidates, who want to raise and spend as much as they think they need to get elected, and by their media constituents, who would like them to spend as much as possible since their compensation depends upon the number of television spots they place. Ironically when voters have tried to control the debate, by passing initiatives and referendums limiting campaign spending . . . the lower courts have struck them down as unconstitutional under *Buckley v. Valeo.*

The revulsion to this state of affairs has spread to every part of society, it seems, except for the judiciary. In poll after poll, by margins of up to 8 to 1, voters have said they want more limits on spending and contributions. After the 1996 election, they told poll takers that the hundreds of millions spent between the conventions and November had no effect on their ultimate votes, but that the way campaigns are paid for was a major reason for their lack of trust in public officials.

For their own part, scores of elected officials express frustration at how the constant begging for money saps their time, hurts their dignity and offends their sense of decency. As George Mitchell said on the floor of the Senate in 1993, after a third attempt to break a filibuster on a campaign reform bill had failed:

"Mr. President, this system stinks. Every senator who participates in it knows it stinks. And the American people are right when they mistrust this system, when what matters most in seeking public office is not integrity, not ability, not judgment, not reason, not responsibility, not experience, not intelligence, but money. . . . Money dominates the system. Money infuses the system. Money is the system."

Just about every legal scholar in the field has criticized the court on campaign finance. Prof. Paul Freund of the Harvard Law School wrote: "Campaign contributors are operating vicariously through the power of their purse rather than through the power of their ideas. I would scale that relatively lower in the hierarchy of First Amendment values. Television ads have their value surely, and yet in terms of the philosophy of the First Amendment seem to be minimally the kind of speech or communication that is to be protected. We are dealing here not so much with the right of personal expression or even association, but with dollars and decibels. And just as the volume of sound may be limited by law so may the volume of dollars, without violating the First Amendment."

The best way to confront the court directly with the need for change is for Congress to reenact the spending limits the *Buckley* case found unconstitutional. To buttress its constitutionality, the law should begin with extensive findings of fact about the corrosive influence of the present system and firmly declare its purposes: to prevent corruption or the appearance of corruption; to enhance the quality of our system of democratic self-government; and to equalize the influence of all citizens in the political process, both as voters and active participants.

The limits themselves should be adjusted for inflation, as could the limit on contributions. This would mean a nominee for president could spend $60 million, someone running for the House could spend $210,000 (and an equal amount if there is a primary), and general election spending for a Senate campaign would be limited to 36 cents per eligible voter. This would limit Senate nominees to around $1.7 million in a mid-size state such as Massachusetts and $3.2 million in a large one such as Illinois. These are reasonable amounts of money, far less than has been spent in recent years. (Each Massachusetts Senate candidate spent more than $7 million in 1996.)

What chance is there, if the current scandal goes deep enough and long enough to produce an effective bill like this, that the court will uphold it? In the past, when the court has reversed its decisions on broad public issues, it was because the previous doctrine was badly out of sync with the way American society now views its social and political requirements and, indeed, the fundamental principles of justice.

Brown v. Board of Education reversed the court's sanctioning of segregated schools. Until the Scottsboro Boys decision in 1932, the right to a fair trial in a criminal case did not necessarily include the right to obtain a lawyer. For most of our history, state legislative districts were rigged to give rural voters greater representation than city people. In its reapportionment decisions in 1962, the court forced state legislatures to redraw their districts so that every person's vote would have an equal weight. In reversing itself those times, the court had the sense and the courage to read the Constitution as a living document, whose interpretation could change with the changing perception of society's needs.

The members of the Supreme Court are intelligent people. They read the same newspapers and watch the same television news as the rest of us. I would be surprised if they were not as offended by what goes on in campaigns as we are. What they can do within the limits of the Constitution is their responsibility. For the rest of us, the scandals of the 1996 election campaign offer a chance to revive the issue, and it behooves us to take it as far as we can.

Campaign Finance Reform:
Phony Cures versus a Workable Solution

Larry J. Sabato and Glenn R. Simpson

The campaign finance system's problems are vexing. Is it possible to fashion a solution to all of them simultaneously? Over the years, the reformers' panacea has been taxpayer financing of elections and limits on how much candidates can spend. Public financing is a seductively simple proposition: if there is no private money, presumably there will be none of the difficulties associated with private money. But in a country such as ours, which places great emphasis on the freedoms of speech and association, it is unrealistic to expect that the general citizenry or even many of the elite activists will come to support greater federal subsidization of our election system at the cost of their individual and group political involvements. Spending limits are also enticing. Are politicians raising and spending too much money? Let's pass a law against it! Yet such a statute may be difficult to enforce in an era when politicians and the public seek less regulation, not more—not to mention the serious, maybe fatal, problem of plugging all the money loopholes (the C(4)s; Supreme Court-sanctioned, unlimited "independent expenditures" by groups and individuals unconnected to a campaign, and so on). Once again, the biggest, the original, and the unpluggable loophole is the First Amendment.

Public financing and spending limits are both also objectionable on the basic merits: the right to organize and attempt to influence politics is a fundamental constitutional guarantee, derived from the same First Amendment protections that need to be forcefully protected. To place draconian limits on political speech is simply a bad idea. . . .

[E]ven if candidates could be persuaded to comply voluntarily with a public financing and spending limits scheme, such a solution would fail to take into consideration the many ways that interest groups such as the Christian Coalition and labor unions can influence elections without making direct contributions to candidates. Even if we passed laws that appeared to be taking private money out, we would not really be doing so. This is a recipe for deception, and consequently—once the truth becomes apparent—for still greater cynicism.

In our opinion, there is another way, one that takes advantage of both current realities and the remarkable self-regulating tendencies of a free-market democracy, not to mention the spirit of the age. Consider the American stock markets. Most government oversight of them simply makes sure that publicly traded companies accurately disclose vital information about their finances. The philosophy here is that buyers, given the

Larry J. Sabato is professor of political science at the University of Virginia and Glenn R. Simpson is in the Washington, D.C. bureau of the Wall Street Journal. *Reprinted from U.S. Congress, Senate, Committee on Rules and Administration,* Hearings, Campaign Finance Reform Proposals of 1996, *104ᵗʰ Cong., 2ⁿᵈ Sess., 1996, pp. 310–16, as excerpted from the original,* Dirty Little Secrets: The Persistence of Corruption in American Politics *by Larry J. Sabato and Glenn R. Simpson, (New York: Times Books, 1996), pp. 328–36. Reprinted by permission of Times Books, a division of Random House, Inc.*

information they need, are intelligent enough to look out for themselves. There will be winners and losers, of course, both among companies and the consumers of their securities, but it is not the government's role to guarantee anyone's success (indeed, the idea is abhorrent). The notion that people are smart enough, and indeed have the duty, to think and choose for themselves, also underlies our basic democratic arrangement. There is no reason why the same principle cannot be successfully applied to a free market for campaign finance.[1] In this scenario, disclosure laws would be broadened and strengthened, and penalties for failure to disclose would be ratcheted up, while rules on other aspects—such as sources of funds and sizes of contributions—could be greatly loosened or even abandoned altogether.

Call it *Deregulation Plus*. Let a well-informed marketplace, rather than a committee of federal bureaucrats, be the judge of whether someone has accepted too much money from a particular interest group or spent too much to win an election. Reformers who object to money in politics would lose little under such a scheme, since the current system—itself a product of reform—has already utterly failed to inhibit special-interest influence. (Plus, the reformers' new plans will fail spectacularly, as we have already argued.) On the other hand, reform advocates might gain substantially by bringing all financial activity out into the open where the public can see for itself the truth about how our campaigns are conducted. If the facts are really as awful as reformers contend (and as close observers of the system, much of what we see is appalling), then the public will be moved to demand change.

Moreover, a new disclosure regime might just prove to be *the* solution in itself. It is worth noting that the stock-buying public, by and large, is happy with the relatively liberal manner by which the Securities and Exchange Commission regulates stock markets. Companies and brokers (the candidates and consultants of the financial world) actually *appreciate* the SEC's efforts to enforce vigorously what regulations it does have, since such enforcement maintains public confidence in the system and encourages honest, ethical behavior, without unnecessarily impinging on the freedom of market players. Again, the key is to ensure the availability of the requisite information for people to make intelligent decisions.

Some political actors who would rather not be forced to operate in the open will undoubtedly assert that extensive new disclosure requirements violate the First Amendment. We see little foundation for this argument. As political regulatory schemes go, disclosure is by far the least burdensome and most constitutionally acceptable of any political regulatory proposal. The Supreme Court was explicit on this subject in its landmark 1976 *Buckley v. Valeo* ruling. The Court found the overweening aspects of the Federal Election Campaign Act (such as limits on spending) violated the Bill of Rights, but disclosure was judicially blessed. While disclosure "has the potential for substantially infringing the exercise of First Amendment rights," the Court said, "there are governmental interests sufficiently important to outweigh the possibility of infringement, particularly when the free functioning of our national institutions is involved."

The Court's rationale for disclosure remains exceptionally persuasive two decades after it was written:

> First, disclosure provides the electorate with information "as to where political campaign money comes from and how it is spent by the candidate" in order to aid the voters

in evaluating those who seek federal office. It allows voters to place each candidate in the political spectrum more precisely than is often possible solely on the basis of party labels and campaign speeches. The sources of a candidate's financial support also alert the voter to the interests to which a candidate is most likely to be responsive and thus facilitate predictions of future performance in office.

Second, disclosure requirements deter actual corruption by exposing large contributions and expenditures to the light of publicity. This exposure may discourage those who would use money for improper purposes either before or after the election. A public armed with information about a candidate's most generous supporters is better able to detect any post-election special favors that may be given in return. And . . . full disclosure during an election campaign tends "to prevent the corrupt use of money to affect elections." Mr. Justice Brandeis' advice: "Publicity is justly commended as a remedy for social industrial diseases. Sunlight is said to be the best of disinfectants; electric light the most efficient policeman."[2]

A new disclosure-based regime, to be successful, would obviously require more stringent reporting rules. *Most important, new reporting rules would require groups such as organized labor and the Christian Coalition to disclose the complete extent of their involvement in campaigns.* Currently, such groups rely on a body of law that holds that under the First Amendment, broadly based "nonpartisan" membership organizations cannot be compelled to comply with campaign finance laws, nor can groups that do not explicitly advocate the election or defeat of a clearly identified candidate. However, expert observers of the current system, such as former Federal Election Commission chairman Trevor Potter, believe the Court has signaled that constitutional protection for such groups extends only to limits on how much they can raise or spend, not to whether they are required to disclose their activities.[3] The primary advantage of this step is that it would formally bring into the political sphere groups that clearly belong there. By requiring organizations such as the Christian Coalition and labor unions to disclose, their role in elections can be more fully and fairly debated.

Another possible objection to broadening the disclosure requirements would be the fear that the rules would drag a huge number of politically active but relatively inconsequential players into the federal regulatory framework. Clearly, no one wants the local church or the Rotary Club taken to court for publishing a newsletter advertisement that indirectly or directly supports candidates of their choice. To our mind, this is easily addressed by establishing a high reporting threshold—something between $25,000 and $50,000 in total election-related expenditures per election cycle. After all, the concern is not with the small organizations, but the big ones. The Christian Coalition, the term limits groups, and organized labor have all raised and spent millions of dollars annually and operated on a national scale. It is not hard to make a distinction between groups such as these and benign small-scale advocacy.

Another necessary broadening of disclosure would involve contributions made by individuals. While most political action committees already disclose ample data on their backers and financial activities, contributions to candidates from individuals are reported quite haphazardly. New rules could mandate that each individual contributor disclose his place of employment and profession, without exception. The FEC has already debated a number of effective but not overly oppressive means of accomplishing this goal (although to date is has adopted only modest changes). The simplest solution is to *prohibit* campaigns from accepting contributions that are not fully disclosed. Disclosure of campaign *expenditures* is also currently quite lax, with many campaign organizations failing to make a detailed statement describing the purpose of each expenditure. It would be no great task to require better reporting of these activities as well.

The big trade-off for tougher disclosure rules should be the loosening of restrictions on fundraising. Foremost would be liberalization of limits on fundraising by individual candidates. This is only fair and sensible in its own right: there is a glaring disconnection between the permanent and artificial limitations on sources of funds and ever-mounting campaign costs. One of the primary pressures on the system has been the declining value in real dollars of the maximum legal contribution by an individual to a federal candidate ($1,000 per election), which is now worth only about a third as much as when it went into effect in 1975. This increasing scarcity of funds, in addition to fueling the quest for loopholes, has led candidates (particularly incumbents) to do things they otherwise might not do in exchange for funding. Perversely, limits appear to have increased the indebtedness of lawmakers to special interests that can provide huge amounts of cash by mobilizing a large number of $500 to $1,000 donors. By increasing contribution limits, candidates would enjoy more freedom to pick and choose among their contributors. Given the option, we hope more candidates would turn primarily to those contributors whose support is based on values and ideological beliefs, spurning the favor-seekers. By lifting disclosure and contribution levels at the same time, politicians' access to "clean" funds would rise while scrutiny of "dirty"funds would be increased. The idea is to concede that we cannot outlaw the acceptance of special-interest money, but the *penalties* for accepting it can be raised via the court of public opinion. So at the very least, the individual contribution limit should be restored to its original value, which would make it about $2,800 in today's dollars, with built-in indexing for future inflation. We would actually prefer a more generous limit of $5,000, which would put the individual contribution limit on a par with the current PAC limit of $5,000 per election.

For political parties, there seems little alternative to simply legitimizing what has already happened de facto: the abolition of all limits. When the chairman of a national political party bluntly admits that millions of dollars in "soft money" receipts mean that the committee will be able to spend millions of dollars in "hard money," it is time for everyone to acknowledge reality. Moreover, such an outcome is not to be lamented. Political parties *deserve* more fund-raising freedom, which would give these critical institutions a more substantial role in elections.

How would the new disclosure regime work? While the FEC has already moved to impose some tighter disclosure requirements, it lacks the resources as currently constituted to enforce the new rules across the board. However, the solution does not necessarily require a massive increase in funding. Under a disclosure regime, the agency could reduce efforts to police excessive contributions and other infractions, devoting itself primarily to providing information to the public. The commission's authority to audit campaigns randomly would have to be restored to ensure compliance, and sanctions for failure to disclose would have to be increased substantially. In addition, the commission should be given the power to seek emergency injunctions against spending by political actors who refuse to comply with disclosure requirements. And to move the FEC away from its frequent three-to-three partisan deadlock, the six political party commissioners (three Democrats and three Republicans) ought to be able to appoint a seventh "tie-breaker" commissioner. Presumably anyone agreeable to the other six would have a sterling reputation for independence and impartiality. Another remedy for predictable partisanship on the FEC would be a one-term limit of six years for each commissioner. Freed of the need to worry about pleasing party leaders in order to secure reappointment, FEC commissioners could vote their consciences more often and get tough with election scofflaws in both parties.

Finally, in exchange for the FEC relinquishing much of its police powers, Congress could suspend much of its power over the FEC by establishing an appropriate budgetary level for the agency that by law would be indexed to inflation and could not be reduced. Another way of guaranteeing adequate funding for a disclosure-enhanced FEC is to establish a new tax check-off on Form 1040 that would permit each citizen to channel a few dollars of her tax money directly to the FEC, bypassing a possibly vengeful Congress's appropriations process entirely. The 1040 solicitation should carefully note that the citizen's tax burden would not be increased by his designation of a "tax gift" to the FEC, and that the purpose of all monies collected is to inform the public about the sources of contributions received by political candidates. It is impossible to forecast the precise reaction of taxpayers to such an opportunity, of course, but our bet is that many more individuals would check the box funding the Federal Election Commission than the box channeling cash to the presidential candidates and political parties. In today's money-glutted political system, the people's choice is likely to be reliable information about the interest groups and individuals investing in officeholders.

CONCLUDING COMMENTS

The purpose of these reforms is to make regulation of campaign financing more rational. Attempts to outlaw private campaign contributions or to tell political actors how much they can raise and spend are simply unworkable. Within broad limits, the political marketplace is best left to its own devices, and when those limits are exceeded, violators should be punished swiftly and effectively. . . .

NOTES

1. We are indebted to attorney Jan Baran of the law firm Wiley, Rein & Fielding for this analogy.
2. *Buckley v. Valeo*, 424 U.S.1. at 66–67 (1976)
3. Interview with Trevor Potter, July 12, 1995.

The Electoral College

At least once every four years, as the nation approaches the election of the president, political commentators raise the issue of the electoral college mechanism for electing the president, claiming that something ought to be done to correct it. One such critic, political scientist Lawrence Longley, in the first of the two selections in this section, argues that the electoral college is both undemocratic and politically dangerous: undemocratic because voters and votes are treated unequally; dangerous because there exists the possibility that it could lead to a major disruption of the normal electoral process.

In the second selection, another political scientist, Robert Weissberg, takes the view that we should retain the electoral college. While acknowledging that the present arrangement is not perfect, he maintains that the defects of the electoral college are not as serious as critics would have us believe. Moreover, he argues that several positive features associated with the electoral college more than compensate for its shortcomings, not the least of which is that it works.

The Electoral College Should Be Abolished

Lawrence D. Longley

The American electoral college is a deplorable political institution. Obscure and even unknown to the average citizen, it nevertheless serves as a crucial mechanism for transforming popular votes cast for president into electoral votes that actually elect the president. If the electoral college were only a neutral and sure means for counting and aggregating votes, it would be the subject of little controversy. The electoral college, however, is neither certain in its operations nor neutral in its effects. It may fail to produce a winner, in which case an extraordinarily awkward contingency procedure comes into play. Even when it operates relatively smoothly, it does not just tabulate popular votes in the form of electoral votes. Instead, it is an institution that works with noteworthy inequality—it favors some interests and hurts others. In short, the electoral college is a flawed means of determining the president. Its workings at best are neither smooth nor fair, and at worse contain the potential for constitutional crisis. Yet it continues to exist as the constitutional mechanism for electing the people's president. It must be abolished. . . .

THE FLAWS OF THE CONTEMPORARY ELECTORAL COLLEGE

The shortcomings of the contemporary electoral college are many, but five major flaws stand out. These are the faithless elector, the winner-take-all system, the "constant two" electoral votes, the uncertainty of the winner winning, and the contingency election procedure.

1. The Faithless Elector

The first of these flaws or problems of the contemporary electoral college arises out of the fact that the electoral college today is not the gathering of wise and learned elders as envisioned by its creators, but is rather little more than a motley state-by-state collection of political hacks and fat cats usually selected because of their past loyalty and support for their party. Neither in the quality of the electors nor in law is there any assurance that the electors will vote as expected by those who voted for them. State laws requiring electors to vote for their party's candidate are in practice unenforceable—and almost certainly unconstitutional. The language of the Constitution directs that "the

Lawrence D. Longley is professor of political science at Lawrence University, Appleton, Wisconsin. Reprinted from Lawrence D. Longley, "Yes, The Electoral College Should be Abolished," Controversial Issues in Presidential Selection. *Second Edition edited by Gary L. Rose by permission of the State University of New York Press.* © 1994.

electors shall vote"—which suggest that they have discretion as to how they cast their votes. As a result, personal pledges—backed up by party and candidate loyalty together with a certain lack of imagination—can be seen as the only basis of elector voting consistent with the will of a state's electorate.

The problem of the "faithless elector" is neither theoretical nor unimportant. Following the 1968 election, Republican elector Doctor Lloyd W. Bailey of North Carolina decided to vote for George Wallace rather than for his pledged candidate, Richard Nixon—after deciding that Republican nominee Nixon was a communist. Another Republican elector Roger MacBride of Virginia, likewise deserted Nixon in 1972 to vote instead for Libertarian Party candidate John Hospers. In the 1976 election, once again there was a faithless elector—and curiously enough once again a deviant Republican elector. Mike Padden, in the state of Washington, decided six weeks after the November election that he preferred not to support Republican nominee Gerald Ford because President Ford had not been forthright enough in denouncing abortion. Instead Padden cast his electoral vote that year for Ronald Reagan, four years before Reagan won the Republican nomination and was elected president. Another variant electoral vote was cast in 1988 by West Virginia Democratic elector Margaret Leach, who cast her presidential vote not for Democratic presidential nominee Michael Dukakis but for vice-presidential nominee Lloyd Bentsen as a protest against the electoral college system. Other defections from voter expectations also occurred in 1948, 1956, and 1960, or in other words, in 7 of the 12 most recent U.S. presidential elections. Even more important is that the likelihood of such deviations occurring on a multiple basis would be greatly heightened should an electoral vote majority rest on only one or two votes, a real possibility in any close presidential election.

In fact, when one looks at the election return for the most recent close U.S. election, 1976, one can observe that if about 5,560 votes had switched from Jimmy Carter to Gerald Ford in the single state of Ohio, Carter would have lost that state and thus had but 272 electoral votes, only two more than the absolute minimum needed of 270. In that case, two or three Democratic individual electors seeking personal recognition or attention to a pet cause could withhold—or threaten to withhold—their electoral votes from Carter, and thus make the election outcome very uncertain.

Republican 1976 vice-presidential nominee Robert Dole provided evidence of the possibilities inherent in such a close presidential contest. Testifying before the U.S. Senate Judiciary Committee on January 17, 1977, in *favor* of abolishing the electoral college, Senator Dole remarked that during the 1976 election night vote count:

> We were looking around on the theory that maybe Ohio might turn around because they had an automatic recount. We were shopping—not shopping, excuse me. Looking around for electors. Some took a look at Missouri, some were looking at Louisiana, some in Mississippi, because their laws are a little bit different. And we might have picked up one or two in Louisiana. There were allegations of fraud maybe in Mississippi, and something else in Missouri. We [would] need to pick up three or four after Ohio. So that may happen in any event. But it just seems to me that the temptation is there for that elector in a very tight race to really negotiate quite a bunch.

2. The Winner-Take-All System

The second problem of the contemporary electoral college system lies in the almost universal state statutory provisions (the only exceptions being the states of Maine and Nebraska) giving *all* of a state's electoral votes to the winner of a state's popular vote plurality (not even a majority). This extraconstitutional practice, gradually adopted by all states during the 19th century as a means of enhancing state power, can lead to bizarre results—such as in Arkansas in 1968 where major party nominees Hubert Humphrey and Richard Nixon together divided slightly over 61 percent of the popular vote, while third-party candidate George Wallace, with less than 39 percent popular support in Arkansas, received 100 percent of the state's electoral votes. Similarly, in the 1992 election, three-way popular vote divisions among George Bush, Bill Clinton, and Ross Perot resulted in a number of states having their blocs of electoral votes decided on the basis of remarkably small pluralities. President Bush won the electoral votes of the Arizona and Kansas with but 39 percent of the popular vote, while Bill Clinton received all the electoral votes of Maine and New Hampshire with 39 percent and Montana and Nevada on the basis of only 38 percent of these states' popular vote. Ross Perot, with fully 30 percent of the popular vote in Maine, was only nine percentage points behind the state's winner, Bill Clinton, and thus came relatively close to winning electoral votes in that state (a goal actually easier because of Maine's unusual district-based determination of two of its four electoral votes).

Even more significant, however, is the fact that the winner-take-all determination of slates of state electors tends to magnify tremendously the relative voting power of residents of the largest states. Each of their voters might, by a vote cast, decide not just one popular vote, but how a bloc of 33 or 54 electoral votes are cast—if electors are faithful. As a result, the electoral college has a major impact on candidate strategy—as shown by the concern of Carter and Ford strategists, in the final weeks of the very close and uncertain 1976 campaign, with the nine big electoral vote states, which together that year had 245 of the 270 electoral votes necessary to win. The vote in seven of these nine megastates proved to be exceedingly close, with both major party candidates that year receiving at least 48 percent. Similarly in 1992, presidential candidates Clinton, Bush, and Perot focused their campaigns generally on the ten largest electoral vote states, which in the 1990s have fully 257 of the 270 electoral votes needed to win; these states are seen as determinants of any presidential contest's outcome.

In short, the electoral college does not treat voters alike—a thousand voters in Scranton, Pennsylvania, are far more important strategically than a thousand voters in Wilmington, Delaware. This inequity also places a premium on the support of key political leaders in large electoral vote states—as can be observed in any presidential election in the candidates' desperate wooing of the mayors of such cities as Philadelphia, Chicago, and Los Angeles. These political leaders are seen as possibly playing a major role in determining the electoral outcome in the large states of Pennsylvania, Illinois, and California, and thus as important to winning those large blocs of electoral votes. The electoral college treats political leaders as well as voters unequally—those in large marginal states are vigorously courted.

The electoral college also encourages fraud—or at least fear and rumor of fraud. In 1976, for example, New York, by itself had more than enough electoral votes to determine the winner of the presidential contest, and that state went to Carter by 290,000 popular votes. Claims of voting irregularities and calls for a recount were made on election night, but were later withdrawn because of Carter's clear national popular vote win. *If* fraud was present in New York, only 290,000 votes determined the 1976 presidential election; under a national direct election plan, at least 1,700,000 votes would have had to have been irregular in the same election to have changed the outcome.

The electoral college at times also provides even relatively minor third-party candidates the opportunity to exercise magnified political influence in the election of the president when they can gather votes in large, closely balanced states. In 1976, third-party candidate Eugene McCarthy, with less than 1 percent of the popular vote, came close to tilting the presidential election through his strength in close pivotal states. In four states (Iowa, Maine, Oklahoma, and Oregon) totaling 26 electoral votes, McCarthy's relatively small popular vote exceeded the margin by which Ford defeated Carter. In those states, McCarthy's candidacy *may* have swung those states to Ford. Even more significantly, had McCarthy been on the New York ballot (he had been ruled off at the last moment on technical grounds), it is likely Ford would have carried that state with its 41 electoral votes, and with it the election—despite Carter's overall national vote majority and lead of well over one and one-half million votes.

3. The "Constant Two" Electoral Votes

A third flaw of the electoral college system lies in the apportionment of electoral votes among the states. The constitutional formula is simple: one vote per state per senator and representative. Another distortion from equality appears here because of the "constant two" electoral votes, regardless of population, which correspond to each state's two senators. Because of this, inhabitants of the smallest states are advantaged to the extent that they "control" three electoral votes (two for the state's two senators and one for the representative) while their small population might otherwise entitle them to but one or two votes. This is weighing by states, not by population—however, the importance of this feature is greatly outweighed by the previously mentioned winner-take-all system. Nevertheless, the constant two feature of the electoral college—as the winner-take-all system—is yet another distorting factor in the election of the president. These structural features of the electoral college ensure that it can never be a neutral counting device and that it instead contains a variety of biases dependent solely upon the state in which voters cast their ballots. The contemporary electoral college is not just an archaic mechanism for counting the votes for president; it is also an institution that aggregates popular votes in an inherently imperfect manner.

4. The Uncertainty of the Winner Winning

The fourth flaw of the contemporary electoral college system is that under the present system there is no assurance that the winner of the popular vote will win the election. This problem is a fundamental one—can an American president operate effectively if he or she clearly has received fewer votes than the loser? I would suggest that the effect upon the legitimacy of a contemporary American presidency would be disastrous if a president were elected by an obscure electoral college after losing in the popular vote.

An American "divided verdict" election, however, *can* happen and *has* in fact occurred two or three times in American history, the most recent undisputable case (the election of 1960 being undeterminable) being the election of 1888, when the 100,000 popular vote lead of Grover Cleveland was turned into a losing 42 percent of the electoral vote. Was there a real possibility of such a divided verdict in the last truly close U.S. election, that of 1976? An analysis of the election results shows that if 9,245 votes had shifted to Ford in Ohio and Hawaii, *Ford* would have been instead elected president with 270 electoral votes, the absolute minimum, despite Carter's 51 percent of the national popular vote and lead of 1.7 million votes.

One hesitates to contemplate the political and constitutional consequences had a nonelected president, such as Ford, been inaugurated for four more years after having been rejected by a majority of the American voters in his only presidential election.

5. The Contingency Election Procedure

Besides the four aspects of the electoral college system so far discussed, one last problem should also be examined: an aspect of the electoral college system that is both probably the most complex and also the most dangerous for the stability of the American political order. The Constitution provides that if no candidate receives an absolute majority of the electoral votes—in recent years 270 electoral votes—the House of Representatives chooses the president from among the top three candidates. Two questions need to be asked: Is such an electoral college deadlock likely to occur in contemporary politics? And would the consequences be likely to be disastrous? A simple answer to both questions is yes.

In some illustrative examples, in 1960 a switch of less than 9,000 popular votes from John Kennedy to Richard Nixon in the two states of Illinois and Missouri would have prevented either man from receiving an electoral college majority. Similarly, in 1968, a 53,000 vote shift in New Jersey, Missouri, and New Hampshire would have resulted in an electoral college deadlock, with Nixon then receiving 269 votes—one short of a majority. Finally, in the close 1976 election, if some 11,950 popular votes in Delaware and Ohio had shifted from Carter to Ford, Ford would have carried these two states. The result of the 1976 election would then have been— *an exact tie* in electoral votes, 269-269! The presidency would have been decided *not* on election night, but through deals or switches at the electoral college meetings the following December 13, or alternatively by means of the later uncertainties of the House of Representatives.

What specifically might happen in the case of an election night apparent electoral college nonmajority or deadlock? A first possibility, of course, would be that a faithless elector or two, pledged to one candidate, might switch at the time of the actual meetings of the electoral college six weeks later, so as to create a majority for the presidential candidate leading in electoral votes. Such an action might resolve the crisis, although it would be sad to think of the president's mandate as based on such a thin reed of legitimacy as faithless electors.

If, however, no deals or actions at the time of the mid-December meetings of the electoral college were successful in forming a majority, then the action would shift to the newly elected House of Representatives, meeting at noon on January 6, only 14 days before the constitutionally scheduled Inauguration Day for the new president. The House of Representatives contingency procedure, which would now be followed, is, as discussed earlier, an awkward relic of the compromises of the writing of the new Constitution. Serious problems of equity would exist, certainly, in following the constitutionally prescribed one-vote-per-state procedure. In the 1990s, for example, the seven Representatives from the seven single member smallest states could outvote the 177 House members from the six largest states. The voters of the District of Columbia would be without any representation at all in the election of the president. Beyond these noteworthy problems of fairness lurks an even more serious problem—what if the House itself should deadlock and be unable to agree on a president?

In a two-candidate race, this would unlikely be a real problem; however, in a three-candidate contest, such as 1968, 1980, or 1992, there might well be enormous difficulties in getting a majority of states behind one candidate as House members agonized over choosing between partisan labels and support for the candidate (such as George Wallace, John Anderson, or Ross Perot) who might have carried their district. The result, in 1968, 1980, or 1992, might well have been no immediate majority forthcoming of 26 states, and political uncertainty and chaos as the nation approached Inauguration Day uncertain as to who was to be the president.

CONCLUSION

The electoral college has disturbing potential as an institution threatening the certainty of U.S. elections and the legitimacy of the American president. But even beyond these considerations, the electoral college inherently—by its very nature—is a distorted counting device for turning popular votes into electoral votes. It can never be a faithful reflection of the popular will, and will always stand between the citizen's and the people's president.

It is for these reasons that substantial efforts have been made in recent years to reform or abolish the electoral college, especially following the close and uncertain presidential elections of 1968 and 1976. The first of these "hairbreadth elections" resulted in a constitutional amendment to abolish the electoral college being overwhelmingly passed by the House of Representatives in 1969, only to be filibustered to death in the U.S. Senate in 1970. Similar constitutional proposals were debated by the Senate once again following the close 1976 election, during the period of 1977 to 1979, prior to failing in that chamber in July 1979 for want of the necessary two-thirds vote. In the early 1990s, electoral college reform proposals are once again before Congress and were the subject of national televised U.S. Senate hearings in 1992.

Inertia, institutional conservatism, and the self-interest of senators from states perceived as advantaged by the existing electoral college, served to preserve the electoral college during the debates of the 1970s, despite the concerted efforts of well-organized and persistent electoral reformers. The politics of electoral college reform are kindled by close U.S. presidential elections, which demonstrate the inadequacies of the electoral college as a means of electing the president. Should . . . subsequent presidential election[s] prove to be uncertain in outcome or unfairly determined by the special characteristics of the electoral college, that institution will become once again a major target of reformers' efforts. Until that time, the electoral college will continue as an important aspect of American politics, shaping and determining the election of the U.S. president.

The problems inherent in the contemporary electoral college are numerous and should be dealt with *prior* to the nightmares and night sweats of a problem election. They cannot be dealt with by patchwork reforms such as abolishing the office of elector to solve solely the problem of the faithless elector. Rather, the distorted and unwieldy counting device of the electoral college must be abolished, and the votes of the American people—wherever cast—must be counted directly and equally in determining who shall be president of the United States: the people's president.

In Defense of the Electoral College

Robert Weissberg

Defending the electoral college is like defending sin. Almost every responsible person is against it; defenders are rare, yet it somehow survives. However, while sin may be beyond eradication, the electoral college is not deeply rooted in human nature. The electoral college can be abolished just as we abolished other archaic portions of the Constitution. Clearly, then, a defense of this system of selecting our President must be defended on grounds other than its inevitability. Our defense will be divided into two parts. We shall first show that its alleged defects are not as serious as some critics would have us believe. Second, we shall argue that there are in fact several virtues of this electoral arrangement, which the American Bar Association has characterized as "archaic, undemocratic, complex, ambiguous, and dangerous"!

CRITICISMS OF THE ELECTORAL COLLEGE

Criticisms of the electoral college basically fall into two groups. The first emphasize the unpredictable and unintended outcomes that are conceivable under the present system. In a nutshell, from the perspective of these critics, here is what *could* have happened in the 1996 presidential election: Bill Clinton wins a plurality of the popular vote but, thanks to a handful of states narrowly going to Ross Perot, fails to win a majority in the Electoral College. Meanwhile, a few Electors refuse to honor their Dole pledges and cast their ballots for Harry Brown, the Libertarian Party candidate. After a six-month-long acrimonious debate, Ross Perot is selected as president by the GOP dominated House with the promise to serve only a single term and pass a balanced budget.

The second basic criticism accuses the electoral college of overvaluing some votes at the expense of other votes. Some disagreement occurs over just who benefits from these distortions, but most experts claim that voters in populous states, especially members of certain urban ethnic and racial groups, are overrepresented. Would-be presidents pay more attention to some New York and California voters at the expense of votes in places like North Dakota.

THE NIGHTMARE OF UNINTENDED CONSEQUENCES

These are serious charges. Let us first consider what may be called the nightmare of unintended political outcomes. Two points may be made concerning this criticism. First, the odds of any one of these events occurring is remote. Only once in U.S. history—in 1888—has the undisputed winner of the popular vote lost the electoral college vote.

Robert Weissberg is professor of political science at the University of Illinois at Urbana-Champaign. This article was written especially for Points of View *in 1983 and updated in 1997.*

Electors have voted contrary to their popular instructions, but this has been extremely rare, and most important, such "unfaithful electors" have never affected who won and have almost never tried to influence the election's outcome (their actions were largely symbolic in a clearly decided contest). Nor has the last 160 years seen a presidential election decided by the House, despite some efforts by minor-party candidates to bring this about. All in all, the odds of any one event happening are low, and the odds of several such events occurring and making a difference in the same election are remote.

A second rejoinder to this nightmare of unintended, undesirable consequences is that hypothetical catastrophes are possible under *any* electoral system. Take, for example, a direct popular election with the provision for a runoff in the event no candidate receives a majority. It is conceivable that the initial election brings forth a wide range of candidates. A large number of moderate candidates each gets 5 or 7 percent from the middle of the political spectrum, and for the runoff, the public faces a contest between two unpopular extremists who together received 25 percent of the vote in the first election. *All* electoral mechanisms contain so-called time bombs waiting to go off.

MISREPRESENTATION CAUSED BY THE ELECTORAL COLLEGE

This alleged defect of misrepresentation derives from both the electoral college as stated in the Constitution plus individual state nonconstitutional requirements that all of a state's electoral votes go to the candidate receiving the largest number of votes (though Maine and Nebraska allow a division of their electoral vote). The effect of this unit voting is that to win the presidency a candidate must win in several populous states. New York, California, Texas, Illinois, and a few other big states are the valuable prizes in the election and thus a few thousand New Yorkers have more electoral clout than a few thousand voters in South Dakota. It supposedly follows, then, that the desires of these strategically placed voters are given greater attention by those seeking the presidency.

Four points can be made in response to this inequality-of-voters argument. First, it is far from self-evident just who those overadvantaged voters are and whether these big groups can be the cornerstone of electoral victory. It has been said, for example, that since there are many African-Americans in New York, the African-American vote can determine who carries New York. However, New York, like all populous states, has a varied population, so in principle the same argument can be applied to farmers, young people, white Protestants, middle-class suburbanites—any group comprising at least 10 percent of the electorate. This "key-voting-bloc-in-a-key-state" argument is largely the creation of statistical manipulation. Of course, it makes considerable sense for a group to *claim* that its vote, given its strategic position, put a candidate in the White House.

Second, it is a great exaggeration to assert that these strategically placed, "overrepresented" voters can exert control or significantly influence the election. Let's suppose that a candidate said that to win the presidency one must win the big states; to win the big states one must do very well among African-Americans, Jews, and union workers because these groups are overrepresented in these big states. Not only might it be difficult to appeal to all groups simultaneously (promising jobs to African-Americans may anger union workers), but also, even if one's appeals are successful, these "key" votes alone are not enough. The idea of certain well-situated minorities running the electoral show via the electoral college ignores the problems of creating large, diverse voting coalitions and the relatively small size of these "key" groups. At best, the electoral college may provide a disproportionate influence to voters—not a specific group—in large states in close elections (and since World War II national elections have been close only about half the time).

Third, the relationship between overrepresentation caused by the electoral college and disproportionate government benefits has never been demonstrated. The relationship has appeared so reasonable and been mentioned so often that it is now reiterated as if it were a truism. Actual evidence, however, has never been marshaled. Obviously, presidents have endorsed some policies favorable to supposed key groups in large states, but presidents have also opposed policies favorable to these same groups. It may be true that presidents have occasionally taken the operation of the electoral college into account in their policy calculations, but such action has not been sufficiently blatant to draw widespread attention.

Finally, the electoral system embodied in the electoral college may be biased in favor of some voters, but bias is part of *every* system of election. To reject a system because it is somehow "unfair" makes sense only if some perfectly fair system did exist. In fact, no such system does exist. As we did before, let us take as an example the simple majority rule plus a runoff system commonly advocated by opponents of the electoral college. This seemingly "pure" system is "unfair" for several reasons. Unlike the systems of proportional representation used by many European democracies, it provides no representation to citizens whose candidate received less than a majority— 49.9 percent of all voters may get nothing. Moreover, it can be easily demonstrated that by allowing each citizen only one yes or no vote, the system does not allow citizens to rank candidates so that the candidate most acceptable to the most people is selected. In other words, a candidate who is not the first choice of a majority, but is still highly acceptable to almost everyone, is shut out under a simple majority system. In short, the issue is not one of "fair" versus "unfair," but what type of unfairness will be present.

DEFENDING THE ELECTORAL COLLEGE

Thus far we have argued that the major criticisms against the electoral college either rest on exaggerations and misunderstandings or are simply unproven. Is there, however, anything positive to be said for the frequently maligned system? At least four virtues of the electoral college seem reasonably clear and are probably advantageous to most people: (1) it is a proven, workable system; (2) it makes campaigns more manageable; (3) it discourages election fraud; and (4) it preserves a moderate two-party system.

The first virtue—*it is a proven, workable system*—is basically a conservative argument. Conservatives believe that when something works, though somewhat imperfectly, it should not be easily abandoned for the promise of perfection. That is, on paper almost every alternative to the electoral college is without defect. However, as anyone familiar with the success rates of proposed reforms knows well, political changes do not always work as intended. The nightmare and inequalities of the status quo are hypothetical and alleged: a change might bring real and consequential problems despite promises of perfection. Constitutional changes should be made only if the *real* costs of the electoral college are heavy.

The second virtue—*it makes campaigns more manageable*—derives from two facts. First, in terms of time, money, and energy, the present electoral system is already very demanding on candidates. Running for president is so exhausting physically that some have said, half jokingly, that only the mentally unbalanced are attracted to this activity. Second, the electoral college, plus the "winner-take-all" role in 48 of the 50 states plus the District of Columbia, means that some votes are not as important as others. Swaying a few thousand uncommitted voters in a closely divided populous state is much more important than an appeal to the same number of voters in a small, one-party-dominated state. Obviously, then, without some division of voters into important and unimportant voters, campaigning for president would become even more hectic and overwhelming than ever. A rational candidate might even lock himself in a television studio rather than attempt the impossible task of trying to wage an effective nationwide personal campaign.

The third virtue—*it discourages election fraud*—also derives from the present system's divisions of votes into important and less important. In a state with a relatively small number of electoral votes, where the outcome is not in much doubt, little incentive exists for widespread election fraud. Such manipulation is only worthwhile in big states like New York or Illinois where presidential elections tend to be close and a large bloc of electoral votes may hinge on a few thousand votes. Under a direct popular election system, however, all votes are equally valuable and thus equally worth manipulating. Practices such as multiple voting, voting the dead, and intimidating the opposition, which were once limited to a few localities, might very well become national in scope.

The fourth and final virtue—*it preserves a moderate two-party system*—is perhaps the most important. Under the existing system, winning the presidency means winning numerous electoral votes. Since to win electoral votes you must win pluralities in many states, it takes a formidable political organization to win these big prizes. A group that won, say, 5 to 10 percent of the vote in a few states would be doomed. Even an organization that wins a few million votes usually comes up with very little where the prizes are big blocs of electoral votes. In contemporary politics, the only organizations capable of such a massive electoral undertaking are large, diverse, compromise-oriented political parties such as the Democratic and Republican parties.

To appreciate this contribution of the existing electoral college system, imagine presidential campaigns *without* the two major parties. Instead of two major candidates and a dozen or two inconsequential candidates, there would be numerous hopefuls with some reasonable chance of success. These candidates would likely draw most of their support from relatively small segments of the population. There might be an anti-abortion candidate, a strong civil rights candidate, an anti-school-busing candidate, and a few others closely associated with one or two specific issues. The incentive to create broad-based coalitions to capture a majority in 20 or 30 states would be considerably reduced and thus the two major parties would virtually disappear.

This type of campaign politics would suffer from several problems. The narrow basis of candidate appeal would likely generate much sharper conflict and deepen group antagonism (for example, African-Americans might see for the first time in modern times an explicitly anti–civil rights candidate who could win). Perhaps most important, postelection governance would become difficult. Not only would a president have a much smaller base of popular support, but he or she would likely have to deal with a Congress composed of people with no party attachment whose primary purpose was to advance a particular group or regional interest. Of course, the present system of Democratic and Republican party politics does not eliminate the advancement of narrow interests and interbranch conflict. However, the situation would probably be even worse if numerous single-issue groups replaced the present two major political parties. In short, the electoral college, plus the winner-take-all-system, encourages the current two-party system, and this system moderates conflict and promotes effective postelection governance.

We began by noting that defending the electoral college is like defending sin. We have argued that, as some have said of sin, it is not nearly as bad as is claimed, and it may even be beneficial. We have not argued that the present system is beyond reproach. The system has been modified numerous times since its inception, and future changes are certainly possible. It is a serious mistake, however, to believe that abolishing the electoral college will be as beneficial as finally ridding ourselves of sin.

8

POLITICAL PARTIES

For something that was unintended by the founders of this nation, political parties have been a remarkably stable feature of the American political landscape. Parties were alive and kicking in the 1790's, and they are alive and kicking in the 1990's. Just as remarkably, the U.S. political party system has featured competition between two major parties—the Democratic and Republican parties—for at least 130 years. True, there have been periods in our history where one party has been fairly dominant (winning most offices, including the presidency and Congress, for example, over a long period of time), but the two-party pattern remains well established.

The 1992 and 1996 presidential elections, however, presented a challenge to this persistent two-party pattern. Third-party candidate Ross Perot mounted extremely well-financed and organized campaigns for the presidency, and while ultimately unsuccessful, he nevertheless threw a scare into the two major parties. Indeed, it was Ross Perot who, in the 1992 election, was able to dominate the airwaves and force the major-party candidates to open up the presidential debates to three viable candidates instead of two.

The emergence of Perot's third party—"United We Stand America" in 1992 and the "Reform Party" in 1996—has prompted a debate within the academic and political communities over (1) the extent to which Perot's two candidacies constituted significant challenges to the two-party system; and (2) the extent to which Perot's or any other third party represents a positive development in American politics.

In the selections that follow, the third party question is addressed first by Theodore J. Lowi, a professor of political science at Cornell University. Lowi argues that the 1992 election was "the beginning of the end of America's two-party system" and the emergence of the Perot party provided a healthy jolt to the political system. Contending that the two major parties are "brain dead," Lowi believes that a viable third party is just the medicine the country needs to encourage parties that address issues instead of focusing on images, and that generate enthusiasm and greater participation instead of apathy and cynicism.

In the second selection, political scientist Paul S. Herrnson of the University of Maryland takes strong exception to Lowi's point of view. Herrnson develops his counterargument on principally two grounds: first, there is too much tradition and institutional bias in favor of the two-party system for it to be cast aside lightly; and second, while third parties have in the past made important contributions to politics and policy, they should not be further encouraged because they only contribute to more division and fragmentation in our political system—a system that is already so overloaded with both that government finds it difficult to act to solve critical national problems.

The Party Crasher:
The Need for a Third Party

Theodore J. Lowi

. . . [H]istorians will undoubtedly focus on 1992 as the beginning of the end of America's two-party system. The extraordinary rise of Ross Perot and the remarkable outburst of enthusiasm for his ill-defined alternative to the established parties removed all doubt about the viability of a broad-based third party. Republicans, Democrats and independents alike have grasped the essential point that the current incumbents will not, and cannot, reform a system that drastically needs overhauling.

A third party would do more than shock the powers that be into a few reforms. Its very existence—never mind its specific policies—would break the institutional gridlock that has paralyzed Washington for most of the past 20 years. Ultimately, it would give us a more parliamentary style of government, in keeping, it seems to me, with what the Founding Fathers had in mind. Perot demonstrated the possibility. It now falls to the rest of us to make the breakthrough to a three-party system. The New Party, self-defined as "broadly Social Democratic," which has been gathering strength over the past . . . months; the John Anderson crowd from the 1980s, of which I am one; the perennial Libertarian Party—we are going to have to get together.

One of the best-kept secrets in American politics is that the two-party system has long been brain dead—kept alive by support systems like state electoral laws that protect the established parties from rivals and by Federal subsidies and so-called campaign reform. The two-party system would collapse in an instant if the tubes were pulled and the IV's were cut.

Back when the Federal Government was smaller and less important, the two parties could be umbrella parties—organizing campaigns, running elections and getting the vote out—without much regard to ideology or policy. But with the New Deal and the rise of the welfare state, the federal government became increasingly vulnerable to ideological battles over policy. None of this was particularly noticeable while the government and the economy were expanding, but in the early 1970's class and ideological conflicts began to emerge more starkly.

Thus were born the familiar "wedge" issues—crime, welfare, prayer, economic regulation, social regulation, taxes, deficits and anti-Communism. No matter what position party leaders took on such issues, they were bound to alienate a substantial segment of their constituency. While the Democrats were the first to feel the cut of wedge issues, particularly concerning race, Republicans are now having their own agonies over abor-

Theodore J. Lowi is John L. Senior Professor of American Institutions, Cornell University and a former president of the American Political Science Association. From Theodore J. Lowi, "The Party Crasher: The Need for a Third Party," the New York Times Magazine, *August 23, 1992, pp. 28–33. Copyright © 1992 by the New York Times Company. Reprinted by permission.*

tion, foreign policy and budget deficits. Wedge issues immobilize party leadership, and once parties are immobilized the government is itself immobilized.

The parties have also atrophied because both have been in power too long. In theory, a defeated party becomes vulnerable to new interests because it is both weaker and more willing to take risks. But for nearly 40 years, both parties have in effect been majority parties. Since each party has controlled a branch of government for much of that time, neither is eager to settle major policy issues in the voting booth. A very important aspect of the corruption of leadership is the tacit contract between the two parties to avoid taking important issues to the voters and in general to avoid taking risks.

Party leaders have responded to gridlock not with renewed efforts to mobilize the electorate but with the strategy of scandal. An occasional exposure of genuine corruption is a healthy thing for democracy, but when scandal becomes an alternative to issues, leaving the status quo basically unaltered, it is almost certain that all the lights at the crossroads are stuck on red. In fact, the use of scandal as a political strategy has been so effective that politicians have undermined themselves by demonstrating to the American people that the system itself is corrupt.

The Perot candidacy differed fundamentally from past independent presidential candidacies, which were basically single-issue appeals. Perot tapped into a genuinely unprecedented constituency—moderates disgusted with the two major parties, regardless of the nominees. Two major polls completed in May and June [1992] found that about 60 percent of Americans favored the establishment of a new political party.

Predictably, the two-party system defenders have devoted considerable energy to shooting down any suggestion that the status quo can be improved upon. They have produced all sorts of scenarios about how a third party could throw presidential elections into the Congress, with the House of Representatives choosing the president and the Senate choosing the vice president—not only delaying the outcome but producing a Bush-Gore, a Clinton-Quayle, or, God forbid, a Quayle-Who-Knows administration. Worse yet, if it survived to future elections, a third party would hold the balance of power and, as a result, wield an influence far out of proportion to its electoral size. It might, by its example, produce a fourth or a fifth party. And if it elected members to Congress, it might even inconvenience congressional leaders in their allocation of committee assignments.

In fact, genuine third parties have been infrequent in the United States, but wherever they have organized they have had significant, generally positive effects. One of these is providing a halfway house for groups wedged out of the two larger parties. In 1924, the progressive movement succeeded in forming the Progressive Party in Wisconsin and other midwestern states, which nominated Robert M. La Follette for president. In the 1930s, the Farmer-Labor Party flourished in Minnesota, where it eventually fused with an invigorated Democratic Party. In the process, both of these third parties provided the channel through which many dissident and alienated groups found their way back into politics, and their influence lingered long after the parties themselves. Similarly, wherever the Dixiecrats organized as a party, that state was later transformed to a genuinely competitive two-party state.

With three parties, no party needs to seek a majority or pretend that it is a majority. What a liberating effect this would have on party leaders and candidates, to go after constituencies composed of 35 percent rather than 51 percent of the voters. A three-party system would be driven more by issues, precisely because parties fighting for pluralities can be clearer in their positions. Third parties have often presented constructive and imaginative programs, which have then been ridiculed by leaders of the two major parties, who point out that third-party candidates can afford to be intelligent and bold since they can't possibly win. In a three-party system, even the two major parties would have stronger incentives to be more clearly programmatic, because their goal is more realistic and their constituency base is simpler.

Flowing directly from this, voting would increase, as would other forms of participation. Virtually our entire political experience tells us that more organized party competition produces more participation. And we already know that genuine three-party competition draws people into politics—not merely as voters but as petition gatherers, door knockers, envelope lickers and $5 contributors—making the three-party system an antidote to the mass politics that virtually everybody complains about nowadays.

Even defenders of the two-party system criticize the reliance of candidates on television, computerized voter lists, mass mailings and phone banks—which dehumanize politics, discourage participation, replace discourse with 15-second sound bites and reduce substantive alternatives to subliminal imagery and pictorial allusion. And the inordinate expense of this mass politics has led to a reliance on corporate money, particularly through the political action committees, destroying any hope of collective party responsibility.

These practices and their consequences cannot be eliminated by new laws—even if the laws didn't violate the First Amendment. A multiparty system would not immediately wipe out capital-intensive mass politics, but it would eliminate many of the pressures and incentives that produce its extremes, because of the tendency of third parties to rely on labor-intensive politics. Third parties simply do not have access to the kind of financing that capital-intensive politics requires. But more than that, there is an enthusiasm about an emerging party that inspires people to come out from their private lives and to convert their civic activity to political activity.

Finally, a genuine three-party system would parliamentarize the presidency. Once a third party proves that it has staying power, it would increase the probability of presidential elections being settled in the House of Representatives, immediately making Congress the primary constituency of the presidency. Congress would not suddenly "have power over" the presidency. It has such power already, in that the Constitution allows it complete discretion in choosing from among the top three candidates. But if Congress were the constituency of the president, the president would have to engage Congress in constant discourse. The president might under those circumstances have even more power than now, but he would have far less incentive to go over the head of Congress to build a mass following.

Even now, with two parties based loosely on mythical majorities, a president cannot depend on his party to provide a consistent congressional majority. The whole idea of a mandate is something a victorious president claims but few members of Congress accept, even for the length of the reputed honeymoon. Thus, current reality already involves the president in bargains with members of the opposition party.

Confronting three parties in Congress, each of whose members is elected on the basis of clear policy positions, the president's opportunities for bargaining for majority support would be more fluid and frequent. In our two-party environment, issues are bargained out within the ranks of each party and often never see the light of day, particularly during the session prior to a presidential election. A third party with a small contingent of members of Congress would insure a more open and substantive atmosphere for bargaining to take place—*after* the election.

A third party would play the role of honest broker and policy manager, because it would hold a balance of power in many important and divisive issues. There would be little fear of the tail wagging the dog, because, unlike European parties, Democrats and Republicans are not ideologically very far apart—they have simply not been cooperating with each other. The presence of a third-party delegation gives the President an alternative for bargaining, but if the new party raised its price too high it would simply give the President a greater incentive to bargain with the other major party.

The point here is that the third party is a liberating rather than a confining force, a force for open debate on politics. Another important myth in the United States is that policy making is a matter of debate between the affirmative and the negative. But simple yea versus nay on clearly defined alternatives is a very late stage in any policy-making process. In sum, just as the rise of the two-party system fundamentally altered the constitutional structure of our government appropriately for the 19th century, so a three-party system would alter the structure appropriately for the 21st century.

Immediately, one must add an important proviso: A genuine third party must be built from the bottom up. It must be an opportunist party, oriented toward the winning of elections. It must nominate and campaign for its own candidates at all levels and not simply run somebody for president. And it must attract regular Democrats and Republicans by nominating some of them to run as candidates with the third-party nomination as well as that of their own party. Joint sponsorship has been practiced by the Liberal and Conservative Parties in New York for decades. Being listed on two lines on the ballot is a powerful incentive for regular Democrats and Republicans to cooperate with a new party, if not to switch over. About 40 states have laws preventing or discouraging this practice, but their provisions will probably not stand up to serious litigation.

By whatever means, the new party must have enough organizational integrity to last beyond one election. Running candidates for office in every election is the only way to secure organizational integrity. And a new, third political party is the best moderate means of breaking the institutional impasse in American politics.

Ross Perot was never the issue. The issue is a third party, and this is a call to arms, not a dispassionate academic analysis. A third party could, it just could, turn the switches at the crossroads from red to green.

Fizzle or Crash and Burn?
Ross Perot's Challenge to the Two-Party System

Paul S. Herrnson

Presidential candidate Ross Perot burst onto the political scene in 1992 like a meteor in a clear night sky and then crashed and skidded along the ground, leaving behind only fragments of an ill-fated candidacy. In 1996 his sun never rose. Perot's entrance, disappearance, and reemergence in the 1992 presidential campaign did little to dissuade most Americans from turning to some familiar choices. His stewardship of the newly created Reform Party in 1996 produced similar results. By the time election day came around in both years, most voters were ready to cast their ballots for one of the major parties' two candidates.

Previous independent or minor-party candidacies have also been largely unsuccessful. It is these results and the persistence of the two-party system that are the most important stories behind the 1992 and 1996 presidential elections. Those who argue that Perot's candidacies will lead to a new permanent minor party just plain have it wrong. Those who believe that the development of a multiparty system would improve American politics are equally mistaken.

Perot's bids for the presidency were built on the discontent that many voters felt toward the major parties and the political system in general. Whatever successes Perot enjoyed at the polls were more a reflection of the disenchantment that the American people had with the performance of the federal government and the two major parties than an endorsement of the candidate's beliefs.

Scandal, gridlock, and the major parties' failure to deal with the nation's sagging economy led to the middle-class frustrations that provided the foundation for Perot's campaigns. The degree to which the major parties deal with these issues in the future will be more influential in determining the survival of Perot's Reform Party than the efforts of Perot himself. This is typical of most of the independent and minor-party presidential candidacies that have occurred in the United States during the 20th century.

IMPEDIMENTS TO MINOR PARTIES

There are a number of reasons that most minor parties fail to root themselves firmly in the American landscape. Institutional impediments rank high among them. The Constitution is hostile to minor parties and party politics in general. Single-member simple-plurality elections, of which the electoral college is a peculiar variant, make it very difficult for minor parties to have much of an impact on the political process. These winner-take-all systems deprive any candidate or party that does not win an election a

Paul S. Herrnson is professor of political science at the University of Maryland and executive director of the Committee for Party Renewal. This article was written especially for Points of View *in 1994 and updated in 1997.*

share of elected offices, even when they come in second place. This is especially harmful to minor-party candidates, who usually consider themselves to have been successful when they come in second at the polls. Other electoral systems, like the proportional multimember representation systems used in much of Europe, on the other hand, virtually guarantee at least some legislative seats to any party—no matter how small, transient, or geographically confined—that wins a threshold of votes. These seats result in minor parties receiving both institutional recognition and political legitimacy.

Institutional recognition also gives the Democratic and Republican parties some critical advantages over minor parties. Because they receive automatic placement on the ballot, federal subsidies for their national conventions, and full funding for their presidential candidates, the two major parties are able to focus most of their energies on winning the support of voters. Minor-party and independent candidates, to the contrary, can obtain full access to the ballot only after they have collected thousands of signatures and met other requirements that have been established by each of the 50 states and the District of Columbia.

Moreover, it is difficult for minor-party and independent presidential candidates to obtain federal funding. Newly emergent minor parties can only qualify for federal subsidies retroactively. Those that do well in a given election are rewarded with campaign subsidies, but these funds are provided too late to have any impact on the election. Minor parties that have made a good showing in a previous election are automatically entitled to some campaign subsidies in advance, but these parties get only a fraction of the money that is made available to the Democrats and the Republicans. Of course, neither money nor ballot access difficulties provided serious obstacles to Ross Perot in 1992, and Perot qualified for federal matching funds in 1996.

Institutional impediments, however, are not the only hurdles that must be cleared in order for minor parties to survive. Americans' moderate views about politics deprive minor parties and their candidates of the bases of support that exist for minor parties in most other modern democracies. The fact that the vast majority of Americans hold opinions that are close to the center of a fairly narrow ideological spectrum means that most elections, particularly those for the presidency, are primarily contests to capture the "middle ground." At their very essence, Democratic strategies involve piecing together a coalition of moderates and voters on the left, and Republican strategies dictate holding their party's conservative base while attracting the support of voters at the center. The distribution of public opinion, particularly the association that each of the major parties has with an ideological pole, leaves little room for a minor party to develop a sizable base of reliable supporters. Democracies whose citizens have a broader array of ideological perspectives or have higher levels of class or ethnic solidarity generally provide more fertile ground for minor-party efforts.

The career paths of the politically ambitious are extremely important in explaining the weakness and short-term existence of most minor-party movements in the United States. Budding politicians learn early in their careers that the Democratic and Republican parties can provide them with useful contacts, expertise, some financial assistance, and an orderly path of entry into electoral politics. Minor parties and independent candidacies simply do not offer these same benefits. As a result, the two parties tend to attract the most talented among those interested in a career in public service. A large part of the parties' hegemony can be attributed to their advantages in candidate recruitment.

Voters are able to discern differences in the talents of minor-party and major-party candidates and, not surprisingly, they hesitate to cast their votes for minor-party contestants for the presidency or other public offices. Even voters who are willing to publicly declare their support for a minor-party or independent candidate early in the election cycle often balk at casting their ballot for one of these candidates on election day. Major-party candidates and their supporters prey upon Americans' desire to go with a winner—or at least affect the election outcome—when they discourage citizens from "throwing away" their votes on fringe candidates.

Finally, mainstream politicians are not stupid. When a minor-party or independent candidate introduces an issue that proves to be popular, Democratic and Republican leaders are quick to co-opt it. In 1992 Ross Perot proclaimed himself to be an agent of change and was championed as someone who would make the tough choices needed to reform the political system and get America's sagging economy moving again. When that proved popular, many major-party candidates, including President George Bush in 1992 and President Bill Clinton in 1996, staked out similar positions. There is nothing disingenuous about these conversions. By adopting positions espoused in popular movements, party leaders are able to better represent their constituents as well as attract votes. Such strategic adjustments are commonplace in American history. By robbing minor party and independent movements of their platforms the two major parties ensure the longevity of the two-party system.

PEROT—PARTY LEADER OR SELF-AGGRANDIZER?

The preceding institutional and structural barriers apply to minor parties equally, but some forces that will impede the transformation of Perot's bids for the presidency into an enduring minor party originate from within the Perot movement itself. American politics have produced two types of enduring minor-party efforts. United We Stand America (UWSA), the vehicle for Perot's 1992 candidacy, and the Reform Party, his vehicle for 1996, resemble neither.

The first type of minor party, which includes the Communist and Libertarian parties, adheres to narrow ideologies and principally pursues educational goals. These parties survive because their supporters are strongly committed to an ideological cause. Their support for a cause is usually stronger than their desire to elect a winning candidate. Freed from electoral imperatives beyond actually fielding a contestant, these parties do not need to moderate their views in order to survive. Indeed, the ideological purity that is largely responsible for their survival tends to render them electorally inconsequential.

The other type of enduring minor party, which was more common in the 19th than the 20th centuries, possesses most of the characteristics of the major parties. These parties, which include the Liberty Party of the 1840s, the Know Nothing (or American) Party of the 1850s, and the Populist (or People's) Party of the 1880s, began as grassroots movements, fielded candidates for state and local office, experienced contested nominations, hosted conventions, took stands on a broad range of issues, and were led by well-respected and established politicians. They persist for several election cycles because they functioned like existing parties rather than independent candidacies.

UWSA and the Reform Party, and Perot's two presidential candidacies, bear little resemblance to either type of minor party. They differ from the first type in that Perot's, UWSA's, and the Reform Party goals were electorally oriented, not ideologically or educationally motivated. Perot has expressed no interest in leading a cause designed to persuade Americans to support an extremist ideology. His goal in both 1992 and 1996 was clearly to win votes.

UWSA, the Reform Party, and Perot's two campaigns also differed significantly from the other type of enduring minor party. Unlike those parties, Perot's campaigns were built entirely around one person who was their sole focus. The Perot campaigns did not originate as grassroots efforts, nor were they bottom-up phenomena. In 1992 Perot publicly offered himself as a candidate for office, stating he would run if the voters had his name placed on every state ballot. He then hired Ed Rollins and Frank Luntz—two high-powered political consultants—to run his campaign, and had "paid" and "real" volunteers make sure he made it onto the ballot. In 1996 Perot and his followers created the Reform Party to serve as a vehicle for Perot's aspirations.

Perot's tightly controlled, high-tech bids for office, which relied primarily on "infomercials" to propagate his message, are probably closer to the model of future protest candidacies than the decentralized, grassroots minor-party campaigns that existed prior to the development of the electronic media and the rise of modern public relations technology. In fact, modern campaign technology, suburban sprawl, and other systemic developments associated with the rise of a mass society and the decline of grassroots party organizations made independent campaigns like Perot's possible.

Unlike either type of minor party, and both major parties, Perot's followers did not encourage state and local candidates to run under either UWSA's or the Reform Party's label. In 1992 UWSA's charter prohibited them from doing so. In 1996 the Reform Party endorsed several major-party candidates for Congress and other offices and did virtually nothing to help Reform Party candidates wage their campaigns.

UWSA's and the Reform Party's operations also differed from those of traditional minor or major parties in other ways. UWSA held secretive strategy meetings and eschewed public conventions. The closed meetings may have been useful for shutting off debate and allowing Perot to dominate party proceedings, but they were not useful for attracting public support or providing the foundation for a broad-based political movement.

The Reform Party has also differed from other parties in the degree to which it has been dominated by one person. First, Perot's money, roughly $6.7 million, was the overwhelming source of the party's revenue in 1996. Second, the party's nomination process was designed to provide a coronation for Perot rather than to select a nominee from among competing aspirants. The balloting process was poorly carried out. Many party members received their ballots late. Others, including such prominent Reform Party members as Perot's opponent for the nomination, former Colorado Governor Richard Lamm, never received a ballot. Still others received several ballots. Flawed balloting procedures and a lack of interest among Reform Party members resulted in less than 5 percent of all Reform Party members participating in the process.

The nomination process also denied Lamm the opportunity to compete on a level playing field. Perot was the only Reform Party candidate who had access to the party's supporter list, and he benefited from a direct-mail piece that featured his but not Lamm's picture. The Reform Party's decision to stack the deck so heavily in favor of Perot suggests that it will have difficulty making the transition from a movement dominated by a single charismatic leader to an enduring comprehensive party. This transition would require the party to develop a formal governing body that is independent of Perot, an independent source of financing, and a routinized system of candidate selection. It would also require the party to nominate candidates for state, local, and congressional office and to develop a permanent organization capable of assisting its candidates with their general election campaigns.

In short, Perot's efforts never really grew beyond his own aspirations. Perot's candidacies began as a one-person, anti-Washington crusade that tapped into the deep-seated frustrations that many Americans felt toward their government and the dissatisfaction that they felt toward the two major parties and their nominees. The 1992 Perot campaign gained some legitimacy when it published an economic program written by some respected national leaders, faltered when the candidate dropped out of and then back into the race, and then suffered immensely when the media began to subject Perot and his running mate to the same level of scrutiny to which all major-party candidates are subjected. After the election, UWSA further harmed its prospects when it resorted to closed-door strategy sessions and decided against fielding candidates in the 1994 elections. Other activities, such as collecting $1,000 contributions from doctors in order to pay a team of researchers to write a health care plan, did little to fuel a populist-style movement.

Perot's 1996 bid for the presidency suffered difficulties from the start. The lack of evenhandedness in how it conducted its nomination caused the Reform Party to lose some of its credibility with its reform-oriented base and other voters. Perot's inability to attract a respected and recognizable running mate posed a second major problem. Economist Pat Choate was unknown in elite political and journalistic circles, did not register with the general public, and did little to strengthen the Perot ticket's vote-getting power. Perot's decision to accept federal matching funds for his general election campaign limited the party's spending to roughly half of that given to the two major parties, hampering its ability to communicate with voters. The Presidential Debate Commission's decision to deny Perot a place in the presidential debates denied the candidate's lackluster campaign a springboard from which it might take off. The decision also reinforced the widely held belief among voters that a vote for a minor-party candidate is a wasted vote. Finally, the fact that the American economy was growing stronger during the Clinton presidency did not bode well for Perot and, at least in the short term, does not bode well for other minor-party or independent candidacies that hope to use economic issues to attract political support.

IS A MULTIPARTY SYSTEM DESIRABLE?

Throughout its history, the United States has had a two-party system that has been punctuated by the appearance of minor parties. The Civil War, the depression of the

1890s, the Great Depression, the Civil Rights era, and the 1992 election are just a few of the many times in which political instability or public dissatisfaction with the existing two parties have given rise to significant minor-party or independent presidential candidacies. These candidacies, including Perot's, have introduced new ideas, raised some issues that the two major parties might have otherwise ignored, altered the policy debate, and in some cases led to major changes in public policy. They have also acted as safety valves, providing peaceful outlets for public discontent. These are all important political functions.

The question remains, "Should Americans want a permanent three- or multiparty system?" The answer I offer is probably not. Just as minor parties and independent candidacies rise and fall in response to voter dissatisfaction, permanent minor parties are likely to contribute to that dissatisfaction. The American system of checks and balances—with its separation of powers, bicameralism, and federal structure—complicates the political process tremendously. By making each federal, state, and local elected official responsible for his or her own tenure in office, it does little to encourage teamwork across different policy-making bodies. More than anything else, the fragmentation of power between an independent executive and separately elected members of Congress has led to a lack of collective responsibility and the political gridlock and public frustration that often accompanies it.

The introduction of one or more permanent minor parties would make majority rule even more difficult to achieve. These parties would probably draw significant votes away from the victor in a presidential race, cutting into the president's popular majority or policy mandate. They would also probably divide opposition, making it easier for an incumbent, even an unpopular one, to win reelection.

If minor-party candidates were able to elect significant numbers of representatives and senators, they could also change the dynamics in Congress. The majority party in the legislature would have to compromise with more than one minor party in order to enact its policies. Legislators from one or more parties could prevent the majority party from dealing with important issues and escape accountability by blaming that party or one or another for not compromising enough. Increasing the number of parties would fragment power more than the framers of the Constitution intended and lead to greater gridlock, not result in the development of the parliamentary style of government—which they vigorously opposed in the first place.

CONCLUSION

With but a few exceptions, the American political system has had a history of two major parties nominating the most qualified candidates and presenting voters with the most meaningful policy choices. The two major parties have also provided most voters with their electoral decision-making cues. Once the election is over, these parties have organized the government, promoted majority rule, translated public opinion into public policy, helped to centralize power within a fragmented political system, worked to sustain a moderate and inclusive style of politics, and provided a measure of political accountability to voters. The parties have also acted as stabilizing and socializing forces in politics.

The dynamics of the American two-party system are such that when independent or minor-party candidates succeed in tapping into public sentiment, majority party candidates usually rob them of their issue and their movement's *raisón d'être,* leaving these candidates and their movements to falter. Ironically, the major contributions that minor-party and independent candidacies make to American politics are to shore up the two-party system. United We Stand America has disappeared from the political universe. And, the Reform Party will probably fizzle out—as have most of its predecessors—that is, if it, too, doesn't crash and burn under Perot's leadership first.

9

INTEREST GROUPS

*O*ne of the most significant political developments in recent times has been the emergence and spectacular growth of political action committees, or PACs. PACs are specially organized political campaign finance groups, functioning outside the traditional political parties, whose primary purpose is to raise and spend money on behalf of candidates running for office. Modern PACs, with members numbering in the thousands, represent all sorts of special interests, from organized labor, to professional and business organizations, to liberal and conservative ideological groups.

Although PACs clearly have every right to exist in a democratic political system and contribute significantly to our free system of elections, there are those who allege that PACs have come to exercise too much political and governmental power—that they affect electoral and legislative outcomes far more than they should, often to the detriment of the public interest.

Among the critics is Philip M. Stern, for many years an "insider" in politics and more recently a forceful critic of the cozy relationship between PACs and members of Congress. Stern's point of view on PACs is revealed by the title of his book, Still the Best Congress Money Can Buy, from which we have excerpted several passages. From firsthand accounts of members of Congress, as well as his own analysis, Stern gives us a pretty lamentable view of the corrupting influence of money and PACs in Congress—a view that is deeply disturbing to those who think elected representatives ought to be above reproach, neither soliciting nor accepting campaign funds from special interests.

The selection offered in rebuttal to Stern is written by political scientist Larry Sabato, considered one of the nation's leading authorities on PACs. While admitting some faults with PACs, Professor Sabato strongly defends the existence of these new political organizations and the contributions they make to our system of democracy. In Sabato's view, PACs have been the victim of a bum rap, neither causing the current excesses in campaign finance nor unduly influencing individual legislators or the Congress as a whole.

Still the Best Congress Money Can Buy:
A PAC Primer

Philip M. Stern

. . . PACs . . . have introduced into modern American politics two phenomena that distort traditional concepts of representative democracy.

First, they have re-introduced "carpetbagging" into American politics, for the
first time since Reconstruction. That is, to the extent candidates and lawmakers
derive their funds from PACs, they are receiving their money from entities *outside*
their state or district, essentially, from people *who are not allowed to vote for them
on election day.*[1]

The second distortion of democracy is the new meaning with which this newfound
money-built connection between interest groups and legislative committees has altered
the word "constituency." Constituents used to be citizens within a candidate's district or
state who were entitled to vote for him or her. Voters. That was all. Today, PACs have
introduced a new definition: members of Congress now represent—first, their voters,
and second (what may be more important to them), their legislative or economic constituencies as well—who may or may not be (probably are not) part of their voting constituency. For example, the members of the Armed Services Committees and Defense
Appropriations Subcommittees have as their natural economic "constituents" the
defense contractors. Similarly, members of the Telecommunications Subcommittees of
the House and Senate have as their legislative and economic "constituents," broadcast-
ers, telephone companies, the cable industry, and others affected by government regulation of communications.

It's an ugly, undemocratic new concept.

How much influence do the PACs *really* have? Do they actually sway votes? Do they
even win preferential access for their lobbyists?

. . . [D]efenders of the PACs argue that PAC donations have a minimal influence on
the outcome of legislation. Lawmakers themselves—the recipients of the PAC's
largess—indignantly protest that the PACs' influence is virtually nil. The typical refrain
is, "I spent $500,000 on my last campaign. It's absolutely preposterous to suggest I
would sell my vote for $1,000—or even $5,000—just one percent of my campaign
budget!"

There are several counterarguments: the first—and most self-evidently powerful—
is the raw evidence of the steady increases in PAC donations to candidates which have
risen, on average, 40 percent annually since 1974. Evidently, the PACs think they

*Philip M. Stern, author of many books on government reform, is a former newspaper
reporter and research director of the Democratic party. From Philip M. Stern, "Still the
Best Congress Money Can Buy: A PAC Primer,"* Still the Best Congress Money Can
Buy, *1992. Regnery Publishing, Inc.: Washington D.C. Reprinted by permission.*

are getting something for their money. After all, they are not charities. Here are the statistics:

Year	Number of PACs	PAC Gifts to Congressional Candidates
1974	608	$ 12.5 million
1978	1,653	$ 35.2 million
1982	3,371	$ 83.6 million
1986	4,157	$135.2 million
1990	4,681	$150.5 million

Second, many legislators acknowledge that money influences their votes. In a 1987 survey of 27 senators and 87 House members, the non-partisan Center for Responsive Politics found that 20 percent of surveyed members told the interviewers that political contributions have affected their votes. An additional 30 percent were "not sure."[2]

Third, there are examples of how contributions influence members of Congress:

- Former Republican Senator Rudy Boschwitz, of Minnesota, after receiving $30,000 from the manufacture of pesticides, pushed an amendment on behalf of the Chemical Specialties Manufacturers Association (CSMA) to block states from writing regulations stiffer than federal requirements. Prior to its consideration by the Senate Agriculture Committee, the Boschwitz amendment was "widely referred to" as the "CSMA" amendment, according to *The Nation.*

- Republican Senator Orrin Hatch, of Utah, received $30,000 from company officials and PACs of the major Health Industry Manufacturers Association (HIMA) members (Eli Lilly, Bristol-Meyers and Pfizer) for his 1988 campaign. After receiving those contributions, Hatch successfully blocked a measure intended to better regulate such items as pacemakers, incubators and X-ray machines.

A more dramatic example is that of a massive campaign by the privately owned utilities to postpone repayment of $19 billion collected from consumers.

Over a period of years utilities collected money from consumers as a reserve from which to pay federal income taxes. But the 1986 tax reform act lowered the corporate tax rate from 46 to 34 percent, thus reducing the utilities' taxes by $19 billion, a savings the companies owed consumers. (The utilities owed the typical residential customer around $100.)

But how quickly should the utilities be required to repay consumers? Ordinarily that question would be left up to state regulators, but in 1986 Congress passed a special provision allowing the refunds in all states to be paid out over as long as a 30-year period.

The following year, North Dakota Democrat Byron Dorgan introduced a bill calling for a faster refund of the $19 billion. Initially, 48 other Democrats and nine Republicans were signed as co-sponsors.

Immediately the utilities responded by stepping up their political contributions. During 1987, 1988, and 1989, PACs sponsored by utilities and their trade associations gave over $5 million to sitting House members. Five hundred and ten thousand of that went to members of the tax-writing House Ways and Means Committee, through which Dorgan's bill had to pass.

The utilities' honoraria increased as well, totaling $446,000 in the years 1987 and 1988.

Slowly, supporters of the Dorgan bill changed their minds. Some examples:

- Missouri Democrat Richard Gephardt, an original co-sponsor of the Dorgan bill, withdrew his co-sponsorship after the utilities donated over $46,000 to his 1988 campaign.
- South Carolina Democrat Butler Derrick switched his position on the Dorgan bill after the utility industry lavished him with trips, honoraria and campaign contributions. Derrick told the *Wall Street Journal* that the money and trips had "nothing to do with [his decision not to renew co-sponsorship of the Dorgan bill]."
- Eight of the nine representatives who formally repudiated the Dorgan bill after co-sponsoring it received campaign donations from utility PACs averaging $13,000 each.

The original Dorgan bill died without a vote in the House Ways and Means Committee at the end of 1988. . . .

PAC proponents strenuously debate the question: how much influence do PACs really have? Do their contributions actually buy lawmakers' *votes*?

Former Wisconsin Senator William Proxmire, a legislator with 31 years experience, says the influence need not be that direct. He has written of the various subtle ways money can influence a legislator's behavior:

> It [the influence of a campaign contribution] may not come in a vote. It may come in a speech not delivered. The PAC payoff may come in a colleague not influenced. It may come in a calling off of a meeting that otherwise would result in advancing legislation. It may come in a minor change in one paragraph in a 240-page bill. It may come in a witness not invited to testify before a committee. It may come in hiring a key staff member for a committee who is sympathetic to the PAC. Or it may come in laying off or transferring a staff member who is unsympathetic to a PAC. . . .

. . . I interviewed several current and former members of Congress. Here is what they told me:

FORMER CONGRESSMAN MICHAEL BARNES OF MARYLAND

Mike Barnes came to national attention when, as the beneficiary of a liberal revolt on the House Foreign Affairs Committee, he became the chairman of the Western Hemisphere Subcommittee and a principal spokesman against the Reagan Administration's policies in Central America.

From 1978 to 1986, Barnes represented Montgomery County, Maryland, a bed-room suburb of Washington, D.C. In 1986, he ran unsuccessfully for the U.S. Senate. Barnes has a mild-mannered bespectacled mien ("I'm criticized by my friends for not being more flamboyant," he once said). But he displays great passion, especially when speaking about the urgent need for campaign finance reform. His convictions on this subject were solidified by his 1986 experience as a senatorial candidate, during which money-raising was a constant preoccupation. ("There was never a waking moment that I was not either raising money or feeling guilty that I was not.")

Barnes practices law in Washington.

As I spoke to political consultants, they all said I should not even consider running for the Senate if I weren't prepared to spend 80 or 90 percent of my time raising money. It turned out that they were absolutely correct. That's an absolute outrage because the candidates should be talking about the issues and meeting with constituents and voters and working on policy questions.

As a congressman, I had plenty of phone calls from political directors of PACs in which the conversation went something like this:

"Mike, we're getting ready to make our next round of checks out, and I just want to let you know that you're right up there at the top. We really think we can help you with a nice contribution."

"Gee, that's great. Really appreciate it. Grateful to have your help."

"Oh, by the way, Mike, have you been following that bill in Ways and Means that's going to be coming to the floor next week? It's got an item in there we're concerned about—the amendment by Congressman Schwartz. You know, we'll be supporting that and we hope you'll be with us on that one. Hope you'll take a good look at it, and if you need any information about it, we'll send that up to you."

That conversation is perfectly legal under the current laws of the United States, and it probably takes place daily in Washington, D.C. It is an absolute outrage!

You know, if that conversation took place with someone in the executive branch, someone would go to jail.

I regard it as really demeaning to both people—the guy who gets the phone call and the guy who has to make it. It's just a terrible, terrible blight on our political process.

I remember standing on the floor of the House one night when we were voting on the issue of regulations affecting the funeral industry that were, in my view, eminently reasonable. The funeral industry was opposed to this regulation. I remember the evening it was voted on; a rumor swept across the floor of the House that anybody who voted against the regulation would get $5,000 from the industry PAC for his or her upcoming campaign. I don't know if that rumor was true or not, but it flew around the place. Everybody was sort of laughing about this. There's not a doubt in my mind that that rumor had an effect on votes. I was standing next to a guy who, as he put his card in the machine [that registers representatives' votes in the House], said, "You know, I was going to vote against the industry on this thing, but what the hell, I can use the $5,000."

During the months preceding an election, I would say that more than half the conversations between congressmen relate to fundraising. "How are you doing with your fundraising? Will you stop by my fundraiser? God, I'm having a tough time getting money out of X—do you know anybody over there that could help? Do you have access to a rock group or a movie star that could help me with my fundraising?"

More often than not the question is not "Who's your opponent?" or "What are the issues in your race?" It's "How much money have you raised?" Money permeates the whole place.

You have to make a choice. Who are you going to let in the door first? You get back from lunch. You got fourteen phone messages on your desk. Thirteen of them are from constituents you've never heard of, and one of them is from a guy who doesn't live in your district, and is therefore not a constituent, but who just came to your fundraiser two weeks earlier and gave you $2,000. Which phone call are you going to return first?

Money just warps the democratic process in ways that are very sad for the country. You have otherwise responsible, dedicated public servants grubbing for money and having to spend inordinate amounts of their time raising money rather than addressing the issues that they came to Washington to deal with. And you have people trying to present their cases on the merits feeling they have no choice but to buy access to the people who will make the decisions. It demeans both sides in ways that are very sad. You've got good people on both sides, a lot of dedicated lobbyists in Washington who are trying in a responsible way to present their points of view and get forced into becoming fundraisers and contributors in a way that's really outrageous.

FORMER CONGRESSMAN TOBY MOFFETT OF CONNECTICUT

Toby Moffett was 30 years old when, as a former Naderite (he was the first director of the Connecticut Citizen Action Group, one of Ralph Nader's early grass-roots organizations), he was elected to Congress as a member of the post-Watergate class of 1974.

He soon won a seat on the House Energy and Commerce Committee, one of the PAC hot-spots, handling legislation regulating the oil, chemical, broadcasting, and health industries.

An unalloyed liberal (he might prefer the term "progressive") with prodigious energy, he initially chafed at the need, in Congress, for compromise and accommodation. As a new congressman, he observed, "After you stay in the House for a while, all the square edges get rounded off, and you get to look like all the other congressmen." Later, though, he took pleasure in the legislative skills he developed, in "working the system."

In 1982, 1984 and 1990, he ran unsuccessfully for, respectively, U.S. Senate, governor, and U.S. representative.

There was always pressure to raise more and spend more, and build up your margin. If you win by 58 percent, it's one heck of a big difference from winning by 52 percent— in terms of what you have to face next time. So the goal is always to try and get yourself up over 60 or 62 and then 64 percent, and then, in many states, if you get up over 70 or 75, maybe you'll be unopposed. That's the dream, to be unopposed. So as a result, you go to where you have to go to get the money to build up that margin.

I remember during the Carter years, right in the middle of the hospital-cost-control vote—the hospitals and the AMA were just throwing money at the [House Commerce]

Committee [which was handling the bill] as fast as they could. It was coming in wheel-barrows.

Our committee was a prime target, because the Commerce Committee had clean-air legislation, we had all the health bills, we had all the energy stuff—you know, nat-ural gas pricing and that sort of stuff. We had all the communications stuff. So there was a lot of PAC money aimed at neutralizing the Committee. The PACs took those ten or fifteen [swing] votes, and they really went to work on 'em. It was just no secret. Everybody in the room knew it.

You're sitting next to a guy on the Committee and you're trying to get his vote on a clean-air amendment, and you suddenly realize that the night before he had a fundraiser, and all the people who were lobbying against the bill were at the fundraiser. Ways and Means members used to boast about the timing of their fundraisers. What kind of system is that?

In my 1982 Senate race, we had some fundraising people, the kinds of people that you bring on when you've got to raise a lot of money—I mean, very cold-blooded. You know, never mind the issues, let's get the money in. And I remember very, very well their telling me in, maybe, September, that we had to come up with $25,000 immedi-ately for a down payment on a television buy. And I remember sitting down with a member of the House from the farm states, and he said, "How's it going?" I said, "Hor-rible, I've got to come up with $25,000." He said, "How about some dairy money?" And I said, "Oh, no! I can't do that." Remember, in the seventies, dairy money had a pretty bad name.[3]

He said, "Well, I can get you ten or fifteen thousand." I said, "Really?" He said, "Yeah. You know, your record has been pretty good on those issues. I think I can do it." Well, I went back to him the next day and said, "Let's do it."

By the time I got to the last month of the campaign, I was telling my wife and my close friends that here I was, somebody who took less PAC money, I think, than any-body running that year, but I felt strongly that I wasn't going to be the kind of senator that I had planned on being when I started out. I felt like they were taking a piece out of me and a piece out of my propensity to be progressive and aggressive on issues. I felt like, little by little, the process was eating away at me. One day it was insurance money, the next day it was dairy money. . . .

CONGRESSMAN JIM LEACH OF IOWA

Congressman Leach is one of a handful of House members who refuse to take cam-paign money from PACs, and is at the forefront of the campaign-reform movement in the House. In 1985 and 1986, he joined with Democratic Representative Mike Synar of Oklahoma in sponsoring a bill to limit the amount of PAC money any House candidate could receive in an election.

Although listed as a Republican, Jim Leach sides with the Democrats in the House on issues such as arms control, the cessation of chemical-warfare weapons production, sanctions against South Africa and denying funds for the Contra forces in Central America.

> I argue that what you have in a campaign contribution is an implicit contract with the person who gave. If you listen carefully to that group's concerns, and abide by them, there is an implicit promise of another contribution for the next election.

What you've done is turn upside-down the American premise of government, which is the idea that people are elected to represent people. Officeholders should be indebted to the individuals that cast the ballots. Today candidates are becoming increasingly indebted to the people that *influence* the people who cast the ballots. It's a one-step removal. And so we're having an indirect, secondary kind of democracy—one that is increasingly group oriented and financially influenced.

If I had my way, I would eliminate all group giving to campaigns. Prohibit group giving, period. I'd make all contributions individual. I would also prohibit giving from outside the state. That is, why allow a Iowan to influence a Nebraskan or a New Yorker to influence a Californian? That's why in my own campaigns I don't accept PACs and I also don't accept out-of-state gifts.

We have $10 or $20 receptions throughout the district. We have hog roasts, we have barbecues in which we seek small contributions. But it's very time-consuming and difficult as contrasted with the people around Washington. Every night of the week, here, there's a reception at the Capitol Hill Club for candidates, and they can raise $10,000 to $150,000. That takes me three weeks. Twenty events. But on the other hand, my way gets more people involved in the process. And I think it makes them feel a little bit more part of it. For example, how much a part of a campaign is someone going to feel if they give $10 to a candidate who just got $10,000 from ten different unions? Or ten different businesses?

There's always an argument that PACs get more people involved. I've never seen it. It think it's exactly the reverse. Not having PACs forces candidates to go to the voters. I don't raise near as much as other candidates. But I raise over $100,000 and sometimes $150,000. That should be adequate to run a campaign in a state like Iowa. The fact that others in our state spend two to four to five times as much is an indication of how sick the system has become. In part, one side raises all that money because the other side does. It amounts to an arms race. What you need is a domestic SALT agreement. . . .

GOVERNOR AND FORMER SENATOR LAWTON CHILES OF FLORIDA

In 1970, an unknown state senator running for the U.S. Senate pulled on a pair of khaki trousers and hiking boots and spent 92 days hiking across Florida. His thousand-mile trek transformed his long-shot candidacy into a seat in the U.S. Senate.

One of his trademarks in the Senate became "sunshine government"—conducting the processes of government out in the open rather than behind closed doors, and subjecting officeholders' personal financial statements and the activities of lobbyists to public disclosure requirements.

In his next campaign, in 1976, Senator Chiles limited contributions to $10 and refused to accept contributions from out-of-state donors. In 1982, when the Republican Party promised to underwrite his opponent heavily, he apologetically raised the donor ceiling to $100, but added a new restriction: he would not accept contributions from political action committees. Much to the frustration of his fundraisers, he retained all of those limits for his would-be 1988 reelection campaign.

In late 1987, Chiles announced he would not seek a fourth Senate term in 1988. But he returned to politics in 1990, winning the governorship after a hard-fought campaign in which he once again limited contributions to $100 and refused to accept out-of-state contributions.

> Today, PACs are running in packs, where segments of industry or segments of labor, or segments of this group, get together with multiple PACs and decide how they are going to contribute. Sometimes you're talking about $250,000 for a campaign. Overall I think they're distorting the electoral system and what I sense is, very strong, that your John Q. Public is saying, "I don't count any more. My vote doesn't count, I can't contribute enough money to count. No one is going to listen to me."
>
> I'm looking at congressmen 50 percent of whom, I don't know exactly, but around half, that get half of their money or more by PACs. They don't even have to come home. Their money is raised at [Washington] cocktail parties.
>
> At the same time, when I sit down with my fellow senators, they say, "The bane of our existence is fund-raising. We're having to do it over six years and we're having to go to Chicago, Los Angeles, New York, Florida. A lot of us spend a lot of time there. But that's what I have to do at night. That's what I have to do on weekends. And, of course, for these big, big PACs, I have to be pretty careful about what my voting record is going to be."
>
> I think if out-of-state contributions were prohibited, you'd have a better chance of those people in your state making the decision based on the merit of the candidate. I think if one candidate, who usually would be an incumbent, can go raise all kinds of out-of-state money, I think he can [distort] his record very much.
>
> A lot of people seem to think that somebody gives you a PAC contribution, then they come in and say, "I expect you to vote for this." It never happens that way. All that person wants you to do is to take and take and take, and then when he comes in, he never says, "I expect." It's always on the basis of, "This is a big one for me, and maybe my job's on the line." He doesn't need to say anything more than that because the hook is already in you and if you've taken it, you know it, and you *know* you know it. . . .

NOTES

1. I consider all PACs to be "outside" PACs unless (a) the decision as to how the PAC's money is distributed is made *within the state or district* of the particular candidate or lawmaker; or (b) unless the PAC's procedures provide for donors from a given district or state to earmark their funds for the local candidate. Many PACs and PAC defenders dispute this line of reasoning, arguing that in instances where a given PAC represents a company that has large plants and many employees in, say, the Fourth District of North Carolina, it is wrong to label that company's PAC an "outside" PAC. I maintain, however, that if that PAC is headquartered in, say, Pittsburgh, and if the decisions as to how that PAC's money is distributed nation-wide are made there rather than in North Carolina, it is wrong to say that those decisions are made with the interests of the people of the Fourth District of North Carolina primarily in mind, no matter how many plants or employees that company may have in that district.

2. In addition, two-thirds of the senators and 87 percent of their staff members said that raising money affected the time they spent on legislative work. Forty-three percent of members participating in the survey said that PACs had a "largely or somewhat negative" influence on the political process. *Not a single one of the 115 staff members surveyed said that PACs had a positive impact* (Emphasis mine).
3. Because of the dairy lobby's offer of $2 million to the 1972 Nixon campaign in exchange for a higher government dairy subsidy.

The Misplaced Obsession with PACs

Larry Sabato

The disturbing statistics and the horror stories about political action committees seem to flow like a swollen river, week after week, year in and year out. Outrage extends across the ideological spectrum: the liberal interest group Common Cause has called the system "scandalous," while conservative former senator Barry Goldwater (R-Ariz.) has bluntly declared, "PAC money is destroying the election process. . . ."[1]

PAC-bashing is undeniably a popular campaign sport,[2] but the "big PAC attack" is an opiate that obscures the more vital concerns and problems in campaign finance. PAC excesses are merely a symptom of other serious maladies in the area of political money, but the near-obsessive focus by public interest groups and the news media on the PAC evils has diverted attention from more fundamental matters. The PAC controversy, including the charges most frequently made against them, can help explain why PACs are best described as agents of pseudo corruption.[3]

THE PAC ERA

While a good number of PACs of all political persuasions existed prior to the 1970s, it was during that decade of campaign reform that the modern PAC era began. Spawned by the Watergate-inspired revisions of the campaign finance laws, PACs grew in number from 113 in 1972 to 4,196 in 1988 [3,982 in 1995—*Editors.*], and their contributions to congressional candidates multiplied more than fifteenfold, from $8.5 million in 1971–72 to $130.3 million in 1985–86 [$188.5 million in 1992—eds.].

The rapid rise of PACs has engendered much criticism, yet many of the charges made against political action committees are exaggerated and dubious. While the widespread use of the PAC structure is new, special interest money of all types has always found its way into politics. Before the 1970s it simply did so in less traceable and far more disturbing and unsavory ways. And while, in absolute terms, PACs contribute a massive sum to candidates, it is not clear that there is proportionately more interest-group money in the system than before. As political scientist Michael Malbin has argued, we will never know the truth because the earlier record is so incomplete.[4]

The proportion of House and Senate campaign funds provided by PACs has certainly increased since the early 1970s, but individuals, most of whom are unaffiliated with PACs, together with the political parties, still supply about three-fifths of all the money spent by or on behalf of House candidates and three-quarters of the campaign expenditures for Senate contenders. So while the importance of PAC spending has grown, PACs clearly remain secondary as a source of election funding. PACs, then,

Larry Sabato is professor of political science at the University of Virginia. From Chapter 1, Larry J. Sabato, Paying for Elections: The Campaign Finance Thicket, *A Twentieth Century Fund Paper. © 1989 by the Twentieth Century Fund, New York. Used with permission of the Twentieth Century Fund, New York.*

seem rather less awesome when considered within the entire spectrum of campaign finance.

Apart from the argument over the relative weight of the PAC funds, PAC critics claim that political action committees are making it more expensive to run for office. There is some validity to this assertion. Money provided to one candidate funds the purchase of campaign tools that the other candidate must match in order to stay competitive.

In the aggregate, American campaign expenditures seem huge. In 1988, the total amount spent by all U.S. House of Representatives candidates taken together was about $256 million, and the campaign cost of the winning House nominee averaged over $392,000. Will Rogers's 1931 remark has never been more true: "Politics has got so expensive that it takes lots of money to even get beat with."

Yet $256 million is far less than the annual advertising budgets of many individual commercial enterprises. These days it is expensive to communicate, whether the message is political or commercial. Television time, polling costs, consultants' fees, direct-mail investment, and other standard campaign expenditures have been soaring in price, over and above inflation.[5] PACs have been fueling the use of new campaign techniques, but a reasonable case can be made that such expenses are necessary, and that more and better communication is required between candidates and an electorate that often appears woefully uninformed about politics. PACs therefore may be making a positive contribution by providing the means to increase the flow of information during elections.

PACs are also accused of being biased toward the incumbent, and except for the ideological committees, they do display a clear and overwhelming preference for those already in office. But the same bias is apparent in contributions from individuals, who ask the same reasonable, perhaps decisive, economic question: Why waste money on contenders if incumbents almost always win? On the other hand, the best challengers—those perceived as having fair-to-good chances to win—are usually generously funded by PACs. Well-targeted PAC challenger money clearly helped the GOP win a majority in the U.S. Senate in 1980, for instance, and in turn aided the Democrats in their 1986 Senate takeover.

The charge that PACs limit the number of strong challengers is true, because by giving so much money so early in the race to incumbents, they deter potential opponents from declaring their candidacies. On the other hand, the money that PACs channel to competitive challengers late in the election season may actually help increase the turnover of officeholders on election day. PAC money also tends to invigorate competitiveness in open-seat congressional races where there is no incumbent. . . .

PAC MONEY AND CONGRESSIONAL "CORRUPTION"

The most serious charge leveled at PACs is that they succeed in buying the votes of legislators on issues important to their individual constituencies. It seems hardly worth arguing that many PACs are shopping for congressional votes and that PAC money buys access, or opens doors, to congressmen. But the "vote-buying" allegation is generally not supported by a careful examination of the facts.[6] PAC contributions do make a difference, at least on some occasions, in securing access and influencing the course of events, but those occasions are not nearly as frequent as anti-PAC spokesmen, even congressmen themselves, often suggest.

PACs affect legislative proceedings to a decisive degree only when certain conditions prevail. First, the less visible the issue, the more likely that PAC funds can change or influence congressional votes. A corollary is that PAC money has more effect in the early stages of the legislative process, such as agenda setting and votes in subcommittee meetings, than in later and more public floor deliberations. Press, public, and even "watchdog" groups are not nearly as attentive to initial legislative proceedings.

PAC contributions are also more likely to influence the legislature when the issue is specialized and narrow, or unopposed by other organized interests. PAC gifts are less likely to be decisive on broad national issues such as American policy in Nicaragua or the adoption of a Star Wars missile defense system. But the more technical measures seem tailor-made for the special interests. Additionally, PAC influence in Congress is greater when large PACs or groups of PACs (such as business and labor PACs) are allied. In recent years, despite their natural enmity, business and labor have lobbied together on a number of issues, including defense spending, trade policy, environmental regulation, maritime legislation, trucking legislation, and nuclear power.[7] The combination is a weighty one, checked in many instances only by a tendency for business and labor in one industry (say, the railroads) to combine and oppose their cooperating counterparts in another industry (perhaps the truckers and teamsters).

It is worth stressing, however, that most congressmen are *not* unduly influenced by PAC money on most votes. The special conditions simply do not apply to most legislative issues, and the overriding factors in determining a legislator's votes include party affiliation, ideology, and constituents' needs and desires. Much has been made of the passage of large tax cuts for oil and business interests in the 1981 omnibus tax package. The journalist Elizabeth Drew said there was a "bidding war" to trade campaign contributions for tax breaks benefiting independent oil producers.[8] Ralph Nader's Public Citizen group charged that the $280,000 in corporate PAC money accepted by members of the House Ways and Means Committee helped to produce a bill that "contained everything business ever dared to ask for, and more."[9] Yet as Robert Samuelson has convincingly argued, the "bidding war" between Democrats and Republicans was waged not for PAC money but for control of a House of Representatives sharply divided between Reaganite Republicans and liberal Democrats, with conservative "boll weevil" Democrats from the southern oil states as the crucial swing votes.[10] The Ways and Means Committee actions cited by Nader were also more correctly explained in partisan terms. After all, if these special interests were so influential in writing the 1981 omnibus tax package, how could they fail so completely to derail the much more important (and, for them, threatening) tax reform legislation of 1986?

If party loyalty can have a stronger pull than PAC contributions, then surely the views of a congressman's constituents can also take precedence over those of political action committees. If an incumbent is faced with the choice of either voting for a PAC-backed bill that is very unpopular in his district or forgoing the PAC's money, the odds are that any politician who depends on a majority of votes to remain in office is going to side with his constituency and vote against the PAC's interest. PAC gifts are merely a means to an end: reelection. If accepting money will cause a candidate embarrassment, then even a maximum donation will likely be rejected. The flip side of this proposition makes sense as well: if a PAC's parent organization has many members or a major financial stake in the congressman's home district, he is much more likely to vote the PAC's way—not so much because he receives PAC money but because the group accounts for an important part of his electorate. Does a U.S. senator from a dairy state vote for dairy price supports because he received a significant percentage of his PAC contributions from agriculture, or because the farm population of his state is relatively large and politically active? When congressmen vote the National Rifle Association's preferences is it because of the money the NRA's PAC distributes, or because the NRA, unlike gun-control advocates, has repeatedly demonstrated the ability to produce a sizable number of votes in many legislative districts?

If PACs have appeared more influential than they actually are, it is partly because many people believe legislators are looking for opportunities to exclaim (as one did during the Abscam scandal) "I've got larceny in my blood!" It is certainly disturbing that the National Republican Congressional Committee believed it necessary to warn its PAC-soliciting candidates: "Don't *ever* suggest to the PAC that it is 'buying' your vote, should you get elected."[11] Yet knowledgeable Capitol Hill observers agree that there are few truly corrupt congressmen. Simple correlations notwithstanding, when most legislators vote for a PAC-supported bill, it is because of the *merits* of the case, or the entreaties of their party leaders, peers, or constituents, and not because of PAC money.

When the PAC phenomenon is viewed in the broad perspective of issues, party allegiance, and constituent interests, it is clear that *merit* matters most in the votes most congressmen cast. It is naive to contend that PAC money never influences decisions, but it is unjustifiably cynical to believe that PACs always, or even usually, push the voting buttons in Congress.

PACS IN PERSPECTIVE

As the largely unsubstantiated "vote-buying" controversy suggests, PACs are often misrepresented and unfairly maligned as the embodiment of corrupt special interests. Political action committees are a contemporary manifestation of what James Madison called "factions." In his *Federalist, No. 10,* Madison wrote that through the flourishing of these competing interest groups, or factions, liberty would be preserved.[12]

In any democracy, and particularly in one as pluralistic as the United States, it is essential that groups be relatively unrestricted in advocating their interests and positions. Not only is that the mark of a free society, it also provides a safety valve for the competitive pressures that build on all fronts in a capitalistic democracy. And it provides another means to keep representatives responsive to legitimate needs.

This is not to say that all groups pursue legitimate interests, or that vigorously competing interests ensure that the public good prevails. The press, the public, and valuable watchdog groups such as Common Cause must always be alert to instances in which narrow private interests prevail over the commonweal—occurrences that generally happen when no one is looking.

Besides the press and various public interest organizations, there are two major institutional checks on the potential abuses wrought by factions, associations, and now PACs. The most fundamental of these is regular free elections with general suffrage. As Tocqueville commented:

> Perhaps the most powerful of the causes which tend to mitigate the excesses of political association in the United States is Universal Suffrage. In countries in which universal suffrage exists, the majority is never doubtful, because neither party can pretend to represent the portion of the community which has not voted.
>
> The associations which are formed are aware, as well as the nation at large, that they do not represent the majority: this is, indeed, a condition inseparable from their existence; for if they did represent the prepondering power, they would change the law instead of soliciting its reform.[13]

[Former] Senator Robert Dole (R-Kan.) has said, "There aren't any Poor PACs or Food Stamp PACs or Nutrition PACs or Medicare PACs,"[14] and PAC critics frequently make the point that certain segments of the electorate are underrepresented in the PAC community. Yet without much support from PACs, there are food stamps, poverty and nutrition programs, and Medicare. Why? Because the recipients of governmental assistance constitute a hefty slice of the electorate, and *votes matter more than dollars to politicians.* Furthermore, many citizens *outside* the affected groups have also made known their support of aid to the poor and elderly—making yet a stronger electoral case for these PAC-less programs.

The other major institution that checks PAC influence is the two-party system. While PACs represent particular interests, the political parties build coalitions of groups and attempt to represent a national interest. They arbitrate among competing claims, and they seek to reach a consensus on matters of overriding importance to the nation. The parties are one of the few unifying forces in an exceptionally diverse country. . . .

However limited and checkmated by political realities PACs may be, they are still regarded by a skeptical public as thoroughly unsavory. PACs have become the embodiment of greedy special interest politics, rising campaign costs, and corruption. It does not seem to matter that most experts in the field of campaign finance take considerable exception to the prevailing characterization of political action committees. PACs have become, in the public's mind, a powerful symbol of much that is wrong with America's campaign process, and candidates for public office naturally manipulate this symbol as well as others for their own ends. It is a circumstance as old as the Republic.

PACs, however, have done little to change their image for the better. Other than the business-oriented Public Affairs Council, few groups or committees have moved to correct one-sided press coverage or educate the public on campaign financing's fundamentals. In fact, many PACs fuel the fires of discontent by refusing to defend themselves while not seeming to care about appearances. Giving to both candidates in the same race, for example—an all-too-common practice—may be justifiable in theory, but it strikes most people as unprincipled, rank influence purchasing. Even worse, perhaps, are PACs that "correct their mistakes" soon after an election by sending a donation to the winning, but not originally PAC-supported, candidate. In the seven 1986 U.S. Senate races where a Democratic challenger defeated a Republican incumbent, there were 150 instances in which a PAC gave to the GOP candidate *before* the election and to the victorious Democrat once the votes were counted.[15] These practices PACs themselves should stop. Every PAC should internally ban double giving, and there should be a moratorium on gifts to previously opposed candidates until at least the halfway point of the officeholder's term.

Whether PACs undertake some necessary rehabilitative steps or not, any fair appraisal of their role in American elections must be balanced. PACs are neither political innocents nor selfless civic boosters. But, neither are they cesspools of corruption and greed, nor modern-day versions of Tammany Hall.

PACs will never be popular with idealistic reformers because they represent the rough, cutting edge of a democracy teeming with different peoples and conflicting interests. Indeed, PACs may never be hailed even by natural allies; it was the business-oriented *Wall Street Journal,* after all, that editorially referred to Washington, D.C., as "a place where politicians, PACs, lawyers, and lobbyists for unions, business or you-name-it, shake each other down full time for political money and political support."[16]

Viewed in perspective, the root of the problem in campaign finance is not PACs; it is money. Americans have an enduring mistrust of the mix of money (particularly business money) and politics, as Finley Peter Dunne's Mr. Dooley revealed:

> I niver knew a pollytician to go wrong ontil he'd been contaminated be contact with a business man. . . . It seems to me that th' only thing to do is to keep pollyticians an' business men apart. They seem to have a bad infloonce on each other. Whiniver I see an alderman an' a banker walkin' down th' street together I know th' Recordin' Angel will have to ordher another bottle iv ink.[17]

As a result of the new campaign finance rules of the 1970s, political action committees superseded the "fat cats" of old as the public focus and symbol of the role of money in politics, and PACs inherited the suspicions that go with the territory. Those suspicions are valuable because they keep the spotlight on PACs and guard against undue influence. It may be regrettable that such supervision is required, but human nature—not PACs—demands it.

NOTES

1. Quotations from Common Cause direct-mail package to members, January 1987.
2. *The New Republic,* May 28, 1984, p. 9.
3. For a much more extended discussion of these subjects, see Larry Sabato, *PAC POWER: Inside the World of Political Action Committees,* rev. ed. (New York: Report of the Twentieth Century Fund Task Force on Political Action Committees, 1984).
4. Michael J. Malbin, "The Problem of PAC-Journalism," *Public Opinion,* December/January 1983, pp. 15–16, 59.

5. See Larry Sabato, *The Rise of Political Consultants* (New York: Basic Books, 1981); see also *National Journal,* April 16, 1983, pp. 780–81.
6. See Sabato, *PAC POWER,* pp. 122–59, 222–28.
7. See, for example, Edwin M. Epstein, "An Irony of Electoral Reform," *Regulation,* May/June 1979, pp. 35–44; and Christopher Madison, "Federal Subsidy Programs under Attack by Unlikely Marriage of Labor and Right," *National Journal,* December 31, 1983, pp. 2682–84.
8. Elizabeth Drew, "Politics and Money, Part I" *The New Yorker,* December 6, 1982, pp. 38–45.
9. Herbert E. Alexander, *Financing the 1980 Election* (Lexington, Mass.: D.C. Heath, 1983), p. 379.
10. Robert J. Samuelson, "The Campaign Reform Failure," *The New Republic,* September 5, 1983, pp. 32–33.
11. From the NRCC publication "Working with PACs" (1982).
12. See *The Federalist, No. 10,* for a much fuller discussion of the role of factions in a democratic society.
13. Alexis de Tocqueville, *Democracy in America,* vol. 1 (New York: Vintage Books, 1954), p. 224.
14. As quoted in Drew, "Politics and Money," p. 147.
15. Common Cause "If At First You Don't Succeed, Give, Give Again" (Press release, Washington, D.C., March 20, 1987).
16. "Cleaning Up Reform," *The Wall Street Journal,* November 10, 1983, p. 26.
17. Finley Peter Dunne, *The World of Mr. Dooley,* edited with an introduction by Louis Filler (New York: Collier Books, 1962), pp. 155–56.

10

CONGRESS

Representation

The three selections in this section are illustrative of a long-standing debate among political theorists and elected officials alike—namely, whose views should prevail on a given issue, the constituents' or the representatives'? In the first selection, taken from an early debate in the General Assembly of Virginia, the argument is made that legislators are obliged to act as instructed delegates—*that is, that they must vote in accordance with the will of their constituents. In the second selection, former Massachusetts senator and president, John F. Kennedy, writing in 1956, argued that legislators should act as* trustees, *voting according to their own conscience, regardless of whether their choices reflect the sentiments of their constituents. Finally, George Galloway, a former staff assistant in Congress, contends that on some occasions legislators must follow public opinion, while on others they are obliged to vote according to their own conscience. This view, which combines both the delegate and the trustee approach, is characterized as the* politico *role.*

The Legislator as Delegate

General Assembly of Virginia

There can be no doubt that the scheme of a representative republic was derived to our forefathers from the constitution of the English House of Commons; and that that branch of the English government . . . was in its origin, and in theory always has been, purely republican. It is certain, too, that the statesmen of America, in assuming that as the model of our own institutions, designed to adopt it here in its purest form, and with its strictest republican tenets and principles. It becomes, therefore, an inquiry of yet greater utility than curiosity, to ascertain the sound doctrines of the constitution of the English House of Commons in regard to this right of the constituent to instruct the representative. For the position may safely be assumed that the wise and virtuous men who framed our constitutions designed, that, in the United States, the constituent should have at least as much, if not a great deal more, influence over the representative than was known to have existed from time immemorial in England. Let us then interrogate the history of the British nation; let us consult the opinions of their wise men.

Instances abound in parliamentary history of formal instructions from the constituent to the representative, of which . . . the following may suffice: In 1640, the knights of the shire for Dorset and Kent informed the commons *that they had in charge from their constituents* seven articles of grievances, which they accordingly laid before the House, where they were received and acted on. In the 33rd year of Charles II, the citizens of London instructed their members to insist on the bill for excluding the Duke of York (afterward King James II) from the succession to the throne; and their representative said "that his *duty* to his electors *obliged* him to vote the bill." At a subsequent election, in 1681, in many places, formal instructions were given to the members returned, to insist on the same exclusion bill; we know, from history, how uniformly and faithfully those instructions were obeyed. . . . In 1741, the citizens of London instructed their members to vote against standing armies, excise laws, the septennial bill, and a long train of evil measures, already felt, or anticipated; and expressly affirm their right of instruction—"We think it" (say they) "our *duty*, as it is *our undoubted right*, to acquaint you, with *what we desire and expect from you, in discharge of the great trust we repose in you,* and what we take to be *your duty as our representative*, etc." In the same year, instructions of a similar character were sent from all parts of England. In 1742, the cities of London, Bristol, Edinburgh, York, and many others, instructed their members in parliament to seek redress against certain individuals suspected to have betrayed and deserted the cause of the people. . . .

Instances also are on record of the deliberate formal knowledgement of the right of instruction by the House of Commons itself, especially in old times. Thus the commons hesitated to grant supplies to King Edward III *till they had the consent of their*

From Commonwealth of Virginia, General Assembly, Journal of the Senate, *1812, pp. 82–89. In some instances, spelling and punctuation have been altered from the original in order to achieve greater clarity*—Editors.

constituents, and desired that a new parliament might be summoned, which might be *prepared with authority from their constituents.* . . .

"Instructions" (says a member of the House of Commons) "ought to be *followed implicitly,*" after the member has *respectfully* given his constituents *his opinion* of them: "*Far be it from me to oppose my judgment to that of 6000 of my fellow citizens.*" "The practice" (says another) "of consulting our constituents was good. I wish it was continued. *We can discharge our duty no better, than in the direction of those who sent us hither. What the people choose is right, because they choose it.*" . . .

Without referring to the minor political authors . . . who have maintained these positions (quoted from one of them)—"that the people have a right to instruct their representatives; that no man ought to be chosen that will not receive instructions; that the people understand enough of the interests of the country to give general instructions; that it was the custom formerly to instruct all the members; and the nature of deputation shows that the custom was well grounded"—it is proper to mention that the great constitutional lawyer Coke . . . says, "It is the *custom of parliament,* when any new device is moved for on the king's behalf, for his aid and the like, that the commons may answer, *they dare not agree to it without conference with their counties.*" And Sydney . . . maintains "that members derive their power from those that choose them; that those who give power do not give an unreserved power; that many members, in all ages, and sometimes the whole body of the commons have refused to vote until they consulted with those who sent them; that the houses have often adjourned to give them time to do so and if this were done more frequently, or if cities, towns and counties had on some occasions given instructions to their deputies, matters would probably have gone better in parliament than they have done." . . . The celebrated Edmund Burke, a man, it must be admitted, of profound knowledge, deep foresight, and transcendent abilities, disobeyed the instructions of his constituents; yet, by placing his excuse on the ground that the instructions were but the clamour of the day, he seems to admit the authority of instructions soberly and deliberately given; for he agrees, "he ought to look to their opinions" (which he explains to mean their permanent settled opinions) "but not the flash of the day"; and he says elsewhere, that he could not bear to show himself "a representative, whose face did not reflect the face of his constituents—a face that did not joy in their joys and sorrow in their sorrows." It is remarkable that, notwithstanding a most splendid display of warm and touching eloquence, the people of Bristol would not reelect Mr. Burke, for this very offense of disobeying instructions. . . .

It appears, therefore, that the right of the constituent to instruct the representative, is firmly established in England, on the broad basis of the nature of representation. The existence of that right, there, has been demonstrated by the only practicable evidence, by which the principles of an unwritten constitution can be ascertained—history and precedent.

To view the subject upon principle, the right of the constituent to instruct the representative, seems to result, clearly and conclusively, from the very nature of the representative system. Through means of that noble institution, the largest nation may, almost as conveniently as the smallest, enjoy all the advantages of a government by the people, without any of the evils of democracy—precipitation, confusion, turbulence, distraction from the ordinary and useful pursuits of industry. And it is only to avoid those and the like mischiefs, that representation is substituted for the direct suffrage of the people in the office of legislation. The representative, therefore, must in the nature of things, represent his own particular constituents only. He must, indeed, look to the general good of the nation, but he must look also, and especially to the interests of his particular constituents as concerned in the commonweal; because the general good is but the aggregate of individual happiness. He must legislate for the whole nation; but laws are expressions of the general will; and the general will is only the result of individual wills fairly collected and compared. In order . . . to express the general will . . . it is plain that the representative must express the will and speak the opinions of the constituents that depute him.

It cannot be pretended that a representative is to be the organ of his own will alone; for then, he would be so far despotic. *He must be the organ of others*—of whom? Not of the nation, for the nation deputes him not; but of his constituents, who alone know, alone have trusted, and can alone displace him. And if it be his province and his duty, in general, to express the will of his constituents, to the best of his knowledge, without being particularly informed thereof, it seems impossible to contend that he is not bound to do so when he is so especially informed and instructed.

The right of the constituent to instruct the representative, therefore, is an essential principle of the representative system. It may be remarked that wherever representation has been introduced, however unfavorable the circumstances under which it existed, however short its duration, however unimportant its functions, however dimly understood, the right of instruction has always been regarded as inseparably incidental to it. . . .

A representative has indeed a wide field of discretion left to him; and great is the confidence reposed in his integrity, fidelity, wisdom, zeal; but neither is the field of discretion boundless, nor the extent of confidence infinite; and the very discretion allowed him, and the very confidence he enjoys, is grounded on the supposition that he is charged with the will, acquainted with the opinions, and devoted to the interests of his constituents. . . .

Various objections have been urged to this claim of the constituent, of a right to instruct the representative, on which it may be proper to bestow some attention.

The first objection that comes to be considered . . . is grounded on the supposed impossibility of fairly ascertaining the sense of the constituent body. The *impossibility* is denied. It may often be a matter of great *difficulty*; but then the duty of obedience resolves itself into a question, not of principle, but of fact: whether the right of instruction has been exercised or not. The representative cannot be bound by an instruction that is not given; but that is no objection to the obligation of an instruction *actually given.* . . .

It has been urged that the representatives are not bound to obey the instructions of their constituents because the constituents do not hear the debates, and therefore, cannot be supposed judges of the matter to be voted. If this objection has force enough to defeat the right of instruction, it ought to take away, also, the right of rejecting the representative at the subsequent election. For it might be equally urged on that occasion, as against the right of instruction, that the people heard not the debate that enlightened the representative's mind—the reasons that convinced his judgment and governed his conduct. . . . In other words, the principle that mankind is competent to self-government should be renounced. The truth is, that our institutions suppose that although the representative ought to be, and generally will be, selected for superior virtue and intelligence, yet a greater mass of wisdom and virtue still reside in the constituent body than the utmost portion allotted to any individual. . . .

Finally, it has been objected, that the instructions of the constituent are not obligatory on the representative because the obligation insisted on is fortified with no sanction—the representative cannot be punished for his disobedience, and his vote is valid notwithstanding his disobedience. It is true that there is no mode of legal punishment provided for this . . . default of duty and that the act of disobedience will not invalidate the vote. It is true, too, that a representative may perversely advocate a measure which he knows to be ruinous to his country; and that neither his vote will be invalidated by his depravity, nor can he be punished by law for his crime, heinous as it surely is. But it does not follow that the one representative is *not bound to obey the instructions* of his constituents any more than that the other is not bound to obey the dictates of his conscience. Both duties stand upon the same foundation, with almost all the great political and moral obligations. The noblest duties of man are without any legal sanction: the great mass of social duties . . ., our duties to our parents, to our children, to our wives, to our families, to our neighbor, to our country, our duties to God, are, for the most part, without legal sanction, yet surely not without the strongest obligation. The duty of the *representative* to obey the instructions of the *constituent* body cannot be placed on higher ground.

Such are the opinions of the General Assembly of Virginia, on the subject of this great right of instruction, and such the general reasons on which those opinions are founded. . . .

The Legislator as Trustee

John F. Kennedy

The primary responsibility of a senator, most people assume, is to represent the views of his state. Ours is a federal system—a union of relatively sovereign states whose needs differ greatly—and my constitutional obligations as senator would thus appear to require me to represent the interests of my state. Who will speak for Massachusetts if her own senators do not? Her rights and even her identity become submerged. Her equal representation in Congress is lost. Her aspirations, however much they may from time to time be in the minority, are denied that equal opportunity to be heard to which all minority views are entitled.

Any senator need not look very long to realize that his colleagues are representing *their* local interests. And if such interests are ever to be abandoned in favor of the national good, let the constituents—not the senator—decide when and to what extent. For he is their agent in Washington, the protector of their rights, recognized by the vice president in the Senate Chamber as "the senator from Massachusetts" or "the senator from Texas."

But when all of this is said and admitted, we have not yet told the full story. For in Washington we are "United States senators" and members of the Senate of the United States as well as senators from Massachusetts and Texas. Our oath of office is administered by the vice president, not by the governors of our respective states; and we come to Washington, to paraphrase Edmund Burke, not as hostile ambassadors or special pleaders for our state or section, in opposition to advocates and agents of other areas, but as members of the deliberative assembly of one nation with one interest. Of course, we should not ignore the needs of our area—nor could we easily as products of that area—but none could be found to look out for the national interest if local interests wholly dominated the role of each of us.

There are other obligations in addition to those of state and region—the obligations of the party. . . . Even if I can disregard those pressures, do I not have an obligation to go along with the party that placed me in office? We believe in this country in the principle of party responsibility, and we recognize the necessity of adhering to party platforms—if the party label is to mean anything to the voters. Only in this way can our basically two-party nation avoid the pitfalls of multiple splinter parties, whose purity and rigidity of principle, I might add—if I may suggest a sort of Gresham's Law of politics—increase inversely with the size of their membership.

John F. Kennedy, 35th President of the United States, was Democratic member of the U.S. Senate from the state of Massachusetts from 1952 to 1960 and a member of the U.S. House of Representatives from 1947 to 1952. Selected excerpts from pp. 33–39 from Profiles in Courage *by John F. Kennedy. Copyright © 1955, 1956, 1961 by John F. Kennedy. Copyright renewed © 1983, 1984, 1989 by Jacqueline Kennedy Onassis. Foreword copyright © 1964 by Robert F. Kennedy. Copyright renewed. Reprinted by permission of HarperCollins Publishers, Inc.*

And yet we cannot permit the pressures of party responsibility to submerge on every issue the call of personal responsibility. For the party which, in its drive for unity, discipline and success, ever decides to exclude new ideas, independent conduct or insurgent members, is in danger. . . .

Of course, both major parties today seek to serve the national interest. They would do so in order to obtain the broadest base of support, if for no nobler reason. But when party and officeholder differ as to how the national interest is to be served, we must place first the responsibility we owe not to our party or even to our constituents but to our individual consciences.

But it is a little easier to dismiss one's obligations to local interests and party ties to face squarely the problem of one's responsibility to the will of his constituents. A senator who avoids this responsibility would appear to be accountable to no one, and the basic safeguards of our democratic system would thus have vanished. He is no longer representative in the true sense, he has violated his public trust, he has betrayed the confidence demonstrated by those who voted for him to carry out their views. "Is the creature," as John Tyler asked the House of Representatives in his maiden speech, "to set himself in opposition to his Creator? Is the servant to disobey the wishes of his master?"

> How can he be regarded as representing the people when he speaks, not their language, but his own? He ceases to be their representative when he does so, and represents himself alone.

In short, according to this school of thought, if I am to be properly responsive to the will of my constituents, it is my duty to place their principles, not mine, above all else. This may not always be easy, but it nevertheless is the essence of democracy, faith in the wisdom of the people and their views. To be sure, the people will make mistakes—they will get no better government than they deserve—but that is far better than the representative of the people arrogating for himself the right to say he knows better than they what is good for them. Is he not chosen, the argument closes, to vote as they would vote were they in his place?

It is difficult to accept such a narrow view of the role of a United States senator— a view that assumes the people of Massachusetts sent me to Washington to serve merely as a seismograph to record shifts in popular opinion. I reject this view not because I lack faith in the "wisdom of the people," but because this concept of democracy actually puts too little faith in the people. Those who would deny the obligation of the representative to be bound by every impulse of the electorate—regardless of the conclusions his own deliberations direct—do trust in the wisdom of the people. They have faith in their ultimate sense of justice, faith in their ability to honor courage and respect judgment, and faith that in the long run they will act unselfishly for the good of the nation. It is that kind of faith on which democracy is based, not simply the often frustrated hope that public opinion will at all times under all circumstances promptly identify itself with the public interest.

The voters selected us, in short, because they had confidence in our judgment and our ability to exercise that judgment from a position where we could determine what were their own best interests, as a part of the nation's interests. This may mean that we must on occasion lead, inform, correct and sometimes even ignore constituent opinion, if we are to exercise fully that judgment for which we were elected. But acting without selfish motive or private bias, those who follow the dictates of an intelligent conscience are not aristocrats, demagogues, eccentrics, or callous politicians insensitive to the feelings of the public. They expect—and not without considerable trepidation—their constituents to be the final judges of the wisdom of their course; but they have faith that those constituents—today, tomorrow, or even in another generation—will at least respect the principles that motivated their independent stand.

If their careers are temporarily or even permanently buried under an avalanche of abusive editorials, poison-pen letters, and opposition votes at the polls—as they sometimes are, for that is the risk they take—they await the future with hope and confidence, aware of the fact that the voting public frequently suffers from what ex-Congressman T. V. Smith called the lag "between our way of thought and our way of life." . . .

Moreover, I question whether any senator, before we vote on a measure, can state with certainty exactly how the majority of his constituents feel on the issue as it is presented to the Senate. All of us in the Senate live in an iron lung—the iron lung of politics, and it is no easy task to emerge from that rarefied atmosphere in order to breathe the same fresh air our constituents breathe. It is difficult, too, to see in person an appreciable number of voters besides those professional hangers-on and vocal elements who gather about the politician on a trip home. In Washington I frequently find myself believing that forty or fifty letters, six visits from professional politicians and lobbyists, and three editorials in Massachusetts newspapers constitute public opinion on a given issue. Yet in truth I rarely know how the great majority of the voters feel, or even how much they know of the issues that seem so burning in Washington.

Today the challenge of political courage looms larger than ever before. For our everyday life is becoming so saturated with the tremendous power of mass communications that any unpopular or unorthodox course arouses a storm of protests. . . . Our political life is becoming so expensive, so mechanized, and so dominated by professional politicians and public relations men that the idealist who dreams of independent statesmanship is rudely awakened by the necessities of election and accomplishment. . . .

And thus, in the days ahead, only the very courageous will be able to take the hard and unpopular decisions necessary for our survival. . . .

The Legislator as Politico

George B. Galloway

One question which the conscientious congressman must often ask himself, especially when conflicts arise between local or regional attitudes and interests and the national welfare, is this: "As a member of Congress, am I merely a delegate from my district or state, restricted to act and vote as the majority which elected me desire, bound by the instructions of my constituents and subservient to their will? Or am I, once elected, a representative of the people of the United States, free to act as I think best for the country generally?

In a country as large as the United States, with such diverse interests and such a heterogeneous population, the economic interests and social prejudices of particular states and regions often clash with those of other sections and with conceptions of the general interest of the whole nation. The perennial demand of the silver-mining and wool interests in certain western states for purchase and protection, the struggle over slavery, and the . . . filibuster of southern senators against the attempt to outlaw racial discrimination in employment are familiar examples of recurring conflicts between local interests and prejudices and the common welfare. These political quarrels are rooted in the varying stages of cultural development attained by the different parts of the country. It is the peculiar task of the politician to compose these differences, to reconcile conflicting national and local attitudes, and to determine when public opinion is ripe for legislative action. Some conflicts will yield in time to political adjustment; others must wait for their legal sanction upon the gradual evolution of the conscience of society. No act of Congress can abolish unemployment or barking dogs or racial prejudices. . . .

TYPES OF PRESSURES ON CONGRESS

One can sympathize with the plight of the conscientious congressman who is the focal point of all these competing pressures. The district or state he represents may need and want certain roads, post offices, courthouses, or schools. Irrigation dams or projects may be needed for the development of the area's resources. If the representative is to prove himself successful in the eyes of the people back home, he must be able to show, at least occasionally, some visible and concrete results of his congressional activity. Or else he must be able to give good reasons why he has not been able to carry out his pledges. The local residence rule for congressmen multiplies the pressures that impinge upon him. Faithful party workers who have helped elect him will expect the

George B. Galloway (1898–1967) formerly was senior specialist in American government with the Legislative Reference Service of the Library of Congress. Selected excerpts from pp. 284–85, 301, 319–22 from Congress at the Crossroads *by George B. Galloway. Copyright 1946 by George B. Galloway. Copyright renewed. Reprinted by permission of HarperCollins Publishers, Inc.*

congressman to pay his political debts by getting them jobs in the federal service. Constituents affected by proposed legislation may send him an avalanche of letters, telegrams, and petitions which must be acknowledged and followed up. The region from which he comes will expect him to protect and advance its interests in Washington. All the various organized groups will press their claims upon him and threaten him if he does not jump when they crack the whip. Party leaders may urge a congressman to support or oppose the administration program or to "trade" votes for the sake of party harmony or various sectional interests. He is also under pressure from his own conscience as to what he should do both to help the people who have elected him and to advance the best interests of the nation. Besieged by all these competing pressures, a congressman is often faced with the choice of compromising between various pressures, of trading votes, of resisting special interests of one sort or another, of staying off the floor when a vote is taken on some measure he prefers not to take a stand on, of getting support here and at the same time running the risk of losing support there. Dealing with pressure blocs is a problem in political psychology which involves a careful calculation of the power of the blocs, the reaction of the voters on election day, and the long-haul interests of the district, state, and nation. . . .

SHOULD CONGRESS LEAD OR FOLLOW PUBLIC OPINION?

It is axiomatic to say that in a democracy public opinion is the source of law. Unless legislation is sanctioned by the sense of right of the people, it becomes a dead letter on the statute books, like Prohibition and the Hatch Act. But public opinion is a mercurial force; now quiescent, now vociferous, it has various moods and qualities. It reacts to events and is often vague and hard to weigh.

Nor is public opinion infallible. Most people are naturally preoccupied with their personal problems and daily affairs; national problems and legislative decisions seem complex and remote to them, despite press and radio and occasional Capitol tours. Comparatively few adults understand the technicalities of foreign loans or reciprocal trade treaties, although congressional action on these aspects of our foreign economic policy may have far-reaching effects upon our standard of living. . . .

In practice, a congressman both leads and follows public opinion. The desires of his constituents, of his party, and of this or that pressure group all enter into his decisions on matters of major importance. The influence of these factors varies from member to member and measure to measure. Some congressmen consider it their duty to follow closely what they think is the majority opinion of their constituents, especially just before an election. Others feel that they should make their decisions without regard to their constituents' wishes in the first place, and then try to educate and convert them afterward. Some members are strong party men and follow more or less blindly the program of the party leaders. Except when they are very powerful in the home district, the pressure groups are more of a nuisance than a deciding influence on the average member. When a legislator is caught between the conflicting pressures of his constituents and his colleagues, he perforce compromises between them and follows his own judgment.

The average legislator discovers early in his career that certain interests or prejudices of his constituents are dangerous to trifle with. Some of these prejudices may not be of fundamental importance to the welfare of the nation, in which case he is justified in humoring them, even though he may disapprove. The difficult case occurs where the prejudice concerns some fundamental policy affecting the national welfare. A sound sense of values, the ability to discriminate between that which is of fundamental importance and that which is only superficial, is an indispensable qualification of a good legislator.

Senator Fulbright* gives an interesting example of this distinction in his stand on the poll-tax issue and isolationism. "Regardless of how persuasive my colleagues or the national press may be about the evils of the poll tax, I do not see its fundamental importance, and I shall follow the views of the people of my state. Although it may be symbolic of conditions which many deplore, it is exceedingly doubtful that its abolition will cure any of our major problems. On the other hand, regardless of how strongly opposed my constituents may prove to be to the creation of, and participation in, an ever stronger United Nations Organization, I could not follow such a policy in that field unless it becomes clearly hopeless."[1]

A TWO-WAY JOB

As believers in democracy, probably most Americans would agree that it is the duty of congressmen to follow public opinion insofar as it expresses the desires, wants, needs, aspirations, and ideals of the people. Most Americans probably would also consider it essential for their representatives to make as careful an appraisal of these needs and desires as they can, and to consider, in connection with such an appraisal, the ways and means of accomplishing them. Legislators have at hand more information about legal structures, economic problems, productive capacities, manpower possibilities, and the like, than the average citizen they represent. They can draw upon that information to inform and lead the people—by showing the extent to which their desires can be realized.

In other words, a true representative of the people would follow the people's desires and at the same time lead the people in formulating ways of accomplishing those desires. He would lead the people in the sense of calling to their attention the difficulties of achieving those aims and the ways to overcome the difficulties. This means also that, where necessary, he would show special interest groups or even majorities how, according to his own interpretation and his own conscience, their desires need to be tempered in the common interest or for the future good of the nation.

Thus the job of a congressman is a two-way one. He represents his local area and interests in the national capital, and he also informs the people back home of the problems arising at the seat of government and how these problems affect them. It is in the nature of the congressman's job that he should determine, as far as he can, public opinion in his own constituency and in the whole nation, analyze it, measure it in

*At the time this article was written, J. William Fulbright was a U.S. senator from Arkansas—*Editors*.

terms of the practicability of turning it into public policy, and consider it in the light of his own knowledge, conscience, and convictions. Occasionally he may be obliged to go against public opinion, with the consequent task of educating or reeducating the people along lines that seem to him more sound. And finally, since he is a human being eager to succeed at his important job of statesmanship and politics, he is realistic enough to keep his eyes on the voters in terms of the next election. But he understands that a mere weather-vane following of majority public opinion is not always the path to reelection. . . .

NOTE

1. In an address on "The Legislator" delivered at the University of Chicago on February 19, 1946. *Vital Speeches,* May 15, 1946, pp. 468–72.

Congressional Reform:
Term Limitation

*T*ake a poll—any poll—and ask people what they think of Congress, and the response is likely to be, "Throw the bums out!" Indeed, in any popularity contest between the three branches of government—Congress, the presidency, and the Supreme Court—the Congress will almost always end up a poor third.

What are the voters so angry about? The easy answer is—almost everything: the budget, pay raises for representatives, abuses of the franking privilege, undue influence by pressure groups, legislative ethics, the seemingly endless gridlock in government—a veritable litany of complaints.

Given the high level of public criticism and disgust, what might be done to improve the situation? The two articles in this section address what has become a favorite reform proposal of late—limiting the term of representatives to twelve years.

The first of these selections, written by newspaper columnist George F. Will, author of Restoration: Congress, Term Limits and the Recovery of Deliberative Democracy, advances the basic argument of those who would limit congressional terms: term limits would encourage real political competition, open up public office to persons who have had serious and successful careers in the private sector, and reduce "careerism." According to Will, we have nothing to fear from term limits because the Congress cannot get any worse than it already is.

Taking issue with Will is political scientist and frequent TV commentator Norman Ornstein, who rejects the "cheap and easy" solution to the problem of congressional incumbency. According to Ornstein, term limits would do little to solve government problems, either substantively or procedurally. He argues that today's policy issues are much too complex to be left to the inexperienced; a government made up of "amateurs" would most certainly weaken the role of Congress vis-à-vis the other branches of government, thereby diminishing rather than strengthening the institution of Congress.

In 1997, Congress considered but defeated a bill to impose term limits. Despite the bill's defeat, the issue remains alive today and the issues raised by term limits still remain important for both critics and supporters alike.

Congress, Term Limits and the Recovery of Deliberative Democracy

George F. Will

In March, 1992, Representative John Paul Hammerschmidt, an Arkansas Republican, announced that he would not seek reelection to a seat he had held, usually without serious challenge, since 1966. (Once, in 1974, he had to exert himself to spank a whippersnapper fresh from Yale Law School: Bill Clinton.) Hammerschmidt, 70 years old in May, 1992, said, "I'd just like a little time in the other world." Such plain language expressed a thought that had become oppressive to many members of Congress and to scores of millions of Americans, including those Bay Area commuters who in 1991 were being warned by billboards about the sinister congressional "they." The thought—and the truth—is that elective office has become another world, inhabited by professionals preoccupied with staying in it. And it is no longer as much fun as it once was.

When, in 1952, the young Barry Goldwater allowed himself to be enticed into politics, he quipped, "It ain't for life and it might be fun." A healthy spirit, that. What is not healthy is that more and more people bring to politics a grim, desperate craving for careers in Congress—this at a time when life in Congress has become, according to much testimony, dreary. In fact, we are today in the presence of a large and dismal paradox: The paralysis of government and the demoralization of those responsible for governing intensify legislative careerism. . . .

. . . It is devoutly to be hoped, if not confidently predicted, that historians will someday say that an epochal change in American politics began not with the many retirements announced in 1992 but with one resignation effected in June, 1991. Representative Bill Gray of Philadelphia, third-ranking Democratic leader in the House and the highest ranking African American in the history of the House, might have become Speaker, in time. And he had time. He was just 50 years old in the summer of 1991. But there were, he thought, better uses for his time. He resigned to become head of the United Negro College Fund.

Washington—or, more precisely, the city's predominantly white political and media sliver—was uncomprehending and aghast. Many liberals were particularly dismayed by this instance of self-determination by an African-American man.

Gray's decision, which gestated for two years, involved a mix of motives. True, he can make more money as a private citizen (and he has a handicapped child for whose future he must provide). However, Gray also knows that not just political empowerment

George F. Will is a syndicated columnist with the Washington Post *and regular panelist on* This Week With, *ABC-TV. From George F. Will, "Congress, Term Limits, and the Recovery of Deliberative Democracy," pp. 201, 206–13. Reprinted with the permission of The Free Press, a division of Simon & Schuster, from* Restoration: Congress, Term Limits, and the Recovery of Deliberative Democracy *by George F. Will. Copyright © 1992 by George F. Will. Notes have been renumbered to correspond with edited text—Editors.*

but social development—particularly enlargement of the African-American middle class—is the crucial challenge for the African-American community. In this, Congress can be at most marginally important. Given the surge of their enrollments—up 17 percent in four years, twice the college average nationally—the 41 colleges served by the UNCF may educate close to 1 million students in the next decade. The students range from needy inner-city and rural African Americans, who for cultural reasons do not test well but who are college material, to upper-middle-class African Americans seeking an intensely black experience—the Huxtable children from *The Bill Cosby Show.* Gray, a preacher who values pastoral duties more than political duties, is a former teacher whose father was president of two African-American colleges. His career change, as an affirmation of fresh starts and of education, is quintessentially American.

So, too, was his decision to stride purposefully away from the prospect of a lifetime in national politics. His retirement from the House displayed an admirable sense of proportion about the importance of politics, and of himself. His decision proclaimed that although politics is important, it is not all-important. And his decision made clear that he did not have delusions of indispensability. From Philadelphia, as from the rest of the American population, will come other people quite capable of conducting the people's business. We can count on that, because America's population is (in the late Eric Hoffer's splendid phrase) lumpy with talent.

Lumpy enough that the nation need not tremble at the prospect of political turbulence producing unusually high rates of turnover in the membership of Congress. As this is being written, in the summer of 1992, Washington is expecting—queasily expecting—the 1992 elections to produce as many as 120 new members of the House. [The actual number of new members was 110.—*Editors*] That would be the largest freshman class in six decades, since the 165 freshmen elected in 1932. The wave of retirements that washed through Congress prior to the 1992 elections, and perhaps a significant number of defeats of incumbents in the elections (do not bet much on this), may temporarily drain some of the steam from the term limits movement. Some people may conclude that the era of careerism and invincible incumbents has passed, permanently, and therefore formal limits are unnecessary. Such a conclusion would be mistaken, for several reasons.

First, the fundamental factors that underlie the power of incumbents to protect their incumbency are unchanged and, given elemental political realities, are not about to be significantly changed in the foreseeable future. Those factors include the many subsidizing and regulating activities of modern government, activities that enable incumbents to curry favor with constituents and cause constituents to place high value on an incumbent's seniority.

Second, the concatenation of events and circumstances that produced 1992's unusually large number of departures from Congress prior to the 1992 elections was peculiar and is not apt to be repeated soon or often. Those events and circumstances included redistricting that forced some incumbents to run in substantially new districts and even to run against other incumbents; the longest recession since the Depression; and the House bank debacle (and, by the way, the cocaine-selling in the House post office), which came after scandals that caused the resignations of a Speaker (Jim Wright) and a Democratic Whip (Tony Coelho).

And there was one more thing, a provision in the law that made 1992 the last year in which members could retire and convert to private use money raised for campaign spending. As of July, 1992, 39 retiring members were eligible to pocket, collectively $10.2 million, or an average of $260,000 apiece.[1] At least 28 of the 39 said they planned to donate the money to their parties or to charities. In the past, some members who made such pledges did not fulfill them. (A question: How many years does it take the average American family to save $260,000? A Clue: In 1989 the median American approaching retirement age had assets—including a house—worth $91,000; adding the capitalized value of pension and Social Security entitlements, the total rose to around $200,000.)[2]

We can not count on and should not wish for regular recurrences of such disagreeable episodes to churn Congress's membership. And if churning is good, what is bad about making it regular, systematic and orderly? Furthermore, the fact that many opponents of term limits can placidly anticipate such a substantial turnover of Congress's membership undercuts one familiar argument against term limits. The argument is that we dare not drain the reservoir of expertise and institutional memory lest . . . but wait.

Lest what, precisely? Lest we have bad government? We have got bad government by the bushel. Of course things can always be made worse. But how probable is it that a Congress operating under term limits will do worse than the Congress that has collaborated with the production of $400 billion deficits, the savings and loan debacle, and many other policy wrecks, and has driven away in despair many of its best members?

Consider a baseball analogy. In 1988 the Baltimore Orioles (on whose board of directors I sit) were dreadful. They were somewhat like today's Congress—expensive and incompetent. They lost their first 21 games, a record, and went on to lose a total of 107. After the season the Orioles' management had a thought: Hey, we can lose 107 games with inexpensive rookies. The 1989 Orioles were major league baseball's youngest team and had the smallest payroll and came within a few October pitches in Toronto of winning the American League East.

Increasingly, the principal argument against term limits turns out to be a somewhat serpentine assertion. It is that limits would be both harmful and redundant—harmful because rotation depletes the reservoir of wisdom, and redundant because there already is a healthily high amount of rotation. Tom Foley, the Speaker of the House of Representatives, arrived on Capitol Hill (actually arrived there for a second time; he had previously been an aide to Senator Henry Jackson) in 1965. He was part of the bumper crop of new congressmen produced by the anti-Goldwater tide. By 1992 Foley was fond—rather too fond—of noting that 93 percent of the members of the House had arrived since he did, that 81 percent had arrived since the thunderous post-Watergate election of 1974, and that 55 percent had come since Reagan rode into town in 1981.[3] However, a more pertinent number is this: Of the 1,692 congressmen who have sat since 1955, when Democratic control of the House began, 35.7 percent of the members, or 604 congressmen, have served seven terms or more. Of the current members of the 102d Congress (1991–92), 37.5 percent are already in at least their seventh term.[4] In the last four elections (1984–90) the turnover in the House due to death, retirement or—much the least important cause—defeat averaged about 10 percent per election.

Much of the turnover comes not from the defeat of incumbents in competitive elections but from the voluntary departure of members who despair of enjoying useful service in a Congress geared to the service of careerism. The leadership of Congress—the ruling class that runs the committees and subcommittees that are the primary instruments for self-promotion—has not been changed nearly as much as Foley's numbers lead people to believe. Systematic changing by term limits would make serious service possible more quickly than it now is. Hence term limits would make Congress more attractive to serious people. In 1991 the economists W. Robert Reed of the University of Oklahoma and D. Eric Schansberg of Indiana University at New Albany argued that term limitations, while eliminating the possibility of long careers, would increase access to leadership positions. Representatives would be eligible for leadership positions much sooner than at present. "Currently," they said, "it takes sixteen years to reach the 80th percentile of seniority." On the basis of certain assumptions about how many members serving under term limitations will choose to serve the maximum permissible number of terms, and how many will die or be defeated, Reed and Schansberg calculated that under a six-term limit the time required to reach the 80th percentile would be cut in half, to eight years.[5]

Some opponents of term limits say that limits are a recipe for institutionalizing ignorance. They say that if all congressional careers are short, no one will have time to master the subtleties and mysteries of the government's vast and increasing penetration of society, a penetration carried out by subsidies, taxation and regulation. But that argument tends to turn around and bite its authors, as follows: If government now is so omnipresent (because it strives to be omniprovident) and so arcane that it makes a permanent legislative class indispensable, that is less an argument in favor of such a class than it is an argument against that kind of government. It is an argument for pruning the government's claims to omnicompetence. It is an argument for curtailing government's intrusiveness at least enough so that the supervision of the government can be entrusted to the oversight of intelligent lay people. Or amateurs. Sometimes called citizens.

Critics of term limitation worry that compulsory rotation of offices will mean that a substantial number of representatives and senators will always be looking ahead to their next employment. This, say the critics, means, at best, that these legislators will be distracted from the public business, and it may mean that they will be corrupted by the temptation to use their last years in power to ingratiate themselves with potential employers. Both of these possibilities are, well, possible. But the critics must confront a question: Would such corruption be worse—morally more reprehensible, and more injurious to the public weal—than legislative careerism has proved to be? Careerism, after all, is the legislator's constant surrender—with an easy conscience—to the temptation to use every year in power to ingratiate himself with all the factions useful to his permanent incumbency.

Also, people who would come to Congress under term limits would be less susceptible than cynics think to the temptation to misuse their congressional service to court future employers. After all, people who will choose to spend a necessarily limited span of time in Congress are apt to come from serious careers and will want to return to them. Furthermore, the political incentive for private interests to hire politically influential people from the ranks of ex-congressmen will be radically reduced by the term limits that will swell those ranks. Think about it. One reason ex-legislators are hired by private interests today is to take advantage of their relationships with ex-colleagues who remain in Congress. But term limits will guarantee that those relationships are short-lived. Those ex-colleagues will soon be ex-congressmen.

Would term limits deplete the pool of talent from which we draw presidents? History, which is all we have to go by, says otherwise. Presidents are rarely launched from long legislative careers. How many people have become president after serving 12 or more consecutive terms in the House or the Senate? Just three, and two became president by accident. The three are James Polk, Lyndon Johnson and Gerald Ford.

Unquestionably term limits would substantially increase the number of competitive congressional races. It is highly probable that this would lead to increased rates of voting. People are apt to vote at the end of campaigns that they have been talking and arguing about. They are more apt to talk and argue about campaigns when the outcomes are in doubt. Every four years the presidency provides the electorate with an election to argue about. Congress could be a much more prolific producer of wholesome arguments. Every four years Congress offers voters 936 elections—two elections of the 435 members of the House and elections of two-thirds of the one hundred senators. Term limits, by reducing the number of incumbents running, would increase the number of competitive races and would thereby enliven the nation's civic conversation.

NOTES

1. Martin Tolchin, "33 Retirees in House Are Eligible for $8.6 Million," *New York Times,* June 7, 1992, p. A22; "Inside Congress: Congressional Departures," *Congressional Quarterly Weekly Report,* June 27, 1992, vol. 50, no. 26, p. 1859.
2. Michael Barone, "On Politics: The New 'Save Our Wealth' Voters," *U.S. News & World Report,* June 22, 1992, p. 45.
3. Norman Ornstein, "The Permanent Democratic Congress," *The Public Interest* (Washington, D.C.: National Affairs, Inc., 1990), no. 100 (Summer 1990), p. 32.
4. D. Eric Schansberg, from a paper, "Moving Out of the House: Analysis of Congressional Quits," Texas A&M University, College Station, June 1992.
5. W. Robert Reed and D. Eric Schansberg, from a paper, "An Analysis of the Impact of Congressional Term Limits," Texas A & M University, College Station, July 1991.

Term Limits Would Just Make Things Worse

Norman Ornstein

Term limit proponents can't believe their good luck. They have been handed two gifts on a platter . . . the California term limit initiative has been upheld by the state Supreme Court, and they have gained a new and influential adherent in George F. Will. Furious over unchecked government spending and checks bouncing in the Capitol, Will succumbed to emotion and joined the clamorous calls for term limits for legislators.

Public fury about legislative crassness, greed and ineptitude will no doubt be exploited by the term limit movement. Momentum is clearly on its side. But before letting emotion rule over reason, we should take careful stock of the consequences. One doesn't have to defend House check bouncers or Senate bozos to realize that these and other problems won't be solved by a nuclear attack on politicians.

George Will's argument for term limits is not a simple "throw the bums out" approach. But it is still based on the idea that there is a cheap and easy way to take arrogance and excessive ambition out of politics, bring enlightened amateurism back to governance (as if it were ever there in the first place), and restore competition to the political marketplace.

Will says term limits for legislators will remove the virus of professionalism that has unnecessarily complicated government to make lucrative careers for lobbyists, lawyers, think tankers and journalists in Washington. It would be nice to have simplified government and policy. But even over many decades, it is impossible to imagine government getting less complicated, given the dizzying pace and complexity of the world economy, and the nature of governance in a $6 trillion domestic economy.

Does anyone really believe that immigration laws, environmental regulations, trade rules, budget decisions, health policy and stock market regulation are complex because professional lawmakers conspire to make them so for their own advantage? They are complex because the world is complex and because a modern society of 250 million people requires a difficult balance among huge numbers of interests. If we had amateurs writing Medicare provisions, drafting laws for food and drug inspection or deciding clean air provisions, it might give us simpler laws. But that would mean not better governance, but clumsier governance, with more likelihood of fouling up the economy, inadvertently shafting some legitimate interest and creating more, not fewer, openings for sharks to fleece the system.

Chances are that if the legislature consisted of junior amateurs, the real policy decisions and the oversight of financial markets and international affairs would be taken away from an overwhelmed Congress out of its league and made instead by seasoned

Norman Ornstein is resident scholar at the American Enterprise Institute, a government and public policy research organization in Washington, D.C. From Norman Ornstein, "Term Limits Would Just Make Things Worse," the Washington Post, *October 20, 1991, p. C7. Reprinted with permission of the author.*

bureaucrats, presidential appointees, judges and the crafty and experienced people now being regulated—those we sometimes call the "special interests."

Weaken the legislature by taking away its expertise and experience, and we strengthen the other arms of government who now compete with Congress along with the various experienced interests in Washington. Some may favor that approach— clearly, it is the main reason that President Bush and Vice President Quayle . . . eagerly embraced term limits for Congress—but I see no reason to expect more enlightened, less corrupting policy with an unchecked executive branch or a newly unleashed judiciary taking over, or by weakening Congress' oversight over Salomon Brothers, AT&T or other forces in the private sector.

I am not surprised that most "special interests" oppose term limits; they have invested a lot in learning how to take advantage of the current system, and any change would involve heavy transition costs. But I have absolutely no doubt that they would have more leverage, not less, over a Congress consisting of inexperienced newcomers.

One rejoinder to that argument is that we will get *enlightened* amateurs with term limits—noble and seasoned citizen-legislators who leave their top careers in commerce, industry and the professions not for political ambition but to spend a few years in Washington before returning to their homes and jobs. Well, look at what it takes to run for office in a congressional district with 550,000 people in the modern telecommunication age. Look at the web of conflict-of-interest and disclosure requirements. Look at the adversarial press. Look at the costs of uprooting one's family and living the nomadic, two-household existence built into Congress.

Are we really going to have a surge in the quality of candidates? Look for comparison to the top political appointments in the executive branch, which are term-limited, prestigious opportunities for enlightened service in Washington without the costs of elective office. We have no surplus of high-quality people clamoring for these posts—instead we have increasing difficulty getting and keeping anybody of quality.

Wouldn't it be worth it if we could check the arrogance and ambition of the current class of career politicians? Maybe it would—but term limits won't have that effect. Instead, they will bring with them even more corrupting ambition. People willing to suffer the upheaval of running for Congress and coming to Washington will be just as ambitious as those here now—but they will channel their ambitions in different ways.

Congressional service will be a stepping stone to the next post, not a place to serve in and of itself. Instead of making any commitment to their institutions or to long-term policy, term-limited members will start on day one thinking about the next step. They will be running for the Senate from the time they enter the House, or cozying up to lawyers and lobbyists to prepare for the next stage of their careers. Some will go back home, to be sure—but the experience of executive political appointees would suggest that they will be in the minority.

As for policy, if you are limited in your service, your incentive to build long-term policy will be gone; instead, you might as well hit and run, do something splashy for effect now—including spending more, not fewer, federal dollars—and let your successors clean up the mess when you've moved on up the ladder.

To be sure, there are serious problems now in governance and standards for politicians. There are ways to solve those problems, through campaign finance reform, disclosure, stiff enforcement of ethical standards and good old-fashioned political leadership. Dramatic and irreversible constitutional change is not the answer.

We tried that with term limits on the presidency and they have failed miserably as a way to bring more competition to presidential elections or bolder leadership to the White House. Did we get presidential leadership on the deficit from the term-limited Ronald Reagan? Did we get more and better leadership from him in his second term, when he was freed from the shackles of reelection? The answer is clearly no. Instead of seeking a nonexistent panacea and moving to limit the terms of lawmakers, we should devote our efforts to repealing the 22nd Amendment and to removing the term limits that now exist for governors—and rolling up our sleeves to accomplish the reforms that would make a positive difference. George Will is right about one thing—term limits would stick it to the lawmakers. They would stick it to the rest of us too.

11

THE PRESIDENCY

In 1973, the noted historian Arthur Schlesinger wrote a book titled The Imperial Presidency, *in which he argued that the powers and prerogatives of the office had grown so extensive that our cherished principle of balanced government was being seriously threatened.*

The resignation of President Richard Nixon, along with the travails of those presidents who followed him, have caused many political observers to conclude that warnings of an imperial presidency are no longer applicable. In the first selection that follows, however, Michael Lind argues quite the contrary. He insists that on the crucial questions of foreign policy presidents can still do pretty much as they please; and, thanks to actions taken by Carter, Reagan, and Bush, future presidents will find their powers considerably greater in the domestic sphere as well. Meanwhile, according to Lind, the imperial character of the office continues to be reinforced by two other disturbing developments that have actually been in place for some time. One is the view of the presidency as the "tribune of the people"—a view first articulated by Andrew Jackson, later embellished by Woodrow Wilson, and now routinely embraced by our presidents; and the second, a White House bureaucracy that has been steadily expanding since the end of the Second World War. According to Lind, we urgently need to cut the presidency down to size, and he proposes a number of changes designed to do so.

R. Gordon Hoxie, the author of the second selection, rejects any notion of an imperial presidency, suggesting instead that "imperiled" would be a more apt description of the office. Where Lind sees power grabs by our recent presidents, Hoxie sees presidents conscientiously exercising their responsibilities under the Constitution; or, making use of options and resources granted to the president by Congress; or, bolstering the institutional presidency so that it can more effectively compete against both an overreaching Congress and hostile bureaucratic interests within the Executive branch.

As Hoxie sees it, presidents, operating as they must in a separation-of-powers system, nearly always have to struggle for what they get. This constitutional fact of life, moreover, has become even more burdensome for presidents in light of the diminished importance of political parties in the American political process.

The Out-of-Control Presidency

Michael Lind

I.

The president is shrinking. The institution of the presidency, magnified by half a century of world war and cold war, is rapidly diminishing in terms of both power and respect. . . . Meanwhile, Congress has become bloated and arrogant, swelling the ranks of its own staff while encroaching on the constitutional prerogatives of the White House. Congressional supremacy would be a disaster, particularly in foreign affairs. We cannot have 535 commanders in chief.

This tale of the decline of the presidency and the rise of Congress is the emerging conventional wisdom in Washington. It is familiar, widely believed—and wrong. . . .

[The president elected in 1996] will be handed the Nixonian imperial presidency, with most of its powers intact and with a few new prerogatives added.

In foreign policy, the [newly elected] president [will] discover that, like every president since Truman, he can wage war at will, without consulting Congress. Though he might consent to a congressional vote as a matter of public relations (as Bush did before the Gulf war), he is more likely to invoke his supposed "inherent" authority as commander-in-chief. If necessary, his aides will concoct legalistic rationalizations, citing dangers to U.S. citizens (Grenada, Panama), authorization by the United Nations (Somalia, Haiti), NATO treaty obligations (Libya). Whether a liberal or a conservative, the [new] president will dismiss the War Powers Resolution as unconstitutional.

Nor is de facto presidential supremacy in foreign affairs limited to war-making, the [new] president will discover. Bush and Clinton will have bequeathed an important technique for ramming economic treaties through Congress with little debate: fast-track legislation, which limits the time allowed for debate and forbids amendments. The Senate, which the Founders wanted to have weight treaty commitments deliberately, was granted a mere 20 hours to consider the treaty that committed the United States to the jurisdiction of the World Trade Organization (WTO). Perhaps the [new] president can insist that it be limited even further—to, say, half an hour or 15 minutes.

In the domestic arena, the [new] president will find even greater enhancements of his prerogatives. Thanks to Jimmy Carter, who reformed the Senior Executive Service to give the White House more control over career bureaucrats, and Ronald Reagan, who politicized the upper levels of the executive branch to an unprecedented degree,

Michael Lind is a staff writer for the New Yorker *magazine and formerly assistant to the director of the Center for the Study of Foreign Affairs, the Foreign Service Institute, U.S. Department of State. From Michael Lind, "The Out-of-Control Presidency," the* New Republic, *August 14, 1995, pp. 18–23. Reprinted by permission of the* New Republic. © 1995, The New Republic, Inc.

the [new] president will find it easy to stack government with his spoilsmen or reward partisan bureaucrats. And he can thank George Bush for a technique that enhances presidential prerogative even further—signing laws while announcing he will not obey them.

Bush engaged in the greatest institutional power grab of any president since Nixon. In 1991 Bush, delivering a commencement address at Princeton, said: "[O]n many occasions during my presidency, I have stated that statutory provisions that violate the Constitution have no binding legal force." As Charles Tiefer points out in the *Semi-Sovereign Presidency,* Bush used "signing statements"—statements accompanying his signing of a bill, during which he announced he would not enforce this or that provision—to exercise an unconstitutional line-item veto (White House counsel C. Boyden Gray concocted the idea). In one such instance, when Congress amended the Clean Air Act in 1990 to permit lawsuits by citizen groups against companies that had violated the act, Bush used a signing statement to declare, on supposed "constitutional grounds," that the executive branch would continue to act as though such citizen lawsuits were prohibited—nullifying the intent of Congress. Ironically, the "take care" clause of the Constitution was intended to compel the president to enforce laws he disapproved of (often, Colonial governors had refused to enforce parts of legislation passed by Colonial legislatures). As Tiefer points out, Bush was asserting a sovereign power to ignore statutes that had been denied the English king in the Seven Bishops case of 1688.

Yet another new instrument of arbitrary presidential power is the "czar." The institution of presidential commissars with vague, sweeping charges that overlap with or supersede the powers of department heads is utterly alien to the American constitutional tradition. Most famous is the celebrated position of "drug czar," which William Bennett held under Bush, and Lee Brown now occupies, which arrogates duties that were previously handled perfectly adequately by agencies of Justice and other departments. Similarly, Vice President Dan Quayle acted as a "czar" as the head of Bush's Council on Competitiveness, designed to circumvent Cabinet heads and Congress in regulatory matters.

The White House staff that has ballooned since World War II seems close to becoming an extra-constitutional "fourth branch" of government. For obvious reasons, presidents have preferred to govern through their staffers, most of whom need not be confirmed by the Senate and many of whom are young and pliant, rather than deal with the heads of Cabinet departments and independent agencies, experienced people who are less likely to be mere tools of the president's will. Nor is it any accident that the major presidential scandals of the past generation—Watergate and Iran-contra—have involved attempts by shadowy and scheming courtiers of law-breaking presidents to circumvent or suborn the older, established executive departments. Every time the high-handed actions of White House courtiers drag a president into scandal, Congress, the press and the public denounce the courtiers—Nixon's plumbers, Ollie North—or the president and then, under a new president, sigh with relief: the system worked. That future presidents will almost certainly be tempted to use their White House staffers as Nixon and Reagan did is ignored.

The imperial presidency, then, is intact, merely waiting to be powered up and taken out of the hangar. If today's Congress has its way, the presidency will become even more imperial. Having captured Congress after half a century, the Republicans are hastening to give away the powers of the branch they control.

Some of these powers are formal, such as the line-item veto. States whose governors have the line-item veto don't balance their budgets any better than states without it. A line-item veto simply shifts the power to protect pork from a legislature to an executive. Giving the president the line-item veto would not balance the budget; it would merely permit the president to zero out the bounties of his enemies while keeping bounties for his allies. It would also wreck the constitutional design, which intended the branch closest to the people to have the last word on spending the people's money.

Other reforms backed by Republicans in Congress would weaken their institution indirectly. Term limits would reduce the expertise of representatives and senators—and boost their reliance on executive-branch experts, as well as on K Street lobbyists and think-tank flacks. Abolishing such independent congressional fact-finding agencies as the Office of Technology Assessment would hardly make a dent in the deficit but would make it easier for Congress to be hoodwinked by the executive branch it is supposed to oversee. A balanced budget amendment would shift the final arena of budgetary policy from the Capitol to federal courts, civil servants or White House staffers. . . .

II.

Madison and other Founders did not conceive of the president as a "representative" with a popular constituency at all. The president was to be a nonpartisan chief magistrate. The Founders designed the Electoral College with the expectation that presidents would frequently be chosen by the House, voting by states, from lists of candidates nominated by special state electors. The idea of the chief executive as chief representative is French, not American. As Louis Napoleon observed, his uncle Napoleon I "earnestly claimed the title of first Representative of the People, a title which seemed about to be given exclusively to members of the Legislative Body."

Andrew Jackson was the first president to claim, like the two Napoleons, to be a tribune of the masses: "The president is the direct representative of the American people." His attempt to act as a democratic monarch produced a backlash against such claims until the 20th century. Lincoln justified his sweeping war powers using legal arguments, not the claim that he was the sole legitimate representative of the nation; indeed, this former Whig opponent of "King Andrew" Jackson was hesitant about suggesting legislation to Congress, for fear of arousing suspicions of executive supremacy. "My political education," he declared, "strongly inclines me against a very free use of any of these means [recommending legislation and using the veto], by the Executive, to control the legislation of the country. As a rule, I think it better that Congress should originate, as well as perfect its measures, without external bias."

The modern conception of the president as an all-powerful tribune of the people comes from Woodrow Wilson. . . . Wilson argued for a different, Rousseauian conception of democracy, in which the president is the nation personified: "The nation as a whole has chosen him, and is conscious that it has no other political spokesman." Wilson was the first president since Washington to address Congress in person. He argued that the American constitutional tradition should never obstruct an activist president: "If he rightly interpret the national thought and boldly insist upon it, he is irresistible; and the country never feels the zest of action so much as when its president is of such insight and caliber. Its instinct is for unified action, and it craves a single leader."

The Great Leader is to lead not only the United States but the world: "Our president must always, henceforth, be one of the great powers of the world, whether he act wisely or not." Not the United States, but the presidency itself, is to be a great power! Wilson called for the president to ignore the prerogatives of the House and the Senate in foreign policy and to present the legislature with treaties as faits accomplis. "He need disclose no step of negotiation until it is complete." This strategy backfired when Wilson tried to impose the League of Nations treaty on the Senate, but later presidents have used it effectively. Bush's military buildup in the Gulf more or less forced Congress to ratify his planned war against Iraq, while the Clinton administration followed its Republican predecessors in ramming through GATT and NAFTA by means of fast-track legislation.

The plebiscitary theory of the presidency, the theory that the president, like Napoleon I, is First Representative of the Nation, is shared by all presidents today, Republican or Democratic. Though most presidents are elected with a plurality, not a majority—meaning most voters wanted someone else—every president today claims a "mandate" from the "majority" of "the people," considered as an undifferentiated mass with one General Will. The nomination of today's presidential candidates by primaries, rather than by congressional caucuses (the first system) or brokered party conventions (the system from the 1830s to the 1960s), has reinforced the illusion that the president represents the popular will, unmediated by either government structures or party organizations. The plebiscitary president is free to run against Washington, and even against political parties, in the manner of Ross Perot.

Running against Washington means running against Congress and "the bureaucracy," which are treated as villains in a morality play. The virtuous heroes are the president, and (for conservatives) state governments and an idealized free market. Presidentialists build up the legitimacy of the presidency by grossly exaggerating the faults of Congress and the parts of the executive branch that the White House does not directly control, such as the civil service and the independent agencies.

Consider the myth that the budgets and staffs of Congress and federal agencies have been escalating out of control. The money spent on the entire legislative branch is minuscule compared to that which goes to the executive. As James Glassman has pointed out, "You can eliminate all of Congress . . . just get rid of the whole darn thing, you'd save exactly as much as you would save if you cut the defense budget by less than 1 percent." What's more, during the 1980s, appropriations for Congress actually fell, in real terms. U.S. representatives are paid much less than their counterparts in many other democracies, such as Japan, and their salaries compare unfavorably with those of professionals and corporate executives, many of whom have less onerous responsibilities. Congressional staff, though it has grown along with government in general, actually declined in the 1980s, while the number of employees in the executive and judicial branches expanded. . . .

Nor has the other half of the hated "Washington establishment," the federal bureaucracy, been growing out of control. Most Americans would be surprised to learn that in terms of manpower—about 2 million—the federal government has hardly grown at all since World War II. State bureaucracies have grown faster, local bureaucracies even faster still. Federal funds, to be sure, have paid for much of the expansion of state and local bureaucracies, but conservatives have been concentrating their attacks not on federal funds, but on federal employees.

But, unlike Congress and the federal civil service, one federal institution does resemble the caricature of an ever-expanding, arrogant, corrupt bureaucracy. Since World War II, the White House staff and the Executive Office of the President have metastasized. Dwight Eisenhower made do with 29 key assistants as his White House staff in 1960; Bush needed 81 in 1992. The Executive Office of the President, created in 1939, has grown to include thousands of bureaucrats functioning in a presidential court, a miniature executive branch superimposed on the traditional departmental executive envisioned by the Constitution.

Meanwhile, the number of presidential appointees and senior executives has ballooned an astonishing 430 percent between 1960 and 1992, from 451 to 2,393. Most of this growth has not been in jobs for the hated career civil servants, but in positions for upper-middle-class political activists who donated money to, or worked in, presidential campaigns, or roomed with somebody in college, or whatever.

Presidents have consistently sought to expand the number of these political appointees. Mostly from elite law, lobbying, business, banking or academic backgrounds, these courtiers have ever more elaborate titles: principal deputy assistant secretary, assistant associate office director. As the titles grow, the average tenure shrinks (down to 18 months from three years during the Johnson years). The in-and-outers, once in, can't wait to get out and cash in their fancy titles for higher lobbyist fees or an endowed professorship of government. If conservatives are serious about cutting back government, why not abolish most of the post-'60s presidential branch? Where is the outcry against the expansion of the presidential bureaucracy? Why is a congressional barbershop a greater enormity than four White House staffers devoted to dealing with flowers? . . .

Ideologues of all persuasions have an interest in promoting presidential prerogative. Why battle over years to build a congressional majority, when you can persuade a president to enact your favored reform—gays in the military or gays out of the military—with a stroke of a pen? This accounts for the spitting fury with which op-ed pundits, think tankers and spin doctors pounce on any president who does not use "the power of his office" to enact their pet projects by ukase, preferably in the next few days or weeks.

Our press also helps the presidentialists of right and left by its obsessive focus on the person of the president at the expense of other executive branch officials, to say nothing of members of Congress and the judiciary. It makes for an easier story, of course, but laziness is no excuse for distorted coverage. Would the country crumble into anarchy if the major networks ignored the president for a week and followed the speaker, or the Senate majority leader, or the chief justice of the Supreme Court? News-paper editors are just as bad. Several times, when I have written op-eds concerning gov-ernment policy, I have been told by an editor, "You need to conclude by saying what the president should do."

Robert Nisbet has it right: "It is nearly instinctual in the political clerisy . . . to por-tray the president as one elected representative of the entire people . . . with congress-men portrayed as like mayors and city councilmen, mere representatives of wards, sec-tions and districts." When appeals to plebiscitary legitimacy are insufficient, presidentialists can turn to the "court party" of legal and constitutional scholars, who are always ready with a defense of this or that supposed presidential prerogative. Judge Robert Bork, for example, has argued "that the office of the president of the United States has been significantly weakened in recent years and that Congress is largely, but not entirely, responsible." If one were comparing Reagan, Bush or Clinton to FDR at the height of his power, this might seem plausible. In a 200-year perspective it is absurd. . . .

III.

Presidential democracy is not democracy. In theory a single politician could be answer-able to a constituency of hundreds of millions—but only in theory. In practice, the more presidential the U.S. government becomes, the less responsive it is to most Americans. Stunts like Jimmy Carter's "Phone the President" notwithstanding, any president will necessarily be remote from most citizens and accessible chiefly to concentric tiers of CEOs, big-money contributors, big-labor leaders, network anchors and movie stars. Any reader who doubts this should try to get appointments with both his or her repre-sentative and the president.

Under the Constitution of 1787, representative democracy in the United States means congressional democracy. Restoring congressional democracy must begin with discrediting in the public mind the plebiscitary theory of democracy. Americans must conclude that democracy does not mean voting for this or that elective monarch every four years and then leaving government to the monarch's courtiers. Democracy means continuous negotiation among powerful and relatively autonomous legislators who rep-resent diverse interests in society.

This battle on the level of theory should be accompanied by a campaign at the level of symbolism. Congress, as an institution, is slighted by our public iconography. "We celebrate Presidents' Day," Thomas Langston notes in his new book about the presi-dency, *With Reverence and Contempt*. "Why not celebrate Speakers' Day? How about a Speakers' Memorial in Washington, D.C., . . . [or] proposing that famous speakers of the House, or senators, also ennoble our currency[?]" The royalism symbolized by pharaonic presidential libraries should be combated by a law requiring that all presi-dential papers hereafter be deposited permanently in a single, modest presidential library in Washington.

Changes in government organization would need to accompany changes in percep-tions of congressional legitimacy. An electoral reform such as proportional representation for the House might actually strengthen the separation of powers; it would encourage a multiparty system, but the same multiparty coalition would not likely hold the House, Senate and White House at once. In a multiparty system, the president might also be forced to appoint coalition Cabinets, as in parliamentary regimes. He would have less influence over a Cabinet secretary of another party than over some servile functionary from his own.

As for the executive branch, the slow seeping of authority from Cabinet secretaries to courtiers needs to be halted and reversed. Congress could drastically cut the White House staff—if representatives aren't intimidated by the divinity that hedges our elected king. The depths of the reverence surrounding the presidential court became clear on Thursday, June 25, when a House Appropriations subcommittee released a plan to abolish the Council of Economic Advisers. "Democrats," the *New York Times* reported, "said they were startled at the lack of respect for a separate and equal branch of government displayed by the gesture, and even the subcommittee chairman, [Republican] Representative Jim Ross Lightfoot of Iowa, said he recognized that they could be accused of 'micromanagement' and lack of proper respect for the office of the president." It is as though the British parliament had threatened to cancel the changing of the guard at Buckingham Palace. The irony is particularly delicious since the Council of Economic Advisers was imposed on the presidency as part of the Employment Act of 1946 by conservatives in Congress hoping to check a free-spending White House.

　　The evolution of the council is typical of the process by which every argumentation of the executive branch in the interest of "efficiency" soon serves to enhance the power and prestige of the presidency. An even better example is the Office of Management and Budget, which was created after World War I as an independent agency (the Bureau of the Budget), drifted under presidential control during the administration of FDR and under Reagan became one of the White House's chief instruments of partisan control of executive agencies. Like a black hole, the presidency grows by absorbing ever more power and light.

Unlike a black hole, however, the presidency can be shrunk. Congress can not only scale back the White House to bring it in line with the staffs of prime ministers, but it can also make the heads of executive departments more independent of the president. The Founders expected department heads to carry out their duties more or less on their own (the Constitution gives the president the modest power to request reports in writing from department heads). The idea that department heads should be mere creatures of particular presidents is a modern misconception. Their duty is to use their own judgment to implement the laws passed by Congress, not to promote an imaginary "mandate" given the president by 40 or 45 percent of the voters. The Constitution permits Congress to vest the appointment of "inferior officers" in the heads of departments. Why not give it a try? It would strengthen their ties to their department head—and make it more likely that they would hang up when a White House staffer phoned to intervene, for the short-run political benefit of his boss, in the department's operations.

　　Reducing the president from a Latin American-style caudillo to something like a 19th- or 18th-century U.S. chief magistrate can be done, then, without revising the

Constitution, merely by passing a few laws. It is hard to see how else the U.S. can avoid the completion of its slow evolution from a congressional republic into a full-fledged presidential state. The real trend in the world at the end of the 20th century, it can be argued, is not so much from "dictatorship" to "democracy" as from unelected dictatorship to elective dictatorship—from Gorbachev to Yeltsin. The executive rulers have to face election, but rule by decree still tends to supplant rule by laws passed by representative legislatures. It could happen here—as the Founding Fathers feared it would. Ben Franklin, among others, predicted, "The Executive will always be increasing here, as elsewhere, till it ends in a monarchy." The new Republican majority in Congress should ponder that warning, as it sets about the further dismantling of the popular branch of government.

The Not-So-Imperial Presidency

R. Gordon Hoxie

In a recent essay entitled "The Out-of-Control Presidency," Michael Lind contends that recent portrayals "of the decline of the presidency and the rise of Congress" are "wrong." He concludes, "The imperial presidency . . . is intact, merely waiting to be powered up and taken out of the hanger."

This perception predated Lind's essay, or even Arthur Schlesinger's 1973 volume, *The Imperial Presidency*. At least one early and strong president, Andrew Jackson (1829–1837) was even termed "King Andrew I" by his political enemies. Many presidents since have enjoyed presidential pomp. However, the American constitutional system, together with the media and public opinion have generally held in check any tendencies toward presidential excesses. Each of the four 20th-century presidents who won the biggest victories, and thereafter engaged in excesses, were slapped down by a combination of Congress, the courts, the media, and public opinion: Franklin Roosevelt in 1937 with his scheme to pack the Supreme Court with additional judges; Lyndon Johnson after 1965 with his escalation of the Vietnam War; Richard Nixon in 1973 with his Watergate cover-up; and Ronald Reagan in 1985 with the Iran-Contra affair.

Michael Lind portrays the president as an all-powerful chief executive. To the contrary, among the leading industrial nations the American president is one of the weakest political leaders. The French president and the British prime minister have the fewest constraints on their power. In the *New York Times,* May 1, 1997, political scientist and pollster Stanley B. Greenberg, comparing British prime minister Tony Blair to the American president, asserted that the difference "could not be more stark. Mr. Clinton was unable to move his party in a new direction. Mr. Blair, however, was able to change his party before his campaign began." Despite our common language and political heritage, the British system of government, with its clear lines of accountability, could not be more different from the American system, with its system of checks and balances, which defies clear lines of accountability and imperialistic aspirations.

Far from being imperial and out of control, presidents are frustrated and unable to carry out the principal programs on their agenda. This frustration comes primarily from two sources: the framers of the Constitution, who distrusted centralization of powers and therefore created a separation-of-powers system; and the contemporary decline of the American political party system, which, in the past has been the engine of presidential strength.

I.

With respect to the decline of political parties, it is not unreasonable to suggest that, except for Washington, whose presidency preceded parties, our strongest presidents—

R. Gordon Hoxie is President-Chairman Emeritus of the Center for the Study of the Presidency, New York, N.Y. This article was written especially for Points of View *in 1997.*

Jefferson, Jackson, Polk, Lincoln, Wilson, and the two Roosevelts—all led through effective *party support*. In the case of Wilson, that support was lost in his last two years in office when Republicans gained control of Congress.

Today party no longer strengthens the presidency. This can be seen in the decline of voting turnout, which, in part, is a reflection of the diminished importance that voters attach to parties; and secondly, the decline of elections of the same party in Congress and the presidency. These factors have weakened the presidency and caused it to seek the means of support that Lind criticizes.

The sharp decline in voting for candidates for the presidency means there is no strong popular mandate for the programs of the candidate who is elected president. By contrast, a high voter turnout coupled with a wide margin of victory sends a strong signal to Congress to support the winning presidential candidate's programs. This was clearly indicated in the record number of voters for the presidency and the landslide victories of Franklin Roosevelt in the 1932 and 1936 presidential elections and in the record number of voters for the presidency in 1964 and Lyndon Johnson's formidable margin of victory. In these instances, Congress responded with overwhelming support for the Roosevelt and Johnson programs, changing the social structure of the nation. By contrast, the low voter turnout in the 1996 elections—a mere 49 percent and the lowest since 1924—is reflected in few presidential program initiatives pending or enacted by the current Congress.

In the election of 1900, only 3.4 percent of congressional districts recorded split results (ie., voting for one party for Congress and another for presidential candidates) for presidential and congressional candidates. Partisanship binding the Congress and the presidency was alive and well. By 1948, however, 21.3 percent of congressional districts recorded split voting. In 1996, split results occurred in 25 percent of congressional districts. In brief, the "coattail" effect of presidential candidates influencing the election of congressional candidates of their own party has diminished considerably, thereby increasing the incidence of divided government in which one party controls the presidency and the other one or both houses of Congress.

II.

While party support may serve to mute the struggle between the legislative and executive branches, it cannot eliminate it altogether, for the separation-of-power systems builds competition into the relationship. From the presidency of George Washington to the present there has been a struggle between the Congress and the president, a struggle that has manifested itself in both foreign and domestic arenas. In foreign policy, the framers of the Constitution made the president both the chief diplomat and the commander-in-chief. Although Jefferson was highly critical of the conduct of foreign policy by President Washington, and proposed roles for Congress in foreign policy, when he became president, he insisted that the conduct of foreign affairs is "executive altogether." The War Powers Resolution of 1973, an attempt to curb presidential war making, and forced upon a weakened President Nixon, has, as Lind acknowledges, been viewed as unconstitutional by Nixon and subsequent presidents. But Lind fails to note that the act gives Congress the authority to contravene the orders of the president as commander-in-chief by forcing the withdrawal of troops from combat at the end of 60 to 90 days. Nixon's successor, Gerald Ford, referring to the 535 members of Congress, where he had been a member, asserted, "Our forefathers knew you could not have 535 commanders-in-chief and secretaries of state."

As for the Gulf War, the congressional vote authorizing the use of force in this military engagement in spring 1991 was not "a matter of public relations," as Lind charges. Indeed, any assertion to that effect wholly misreads the seriousness of the entire war and the historic debate that transpired on the floors of Congress as it considered whether or not to authorize military action. The fact is President Bush sought, and by a narrow voting margin, got congressional support. Other presidents as early as John Adams and Jefferson engaged in undeclared wars *without* congressional authorization: In the case of Adams there was a naval war with France and in the case of Jefferson a punitive expedition led by the United States Navy and Marines against the Barbary pirates in the Tripolitan War. Adams and Jefferson acted in their capacity as commander-in-chief as many presidents have since. By contrast, Bush did earnestly seek congressional support, even while necessarily readying a force to repel Iraqi aggression.

There are, of course, times of grave emergency when the very security of the nation is so threatened that a president must in his position as commander-in-chief assume authority, even before turning to Congress for legislative authorization. Indeed, such was the action taken by President Lincoln in the Civil War and by President Roosevelt in aiding Great Britain in the desperate 1940–41 period before the United States, by congressional declaration, entered World War II.

In another area related to the separation-of-powers issue, Lind charges Bush with "the greatest institutional power grab of any president since Nixon." He portrays Bush's White House counsel, C. Boyden Gray, as having "concocted" the idea of using the "signing statements" that accompany the signing of a bill to declare invalid provisions of a law with which the president disagreed. President Bush's signing statement policy of ignoring what he views as unconstitutional provisions is nothing more than a reflection of his oath to see that the laws are faithfully executed, pursuant to which the Constitution always supersedes a statute—for all three branches of government. Prudentially, of course, the president has to have a high degree of certainty about constitutionality, higher than the other two branches, but this factor does not negate his oath to uphold the Constitution. And even in this context, the president can rarely act unilaterally in any event. Every president, while enforcing the law, has the right to inquire as to the wisdom of any legislation and seek revision or repeal of legislation deemed unwise. However, as for example, the War Powers Resolution, which presidents have deemed unconstitutional, it remains on the statute books and presidents go through the motions of seeking to comply.

In the domestic arena, Lind charges that President Bush created "a new instrument of arbitrary presidential power" called the "czar," and calls this action "entirely alien to the American constitutional system." He also chastises Bush for making his vice-president, Dan Quayle, a czar in the Council on Competitiveness. It is perhaps a compliment that any vice-president—the occupant of the weakest political office in the American political system—could be considered a "czar" of anything.

Actually, the term "czar" was coined to emphasize the urgent need to combat the drug problem. Moreover, the drug czar is a statutory office *set up by Congress itself* to compensate for its own hopeless fragmentation of responsibility among 50 or more committees and subcommittees.

Lind charges that the Republican's newly won control of Congress is contributing to a new imperial presidency. He asserts that "having captured Congress [in 1994] after a half century, the Republicans are hastening to give away the powers of the branch they control." He cites their advocacy of the line-item veto and term limits. These are not advocacies only of Republicans, however. True, the line-item veto was a favorite of Reagan, but it has also been advocated by Democrats, as has congressional term limits.

Mr. Lind laments the large executive branch staffs in the American system. These staffs, however, grow out of weakness rather than strength, as the president seeks to respond to the pressures of both the Congress and the courts as they relate to presidential proposals and programs. It is Congress that often creates executive agencies as it did the National Security Council, Council of Economic Advisers, and Bureau of the Budget, the latter restructured as the Office of Management and Budget. Nor should it be forgotten that the strength of the judicial system in our three-part government causes the executive departments as well as the president and vice-president to appoint large numbers of government counsels to see how far they can go in testing the limits of our checks-and-balances system. Finally, the enormous growth of entitlements since the beginning of the Social Security system in 1935, and the social sensitivity that is aroused whenever there are proposals for reductions, indicates that it is the public, not the presidents, which has demanded the growth in government. In this connection, let us not forget that President and Mrs. Clinton's efforts to revise the health care system were completely defeated when it became known that the public opposed the plan.

Lind laments, in particular, the growth of the White House staff, but much of that growth, it should be noted, was a reaction to the growth of the congressional staff. By creating its own budget office, the Congress challenged the White House Office of Management and Budget to further growth in order to address the questions posed to it by the Congressional Budget Office. Further, ever since the Senate Watergate Hearings in 1973–74, the Congress has continued to increase its oversight activity. In 1961, only 8.2 percent of congressional committee hearings and meetings related to oversight of the executive branch. Between 1961 and 1983, however, oversight activity rose 207.3 percent. Currently, there is a record amount of congressional oversight in all areas of public policy. Congressional efforts to micromanage both foreign and domestic policy causes increase in all executive branch staffs as they constantly seek to respond to questions and defend executive positions.

III.

Lind concludes that "like a black hole, the presidency grows by absorbing ever more power and light." What this comparison overlooks, however, is that the policy-making machinery in our government has for a long time been characterized by "iron triangles" or, if you will, subgovernments consisting of three key actors that together comprise a powerful policy-making machine. One part of the triangle are the special interest lobbyists, the second are the members of Congress located in the congressional subcommittees, and the third are the federal bureaucrats working within the myriad administrative agencies in the executive branch of government. Whether it is in agriculture, defense policy, education, labor, veterans affairs, or whatever, as Hedrick Smith has written, "The object of the Iron Triangle is a closed power game," and they are often arrayed against the president. Lind denies this, asserting that "Presidentialists build up the legitimacy of the presidency by grossly exaggerating the faults of Congress and the parts of the executive branch that the White House does not directly control, such as the civil service and the independent agencies." In point of fact, Lind makes no reference to the reality of these "iron triangles."

Lind perceives in any presidential reforms a scheme to grab power. He does so even with President Carter's proposal to enhance the civil service by the addition at the top of the Executive Service Corps. Lind finds in this a scheme to tie the civil service more closely to the presidency. Given the influence of the iron triangles, any president is to be applauded for his efforts to more effectively relate the civil service to the presidency.

In the final analysis, there is a need for a strong and vigorous presidency. This was so very well set forth by Alexander Hamilton on March 15, 1788, during the period when the ratification of the Constitution was being debated. In *Federalist* 70 he wrote, "Energy in the executive is a leading character in the definition of good government. It is essential to the protection of the community against foreign attacks. It is not less essential to the steady administration of the laws. . . ." Hamilton concluded, "The ingredients, which constitute energy in the executive, are first unity, secondly duration, thirdly an adequate provision for this support, fourthly competent powers." In *Federalist 69,* in 1788, Hamilton made clear that there is nothing imperial in the presidency as created by the Constitution and in 70 he points to the fallacy that vigor in the executive "is inconsistent with the genius of republican government." To the contrary, Hamilton states "a feeble executive" is a source of "bad government." In *Federalist 71,* Hamilton goes further and warns of "the tendency of the legislative authority to absorb every other." He adds, "The representatives of the people, in a popular assembly seem sometimes to fancy that they are the people themselves." That is what Lind would invite with his call for congressional democracy.

True, strong presidents, including Jackson and the two Roosevelts, have viewed themselves as the tribune of the people—a formulation denounced by Lind as a "plebiscitary presidency" (i.e., representing the will of the whole people). But that is precisely what the two Roosevelts stated they were doing: Theodore representing the people against the powerful moneyed interests, the railroads, monopolies, the trusts; and Franklin in combating unemployment, lack of social security, and in defense of the nation. Quite unfairly, Lind describes presidents as elective monarchs, and presidential libraries as symbols of royalism. Quite the contrary, it is not a question of monarchy, but a matter of leadership. In a dangerous world, bold leadership is required, and that leadership, thrust upon the United States more than a half-century ago, must, of necessity, be exercised by the president. As for presidential libraries, they are not symbols of royalism, but rather valuable depositories of our historical heritage.

So far as the separation of powers is concerned, we would do well to recall Madison in *Federalist 47*. Therein he contended that the Constitution set forth not so much a *separation* as it did a *sharing* of powers, asserting that "the legislative, executive, judiciary departments are by no means totally separate and distinct from each other." He perceived not so much a struggle as, by necessity, a working together of Congress and the presidency. Former Senator Nancy Landon Kassebaum (R-Kansas) likened it to two people in a three-legged race: "If one balks the other trips." What is needed is more coming together of the Congress and the presidency, not a shutdown of government as the Congress caused in 1996 over the budget. Bipartisan consensus with the president peaked at nearly 70 percent during the two terms of Eisenhower, and unfortunately, steadily went down thereafter, reaching a low point in 1995–96. Far from Lind's contention that we have been moving into "a full-fledged presidential state," we have been moving into a congressional state. What we have seen from the Nixon presidency to the present is a constantly more constrained and impeded presidency. Contrary to Lind's view we are *not* witnessing an imperial presidency. Rather we are witnessing a presidency more and more in a state of siege, and a Congress more and more unwilling to work with the president. A balance must be restored. One can only hope that the budget agreement that, as of this writing (spring 1997), appears to have been reached between Congress and the Clinton administration, signals an effort to restore that balance.

Lind concludes with a quote from Benjamin Franklin about our executive becoming a monarch. There is another quote, however, that Lind might have recalled. When asked after the Constitutional Convention what kind of government had been created, Franklin replied, "a Republic if you can keep it." We have kept it, and will continue to do so.

12

THE PRESIDENT AND CONGRESS

If the critical problems facing our nation are to be addressed in a timely and effective way, cooperation between the president and the Congress is essential. For this reason, the relationship between these two branches is arguably the most important institutional relationship in our government.

The Founding Fathers, of course, fully expected that the division of power in our national government would create conflict between the executive and legislative branches. Indeed, they welcomed it, believing that interbranch rivalry would help prevent government from becoming too powerful. But has this relationship grown too confrontational in recent years, and if so, with what effects? Each of the following three selections offers a different perspective on this much discussed question.

In the first selection, political scientist James Sundquist insists that the relationship is in serious trouble and lays the blame at the doorstep of divided government. Specifically, for most of the time between 1956 and 1992, the presidency has been controlled by one party (Republicans) and Congress by the other (Democrats); and, of course, between 1992 and 1999, Democrats held the White House and Republicans controlled Congress for most of these years. Consequently, the constitutional tension which normally exists between the two branches has been compounded by partisanship. According to Sundquist, this state of affairs has had an impact on the government's capacity to act and to administer the laws and has affected as well the public's ability to hold government accountable. The remedy, he insists, lies in instituting reforms that are designed to reduce the occurrence of divided government.

A rather different view comes from David Mayhew, also a political scientist. In the second article, he contends that a careful review of the hard evidence, namely, the legislative output of Congress over a 44-year period, does not support the claim that divided government equals stalemated government.

In the final selection, political columnist David Broder approaches the relationship between the president and Congress from a somewhat broader perspective. While not disputing the fact that divided government has complicated the task of governing, he maintains that government's ability to produce timely and coherent policies has become more difficult even when the president and Congress are controlled by the same party. The reasons for this are traceable to the weakened state of our political institutions—notably, political parties, the presidency, and Congress—and also to the attitudes of the American people.

A Government Divided against Itself

James L. Sundquist

Public esteem for Congress has hit a record low, the polls tell us. Popular approval of the president is . . . low . . ., too. More than half of the voters [in 1992] [told] poll takers that they would like the chance to vote for somebody other than the candidates the presidential selection process [gave] us—witness the groundswell of public support for Ross Perot. Fewer voters than in previous years . . . bothered to vote in the Republican and Democratic primaries. Disillusionment, apathy, and cynicism dominate the public mood.

Why? Because it is clear to just about everyone that the government of the United States simply is not working. The budget deficit remains out of control. The national debt has reached $4 trillion—four times what it was barely a decade ago. . . . [U]nemployment [is at a level] that would not have been tolerated in the past. . . . The poverty, squalor, and lack of opportunity for millions in our inner cities, now so vividly illuminated by the violence in Los Angeles, have been plainly visible all along, but have been ignored. [In 1992] more than 30 million people lack[ed] health insurance. . . .

Individual voters, frustrated because they see no ready solution to failing and gridlocked government, look for scapegoats. They want to "throw the rascals out" of Congress and limit the terms of their replacements, or they chase after so chimerical a source of salvation as Ross Perot.

But there is something all citizens can do—or, rather, stop doing—to help make the governmental system work. They can stop splitting their tickets in presidential elections, putting one party in control of the executive branch and the opposing party in control of Congress.

Divided government is a new phenomenon in American political life. Until the mid-20th century, the norm was a government in which the president and the majorities in Congress were of the same political faith. Indeed, from 1884 to 1956, in 17 successive elections, not once did the voters force their newly chosen president to contend with an opposition majority in either chamber of the Congress.

But with the second election of president Eisenhower in 1956, the long era of unified party government gave way to the current era of divided government. Since 1956 the country has had Republican presidents 68 per cent of the time; since 1968, 83 percent of the time. During those years, the Democrats have controlled the House all of the time and the Senate for all but six years. [Since 1994, Republicans have held both houses—Editors]

Scholars of politics have been slow to recognize that, in times of divided government, fundamental tenets of their discipline are rendered obsolete. During the long period of unified party government, it became a settled doctrine of political science that

James L. Sundquist is senior fellow emeritus at The Brookings Institution, a government and public policy research organization in Washington, D.C. From James L. Sundquist, "A Government Divided against Itself," the Chronicle of Higher Education, *June 24, 1992, B1–2. Reprinted with permission of the author.*

the political party was the indispensable instrument that brought together the institutions of government that the Founding Fathers had so carefully separated. In a variety of metaphors, the political party was extolled as the bridge across the constitutional chasm, the web that unites the separated branches, the tie that binds.

A corollary to the doctrine of party government was that of presidential leadership: No government could be dynamic without a leader. And the logical point of leadership was the head of the governing party, the leader of the legislative as well as the executive branch.

But the party cannot be the tie that binds the branches unless it controls them both, nor can the president lead the entire government when the Senate or the House or both are controlled by the opposing party. . . .

Does divided government create stalemate in the legislative process? Do policy differences between the branches lead to incoherence and breakdown in the administration of the laws? Does the conflict growing out of partisan division of government undermine public confidence in governmental institutions and their leaders? Does divided government destroy the accountability that is essential for democratic control of government by voters?

Not all political scientists now writing on the subject will agree, but to me the answers to all four questions are affirmative. The problems constitute a four-point indictment of divided government as a model for our third century of national life and argue for a return to the unified party government that prevailed through most of our history.

How does divided government affect the legislative process? For anything constructive to happen when government is divided, the Democrats who control the House and the Senate must reach agreement with the Republican president. Such agreement is always arduous and at times impossible. People divide into parties, after all, because they disagree in fundamental ways about what government should do, for whom, and how. The clash of opposing philosophies and program ideas—with the voters as arbiters—is what gives government its spirit and its meaning.

When the government is divided between the parties, that normal and healthy debate is transformed into conflict between the branches of government themselves. The president vetoes congressional proposals; the Congress labels his recommendations "dead on arrival." It is at such times that the Congress is "stymied by relentless . . . maneuvering for short-term political advantage," as Democratic Sen. Timothy E. Wirth of Colorado put it when in "anger and frustration" he announced his retirement in April.

The political scientists Allen Schick and Matthew McCubbins, among others, have convincingly blamed divided government for the decade-long impasse on fiscal policy that created the current $400 billion deficit and $4 trillion national debt. Republicans in full control of the government would have reduced the deficit by further cutting domestic spending; Democrats would have decreased it by raising taxes. With government divided, each party had the power to thwart the other's program but not enough to enact and carry out its own. The country got the spending without the taxes.

This year [1992], each party had at least something of a program designed to speed the nation's recovery from recession. Reflecting the differences in party philosophies, programs, and sources of support, the Republican proposal featured the capital-gains tax cut sought by the financial community, while the Democrats offered a tax cut designed to favor (although it was not necessarily sought by) the middle class. The president's program was rejected out of hand by the Congress, and Congress's program, in turn, was killed by a presidential veto. Either plan, presumably, might have been better than nothing at all.

Does divided government lead to inefficient administration? When government is unified, the congressional majorities are more willing to delegate to administrators the flexibility and discretion they require to execute the laws, because they are delegating power to an executive branch headed by their own party leader, the president. In a divided government, in contrast, delegations of authority go to administrators of the opposing political faith, who are intent on steering the course of government in their direction, rather than in the legislators'. Thus, the power to enforce laws written by the Democrats to protect the environment or consumers or workers' safety or opportunity for members of minority groups is in the hands of Republican officials who may be less than fully sympathetic to the Democratic policies.

Inevitably, legislators try to tighten their control of administration by withholding discretion and writing detailed prescriptions into law, often to the point of unworkability. Congressional staffs multiply for the purpose of supervising administration. Administrators, in turn, complain of meddling and "micromanagement," of being torn between conflicting directives from their White House and Capitol Hill supervisors, and of administrative paralysis when the two branches cannot reconcile their partisan differences.

What does divided government do to public confidence? As the partisan debate turns into a feud between the branches, not only does Washington appear impotent to solve the nation's problems, but its affairs are conducted in an atmosphere of conflict and rancor. The president condemns Congress as being run by spendthrifts and wastrels, tainted with corruption. Legislators, in turn, denounce him as incompetent, lacking in vision and in compassion. In time, the evidence suggests, the people come to believe both sides.

Lastly, *what is the impact of divided government on accountability to the public?* Divided government lends itself to passing the buck and avoiding blame. In the days of unified party government, a president and his party won, for at least two years and usually for four, the power to carry out the policies for which they had received their mandate. At the end of four years, the party in power was accountable to the electorate. If it had satisfied the voters' expectations, it was returned to office. If it had failed, it was turned out and the opposing party given the reins of government. But now, when the government fails, the president heaps the blame upon the Congress—as we [could] see in [the 1992] campaign—while the Democrats cry that the fault is his. How can the voters hold anybody responsible for the massive deficits and debt or the savings-and-loan debacle or the plight of cities like Los Angeles, when in fact nobody has been?

Divided government is caused, of course, by voters' splitting the ticket. Scholars, like the political scientist Gary Jacobson, suggest that ticket splitting will continue because people use different criteria in selecting among candidates for different offices: They look to presidents to handle large national problems, such as foreign crises and economic policy, and they have greater trust for Republicans in those areas. They expect Congress to look after matters affecting local constituencies, and they find the Democrats more effective there. Some people have put it more crudely: The voters elect Democrats to Congress to enact spending programs, then put a Republican in the White House to make sure they won't have to pay for them.

Ticket splitting could be prohibited only by constitutional amendment. Voters could be required to select among party "team tickets" that included their candidates not just for president and vice-president, but also for the Senate and the House of Representatives. Clearly, no such amendment would ever be considered by Congress, for what legislator would want to risk being dragged to defeat by an unpopular presidential candidate? Nor would the public at large ever consent to such a limitation on its freedom of choice.

The Committee on the Constitutional System, made up of former Congressmen, high executive-branch officials, and other elder statesmen, has recommended that each state give its voters the option of voting a straight ticket by making a single mark on the ballot or by pulling a single lever on the voting machine. But some states already do so, and the proportion of ticket splitters is not significantly reduced.

Lloyd Cutler, co-chairman of the committee, has advocated sequential elections, with the congressional choices to be made two or three weeks after the presidential balloting. Knowing who would be inaugurated president, the voters might heed his or her plea to send to Congress a majority of the same party. But perhaps, because of their distrust of past leaders, they would react in opposite fashion, deliberately electing to Congress members of the opposing party to restrain the president.

In the absence of a constitutional amendment, scholars, policy makers, and in fact anyone who would like to see a more harmonious, cohesive, and hence more effective government (or at least more accountable government) can only exhort the voters: If you want [a Republican] as president and want him to succeed in his purposes, then give him a Republican Congress to support him. Or, if you prefer the policies and legislative potential of a Democratic Congress, give it a Democratic president who will lead it and sign its bills.

Divided Party Control:
Does It Make a Difference?

David R. Mayhew

Since World War II, party control of the U.S. national government has been formally divided for 26 years and unified for 18. (That is the span between the elections of 1946 and 1990.) Truman, Eisenhower, Nixon, Ford, Reagan, and Bush have had to coexist—for at least a two-year stretch in each case—with opposite-party majorities in the Senate or House or both. Truman, Eisenhower, Kennedy, Johnson, and Carter have had—again, for at least a two-year stretch—House and Senate majorities of their own party.

In other respects bearing on relations between the president and Congress, this postwar era shows a high degree of continuity or commonality stemming from events or precedents of the 1930s and 1940s. The New Deal and the war ratcheted the government to new levels of activity, and Franklin Roosevelt permanently strengthened the presidency. The La Follette-Monroney Act of 1946 streamlined the congressional committee system. Soon after the war the government took on new commitments in defense, foreign policy, and macroeconomic management that are with us still. Truman developed the custom of presenting "the president's program" to Congress each year. Televising of major congressional investigations began in 1948 with HUAC's [House Un-American Activities Committee's] probe of Alger Hiss.

The postwar era presents, then, a checkered pattern of unified-versus-divided party control set against a background of commonalities. That makes 1946–90 a good span of experience to look into if one wants to track the consequences of unified party control against divided party control, with at least one congressional house organized by the party not holding the White House. How well any generalizations based on 1946–90 would hold for previous eras in American history is not clear, though they might well hold for the near future.

. . . I have tried to find out how well two pieces of conventional wisdom about party control stand up against the experience of 1946–90.[1] The first conventional view is: *Congressional committees, acting as oversight bodies, will give more trouble to administrations run by the opposite party than to those of their own party.*[2] The second view, which comes close to being an axiom of political science, is: *Major laws will pass more frequently under unified party control than under divided control.*[3] A party that controls the House, the Senate, and the presidency, the logic goes, can put through a program. Absent such party control, legislative "deadlock" or "stalemate" will set in. In Woodrow Wilson's words, "You cannot compound a successful government out of antagonisms."[4]

David R. Mayhew is Alfred Cowles Professor of Government at Yale University. From David R. Mayhew, "Divided Party Control: Does It Make a Difference?" P.S.: Political Science and Politics 24 (December 1991), pp. 637–40. Reprinted by permission of the American Political Science Association. The author's references have been adjusted to conform to endnote style of presentation—Editors.

My conclusion is that both assertions are false—or at least largely or probably false. (I hedge because I use evidence that requires many individual judgments that can be disputed.) On balance, neither the "beat up on the other party's administration" effect nor the "divided control causes deadlock" effect makes a significant showing in the political record of 1946–90.

HIGH-PUBLICITY INVESTIGATIONS

The evidence on oversight is for a particular variety of that activity—congressional investigations that deal with alleged executive misbehavior and draw media attention. Included are such amply reported enterprises as HUAC's Hiss-Chambers probe of 1948, Senator McCarran's investigation of China policy in 1951–52, Senator McCarthy's Army and State Department hearings of 1953–54, the House probe of corruption in the regulatory agencies in 1958, Senator Fulbright's hearings on the Indochina war during 1966–70, the Senate and House Watergate inquiries of 1973–74, and the Iran-Contra investigations of 1987.

"Misbehavior" here means anything from treason or usurpation through corruption to simply making mistakes. The charges could be true, partly true, or fantasy. The target could be any present or past executive official or agency. An investigation made it onto a final list if it inspired front-page stories in the *New York Times* on at least 20 days. For any day, the test for content was whether anyone connected with a congressional committee made a charge against the executive branch, or someone in the executive branch answered such a charge.

Thirty-one investigations between 1946 and 1990 made the list. First prize went to the McCarthy hearings of 1953–54, which generated front-page stories on 203 days. The Senate and House Watergate inquiries ranked second and third. The results do not sort in any remarkable way according to divided versus unified party control. Probes of corruption split about equally between times of unified and divided control; it is a good bet that the ones conducted by Democratic Congresses against the Truman administration caused the most damage politically.[5] The Watergate inquiries, which occurred under divided control, may deserve a status all their own. Still, for overall significance it is hard to surpass the loyalty investigations of 1948 through 1954, and notwithstanding the 1948 Hiss probe, those occurred mostly under unified control. . . .

For 1946–90, at least, there is not a convincing case that Congress increases its high-publicity probes of the executive branch during times of divided party loyalty.

IMPORTANT LAWS

The evidence here is a list of 267 major statutes enacted between 1947 and 1990—ranging from the Taft-Hartley Labor-Management Relations Act and Marshall Plan of 1947–48 through the Clean Air Act and Americans with Disabilities Act of 1990. The 267 items are the product of two sweeps through the 44-year history. Sweep One picked up enactments that observers of the Washington scene judged (according to my coding)

to be particularly important at the times the laws passed. Those observers were journalists who wrote "wrapup stories" at the close of each congressional session, or other
witnesses whose appraisals have been relayed or embodied in secondary works. Sweep
Two picked up enactments that policy specialists, writing recently in 43 policy areas,
have indicated to be particularly important in discussing the postwar histories of their
areas. "Important" in these contexts means both innovative and consequential—or at
least expected at the time of passage to be consequential.

As expected, Johnson's Great Society Congress of 1965–66 emerges in first place (or
at least in a tie for it) with 22 major laws—Medicare, the Voting Rights Act (VRA), the
Elementary and Secondary Education Act (ESEA) and many others. Eisenhower's last
Democratic Congress of 1959–60, which ended in classic deadlock, finishes in last place
with five enactments. Taken alone, these reports ratify the triumph-of-party-government
story that Sundquist wrote concerning the mid-1950s through the mid-1960s.[6]

But precious little else during these decades follows that "party government"
script. On average, about as many major laws passed per Congress under divided control as under unified control. In several policy areas where specialists' judgments come
through clearly—for example, foreign aid, foreign trade, immigration, agriculture, and
tax reform—sets of key enactments became law in time patterns unrelated to conditions
of party control. For example, the three post-1950 "major expansions" of Social Security occurred with disability insurance in 1956 (divided control), Medicare in 1965 (unified), and a "quantum increase" in cash benefits in 1969–72 (divided).[7] Otherwise, several notable statutes emerged from Congress and won out over presidential vetoes—for
example (besides the Taft-Hartley Act), the McCarran Internal Security Act of 1950, the
McCarran-Walter Immigration Act of 1952, the Water Pollution Control Act of 1972,
the War Powers Act of 1973, and South Africa sanctions in 1986. The "do-nothing"-
ness of Truman's Republican Congress of 1947–48 was largely Democratic propaganda; policy specialists point back, for example, to the precedent-setting Federal
Insecticide, Fungicide, and Rodenticide Act (FIFRA) of 1947 and the Water Pollution
Control Act of 1948. Under Reagan and Bush, the last few years . . . featured, for example, the Tax Reform Act of 1986, Speaker Jim Wright's considerable program of
1987–88, and Bush's controversial $500 billion budget-reduction package of 1990.

At the level of ambitious presidential programs, Johnson succeeded memorably in
1964 through 1966 with a Congress of his own party, but so did Reagan in 1981 despite
having to deal with a House of the opposite party. Truman's Fair Deal and Kennedy's
New Frontier largely failed as legislative enterprises, despite the availability of Congresses of the same party. Carter's years proved a washout for his party's lawmaking
aspirations, despite sizable Democratic House and Senate majorities of 292–143 and
62–38 during 1977–78. On the only occasion since 1840 when a party took over the
House, Senate, and presidency all at once—in 1952 when the Republicans did—that
party turned out not to have much of a program to enact. As a result, virtually no laws
of importance passed in the seemingly favorable circumstances of 1953, though Eisenhower won some victories later.

The real story of these decades is the prominent, continuous lawmaking surge that
lasted from late 1963 through 1975 or 1976. That was under Johnson, Nixon, and Ford.

Whether one looks at legislative workload in general[8] or major laws passed,[9] it was during that span of years—or roughly that span; assessments of boundaries differ a bit—that the postwar legislative mill operated at full steam. Everyone knows that happened under Johnson, but the Vietnam war, wrangling over "social issues," and Watergate have clouded our picture of legislating under Nixon and Ford. In fact, the state-enhancing thrust of the 1960s toward greater expenditure and regulation continued with great force in the 1970s. Budget growth owed to Johnson's Great Society programs, but also to post-1968 legislative initiatives in the areas of, for example, food stamps, Supplementary Security Income (SSI), CETA [Comprehensive Employment and Training Act] jobs, unemployment compensation, housing block grants, mass transit, and water pollution, as well as Social Security benefits.[10] The "new social regulation," to use Vogel's term,[11] came to pass largely by statute under Nixon.[12] That featured, to cite some highlights, the National Environmental Policy Act (NEPA) of 1969, the Occupational Safety and Health Act (OSHA) of 1970, the Clean Air Act of 1970, the Equal Employment Opportunity Act of 1972, and the Consumer Product Safety Act of 1972. Campaign finance and private pensions came under comprehensive regulation for the first time through laws enacted in 1974. Statutory regulation of state governments reached new heights under Nixon.[13] The Equal Rights Amendment (ERA) cleared Congress in 1972, though the states would not buy it.[14] These and many other items from the Nixon-Ford years are probably familiar to readers, but I do not think we have appreciated their volume or sifted them through our doctrines about party control and legislative action. In terms of volume and also ideological direction of lawmaking, there arguably existed an era of Johnson-Nixon (or Johnson-Nixon-Ford), and it overlapped different circumstances of party control.

Since World War II, to sum up, neither high-publicity investigations nor major laws have accumulated on a schedule that the rules of party control would predict. Why not? That is too complicated a question to tackle here. The material cited above makes it obvious that no simple arithmetic theory involving Democratic presidents and sizes of cross-party "conservative coalitions" on Capitol Hill can work very well. If that were the key factor, why all the lawmaking under Nixon? Why the slump under Carter? Evidently, speculation about causes needs to center on features of the modern U.S. regime that dominate, override, or blot out parties to a greater degree than we may have supposed. Some good candidates for that role seem to be Capitol Hill electoral incentives that foster lawmaking and investigating, presidential leadership qualities that operate more or less independently of party, the practical need for non-narrow roll-call majorities to pass laws regardless of conditions of party control, forcing public events, public opinion cleavages that crosscut parties, and "public moods" like that of 1963–76 that seem capable of overriding everything else.[15]

NOTES

1. David R. Mayhew, *Divided We Govern: Party Control, Lawmaking, and Investigations, 1946–1990* (New Haven, CT: Yale University Press, 1991).

2. Morris S. Ogul, *Congress Oversees the Bureaucracy: Studies in Legislative Supervision* (Pittsburgh: University of Pittsburgh Press, 1976), p. 18; Seymour Scher, "Conditions for Legislative Control," *Journal of Politics* 25 (1963), 526–51.

3. James L. Sundquist, "Needed: A Political Theory for the New Era of Coalition Government in the United States," *Political Science Quarterly* 103 (1988–89), 616–24; V. O. Key, Jr., *Politics, Parties, and Pressure Groups,* 5th ed. (New York: Crowell, 1964), pp. 656, 687–88; Randall B. Ripley, *Congress: Process and Policy* (New York: W. W. Norton, 1983), pp. 347–56; Lloyd N. Cutler, "Some Reflections About Divided Government," *Presidential Studies Quarterly* 18 (1988), 485–92.

4. Quoted in James L. Sundquist, "Needed: A Political Theory for the New Era of Coalition Government in the United States," p. 618.

5. Andrew J. Dunar, *The Truman Scandals and the Politics of Morality* (Columbia: University of Missouri Press, 1984).

6. James L. Sundquist, *Politics and Policy: The Eisenhower, Kennedy and Johnson Years* (Washington, DC: Brookings, 1968).

7. Martha Derthick, *Policymaking for Social Security* (Washington, DC: Brookings, 1979), p. 296.

8. Roger H. Davidson, "The New Centralization on Capitol Hill," *Review of Politics* 50 (1988), 345–64.

9. David R. Mayhew, *Divided We Govern: Party Control, Lawmaking, and Investigations, 1946–1990,* ch. 4.

10. Robert J. Lampman, *Social Welfare Spending: Accounting for Changes from 1950 to 1978* (New York: Academic Press, 1984), pp. 8–9; Timothy Conlan, *New Federalism: Intergovernmental Reform from Nixon to Reagan* (Washington, DC: Brookings, 1985), p. 81; Robert X. Browning, *Politics and Social Welfare Policy in the United States* (Knoxville: University of Tennessee Press, 1986), pp. 79–83; David R. Mayhew, *Divided We Govern: Party Control, Lawmaking, and Investigations, 1946–1990,* ch. 4.

11. David Vogel, "The 'New' Social Regulation in Historical and Comparative Perspective," in Thomas K. McCraw (ed.), *Regulation in Perspective: Historical Essays* (Cambridge, MA: Harvard University Press, 1981).

12. See also Murray L. Weidenbaum, *Business, Government, and the Public* (Englewood Cliffs, NJ: Prentice-Hall, 1977), pp. 5–10; Robert Higgs, *Crisis and Leviathan: Critical Episodes in the Growth of American Government* (New York: Oxford University Press, 1987), pp. 246–54.

13. Timothy Conlan, *New Federalism: Intergovernmental Reform from Nixon to Reagan,* pp. 84–89.

14. Jo Freeman, *The Politics of Women's Liberation* (New York: David McKay, 1975), ch. 6.

15. David R. Mayhew, *Divided We Govern: Party Control, Lawmaking, and Investigations, 1946–1990,* chs. 5, 6.

Gridlock Begins at Home:
How We Build Political Failure into the System
David S. Broder

. . . Governments in democratic societies around the globe are notably weak these days [1994]. From the struggling Hosokawa regime in Japan, through the just-resigned Italian government, embattled Balladur in France and Kohl in Germany, to Major in Great Britain and Chretien in Canada, leaders are struggling to maintain enough political traction to advance their agendas.

More than a year ago, Bill Brock, the former senator from Tennessee, secretary of labor and special trade representative, linked the phenomenon to the revolutionary economic changes sweeping the world: The virtual erasure of national boundaries to the flow of capital and the location of manufacturing and service facilities were lessening the ability of governments to control their national economies. Left of center or right of center, regimes of all kinds are finding it nearly impossible to enact and carry through policies that will cushion the shock waves of this economic transformation. Even if the policies are correct—and often they are not—another election is upon them before leaders can demonstrate they are on the right path.

Brock's analysis also applies to the United States, where George Bush struggled and failed and now Bill Clinton is being buffeted by forces he finds hard to tame. But beyond those elemental forces, there are additional factors in this country that have made the task of governing far more difficult than it used to be.

The weakened condition of our three principal governing institutions—parties, Congress and the presidency—has damaged the capacity of our system to develop and sustain coherent policy. And their weakness has fed the growth in power of two other sets of institutions—interest groups and the press—that, whatever their utility in other respects, are notably ill-equipped to develop national consensus.

The decline of political parties, which have supplied the necessary connective tissue between executive and legislative authority since the first decades of the American republic, is a familiar tale. It reflects, among other things, the suburbanization of America and the emergence of television as a principal means of communication. But the weakness comes into focus at a time when both elected branches of the national government are nominally controlled by the same party—and still the president must struggle to advance an agenda.

The opposition to [the North American Free Trade Agreement] [was] led by the Democratic majority leader and majority whip of the House. Two of the top three Democrats in the Senate also [opposed] him. He [put] forward a high-priority health care plan, only to find it sandwiched between competing plans advanced by other

David S. Broder is a syndicated columnist with the Washington Post *and a former member of the governing council of the American Political Science Association. From David S. Broder, "Gridlock Begins at Home," the* Washington Post, *January 23, 1994, p. C1. © 1994, The Washington Post Writers Group. Reprinted with permission.*

groups of Democrats. (The Republicans, no better off, [advanced] at least four health plans.)

The reality is that we do not have two parties in Washington. We have 536. The president, the 100 senators and the 435 representatives are each a political party of one. Every one of them picked out the particular office he or she wanted, raised the campaign funds, hired the pollster, the media adviser, the consultants, recruited the volunteers, chose the issues—and ran as if it were the only office on the ballot. Once in office, they quickly discovered that governing is a lot tougher than campaigning, that without genuine bonds of party loyalty, coalitions are hard to build.

Like his predecessors, Clinton found that dealing with members of Congress was often tougher than negotiating with heads of other sovereign states. The president soon found himself trying to cut deals with people who operate in a ruthlessly self-interested fashion. The classic case, perhaps, came when Sen. Herbert Kohl (D-Wis.), a multimillionaire who paid for his own campaign, informed the president of the United States that the ceiling on a gas tax increase was precisely 4.3 cents. Because Kohl was a potential swing vote, Clinton had to accept.

That was just one of many "deals" that permitted the president to pass a budget [in 1994] by a single vote in the House and by Vice President Gore's tie-breaking vote in the Senate. NAFTA and other issues brought on more such bargaining. While Clinton won more often than he lost on final passage, the bargaining process too often involved the sacrifice of important national goals—like a rational energy policy, for example.

And it also cost government some of its moral authority, for the public generally reacted with revulsion to the spectacle of this crude bargaining, not realizing that it is the inevitable byproduct of a system in which every office-seeker and officeholder constitutes his or her own party.

The weakening of the presidency is the result of many forces, including party-splintering. The growth of government programs has sapped the president's ability to manage anything. Too many people beyond his reach—federal bureaucrats and even more state and local officials spending federal dollars—do the day-to-day work of governing for which he is in theory accountable. This president has struggled even to manage his own White House staff. . . .

A series of credibility crises has weakened Americans' trust in their presidents, from Lyndon Johnson and Vietnam to George Bush on Iran-contra, Iraqgate and "Read my lips, no new taxes." Clinton has added to the list, with everything from his excuses for missing military service to the special prosecutor on Whitewater.

But this president, unlike several of his predecessors, has an activist agenda; [in 1994] alone, he hopes to restructure three basic social programs—education, welfare and health care.

Historically, major changes in domestic policy have occurred only under special circumstances, either when the country was deep in a recognized crisis (the Great Depression setting the stage for the New Deal) or when a president has just won a landslide election victory (Lyndon Johnson and the Great Society of 1965 or Ronald Reagan and the tax-and-budget revolution of 1981).

Neither of these fit Clinton's situation today. The doubts he raised in the campaign limited his victory to a modest plurality of 43 percent, which in turn has reduced his political clout in the hand-to-hand combat with the leaders of the other 535 parties in Washington. Even as the economic recovery bolsters him, his repeated imbroglios, personal and political, drag him back down.

If the parties are weak and the presidency is weak, then *what word applies to Congress and its reputation?* The lawmakers have long been the butt of jokes, but the *contempt* in which they are held these days bespeaks something darker and more sinister. An NBC-Wall Street Journal poll [in December 1993] found only 3 of 10 respondents expressing approval of the national legislature.

The effect of this on the legislators can be measured in several ways. They are bailing out in record numbers. In 1992, 65 House members retired from Congress; the early pace suggests the numbers may be even higher [in 1994]. Many are relative youngsters like Rep. Tim Penney (D-Minn.), 42, who said that he had been worn down after seven years by frustration with a Congress "that is constantly fragmented and seldom gets anything done."

For those who stay behind, the public mood feeds serious anxiety attacks. Members of the largest freshman class in almost half a century face with dread the prospect of running for the first time with the awful label "incumbent" attached to their names. Even upperclassmen weigh and measure each vote for the hidden time bomb it may contain, seeking constant reassurance that an opponent will not zap them with a 30-second spot for their vote or that a single slip will not be fanned into white-hot flames by the talk-show network. A House member who came to Congress a quarter-century ago says, "I have never served with more chickens than there are today. They don't want to cast *any* tough votes."

Politics abhors a power vacuum. *The authority that has been lost by the legitimate organs of government—parties, presidents and legislators—flows elsewhere. In this country, much of it has been taken over by interest groups,* which claim to "represent" their members in ways that elected officials and politicians can't or won't.

I do not take a purist view of "special interests" or their financial and political clout. In a diverse, pluralistic society like ours, representation has to go beyond the mere act of voting on Election Day.

But there is a question of proportion. When scores of House members receive more than half their campaign funds from PACs, the balance has shifted in ways that make it virtually impossible for any issue to be considered on its merits. Health care provides the classic case. The White House has logged into its computers the names of more than 1,100 interest groups with substantial stakes in the health care battle. Framing national policy is difficult enough in an arena with 536 separate political parties. When the concurrence or acquiescence of more than twice that number of interest groups also must be obtained, the task of forging a governing consensus becomes nigh impossible.

The other recipient of the power that has flowed out of the governing institutions is the press. Willy-nilly, much of the agenda-setting that was done by political parties and elected officials in times past has drifted into the hands of news organizations.

We are ill-equipped for the job. Reporters are instinctively fight promoters. Consensus-building is not our forte—or our job. Launching and carrying through public policy requires sustained effort. The press in all its forms is episodic. We flit from topic to topic. We hate repetition. Our attitude toward institutions is cavalier. All this hobbles our ability to substitute for political leadership—even if we had any claim to do so, which we do not.

Does this mean that governing is impossible? No, but it is increasingly difficult. This is not to make alibis for President Clinton. He promised national leadership, and it is up to him to deliver. But we ought to be honest and say that the decayed condition of our vital institutions makes the odds against his—or any president's—success pretty daunting.

And we might acknowledge one other fact—our own complicity in these problems. Weak as our governing institutions may be, they have not lost their responsiveness. When the American people send an unequivocal signal of what they want done, Washington still gets the message—and acts.

Look at what happened on gun control. For years, polls had shown majority support for stricter measures, but there was so little passion behind the polling numbers that aggressive lobbying could defeat measures like the Brady bill. When voters finally became aroused by repeated incidents of slaughter by gun-toting crazies, Congress, the president and both parties got on the ball.

But often, we send confusing, contradictory signals to Washington. Again, health care provides a good example. Most of us say we're satisfied with our own care, but we'd also like to see health insurance made available to everyone. We'd like government to crack down on the excesses, frauds and ripoffs we think are occurring in the health care system. But we don't want a big government bureaucracy or any government official standing between us and our doctor or hospital. And, by the way, we also don't want to pay more taxes for more protection.

When we begin to resolve some of these contradictions in our own minds, we may be able to start repairing our battered institutions.

13

BUREAUCRACY

It has become commonplace among business leaders, politicians, and the public alike to criticize government for waste and inefficiency. Former U.S. senator William Proxmire (D-Wis.), for example, used to present the Golden Fleece award to bureaucrats or government agencies that wasted the taxpayers' money. And former president Ronald Reagan made one of his administration's major themes the elimination of government waste. So it was not surprising that, shortly after taking office, Reagan took the lead in establishing a commission charged with finding ways to reduce government spending and eliminate bureaucratic waste and mismanagement. Known as the Grace Commission (for its chairman, Peter Grace, at the time one of America's top corporate executives), it issued a thick report outlining ways to make the government more efficient.

In the first of the articles in this chapter, Edward Meadows reviews the work of the Grace Commission and agrees with its conclusion that "the government is the worst-run enterprise in America." Citing examples from the report, Meadows paints a dismal picture of bureaucratic waste, including a government that overly indulges its workers, tolerates the spending of the taxpayers' money to an excessively high degree, and is blind to the need to get government out of the business of doing what the free market itself should be doing.

In the second selection, Steven Kelman offers a rebuttal to the Grace Commission findings. In a point-by-point refutation of 10 of the commission's examples of bureaucratic waste, Kelman concludes that popular conceptions of waste in the federal government, fueled by the commission and others, are, at best, "gross exaggerations." According to Kelman, the government is simply not as poorly run as everyone supposes. The reader is left to judge, of course, which is the more accurate view, on the basis of the evidence.

The Government Is the Worst-Run Enterprise in America

Edward Meadows

. . . When President Reagan named Peter Grace chairman of his new budget-study commission, back on February 18, 1982, the President bade him and his men go forth like tireless bloodhounds. The President asked Mr. Grace to command troops of corporate volunteers—accountants, staff officers, management experts—who would stalk the government's red-tape jungle, sniffing out inefficiency. In order not to add to the problem it was investigating, the commission would be funded privately, the President decreed, by corporate donations of time and money. Such a scheme had worked in California under his governorship, and it would work again in Washington. . . .

Bloodcurdling pig screams echoed down the Washington Mall as the Grace Commission began to release its findings in 1983. One task force proposed, for instance, that military commissaries be shut down. The military press ranted, and Defense Secretary Weinberger agreed that the matter needed "more study." This was typical and predictable.

A listing of the commission's executive committee reads like an honor roll of blue-chip corporate America, names like Frank Cary, chairman of IBM; William Agee, chairman of Bendix; John W. Hanley, chairman of Monsanto; and 157 other top-ranking executives. They remanded some two thousand of their employees to root in government files for evidence of mismanagement. The volunteer inspectors ended up writing 47 hefty blue-bound reports, many of them two inches thick, all chock-full of fascinating detail. They wrote 23,000 pages in all, suggesting budget cuts ranging from half a million dollars to $59 billion. All the work was done at a cost of $75 million in donated manpower, equipment, and materials, plus $3.3 million in cash contributions. Corporations footed the entire bill. Not a cent of the money came from the federal government. . . .

. . . The government is the worst-run enterprise in America. Thus it is the thesis of the Grace Commission that the country can save that $454 billion simply by curbing outright, blatant, casebook mismanagement, without ripping the social safety net, or even cutting some government services that many people, libertarians especially, would deem unwarranted on principle.

To begin, here is a random sampler of this mismanagement. Read and be outraged:

- The Health and Human Services Department has been paying Medicare benefits to 8,500 dead people.
- A Mississippi supplier bought a gravity timer from the sole manufacturer for $11 and sold it to the Navy for $256—a 2,227 percent markup.

Edward Meadows is a professional journalist and writer who frequently comments on economic issues. From Edward Meadows, "Peter Grace Knows 2,478 Ways to Cut the Deficit," National Review, *March 9, 1984, pp. 26–36. © 1984 by National Review, Inc., 215 Lexington Avenue, New York, NY 10016. Reprinted by permission.*

- The Minority Business Development Agency didn't notice when a management consulting firm used part of its $4 million MBDA grant to rent a townhouse and two cars for its executives, buy unauthorized gifts for its employees, and promote "questionable activities." The firm also neglected to pay some $315,000 in federal and state taxes, consulting fees, and salaries.
- It costs the Veterans Administration from $100 to $140 just to process a single medical claim, while the average for private insurance companies is $3 to $6 per claim.
- But the VA is a paragon of efficiency in letter-writing. It requires only 20 days to finish a letter. Compare with Health and Human Services, where a single piece of correspondence needing the signature of the Secretary takes 47 days to get done and involves about 60 people.
- The Army spends $4.20 to issue each payroll check, compared to the private-sector cost of $1. This wastes $40 million a year.
- Some unsuspecting citizens open their mailboxes to find 29 or more copies of pamphlets with titles like *How to Serve Nuts,* because the Government Printing Office uses out-of-date, duplicate, and incorrect mailing lists to post its myriad free publications. The lack of centralized correct mailing lists costs an estimated $96 million a year.

Say, is this Ubanga or the Central Banana Republic we're talking about? No, it's glittering Washington, and you're paying the tab. How does one get a firm hold on such maddeningly diverse ways of wasting taxpayers' money? The Grace Commission has broken down the inefficiencies by government agency and by function. For simplicity's sake, here are some specific categories of inefficiency, and what the Grace Commission thinks ought to be done to get things in shape.

INFORMATION PROCESSING

The federal government uses 17,000 computers, operated by 250,000 employees. But they are mostly obsolete—on average, they are twice as old as computers in private business. Half of them are so old they can no longer be supported by the manufacturer. And these ancient computers can't tie in with each other. Beyond that, government decision-makers mostly don't know what information they need, where to get it, or how to analyze it. Witness the results:

- The Social Security Administration's computers stay four to six weeks behind in issuing new Social Security cards, and the agency has a three-year backlog in posting retirement contributions. It is unable to process the 7.5 million new claims each year on time or correctly.
- Some 20 percent of all tax returns for 1978, that's right, 1978—have yet to be entered into the IRS computer system, a 20-year-old dinosaur that predates most modern computer technology. Delinquent accounts are therefore at $23.2 billion and growing.

- Though the Urban Mass Transportation Administration spent $10 million to buy new computers to keep track of the $25 billion in grants it hands out, the agency has been unable to close its accounting books since 1979. No account reconciliations have been possible since 1977. The UMTA has no central ledger showing who owes what to whom. Despite the computers, the agency must do its financial data by hand.
- The cost of the Army's business computer systems can only be estimated (at $1.5 billion), because the Army simply doesn't know how much it has spent on these computers, what kinds of computers it has, where they are, how many there are, or whether they should be replaced.

The Grace Commission argues that, for starters, some $20 billion can be saved over a three-year period by straightening out the computer mess. The commission recommends naming a manager to oversee computer operations throughout the government; hiring competent professionals; upgrading the obsolete systems; and using common payroll, personnel, property-management, and other such systems throughout the government. And if the government went even further in closing its information gap, by such means as figuring out what information it needs and then setting up mechanisms to get it, some $78 billion could be saved.

ASSET MANAGEMENT

Any businessman worth his P&L statement knows how to manage financial assets, mainly by putting idle money in interest-bearing accounts, and timing his own payments to avoid costing himself interest. Another way is to cut down the "float" that offers free credit as a payment takes its time getting to its destination. The federal government, however, is ignorant of these common techniques. Because of this, it loses millions of your dollars a year. Consider the evidence:

- In 1982 the Justice Department seized $317 million in the form of cash and of property, such as dope-smuggling planes. But the captured cash, $79 million of the total, wasn't put into interest-bearing bank accounts. Instead, the Justice Department just let it sit. Noncash assets are allowed to depreciate to as little as 65 percent of their value before they are sold off.
- At the Transportation Department, some $473 million in recent grants was paid to contractors an average of 13 days sooner than necessary, costing the government $13 million in interest payments. If payments were made only when due, and bills collected promptly, the department could save $144 million per year.
- The State Department squandered some $17 million over a three-year period by failing to acquire foreign currency before it was actually needed. (And when the dollar weakens, State should delay buying foreign currency.)
- Some $635 million could be saved over three years if the government used direct deposit for the 48 million payments it makes each month. This would allow the money to remain on deposit longer.

- The Education Department could generate some $4.68 billion in cash-flow improvements and $1 billion in interest savings over three years merely by making loans to students in increments rather than in lump sums. Consolidating the student-loan programs could return at least $290 million per year to the Treasury.

In spite of a daily cash flow of $6.8 billion, the federal government obviously hasn't got a handle on the management of its financial assets. The Grace Commission says the government could save up to $79 billion if it ran its asset management as business does.

PERSONNEL

The federal government employs nearly three times the number of high-grade white-collar workers found in the private sector. They tend to be overpaid and underworked, given to absenteeism and job-hopping. They get 35 percent more vacation time than private-industry workers and health benefits that cost $134 a month per family, versus the private-sector average of $93. They like to file such things as on-the-job injury claims (6.3 percent of federal employees filed in 1980, versus 1.7 percent of private-industry employees).

- In 1981, a typical year, Postal Service workers took an average of nearly nine sick days each, versus the 5.3-day average in private enterprise. This lost 21.734 work-weeks, at a cost to the taxpayers of $652 million.
- The Department of Energy has one supervisor for every three employees, twice the number of supervisors in the rest of the federal government, not to mention the private sector. Just bringing the Energy Department into line with the rest of the government would save a tidy $19 million over three years.
- The Education Department overpays nearly 30 percent of its workers, since that many are "overclassified" and there hasn't been a classification audit since the department was formed in 1980. Education Department employees don't mind. Nor do they complain about cost-of-living raises. The average increase was 17.3 percent in 1980 and 27.3 percent in 1981.
- Government pensions are twice as generous as private ones, and military pensions are 600 percent higher than those in the private sector. These pensions are sweetened by lavish cost-of-living increases, such that between 1977 and 1981, civil-service pension pay rose by 50 percent. Between 1973 and 1982, the government handed out more than $200 billion in pension checks to civil-service and military retirees. These costs will more than double over the next decade, rising to $500 billion, not including an unfunded pension liability of a trillion dollars over that period. (For example, there are a million retired railroad workers and only 450,000 active workers in the Railroad Retirement System—that is, 2.2 retirees per worker. The system already has an unfunded liability of $30 billion and will run out of funds sometime before next year.)
- To decide how much to pay its workers, the government surveys salaries in the private sector. But this "comparability survey" covers only a quarter of federal jobs

and excludes 95 percent of companies in major industries. Thus the survey is biased toward high salaries. The average blue-collar salary is 8 percent higher in government enterprises than in private industry. In any case, about half of all federal job-classification standards are more than ten years out of date, with excessively detailed requirements and time-consuming procedures.

- One government study determined that word-processing operators weren't as skilled as regular secretaries, so it cut word-processing pay by $3,000 a year. The predictable result was that word-processing operators disappeared from federal word-processing pools, only to turn up as secretaries. Some word-processing centers went idle for lack of operators. Productivity fell.
- The VA has a hospital construction staff of 800, while the Hospital Corporation of America does the same work with a staff of 50. As a result of overstaffing, it takes the VA seven years to finish a project, versus two years at the HCA. Administrative costs are 8 percent, versus 2 percent in the private sector.

The Grace Commission says the government could save a neat $58 billion over three years by such things as raising the retirement age to 62 (it now can be as low as 55 for civil service and 40 for the military), imposing early-retirement penalties, offering more reasonable cost-of-living adjustments, and redesigning the job-comparability surveys and the job-classification system. More savings would come just from bringing government pay and work customs into line with those in private business.

PROCUREMENT

One-fifth of the federal budget goes for buying equipment and supplies. In fiscal 1982, for instance, procurement totaled nearly $160 billion, with more than three-fourths of that sum going for Defense Department purchases. Add to the total some $88 billion in inventories that government agencies hold stored all over the country in hundreds of locations.

To do all the federal shopping, some 130,000 federal procurement officers take part in about 18 million "procurement actions" per year. They do all this while entangled in more than eighty thousand pages of regulations, plus twenty thousand new pages of revisions each year.

Here are some examples of what federal procurement has wrought:

- The Navy's Training Equipment Center in Orlando paid $511 for bulbs that cost 60 cents in the grocery store.
- The Navy paid $100 last year for aircraft simulator parts that cost a nickel at the hardware store.
- Costs for 25 major weapons systems that were started between 1971 and 1978 have risen an average of 323 percent. One reason is that defense contractors typically underbid on contracts—sometimes as much as 80 percent below true costs—to get government work. Then, as they proceed, they double and even triple the cost estimates. But by then it is too late to do anything about it.

- The government compounds the cost-overrun problem by allowing a defense contractor that underbids to become the government's monopoly supplier of a system or product for up to 20 years. During that time, the contractor has a free hand to raise and re-raise the price as much as he pleases. Costs are typically doubled and tripled again by these monopoly contractors.
- When the Agency for International Development bought 399 cars and trucks for projects in the Middle East, an audit found that 5 were missing, 93 had been diverted to personal or nonproject use; 84 had been sitting idle in parking lots, some for two years; and many of the remaining vehicles had been commandeered by host-country government officials for their private use.
- The U.S. Coast Guard pays $100 per week for the use of an office trailer, while the Environmental Protection Agency pays $100 per day to the same supplier for the identical trailer. The EPA's unwitting generosity is blamed on the way the agency deals with its suppliers, and on the fact that the contractor forgot to mention that the $100 was a weekly rate, not a daily one.

More than $28 billion could be saved in procurement over a three-year span, says the Grace Commission, if the government would tighten up its procedures. It could cure cost overruns by using two competing contractors for production of things like weapons systems; by spreading procurement funding over several years to allow better monitoring; and by purchasing spare parts from a source other than the manufacturer (who tends to mark up spare parts outrageously). Federal agencies should also hold smaller inventories, in line with the practice in private business, and they should consider past performance when deciding on a bid award, and ride herd on bidders' cost estimates.

PRIVATIZATION

The federal government is the world's largest (and worst-run) conglomerate. It is at once the nation's largest insurer, lender, borrower, hospital-system operator, power producer, landowner, tenant, holder of grazing land and timberland, grain owner, warehouse operator, ship owner, and truck-fleet operator.

This unnatural situation evolved from the assumption that only government can provide some services. That might have been true years ago when the feds got into most of the businesses they run today. But now it is often nonsensical:

- In the 1860s the government decided to provide cheap food for soldiers in isolated frontier outposts by setting up government grocery stores, the military commissaries. Nowadays, a wild frontier town like Washington, D.C., has six commissaries; San Francisco and San Antonio have five each; there are four each in San Diego and in Norfolk. The government has 358 commissary stores, 238 of them in the continental United States, duplicating private supermarkets, but without the profit motive. The result is an uncompetitive and inefficient government grocery chain with annual sales of $4.2 billion, at an annual cost to taxpayers of $597 million.

- Europe and Japan are beginning to cut into the U.S. monopoly on outer space, because semiprivate companies like Arianespace can undercut NASA. If the United States is to compete in this growing high-tech business, it should let private companies in on space launches, especially since, by the government's own estimates, it won't be able to meet the commercial demand for space launches in this decade.
- The Department of Energy operates 123 hydroelectric dams and 622 substations, supplying 45 percent of the nation's hydroelectric power. But revenues aren't enough to cover the federal investment, the pricing doesn't make sense, and the account books are a mess.
- Federal agencies try to do everything in-house. The Defense Department has 11,700 employees doing such things as providing food service, maintenance, laundry service, firefighting, etc. Contracting out this kind of work would save $70 million a year at the Department of Defense.

The Grace Commission has found $28.4 billion of potential savings over three years through privatization. Of these savings, $20 billion would come from selling off the government's hydroelectric dams and substations, some $2.5 billion would come from selling off military commissaries, and the rest would come from contracting out services like VA hospital management and turning over redundant operations to the private sector.

SUBSIDIES

The federal government handed out nearly $500 billion in 1983 to individuals, businesses, and other government agencies. The Department of Health and Human Services alone gives away two out of every five tax dollars—$269 billion last year. Not counting such earned entitlements as Social Security and VA benefits, the federal government offers 64 different welfare programs, costing close to $100 billion a year. In 1983, there were an estimated 22 million Medicaid recipients, 19 million food-stamp recipients, 4.1 million Supplemental Security Income recipients, and 11 million recipients of Aid to Families with Dependent Children. Aside from welfare, there are billions more in subsidies paid to industry and even foreign governments. Without debating the basic validity of some of those programs, here are a few of the obvious abuses:

- Food-stamp cheating amounted to $1 billion in 1981, 10 percent of the whole program. It happens largely because recipients lie about their income and the government never checks.
- An estimated 206,100 aliens living abroad collect U.S. Social Security benefits. The average alien family gets $24 in benefits for every dollar paid in FICA taxes.
- Most of the subsidized mortgage loans made by the government in 1982 went to folks who could have bought homes without help. The typical mortgage revenue bond buyer had an income between $20,000 and $40,000. Some 53 percent were among the more affluent families in their states, with several making over $50,000 a year.

- An audit revealed nearly $1 billion in rail-modernization money lying idle at the Urban Mass Transportation Administration because the agency has no system for awarding urban discretionary grants.

Some $59 billion could be saved over three years, according to the Grace Commission, by better management of subsidy programs. One recommendation is to tax subsidy payments above a certain income level or corporate tax bracket. Benefit programs ought to be consolidated, and agency accounting systems need to be improved to provide accurate, up-to-date information. The commission says poverty statistics should be redefined to include in-kind transfer payments such as food stamps and Medicaid.

These broad management categories account for some $330 billion in savings over three years, 78 percent of the total. The rest comes from applying the principles of good business management in diverse cases; for example, the Agriculture Department could save an extra $7 billion over three years by cutting out the overlap and duplication in its services; by shifting the FHA's activities from direct loans to loan guarantees and transferring its housing functions to HUD; by charging for such things as maps, soil survey reports, and firewood, all of which are now given away free; and by increasing user fees for grazing, recreation, and the like.

The Grace Commission calls for an Office of Federal Management to be set up in the executive office of the president. Such an office would guide and coordinate management of the government's $800 billion conglomerate. It would institute the kind of budgeting and strategic planning that large corporations practice, and develop common government-wide software for standardized receivables, payroll, pension-plan, and fixed-asset accounting.

After Peter Grace presented the final report to the president in a White House ceremony on January 16 [1984,] the networks dutifully ran stories on the evening news, usually ending with the remark that here is another commission report to be filed away. Who, in an election year, was going to propose serious budgetary pigsticking? The *New York Times* wanly editorialized that the Grace Commission was "wishful, but worthwhile, on waste." Some of the Grace Commission's recommendations are already being carried out, but three-quarters of them need congressional approval. Hence, the question lingers: Can it really be done? And we are led to the crux of the issue: psychology.

News that the government pays $30 million in Medicare checks to the deceased, and loses track of $10 billion in block-grant money, seems almost beyond reality, somewhere in the realm of the absurd. It makes neat newspaper filler material, American black humor, good for a chuckle over coffee. It's another little confirmation of what most Americans have suspected of the government since the time of Thomas Jefferson.

Upon reflection, the unreality of the abuses becomes as overwhelming and unimaginable as the sheer size of the expenditures. More discouraging still is the realization that this sort of thing has obviously been going on for ages. So one shakes one's head and flips the page. What's to be done. *Nada, niente, rien du tout.*

The irony is that something can indeed be done, if enough citizens believe it can be, and make their wish known in Washington. Only by the force of widespread dissatisfaction can Congress find the courage to stick some pigs. In this sense, Peter Grace's work has only begun.

How Much Waste in Government?
An Alternate View

Steven Kelman

There are few beliefs more deeply embedded in the popular consciousness than that government wastes a lot of money. Seymour Martin Lipset and William Schneider, in their book *The Confidence Gap,* report that in surveys asking people how much of each tax dollar they think the federal government wastes, the median response is 48¢. Lipset and Schneider argue that the paradox of simultaneous public support for tax cuts, and for maintaining or increasing spending in all major categories of government programs, is explained by the perception that waste in government is so rampant that there can be big spending reductions without service rollbacks.

Last January the President's Private Sector Survey on Cost Control (generally known as the "Grace Commission" after its head, J. Peter Grace, Chief Executive Officer of W.R. Grace & Co.) delivered its final reports. The Grace Commission recruited over 2,000 corporate executives to scrutinize the government. Announcing the report, Peter Grace told the press that President Reagan had asked him to look at government agencies as if considering a merger or takeover. "The President's private sector survey would not acquire the government" was the conclusion, he stated. No wonder. He found that, over a three-year period, a total of $424 *billion* in savings could be obtained from controlling waste, "without weakening America's needed defense build-up and without in any way harming necessary social welfare programs." These were stupendous numbers, almost enough to eliminate federal deficits.

But they were not uncontroversial. With the perspective of someone interested in how government can be managed better, I spent time examining some specific allegations of waste the Grace Commission made in areas where, first, there is general agreement—public and governmental—that the activity being undertaken is worthwhile, and second, there are examples of the private sector producing the same output, so that the relative costs to government and to the private sector can be compared. The Grace Commission issued 48 reports and made a now-notorious 2,478 recommendations, so it was obviously impossible to examine any significant percentage. But in the press packet accompanying the Grace Commission report, there was a chart entitled "Ten Random Examples of Bureaucratic Absurdity" (which was picked up in the *New York Times* story on the Commission), and I examined those ten.[1] Also, I examined recommendations the Commission made involving the General Services Administration (GSA) and the Veterans Administration (VA), because the responsibilities of both agencies include tasks very similar to ones private firms undertake.

Steven Kelman is professor of public policy at the Kennedy School of Government at Harvard University and since 1993, administrator of the U.S. Office of Federal Procurement Policy, Office of Management and Budget, the Executive Office of the President, Washington, D.C. From Steven Kelman, "The Grace Commission: How Much Waste in Government?" Public Interest, No. 78 (Winter 1985), pp. 62–74, 77–78. © 1985 by National Affairs, Inc. Reprinted with permission of the author and Public Interest.

THE CASE OF THE $91 SCREW

(1) *"The Pentagon has been buying screws, available in any hardware store for 3 cents, for $91 each."*

There have been many widely publicized examples of the apparently outrageous prices paid for spare parts for weapons—$110 for a 4¢ diode, $9,609 for a 12¢ Allen wrench, and $1,118 for a plastic cap for a navigator's seat.

One has reason to doubt these stories, even before further investigation, on strictly logical grounds. To suggest that defense contractors could routinely charge the government $110 for something they got for a few pennies is to suggest that the defense contracting business is the easiest avenue to unearned fortune since the invention of plunder. In fact, it turns out that the Defense Department has not negligently allowed itself to be hoodwinked. Most of these cases have a common explanation, which involves an accounting quirk in pricing material purchased from contractors.

Any time anybody buys something, the price includes not only the direct cost of the materials, machines, and labor to produce it, but also a share of the company's overhead expenses—ranging from running the legal department to renting corporate headquarters. Defense Department acquisition rules prescribe that a defense contractor's overhead expenses be allocated to each shipment at some fixed proportion of the value of the procurement. Thus, if the direct cost of a weapon is $5 million, a company might be authorized to tack on, illustratively, 20 percent or $1 million, for overhead expenses. The same percentage may also be added to the direct costs of other items procured, such as spare parts. Thus $1 million would be added to a spare parts order for $5 million, just as it would be to a fighter plane order.

The Pentagon orders many different spare parts at one time. Often in the past, contractors have, simply as a matter of accounting convenience, allocated the overhead to the individual parts on an "item" basis rather than a "value" basis. Say that the $20 million order is for 10,000 parts, some of which have a direct cost of $25,000 each and others of 4¢ each. Instead of apportioning the $1 million total overhead such that the $25,000 part gets a lot and the 4¢ part a little, the computer printout will allocate $100 to each part. This produces a charge to the government of $25,100 for the expensive part and $100.04 for the cheap one.

Although this produces horror stories, nothing horrible has occurred. The total overhead represents real resources legitimately charged to the government. If the $100 doesn't get allocated to the 4¢ diode, the diode no longer appears to be so outrageously expensive. But the $100 doesn't disappear, nor should it. The overhead is just allocated elsewhere.

There is one mildly distressing aspect of this practice. The spreading of overhead costs over a contractor's entire production appears to reduce the upfront costs of new weapons systems, since research and development for the weapon is charged to spare parts as well. This, in turn, makes new weapons systems appear less expensive than they really are, and distorts political discussions of a system's costs and benefits. But that has nothing to do with "not minding the store."

Other horror stories have a different explanation. Many parts the Defense Department procures are "common use items," the same as commercially produced parts that might be used in a car as well as a tank. Other items need to be custom designed, which often produces an extremely high price per unit, because, unlike Chevrolets, much military equipment is produced in very small quantities and thus requires only a few of the same spare parts. The initial cost to design the part, and make the machine die or molding to produce it, must then be spread out over only a few units. (If it costs $3,000 to design and tool up a plastic cap, that will add only 1¢ to the cost of the cap if 300,000 are produced, but $1,000 if three are produced.)

The economics of tooling-up do suggest that common-use parts be used when possible, and the Defense Department does make efforts to get common-use items. Spare parts are frequently procured on a sole-source basis from the contractors for the original weapon. When the contractor submits designs for spare parts, he must designate those which are common-use. This list is reviewed by a Defense Department contracting officer, who makes suggestions for expanding common-use procurement when appropriate. After the contractor proposes prices, the contracting officer requests an independent evaluation of the offer by Defense Department value engineers, who may question whether a newly designated part is sufficiently different from common-use items to justify special tooling-up. But special design *is* sometimes necessary.

Contractors have something of an incentive to propose custom-designed parts, since a contractor is allowed to take a standard percentage profit, which in dollar terms is of course far greater for a $1,000 item than a $1 item. Cheating is presumably discouraged by the negative impact repeated discovery would have on the contractor's relations with the Defense Department. But the Department has an enormous review task—there are about 300,000 parts in an airplane—and sometimes an item that should have been classified as common-use ends up getting designed to order. This is what happened in the case of the $1,118 plastic cap. In the widely publicized case of the $9,609 Allen wrench, however, the system did work. General Dynamics proposed a custom-designed wrench, but the Pentagon's value review engineer found that the function could be performed equally well by an ordinary wrench. The Defense Department never ordered the custom-designed version, and is now increasing its scrutiny for common-use items. The additional scrutiny may cost more than it saves, but the issue to the Defense Department at this point is the credibility of the defense buildup.

THE OUTRAGEOUS CASE OF BUILDING MANAGEMENT

(2) *"In comparison to a private sector company, managing comparable building space, the General Services Administration employs 17 times as many people and spends almost 14 times as much on total management costs."*

This contention is so wildly inaccurate that it is hard to know where to begin. The best place to start is with two whopping errors in the numbers the Grace Commission provided on the private sector firm being compared with GSA. The chart the Commission provided stated that the property management division of a large life insurance firm was managing 10,000 buildings, "comparable building space" to GSA. In fact, no insurance company has a portfolio anywhere near that large. The correct number for the insurance company is not 10,000 buildings, but *1,000,* which is not comparable to GSA at all. Furthermore, the Grace Commission states that the insurance company employs a total of 300 professionals, 100 in central administration, and 200 under contract. It turns out, however, that the company in question does not employ 200 *individuals* under contract, but rather hires 200 property management *firms* actually to manage its buildings. Each of these firms in turn has many professionals working for it.

The figure the Commission chart provided for GSA professionals—5,000—is also exaggerated. About one-third of these are clerical and often non-professional employees (the Grace Commission simply looked at total white-collar employment at the Public Buildings Service). And about 800 of this number manage GSA design and construction, overseeing the contract process for construction of new buildings as well as repairs and alterations of existing buildings; the people who do this for the insurance company work in a different division, and thus aren't included in the employment figures the Grace Commission provided. So the number of professionals working on building management at GSA is really around 2,700, rather than 5,000.

Although all this indicates that the Grace Commission is monumentally mistaken, a precise comparison is difficult to make. One would need to know how many professionals the building management contractors employ, and the insurance company itself doesn't know that. Beyond that, the nature of the GSA portfolio and the insurance company's portfolio is different. Over two-thirds of the GSA buildings are leased space rather than owned space; this requires people to work on initial lease bids and on lease renewals (neither of which applies to the insurance company), but does not require government-provided building management services. Over 1,000 of the GSA buildings are (owned or leased) local social security offices, which are considerably smaller than the properties an insurance company owns. GSA officials would themselves concede that they probably have a larger staff for comparable functions than a private sector counterpart, because GSA requires more levels of review on contracting and leasing decisions to assure due process and to minimize corruption. But the difference is nothing like 17 to 1.

THE $61,250 NURSING HOME BED

(3) *"The VA spends $61,250 per bed to construct nursing homes—almost four times the $16,000 per bed cost of a major private sector nursing home operator."*

The Grace Commission averaged the cost of six VA nursing homes, and the average was raised dramatically by the reported $113,500 per-bed cost of construction of a home in Martinsburg, West Virginia. This nursing home was being built simultaneously with a VA hospital adjacent to it, and the cost the Grace Commission reported included construction costs for a domiciliary that was part of the whole medical center, as well as site preparation and utilities for the entire complex. The actual cost for the nursing home at that site was $29,000 per bed, bringing the average cost per bed for the six facilities down from $61,000 to $47,000. Furthermore, the cost of three of the VA homes was significantly higher than usual because of unfavorable site conditions (such as confined space for construction, thus requiring off-site warehousing of building materials). Site conditions were unfavorable because the nursing homes were being built next to already-existing VA hospitals, pursuant to VA policy. The average cost of the remaining three homes, built under normal site conditions, was $39,000 a bed. So while the Commission exaggerates, there remains a substantial difference compared with the private sector, even if one considers only the homes constructed on normal site conditions.

Why these differences? Whatever the answer, one can be relatively confident that it is not the result of lazy government construction workers or bloated construction material prices paid by government. In fact, the VA does not construct nursing homes itself. It takes its nursing home specifications and puts them out to bid by building contractors. The low bid wins.

The truth is that what the VA calls a nursing home is in many ways of much higher quality than what private-sector chains produce. These quality differences increase the cost of a VA nursing home relative to a private one.

The most obvious differences involve the physical designs. VA facilities have been top-of-the-line. Homes have routinely included balconies in each room, occupational therapy areas, quiet rooms, extensive recreation space, and on-premises artwork. The VA policy of building homes contiguous to VA hospitals rather than freestanding, as the private company Beverly does, is also quality-driven; it provides nursing home residents quick access to hospital services and allows more rapid treatment of medical emergencies. That policy drives up costs in a number of ways, however. The VA got into the nursing home business relatively recently, and most homes are built on existing hospital sites. Often, however, these sites are too small to be ideal for new construction. That can raise costs by requiring construction in cramped or otherwise difficult situations. And frequently there is not enough land to build single-story homes, which are marginally cheaper to construct than the two-story homes the VA often must build. Is it worthwhile to produce this level of quality? That is a matter of debate. But it is not an issue of "waste," as the term is typically used.

The cost of constructing VA nursing homes *can* be reduced by decreasing quality. In 1981 the VA established a task force on nursing home construction cost reduction, after private nursing home chains had called cost differences to the attention of congressional oversight committees. The task force proposed a number of design changes that will reduce the cost of new VA nursing homes by about $12,000 per bed. They include eliminating balconies, making ceilings eight rather than nine feet high, reducing recreation room and dining room space by 35 percent, and reducing landscaping by half.

Another part of higher VA construction costs stems from the special requirements of government procurement. The most obvious are ones such as Davis-Bacon, and the preference given to American-made products and to minority and small-business enterprises. When the government builds a nursing home, it has decided not just to build a home but also to aid small business and American-made products. Again, this is not "waste," but rather government policy.

The entire mode of procurement in government is a less obvious, but very important, source of additional costs. Private sector nursing home chains generally establish ongoing relationships with construction firms in an area (often two firms, each to serve as a competitive check on the other), to whom they turn again and again. This allows them to avoid the costs of gearing up for new bidding procedures for each job. By contracting for several jobs at the same time, it allows the general contractor to obtain lower prices from subcontractors and suppliers, who give quantity discounts for the larger volume of work. It allows the contractors to become familiar with the details of how the firm wants the home built and to look for ways to build more economically, since investments in such efforts can be capitalized over a number of projects. The VA, by contrast, must gear up for a *de novo* bidding procedure, open to all, for each construction contract, with detailed functional specifications (rather than brand-specific ones) so that nobody is excluded from bidding. There are many layers of review within the VA to ensure that specifications inhibit no one, and to clear any deviations by the procurement or project staff from the rule that the lowest bid must be accepted. These procurement methods entail extensive additional costs, both because any individual act of procurement is more complicated (developing functional specifications, layers of review) and personnel-intensive, and because there are far more separate procurement decisions to be made (the *de novo* bidding process). Although the monetary costs of these procedures outweigh their monetary benefits (or else private firms would follow similar procedures) none of them, again, constitutes a clear example of waste. At worst, they reflect mistaken policies. They produce outputs with "quality" features not found in private home construction such as equal opportunity for all businesses to compete and a minimization of kickbacks.

Where does all this leave the VA/private sector comparison? I start with a $39,000 per bed average figure for the nursing homes built on normal site conditions, and I subtract $6,000 per bed in savings from the cost-control task force.[2] This brings the VA cost down to $33,000 a bed, compared with $16,000 in the private sector: about twice as much, rather than four times as much. The costs of Davis-Bacon and various statutory procurement preferences, of complex procurement procedures that must be repeated each time a home is built, of any remaining quality difference compared with private sector homes, and of any extra costs from two-story construction, reduce the differences further. Since no study exists of the accumulated effect of those factors, it is impossible to say how much of the VA/private sector difference that does remain is simple waste. My suspicion is that something does remain, but that the differences are not dramatic.

THE FREIGHT-CHARGES BOONDOGGLE

(4) *"The government spends almost $5 billion annually on freight charges but doesn't bother to negotiate volume discounts with suppliers."*

The Grace Commission's own backup material regarding this claim turns out not even to make the contention that the government "doesn't bother to negotiate volume discounts." In fact, it turns out that virtually all government freight is moved at rates discounted for volume.

The problem is a more subtle one. Before trucking deregulation, freight tariffs were fixed. Deregulation in 1980 produced an avalanche of different rates (similar to the situation for airline travelers). Suddenly, there were differences in fares charged for a given route and many lower tariffs for full-load shipments.

Deregulation opened up opportunities for savings on freight expenses, but the proliferation of rates increased the information-processing requirements for taking advantage of those possibilities. Very quickly, computer software companies began offering packages that allow a shipper to determine the cheapest available rate, and also to determine what shipments from several sources within the organization might be going to the same place at the same time, so that full-load discounts can be obtained. These systems have spread quickly in the private sector since 1980.

In 1981 the General Services Administration, which administers shipping for most of the government, began to look at these new computer systems, but decided they were still too new to try. In the summer of 1983 they decided to procure one, and the system they selected went on-line in March 1984.

THE MAILING LIST FIASCO

(5) *"Government mailing lists erroneously repeat the same addresses as many as 29 times."*

This statement, though ambiguous, seems to suggest that somewhere there is a government mailing list that has the same address on it 29 times, causing 29 copies of the same publication to be sent to one location. The implication is that government officials simply never bothered to check the list for such wasteful duplication.

This example of 29 repetitions comes from a 1980 effort by the Office of Human Development Services in HHS to improve its management of mailing lists. The Office was formed in the mid-1970s as an umbrella organization for a large number of already existing agencies, such as the Administration on Aging and the Administration for Children, Youth and Families. Each of these separate organizations, quite naturally, maintained its own mailing lists—usually, in fact, a number of different mailing lists, such as lists of subscribers to an agency magazine, media contacts, libraries, or recipients of grant award information. There were about 300 different mailing lists in all.

In 1979, a newly appointed manager of the Office of Public Affairs at Human Development Services persuaded his boss to authorize a project to centralize and modernize the organization's mailing list. The 300 lists were combined into one master list. A "positive purge" was conducted, whereby every person on any of the lists had to return a card in order to stay on. The Public Affairs Office also began to rent commercially available lists—of libraries, professors of social work, etc.—as an alternative to maintaining and updating its own lists.

In the course of this project, it was discovered that one address (a social service agency) appeared 29 times. But this was 29 times on 300 different lists, and these 300 lists generally received different publications. In other words, the addressee might have been on one list to receive the *Mental Disability Law Reporter,* on another for press releases from the Administration on Aging, and on a third for information about grant availability from the Office of Handicapped Individuals. The addressee wasn't receiving 29 copies of any one publication. At worst, as the person in charge of the reform effort told me, an addressee appearing 29 times might receive five copies of a single publication—but only in the rare cases when a mailing went to several of the agency's *different* lists. There were certainly some examples of duplications on the same list: Although federal law requires annual canvassing of individual agency lists for duplication, compliance is mixed.

Although the quality of mailing list management within the government varies, there is no doubt that significant improvements could be made. There have been major changes in the mailing list business during the last decade, with the increased use of computers for list generation and management. Simple software now exists to purge lists of duplication, and with the growth of list brokers there is no longer any need for an organization to attempt to maintain its own lists of nursing home administrators, libraries, or public health professors. The government is now beginning to adapt to these changes.

THE SCANDAL OF SEIZED ASSETS

(6) *"The Justice Department just sits on the cash seized from criminals, not bothering to deposit the money in interest-bearing accounts while cases are being adjudicated."*

Traditionally, cash seized from criminals was indeed not deposited in interest-bearing accounts. "Not bothering," however, was not the reason. Prosecuting attorneys wanted the actual bills in hand, to impress juries with wads of ill-gotten lucre. Depositing the money would have meant losing the ability to show it to juries: The only thing available would have been a statement in a government bank account! Furthermore, some jurisdictions require that actual bills be submitted as evidence.

Until quite recently, very little cash was seized from criminal suspects. In the late 1970s, however, the Justice Department began actively to seize cash and physical assets (such as cars and boats)—and to seek their forfeiture—as a tactic against organized crime.

Soon thereafter, the Department realized that this vast quantity of physical assets had created a management problem. The Justice Department's policy was not to question legitimate third-party liens on seized assets, so that if there was a $110,000 loan outstanding on a $150,000 boat, the government would not contest the bank's right to collect $110,000 from the sale of the boat. The frequent problem is that the hypothetical boat might deteriorate badly while in the government's possession. When sold after being forfeited, less than $110,000 might be realized; the government would have to make up the difference. The local U.S. Attorney offices had no capability to manage seized assets while they awaited disposition (lawyers are experts at trying cases, not managing property), and no centralized management system had ever been developed because there were so few seized assets.

In 1981, the Justice Department appointed a task force to examine the management of seized assets. It issued a report in 1982, recommending that the Department establish a central organizational capability, through the U.S. Marshal Service, to manage seized assets for local U.S. Attorney offices. Agreement having been obtained within the Department (including from the U.S. Attorney offices), this new capability is now being established.

THE SHOCKING SLOTH OF LOAN COLLECTORS

(7) *"HUD makes only 3 attempts to collect loans versus 24 to 36 tries in the private sector."*

This refers to loan collection procedures for two programs—a Housing and Urban Development credit insurance program for regular property improvement loans (Title I), and HUD's direct, subsidized loan program for property-improvement loans in disadvantaged areas (Section 312). Title I is an old program (enacted in 1934) that does not have income restrictions; Section 312 is a War on Poverty-era program that is targeted to poorer neighborhoods.

Again, the comparison the Grace Commission presents is exaggerated. First, the Grace Commission's own backup material refers to two or three loan collection tries per month in the private sector (compared to a total of three in HUD), but collection activity, in both the private sector and HUD, proceeds for only four months before legal action is commenced or the loan abandoned. The press packet figure of "24 to 36 tries in the private sector" comes from incorrectly assuming that collection activity at private banks goes on for an entire year. Even accepting the Grace Commission comparison at face value, the proper number is thus eight to 12 tries in the private sector, not 24 to 36. Second, HUD loan collection officers generally do not make a written record of telephone calls they make to delinquents, so Grace Commission investigators looking only at the written record underestimated the number of collection tries HUD made. Finally, and crucially, there has been collection activity on these loans *before* they are sent to HUD. Title I loans are made by regular banks, and Title I regulations mandate that the banks pursue their own normal debt-collection efforts before passing the loans on to HUD; for the Section 312 loans that HUD makes directly, Fannie Mae (the Federal National Mortgage Association), which services the loans, engages in some mild collection activity (dunning letters but no phone calls or contacts with an employer) before passing the loans on. HUD isn't starting from scratch on collections, as the Grace Commission's comparison suggests.

None of this is to suggest that there have been no problems with debt-collection at HUD. Although the regulations call for banks to pursue normal debt-collection efforts at first, HUD officials concede that compliance is mixed. Also, when their own collection efforts fail, private banks give potentially collectible loans to private-collection agencies, and HUD gives them to the Department of Justice for prosecution. Attorneys there have regarded these as low-priority cases and have not prosecuted them in a timely way—something that debt-collection experts regard as crucial to any chance of recovery. Finally, at least for Section 312 loans, management at HUD has probably always regarded these loans as a sort of disguised social assistance program, and has seen the idea of banging on the doors of poor people to get them to pay as distasteful. Loan collection efforts for the 312 program traditionally received little attention from top management. (The Title I program, by contrast, turns a profit for the government.)

The organization of debt collection at HUD has also failed to reflect changes in private debt collection practices. HUD standard operating procedures continued to call for personal dunning visits to delinquents, although banks had concluded over a decade ago that such efforts (earlier traditional in the industry) were generally not cost-effective. And HUD was very slow to computerize debt information, which resulted both in a great deal of clerical work for loan collectors (reducing the time available for collection activities) and in poor control over the status of files. The Section 312 program began to move toward computerization (and now to contracting out its debt collection to a private firm) after a critical report by the General Accounting Office in 1979; Title I has only recently computerized its collection activities, after a decision to do so was made by the assistant secretary appointed by President Reagan. . . .

WASTE IN GOVERNMENT

There are a number of conclusions one can draw from all of this. First, the horror stories one hears are almost always gross exaggerations. What we have seen suggests that those responsible for the activities in question generally pay attention to costs, and have a fairly good sense of ways to keep them down. People are too quick to conclude that programs are wasteful when they think the programs are not worthwhile. But if the government efficiently delivers a worthless product, the criticism should be directed at the decision to deliver the product, not vented in charges of incompetence and venality against those making the deliveries.

Second, some differences between relative costs to government and to the private sector occur because the government, superficial similarities notwithstanding, is in fact producing something very different. This is most obviously the case when, for instance, the VA puts balconies outside its nursing home rooms. But it is also the case when agencies follow cumbersome procurement procedures designed not solely to procure certain goods, but also to ensure due process for vendors and special aid for disadvantaged businesses. There may indeed be incentives in some government programs, such as those administered by the VA, to overproduce quality. And it may be that we are spending too much for due process. But the extra money entailed has not simply disappeared down a black hole.

Third, even after taking account of quality differences, it is probably true that government generally produces a given output less efficiently than the private sector. If I had to hazard a guess, I would say that the government might typically use, not 4 times or 17 times as many resources as the private sector to produce a given output, but perhaps 1.2 times. That is less dramatic, but it does add up. Even if it adds up only to several billion dollars, rather than to the Grace Commission's fantasy figures, such a sum is negligible only to those who, to paraphrase [former U.S. senator] Everett Dirksen, have gotten so used to spending a billion here and a billion there that they forget it eventually adds up to real money.

Fourth, government is not very good at turning on a dime. As we have seen, there are many situations in which the environment changed—computer programs becoming available, for example—and it took more time for government to adapt than for the private sector. But, as we have also seen, the government does in fact adapt. . . .

NOTES

1. Of these, four proved not to be "bureaucratic absurdity" after all, but rather policies enacted by Congress. So only six cases were investigated. In addition, I examined the issue of Defense Department spare parts prices (which appeared in the press packet under another listing) because the issue had received so much media attention and because it had the horror-story sound of the other examples of "bureaucratic absurdity."

2. I subtract $6,000 rather than the estimated $12,000 in savings because some of the changes the VA is making bring VA nursing homes below Beverly's standards—for example, the ceilings in VA homes will now be lower than those in Beverly homes. Lacking time, or expertise in architecture, to allow an exact estimate of the cost-reduction steps that bring the VA homes to the *same* level as Beverly's, I have taken a figure of one-half, the arbitrary nature of which the reader should be aware. . . .

14

THE JUDICIARY

The Supreme Court

While few would question the Supreme Court's authority to interpret the Constitution, there has long been disagreement over how the nine justices should approach this awesome responsibility. This debate grew in intensity during the Reagan era as the president and his attorney general inveighed against the Supreme Court, charging that justices had all too often substituted their own values and principles for those contained in the Constitution.

In the selection which immediately follows, Edwin Meese, U.S. attorney general during part of the Reagan administration, calls upon judges to interpret the Constitution in accordance with the intent of those who wrote and ratified it. Insisting that the Founding Fathers expected as much from the members of the Supreme Court, Meese goes on to suggest how the justices should approach this task. He remains convinced that the application of original intent—undistorted by the personal values of well-meaning judges—will best preserve the principles of democratic government.

The second selection offers a markedly different perspective from someone who has had the responsibility of interpreting our Constitution. Irving Kaufman, chief judge of the United States Court of Appeals for the Second Circuit, maintains that ascertaining the original intent of the Founding Fathers is decidedly more difficult than Edwin Meese would lead us to believe. Nor, for that matter, is the strict application of original intent necessarily desirable in every instance. This is not to say that judges are at liberty to read whatever they choose into the wording of our Constitution. On the contrary, Kaufman points to several factors that serve to restrain judges from doing so.

A Jurisprudence of Original Intention

Edwin Meese III

. . . Today I would like to discuss further the meaning of constitutional fidelity. In particular, I would like to describe in more detail this administration's approach.

Before doing so, I would like to make a few commonplace observations about the
original document itself. . . .

The period surrounding the creation of the Constitution is not a dark and mythical
realm. The young America of the 1780s and '90s was a vibrant place, alive with pamphlets, newspapers and books chronicling and commenting upon the great issues of the
day. We know how the Founding Fathers lived, and much of what they read, thought,
and believed. The disputes and compromises of the Constitutional Convention were
carefully recorded. The minutes of the convention are a matter of public record. Several
of the most important participants—including James Madison, the "father" of the Constitution—wrote comprehensive accounts of the convention. Others, Federalists and
Anti-Federalists alike, committed their arguments for and against ratification, as well as
their understandings of the Constitution, to paper, so that their ideas and conclusions
could be widely circulated, read, and understood.

In short, the Constitution is not buried in the mists of time. We know a tremendous
amount of the history of its genesis. . . .

With these thoughts in mind, I would like to discuss the administration's approach
to constitutional interpretation. . . .

Our approach . . . begins with the document itself. The plain fact is, it exists. It is
something that has been written down. Walter Berns of the American Enterprise Institute has noted that the central object of American constitutionalism was "the effort" of
the Founders "to express fundamental governmental arrangements in a legal document—to 'get it in writing.'"

Indeed, judicial review has been grounded in the fact that the Constitution is a written, as opposed to an unwritten, document. In *Marbury* v. *Madison* John Marshall rested
his rationale for judicial review on the fact that we have a written constitution with
meaning that is binding upon judges. "[I]t is apparent," he wrote, "that the framers of
the Constitution contemplated that instrument as a rule for the government of *courts,* as
well as of the legislature. Why otherwise does it direct the judges to take an oath to support it?"

The presumption of a written document is that it conveys meaning. As Thomas
Grey of the Stanford Law School has said, it makes "relatively definite and explicit
what otherwise would be relatively indefinite and tacit."

We know that those who framed the Constitution chose their words carefully. They
debated at great length the most minute points. The language they chose meant some-

*Edwin Meese III served as U.S. Attorney General under President Ronald Reagan.
Excerpted from a speech by Attorney General Meese before the Washington, D.C.,
chapter of the Federal Society, Lawyers Division, November 15, 1985, pp. 2–14.*

thing. They proposed, they substituted, they edited, and they carefully revised. Their words were studied with equal care by state ratifying conventions.

This is not to suggest that there was unanimity among the framers and ratifiers on all points. The Constitution and the Bill of Rights, and some of the subsequent amendments, emerged after protracted debate. Nobody got everything they wanted. What's more, the framers were not clairvoyants—they could not foresee every issue that would be submitted for judicial review. Nor could they predict how all foreseeable disputes would be resolved under the Constitution. But the point is, the meaning of the Constitution can be known.

What does this written Constitution mean? In places it is exactingly specific. Where it says that Presidents of the United States must be at least 35 years of age it means exactly that. (I have not heard of any claim that 35 means 30 or 25 or 20.) Where it specifies how the House and Senate are to be organized, it means what it says.

The Constitution also expresses particular principles. One is the right to be free of an unreasonable search or seizure. Another concerns religious liberty. Another is the right to equal protection of the laws.

Those who framed these principles meant something by them. And the meanings can be found. The Constitution itself is also an expression of certain general principles. These principles reflect the deepest purpose of the Constitution—that of establishing a political system through which Americans can best govern themselves consistent with the goal of securing liberty.

The text and structure of the Constitution is instructive. It contains very little in the way of specific political solutions. It speaks volumes on how problems should be approached, and by *whom.* For example, the first three articles set out clearly the scope and limits of three distinct branches of national government. The powers of each being carefully and specifically enumerated. In this scheme it is no accident to find the legislative branch described first, as the framers had fought and sacrificed to secure the right of democratic self-governance. Naturally, this faith in republicanism was not unbounded, as the next two articles make clear.

Yet the Constitution remains a document of powers and principles. And its undergirding premise remains that democratic self government is subject only to the limits of certain constitutional principles. This respect for the political process was made explicit early on. When John Marshall upheld the act of Congress chartering a national bank in *McCulloch* v. *Maryland* he wrote: "The Constitution [was] intended to endure for ages to come, and, consequently, to be adapted to the various crises of human affairs." But to use *McCulloch,* as some have tried, as support for the idea that the Constitution is a protean, changeable thing is to stand history on its head. Marshall was keeping faith with the original intention that Congress be free to elaborate and apply constitutional powers and principles. He was not saying that the Court must invent some new constitutional value in order to keep pace with the times. In Walter Berns's words: "Marshall's meaning is not that the Constitution may be adapted to the 'various crises of human affairs,' but that the legislative powers granted by the Constitution are adaptable to meet these crises."

The approach this administration advocates is rooted in the text of the Constitution as illuminated by those who drafted, proposed, and ratified it. In his famous

Commentary on the Constitution of the United States Justice Joseph Story explained that:

> The first and fundamental rule in the interpretation of all instruments is, to construe them according to the sense of the terms, and the intention of the parties.

Our approach understands the significance of a written document and seeks to discern the particular and general principles it expresses. It recognizes that there may be debate at times over the application of these principles. But it does not mean these principles cannot be identified.

Constitutional adjudication is obviously not a mechanical process. It requires an appeal to reason and discretion. The text and intention of the Constitution must be understood to constitute the banks within which constitutional interpretation must flow. As James Madison said, if "the sense in which the Constitution was accepted and ratified by the nation . . . be not the guide in expounding it, there can be no security for a consistent and stable, more than for a faithful exercise of its powers."

Thomas Jefferson, so often cited incorrectly as a framer of the Constitution, in fact shared Madison's view: "Our peculiar security is in the possession of a written Constitution. Let us not make it a blank paper by construction."

Jefferson was even more explicit in his personal correspondence:

> On every question of construction [we should] carry ourselves back to the time, when the constitution was adopted; recollect the spirit manifested in the debates; and instead of trying [to find], what meaning may be squeezed out of the text, or invented against it, conform to the probable one, in which it was passed.

In the main a jurisprudence that seeks to be faithful to our Constitution—a jurisprudence of original intention, as I have called it—is not difficult to describe. Where the language of the Constitution is specific, it must be obeyed. Where there is a demonstrable consensus among the framers and ratifiers as to a principle stated or implied by the Constitution, it should be followed. Where there is ambiguity as to the precise meaning or reach of a constitutional provision, it should be interpreted and applied in a manner so as to at least not contradict the text of the Constitution itself.

Sadly, while almost everyone participating in the current constitutional debate would give assent to these propositions, the techniques and conclusions of some of the debaters do violence to them. What is the source of this violence? In large part I believe that it is the misuse of history stemming from the neglect of the idea of a written constitution.

There is a frank proclamation by some judges and commentators that what matters most about the Constitution is not its words but its so-called "spirit." These individuals focus less on the language of specific provisions than on what they describe as the "vision" or "concepts of human dignity" they find embodied in the Constitution. This approach to jurisprudence has led to some remarkable and tragic conclusions.

In the 1850s, the Supreme Court under Chief Justice Roger B. Taney read blacks out of the Constitution in order to invalidate Congress's attempt to limit the spread of slavery. The *Dred Scott* decision, famously described as a judicial "self-inflicted wound," helped bring on civil war.

There is a lesson in this history. There is danger in seeing the Constitution as an empty vessel into which each generation may pour its passion and prejudice.

Our own time has its own fashions and passions. In recent decades many have come to view the Constitution—more accurately, part of the Constitution, provisions of the Bill of Rights and the Fourteenth Amendment—as a charter for judicial activism on behalf of various constituencies. Those who hold this view often have lacked demonstrable textual or historical support for their conclusions. Instead they have "grounded" their rulings in appeals to social theories, to moral philosophies or personal notions of human dignity, or to "penumbras," somehow emanating ghostlike from various provisions—identified and not identified—in the Bill of Rights. The problem with this approach, as John Hart Ely, Dean of the Stanford Law School, has observed with respect to one such decision, is not that it is bad constitutional law, but that it is not constitutional law in any meaningful sense, at all.

Despite this fact, the perceived popularity of some results in particular cases has encouraged some observers to believe that any critique of the methodology of those decisions is an attack on the results. This perception is sufficiently widespread that it deserves an answer. My answer is to look at history.

When the Supreme Court, in *Brown* v. *Board of Education,* sounded the death knell for official segregation in the country, it earned all the plaudits it received. But the Supreme Court in that case was not giving new life to old words, or adapting a "living," "flexible" Constitution to new reality. It was restoring the original principle of the Constitution to constitutional law. The *Brown* Court was correcting the damage done 50 years earlier, when in *Plessy* v. *Ferguson* an earlier Supreme Court had disregarded the clear intent of the framers of the Civil War amendments to eliminate the legal degradation of blacks, and had contrived a theory of the Constitution to support the charade of "separate but equal" discrimination.

Similarly, the decisions of the New Deal and beyond that freed Congress to regulate commerce and enact a plethora of social legislation were not judicial adaptations of the Constitution to new realities. They were in fact removals of encrustations of earlier courts that had strayed from the original intent of the framers regarding the power of the legislature to make policy.

It is amazing how so much of what passes for social and political progress is really the undoing of old judicial mistakes.

Mistakes occur when the principles of specific constitutional provisions—such as those contained in the Bill of Rights—are taken by some as invitations to read into the Constitution values that contradict the clear language of other provisions.

Acceptances to this illusory invitation have proliferated in recent decades. One Supreme Court justice identified the proper judicial standard as asking "what's best for this country." Another said it is important to "keep the Court out in front" of the general society. Various academic commentators have poured rhetorical grease on this judicial fire, suggesting that constitutional interpretation appropriately be guided by such standards as whether a public policy "personifies justice" or "comports with the notion of moral evolution" or confers "an identity" upon our society or was consistent with "natural ethical law" or was consistent with some "right of equal citizenship."

Unfortunately, as I've noted, navigation by such lodestars has in the past given us questionable economics, governmental disorder, and racism—all in the guise of constitutional law. Recently one of the distinguished judges of one of our federal appeals courts got it about right when he wrote: "The truth is that the judge who looks outside the Constitution always looks inside himself and nowhere else." Or, as we recently put it before the Supreme Court in an important brief: "The further afield interpretation travels from its point of departure in the text, the greater the danger that constitutional adjudication will be like a picnic to which the framers bring the words and the judges the meaning."

In the *Osborne* v. *Bank of United States* decision 21 years after *Marbury,* Chief Justice Marshall further elaborated his view of the relationship between the judge and the law, be it statutory or constitutional:

> Judicial power, as contradistinguished from the power of the laws, has no existence. Courts are the mere instruments of the law, and can will nothing. When they are said to exercise a discretion, it is a mere legal discretion, a discretion to be exercised in discerning the course prescribed by law; and, when that is discerned, it is the duty of the Court to follow it.

Any true approach to constitutional interpretation must respect the document in all its parts and be faithful to the Constitution in its entirety.

What must be remembered in the current debate is that interpretation does not imply results. The framers were not trying to anticipate every answer. They were trying to create a tripartite national government, within a federal system, that would have the flexibility to adapt to face new exigencies—as it did, for example, in chartering a national bank. Their great interest was in the distribution of power and responsibility in order to secure the great goal of liberty for all.

A jurisprudence that seeks fidelity to the Constitution—a jurisprudence of original intention—is not a jurisprudence of political results. It is very much concerned with process, and it is a jurisprudence that in our day seeks to depoliticize the law. The great genius of the constitutional blueprint is found in its creation and respect for spheres of authority and the limits it places on governmental power. In this scheme the framers did not see the courts as the exclusive custodians of the Constitution. Indeed, because the document posits so few conclusions it leaves to the more political branches the matter of adapting and vivifying its principles in each generation. It also leaves to the people of the states, in the Tenth Amendment, those responsibilities and rights not committed to federal care. The power to declare acts of Congress and laws of the states null and void is truly awesome. This power must be used when the Constitution clearly speaks. It should not be used when the Constitution does not.

In *Marbury* v. *Madison,* at the same time he vindicated the concept of judicial review, Marshall wrote that the "principles" of the Constitution "are deemed fundamental and permanent," and except for formal amendment, "unchangeable." If we want a change in our Constitution or in our laws we must seek it through the formal mechanisms presented in that organizing document of our government.

In summary, I would emphasize that what is at issue here is not an agenda of issues or a menu of results. At issue is a way of government. A jurisprudence based on first principles is neither conservative nor liberal, neither right nor left. It is a jurisprudence that cares about committing and limiting to each organ of government the proper ambit of its responsibilities. It is a jurisprudence faithful to our Constitution.

By the same token, an activist jurisprudence, one which anchors the Constitution only in the consciences of jurists, is a chameleon jurisprudence, changing color and form in each era. The same activism hailed today may threaten the capacity for decision through democratic consensus tomorrow, as it has in many yesterdays. Ultimately, as the early democrats wrote into the Massachusetts state constitution, the best defense of our liberties is a government of laws and not men.

On this point it is helpful to recall the words of the late Justice Frankfurter. As he wrote:

> [T]here is not under our Constitution a judicial remedy for every political mischief, for every undesirable exercise of legislative power. The framers carefully and with deliberate forethought refused so to enthrone the judiciary. In this situation, as in others of like nature, appeal for relief does not belong here. Appeal must be to an informed, civically militant electorate. . . .

What Did the Founding Fathers Intend?

Irving R. Kaufman

. . . In the ongoing debate over original intent, almost all federal judges hold to the notion that judicial decisions should be based on the text of the Constitution or the structure it creates. Yet, in requiring judges to be guided solely by the expressed views of the framers, current advocates of original intent seem to call for a narrower concept. Jurists who disregard this interpretation, the argument runs, act lawlessly because they are imposing their own moral standards and political preferences on the community.

As a federal judge, I have found it often difficult to ascertain the "intent of the framers," and even more problematic to try to dispose of a constitutional question by giving great weight to the intent argument. Indeed, even if it were possible to decide hard cases on the basis of a strict interpretation of original intent, or originalism, that methodology would conflict with a judge's duty to apply the Constitution's underlying principles to changing circumstances. Furthermore, by attempting to erode the base for judicial affirmation of the freedoms guaranteed by the Bill of Rights and the 14th Amendment (no state shall "deprive any person of life, liberty, or property without due process of law; nor deny to any person . . . the equal protection of the laws"), the intent theory threatens some of the greatest achievements of the Federal judiciary.

Ultimately, the debate centers on the nature of judicial review, or the power of courts to act as the ultimate arbiters of constitutional meaning. This responsibility has been acknowledged ever since the celebrated 1803 case of *Marbury* v. *Madison,* in which Chief Justice John Marshall struck down a congressional grant of jurisdiction to the Supreme Court not authorized by Article III of the Constitution. But here again, originalists would accept judicial review only if it adhered to the allegedly neutral principles embalmed in historical intent.

In the course of 36 years on the federal bench, I have had to make many difficult constitutional interpretations. I have had to determine whether a teacher could wear a black armband as a protest against the Vietnam War; whether newspapers have a non-actionable right to report accusatory statements; and whether a school system might be guilty of de facto segregation. Unfortunately, the framers' intentions are not made sufficiently clear to provide easy answers. A judge must first determine what the intent was (or would have been)—a notoriously formidable task.

An initial problem is the paucity of materials. Both the official minutes of the Philadelphia Convention of 1787 and James Madison's famous notes of the proceedings, published in 1840, tend toward the terse and cursory, especially in relation to the judiciary. The congressional debates over the proposed Bill of Rights, which became effective in 1791, are scarcely better. Even Justice William Rehnquist, one of the most articulate spokesmen for original intent, admitted in a recent dissent in a case concerning

Irving R. Kaufman is a judge of the 2d U.S. Circuit Court of Appeals. From Irving R. Kaufman, "What Did the Founding Fathers Intend?" New York Times Magazine, February 23, 1986, pp. 59–69. Copyright © 1986 by The New York Times Company. Reprinted by permission.

school prayer that the legislative history behind the provision against the establishment of an official religion "does not seem particularly illuminating."

One source deserves special mention. *The Federalist Papers*—the series of essays written by Alexander Hamilton, James Madison and John Jay in 1787 and 1788—have long been esteemed as the earliest constitutional commentary. In 1825, for example, Thomas Jefferson noted that *The Federalist* was regularly appealed to "as evidence of the general opinion of those who framed and of those who accepted the Constitution of the United States."

The Federalist, however, did not discuss the Bill of Rights or the Civil War amendments, which were yet to be written. Moreover, the essays were part of a political campaign—the authors wrote them in support of New York's ratification of the Constitution. The essays, therefore, tended to enunciate general democratic theory or rebut anti-Federalist arguments, neither of which offers much help to modern jurists. (In light of the following passage from *The Federalist,* No. 14, I believe Madison would be surprised to find his words of 200 years ago deciding today's cases: "Is it not the glory of the people of America that . . . they have not suffered a blind veneration for antiquity . . . to overrule the suggestions of their own good sense. . .?")

Another problem with original intent is this: Who were the framers? Generally, they are taken to be the delegates to the Philadelphia Convention and the congressional sponsors of subsequent amendments. All constitutional provisions, however, have been ratified by state conventions or legislatures on behalf of the people they represented. Is the relevant intention, then, that of the drafters, the ratifiers or the general populace?

The elusiveness of the framers' intent leads to another, more telling problem. Originalist doctrine presumes that intent can be discovered by historical sleuthing or psychological rumination. In fact, this is not possible. Judges are constantly required to resolve questions that 18th-century statesmen, no matter how prescient, simply could not or did not foresee and resolve. On most issues, to look for a collective intention held by either drafters or ratifiers is to hunt for a chimera.

A reading of the Constitution highlights this problem. The principles of our great charter are cast in grand, yet cryptic, phrases. Accordingly, judges usually confront what Justice Robert Jackson in the 1940s termed the "majestic generalities" of the Bill of Rights, or the terse commands of "due process of law," or "equal protection" contained in the 14th Amendment. The use of such open-ended provisions would indicate that the framers did not want the Constitution to become a straitjacket on all events for all times. In contrast, when the framers held a clear intention, they did not mince words. Article II, for example, specifies a minimum Presidential age of 35 years instead of merely requiring "maturity" or "adequate age."

The First Amendment is a good example of a vaguer provision. In guaranteeing freedom of the press, some of our forefathers perhaps had specific thoughts on what publications fell within its purview. Some historians believe, in light of Colonial debates, that the main concern of the framers was to prevent governmental licensing of newspapers. If that were all the First Amendment meant today, then many important decisions protecting the press would have to be overruled. One of them would be the landmark *New York Times* v. *Sullivan* ruling of 1964, giving the press added protection in libel cases brought by public figures. Another would be *Near* v. *Minnesota,* a case involving Jay Near, a newspaper publisher who had run afoul of a Minnesota statute outlawing "malicious, scandalous and defamatory" publications. The Supreme Court struck down the statute in 1931, forbidding governmental prior restraints on publication; this ruling was the precursor of the 1971 Pentagon Papers decision.

The Founding Fathers focused not on particularities but on principles, such as the need in a democracy for people to engage in free and robust discourse. James Madison considered a popular government without popular information a "Prologue to a Farce or a Tragedy." Judges, then, must focus on underlying principles when going about their delicate duty of applying the First Amendment's precepts to today's world.

In fact, our nation's first debate over constitutional interpretation centered on grand principles. Angered at John Adams's Federalist Administration, advocates of states' rights in the late 18th century argued that original intent meant that the Constitution, like the Articles of Confederation, should be construed narrowly—as a compact among separate sovereigns. The 1798 Virginia and Kentucky Resolutions, which sought to reserve to the states the power of ultimate constitutional interpretation, were the most extreme expressions of this view. In rejecting this outlook, a nationalistic Supreme Court construed the Constitution more broadly.

The important point here is that neither side of this debate looked to the stated views of the framers to resolve the issue. Because of his leading role at the Philadelphia Convention, Madison's position is especially illuminating. "Whatever veneration might be entertained for the body of men who formed our Constitution," he declaimed on the floor of Congress in 1796, "the sense of that body could never be regarded as the oracular guide in expounding the Constitution."

Yet, I doubt if strict proponents of original intent will be deterred by such considerations. Their goal is not to venerate dead framers but to restrain living judges from imposing their own values. This restraint is most troublesome when it threatens the protection of individual rights against governmental encroachment.

According to current constitutional doctrine, the due process clause of the 14th Amendment incorporates key provisions of the Bill of Rights, which keeps in check only the Federal Government. Unless the due process clause is construed to include the most important parts of the first eight amendments in the Bill of Rights, then the states would be free, in theory, to establish an official church or inflict cruel and unusual punishments. This doctrine is called incorporation.

Aside from the late Justice Hugo Black, few have believed that history alone is a sufficient basis for applying the Bill of Rights to the states. In his Georgetown University address, Justice Brennan noted that the crucial liberties embodied in the Bill of Rights are so central to our national identity that we cannot imagine any definition of "liberty" without them.

In fact, a cramped reading of the Bill of Rights jeopardizes what I regard as the true original intent—the rationale for having a written Constitution at all. The principal reason for a charter was to restrain government. In 1787, the idea of a fundamental law set down in black and white was revolutionary. Hanoverian England in the 18th century did not have a fully written, unified constitution, having long believed in a partially written one, based on ancient custom and grants from the Crown like the Magna Carta. To this day, the British have kept their democracy alive without one. In theory, the "King-in-Parliament" was and is unlimited in sovereign might, and leading political theorists, such as Thomas Hobbes and John Locke, agreed that governments, once established by a social contract, could not then be fettered.

Although not a Bill of Rights, the Magna Carta—King John's concessions to his barons in 1215—was symbolic of the notion that even the Crown was not all-powerful. Moreover, certain judges believed that Parliament, like the king, had to respect the traditions of the common law. This staunch belief in perpetual rights, in turn, was an important spark for the Revolutionary conflagration of 1776.

In gaining independence, Americans formed the bold concept that sovereignty continually resided with the people, who cede power to governments only to achieve certain specific ends. This view dominated the Philadelphia Convention. Instead of merely improving on the Articles of Confederation, as they had been directed to do, the framers devised a government where certain powers—defined and thereby limited—flowed from the people to the Congress, the President and the Federal judiciary.

Alexander Hamilton recognized that the basic tenets of this scheme mandated judicial review. Individual rights, he observed in *The Federalist,* No. 78, "can be preserved in practice no other way than through the medium of courts of justice, whose duty it must be to declare all acts contrary to the manifest tenor of the Constitution void." Through a written constitution and judicial enforcement, the framers intended to preserve the inchoate rights they had lost as Englishmen.

The narrow interpretation of original intent is especially unfortunate because I doubt that many of its proponents are in favor of freeing the states from the constraints of the Bill of Rights. In fact, I believe the concern of many modern "intentionalists" is quite specific: outrage over the right-of-privacy cases, especially *Roe v. Wade,* the 1973 Supreme Court decision recognizing a woman's right to an abortion. (The right of privacy, of course, is not mentioned in the Constitution.) Whether one agrees with this controversial decision or not, I would submit that concern over the outcome of one difficult case is not sufficient cause to embrace a theory that calls for so many changes in existing law. . . .

. . . [I]f original intent is an uncertain guide, does some other, more functional approach to interpreting the Constitution exist?

One suggestion is to emphasize the importance of democratic "process." As John Hart Ely, dean of the Stanford Law School forcefully advocates, this approach would direct the courts to make a distinction between "process" (the rules of the game, so to speak) and "substance" (the results of the game). Laws dealing with process include those affecting voting rights or participation in society; the Supreme Court correctly prohibited segregation, for example, because it imposed on blacks the continuing stigma of slavery. Judges, however, would not have the power to review the substantive decisions of elected officials, such as the distribution of welfare benefits.

Basically, such an approach makes courts the guardians of democracy, but a focus on process affords little help when judges decide between difficult and competing values. Judicial formulation of a democratic vision, for example, requires substantive decision-making. The dignities of human liberty enshrined in the Bill of Rights are not merely a means to an end, even so noble an end as democratic governance. For example, we cherish freedom of speech not only because it is necessary for meaningful elections, but also for its own sake.

The truth is that no litmus test exists by which judges can confidently and consistently measure the constitutionality of their decisions. Notwithstanding the clear need for judicial restraint, judges do not constitute what Prof. Raoul Berger, a retired Harvard Law School fellow, has termed an "imperial judiciary." I would argue that the judicial process itself limits the reach of a jurist's arm.

First, judges do not and cannot deliberately contravene specific constitutional rules or clear indications of original intent. No one would seriously argue or expect, for instance, that the Supreme Court could or would twist the Presidential minimum-age provision into a call for "sufficient maturity," so as to forbid the seating of a 36-year-old.

I doubt, in any event, that federal judges would ever hear such a question. The Constitution limits our power to traditional "cases" and "controversies" capable of judicial resolution. In cases like the hypothetical one regarding the presidential age, the High Court employs doctrines of standing (proving injury) and "political question" to keep citizens from suing merely out of a desire to have the government run a certain way.

Moreover, the issues properly before a judge are not presented on a tabula rasa. Even the vaguest constitutional provisions have received the judicial gloss of prior decisions. Precedent alone, of course, should not preserve clearly erroneous decisions; the abhorrent "separate but equal" doctrine survived for more than 50 years before the Warren Court struck it down in 1954.

The conventions of our judicial system also limit a jurist's ability to impose his or her own will. One important restraint, often overlooked, is the tradition that appellate judges issue written opinions. That is, we must support our decisions with reasons instead of whims and indicate how our constitutional rulings relate to the document. A written statement is open to the dissent of colleagues, possible review by a higher court and the judgment, sometimes scathing, of legal scholars.

In addition, the facts of a given case play a pivotal role. Facts delineate the reach of a legal decision and remind us of the "cases and controversies" requirement. Our respect for such ground rules reassures the public that, even in the most controversial case, the outcome is not just a political ruling.

Judges are also mindful that the ultimate justification for their power is public acceptance—acceptance not of every decision, but of the role they play. Without popular support, the power of judicial review would have been eviscerated by political forces long ago.

Lacking the power of the purse or the sword, the courts must rely on the elected branches to enforce their decisions. The school desegregation cases would have been a dead letter unless President Eisenhower had been willing to order out the National Guard—in support of a decision authored by a Chief Justice, Earl Warren, whose appointment the President had called "the biggest damned-fool mistake I ever made."

Instead of achieving the purple of philosopher-kings, an unprincipled judiciary would risk becoming modern King Canutes, with the cold tide of political reality and popular opprobrium lapping at their robes.

My revered predecessor on the Court of Appeals, Judge Learned Hand, remarked in a lecture at Harvard in the late 1950s that he would not want to be ruled by "a bevy of Platonic Guardians." The Constitution balances the danger of judicial abuse against the threat of a temporary majority trampling individual rights. The current debate is a continuation of an age-old, and perhaps endless, struggle to reach a balance between our commitments to democracy and to the rule of law. . . .

Crime and the Courts

Courts have a special role to play in our society. Unlike the two political branches of our government—Congress and the President—which are most sensitive to majority public opinion, courts must protect and defend minorities. Indeed, courts most often are called upon to ensure that the government acts in a fair and reasonable manner and to make certain that individual rights are protected.

Courts have a particularly important role to play in the protection of criminal rights, for in this area they must see that no injustice is done to the person accused of a crime.

In the last 30 years, the U.S. Supreme Court has taken great care in enforcing the constitutional rights of persons accused of a crime. These include such protections as the right to remain silent and the right to counsel. Some of these criminal procedural safeguards have evoked considerable controversy among law-enforcement officials, political leaders, commentators, and the general public. Typically, critics of the criminal justice system point to its failures—failures that either put criminals back on the streets or penalize innocent and unsuspecting people.

In the two articles that follow, the role of the courts in the criminal justice system is examined. In the first article, journalist Bernard Gavzer reports on the views of New York State judge, Harold Rothwax, an outspoken critic of today's criminal justice system and author of Guilty: The Collapse of Criminal Justice. *According to Judge Rothwax, the criminal justice system, with all its procedural guarantees, is tilted too much in favor of criminal suspects, so much so that he believes "We're in the fight of our lives" to preserve a law-abiding society.*

In the second article John Kilwein, a professor of political science at West Virginia University, challenges the views of Judge Rothwax. While conceding that crime continues to be a major problem in the United States, Professor Kilwein argues that it would be unwise to adopt Judge Rothwax's "reforms" of the criminal justice system. Kilwein contends that the real issue in the criminal justice system is whether all citizens are fully protected from the possible abuses and excesses of law-enforcement officials. The many procedural guarantees of the Constitution and the courts, he argues, are merely the means to assure a "fair fight" between a criminal defendant and a criminal justice system that is stacked heavily in favor of the government. Without these guarantees, he contends, there exists the very real possibility that innocent persons might be accused, tried, convicted, and punished without adequate protection of the law.

'We're in the Fight of Our Lives'

Bernard Gavzer

At 2 A.M. on November 20, 1990, Leonardo Turriago was pulled over for speeding by two state troopers. They asked if they could look into his van, and Turriago said they could. Inside, the troopers saw a trunk and asked Turriago about it. He sprang open its lock, then ran away. Opening the trunk, the troopers found the body of a man shot five times.

Turriago was quickly caught. In his apartment, police found 11 pounds of cocaine and guns. The suspect told them where to look for the murder weapon, and it was recovered. Turriago was convicted of second-degree murder and sentenced to 45 years to life.

The defense appealed, saying the troopers had no right to search the van. On June 6, 1996, Turriago's conviction was overturned. A New York appellate court ruled that the police search was not justified and had been coerced.

"Criminal justice in America is in a state of collapse," says Judge Harold J. Rothwax, who has spent 25 years presiding over criminal cases in New York City. "We have formalism and technicalities but little common sense. It's about time America wakes up to the fact that we're in the fight of our lives."

Rothwax believes cases such as Turriago's illustrate that the procedural dotting of every "i" and crossing of every "t" has become more important than the crime's substance. "The bottom line is that criminals are going free," he says. "There is no respect for the truth, and without truth, there can be no justice."

While the search for truth should be the guiding principle of our courts, instead, the judge says, "our system is a carefully crafted maze, constructed of elaborate and impenetrable barriers to the truth.". . .

Practices we have taken for granted—such as the *Miranda* warning, the right to counsel, even unanimous jury verdicts—need to be reconsidered, says the judge. "You know." Rothwax confides, "more than 80 percent of the people who appear before me are probably guilty of some crime."

Rothwax insists there is a fundamental difference between the investigative and the trial stages of a case. The investigative stage is marked by the notion of probable guilt, he asserts, not the presumption of innocence. "Until a defendant goes on trial, he is probably guilty," the judge says, noting that by the time a person reaches trial he has been deemed "probably guilty" several times. "When a person is arrested, indicted by a grand jury, held in detention or released on bail, it is all based on probable guilt." Rothwax adds. "Once *on trial,* he is presumed innocent.". . .

The positions the judge has staked out in what he regards as his crusade to bring sense to the criminal justice system have shocked those who long associated him with strong liberal causes. A lifelong Democrat, Rothwax was a senior defense trial attorney

Bernard Gavzer is a contributing editor for Parade *magazine. From Bernard Gavzer, "We're in the Fight of Our Lives,"* Parade, *July 28, 1996, pp. 4–6. Reprinted with permission from* Parade, *Copyright © 1996.*

for the Legal Aid Society in New York and a stalwart of the New York Civil Liberties Union early in his career.

"I represented Lenny Bruce and Abbie Hoffman, the Black Panthers and the Vietnam war protesters," he says, "I am today as much a civil libertarian as ever. But that does not mean I must close my eyes to the devastation that has occurred in criminal justice. We have the crime, but where is the justice? It is all tilted in favor of the criminal, and it is time to bring this into balance."

The interests of the victim weigh solidly in Rothwax's courtroom in the Criminal Court Building in Manhattan. However, he is troubled by some decisions of the U.S. Supreme Court, saying: "Its rulings over the last 35 years have made the criminal justice system incomprehensible and unworkable."

Although neither the Supreme Court nor the Courts of Appeals decide the guilt or innocence of a defendant, they do make rulings on the constitutionality of acts by the police and lower courts and thus have a significant impact on our justice system. Key practices of our current system—which have come about as a result of Supreme Court rulings in recent decades—need to be changed, Rothwax believes. Among them are:

The Miranda Warning   In New York, Alfio Ferro was arrested in 1975 in connection with a fur robbery that turned into a murder. In the lockup, a detective—without saying a word—dropped some of the stolen furs in front of Ferro's cell. Ferro then made incriminating statements that led to his conviction for second-degree murder.

In 1984, an appellate court overturned the conviction, saying that the detective's action amounted to interrogation and violated Ferro's *Miranda* rights. The *Miranda* warning requires that the suspect be told he has a right to remain silent, that any statement he makes might be used against him and that he has the right to have a lawyer present.

"*Miranda* came about because of abuses such as prolonged custodial interrogation, beatings and starving in order to get a confession," says Rothwax. "I think those abuses have been largely dealt with. Now the police officer is put in the position of telling a suspect in a murder or rape, 'Look, you don't have to tell us anything, and that may be the best thing for you.' And it produces a situation in which a proper confession is thrown out because of the way in which it was read or that it wasn't read at the right time."

Rothwax believes *Miranda* can be replaced by the recording of an arrest and interrogation through videotapes, tape recorders and other technology. This would probably show whether a confession or statement was coerced.

The Exclusionary Rule   [In the winter of 1996] Federal Judge Harold Baer Jr. refused to admit as evidence 80 pounds of cocaine and heroin obtained in the arrest of a drug courier in the Washington Heights neighborhood of New York City. The evidence was excluded because, said Baer, the police had violated the Fourth Amendment protection against unreasonable search and seizure when they searched the car in which the drugs were found.

The police said their search was proper in view of the fact that they saw men hastily loading bags into an out-of-state car in a high drug area in the middle of the night, and the men ran away when the police approached. Judge Baer, however, said just because the men ran off was no reason to suspect them of a crime. In Washington Heights, the judge said, it was not unusual for even innocent people to flee, because police there were regarded as "corrupt, violent and abusive."

Under a growing chorus of criticism. Judge Baer first reversed himself and then asked that the case be assigned to another judge. It was. Rothwax says this is the sort of muddled episode which arises from the exclusionary rule, producing "truth and justice denied on a technicality."

"The Supreme Court has consistently ruled that evidence seized in violation of the Fourth Amendment *should* be excluded from a criminal trial. But if you read the Fourth Amendment, nowhere does it say that *illegally* obtained evidence *must* be excluded," says Rothwax. "In my view, when you exclude or suppress evidence, you suppress the truth."

Judge Rothwax has a remedy: "Make the exclusionary rule *discretionary* instead of mandatory. If it was at the discretion of the judge, there could be a test of reasonableness. A judge could consider factors such as whether a police officer acted with objective reasonableness and subjective good faith. As it is now, the exclusionary rule is irrational, arbitrary and lacks proportion. No wonder that in 90 percent of exclusionary cases, the police don't know what the law is."

The Right to Counsel   In 1982, Kenneth West of New York, an alleged drug dealer, was suspected of being involved in killing a man who had taken his parking place. His lawyer, at a police lineup, told the police not to question West in his absence. Nothing came of the case for three years. Then police arrested a former cohort of West who said West had been one of the shooters. The informer secretly taped West talking about the killing. West was convicted, but in 1993 the New York Court of Appeals reversed the conviction, saying the secret taping amounted to questioning him without the presence of counsel.

The right to counsel is provided by the Sixth Amendment. "It is essential there be a right to counsel," Judge Rothwax says. "But the amendment doesn't say it has to be during police questioning and investigation. As a result of technicalities over this issue of counsel, I have seen murderers go free. Make it clear that the right to a lawyer shouldn't be a factor in the *investigative* stage but only in pre-trial and trial stages."

Instructions to the Jury   After closing arguments in the O. J. Simpson murder trial, Judge Ito took great care in telling jurors that Simpson's failure to take the stand in his own defense should in no way be taken to mean anything negative or to draw any other adverse conclusion.

This instruction to the jury occurs in all cases in which the defense asks for it, because of a Supreme Court ruling in 1981 that said not to do so amounted to a violation of the Fifth Amendment. [The Fifth Amendment states that no person shall be forced to testify against himself.] "The Fifth Amendment does *not* say that one might not draw reasonable inferences from the silence of a defendant," Judge Rothwax says. "I think we must find a way to return to the standard that existed before, that the judge could tell the jury that the failure to explain could amount to an inability to explain."

The judge would like to see other changes made to the jury system. Among them:

1. *Unanimous jury verdicts should no longer be required.* Why? Rothwax cites a murder case he presided over. "It was an overwhelming case of clear guilt. Yet there was a hung jury. One juror was convinced the defendant was not guilty. How did she know? Well, as she explained it, 'Someone that good-looking could not commit such a crime.' We had to retry the case, and the man was quickly found guilty."

   By allowing verdicts to be decided by a vote of 11-1 or 10-2, Rothwax says, there could be a reduced risk that a single juror could cause a retrial or force a compromise in the face of overwhelming evidence of guilt.

2. *Preemptory challenges to prospective jurors should be strictly limited or abolished.* Peremptory challenges allow lawyers to knock someone off the jury without giving any reason. "As we saw in the Simpson case," Rothwax says, "it makes it possible to stack a jury so that the most educated juror is excused, and you end up with a jury that can be manipulated to accept innuendo as evidence."

Judge Rothwax regards the entire conduct of the Simpson trial as an unspeakable insult to the American people, one that left them "feeling wounded and deeply distrustful of the system." He adds: "There was an opportunity to show a vast audience the potential vitality of justice at work. Instead we are assaulted by an obscene circus. We saw proof that the American courtroom is dangerously out of order.". . .

To sit with Rothwax in court, as this writer did, is to get a sense of his urgency for reform. In three hours, there was a procession of men and women charged with felonies from murder to drug dealing. Rothwax was all business, and he was tough with everyone. After 47 cases had been considered and dealt with, the judge turned to me and asked, with irony, about the defendants we had seen: "Did you notice the huge display of remorse?" There hadn't been any. "That's why" he said, "we are in the fight of our lives."

Just Make It a Fair Fight

John C. Kilwein

Crime is a significant problem in this country. Almost 25,000 persons are the victims of homicides each year. Property loss and medical expenses related to crime exceed $17 billion per year. Responding to these and other troubling statistics, President Clinton has promised 100,000 new police officers on the streets in American cities and towns. Congress has "federalized" dozens of crimes that were formerly only state offenses, and state legislatures have passed mandatory minimum sentence laws that require convicted criminals to spend more time in prison. The U.S. Bureau of Justice Statistics reports that as a result of these changes the number of people incarcerated in federal and state prisons more than tripled, increasing from 319,600 in 1980 to 999,800 in 1994. In addition, Congress has made it much more difficult for prisoners to use the federal courts, the Constitution, and writs of *habeas corpus* to appeal their convictions. All of this is evidence of a concerted national effort, some might argue excessive effort, to deal with the crime problem.

But efforts such as these are not enough for New York Judge Harold Rothwax. He wants to shock us into taking action in the criminal courts, and in so doing he uses arguments that are based on fear.[1] Judge Rothwax warns Americans, as they read their Sunday papers, of the ominous threats of such dark predators as Leonardo Turriago, who cart murder victims around in the trunks of their automobiles and who walk the streets thanks to legal "technicalities." But as Judge Rothwax spins his frightening yarn, he fails to tell the reader that the crime rate is actually dropping, in spite of the alleged flaws of the criminal justice system. Violent crime, for example, dropped 12.4 percent in 1995, the largest drop since 1973.[2] Why the paradox: A reduction in crime, while Judge Rothwax thinks we are in "the fight of our lives."?

Judge Rothwax offers us a new system of criminal justice that assumes that all police officers and prosecutors do their jobs in a fair and objective manner, free of any systematic bias against groups or individuals in society. The Rothwax system assumes that prosecutors will base their prosecutorial decisions strictly on legal grounds, ignoring other factors such as political gain or racial animus. Judge Rothwax believes that as a society we have largely solved the problem of police brutality; that American law-enforcement officials no longer use uncomfortable detention, physical violence, or psychological coercion to secure convictions. The Rothwax system assumes that criminal defendants in the United States have more legal representation than they deserve, and that the system would benefit by reducing the formal rules that lawyers bring to the pretrial process. Unfortunately, the real world of American criminal justice is far more complex than the "good vs. evil" morality play suggested by Judge Rothwax.

John C. Kilwein is a professor of political science at West Virginia University. This article was written especially for Points of View *in 1997.*

THE GOVERNMENT VS. THE CRIMINAL DEFENDANT: A FAIR FIGHT?

The legal system in the United States is based on the belief that the best way for a court to discover the truth in a legal dispute is to allow the parties to battle it out in the courtroom before a jury or judge. The judge acts as an independent and objective arbiter or referee who makes sure that the disputants battle fairly by following the rules of law. The disputants are responsible for developing the case they will bring into the courtroom and will understandably have a strong incentive to seek out any evidence or witnesses that might assist them. The disputants also have the right to challenge the veracity of their opponent's presentation. The confrontation in court between these two competing sides, each presenting a very different version of a contested dispute, will, in theory, maximize the likelihood that the truth will come out.[3] Of course, the difficult job for the judge or the jury is sifting through the two accounts to arrive at a sense of what actually took place and what justice should be.

When applied to disputes involving a crime, the disputants in the adversarial system are the defendant, or the person charged with committing the crime, and the state. The state, rather than the victim, is the litigant in criminal cases because by definition crimes not only harm victims, they also harm and threaten society as a whole. In a criminal case, therefore, the battle to be played out in the courtroom is between a person charged with a crime and a prosecutor who represents the interests of society—a battle that strains the notion of a fair fight. The government clearly has a lot more advantages than the criminal defendant. The extent of this mismatch is underscored by the fact that prosecutors have available to them the machinery of government, including the vast investigative powers of law enforcement, whereas defendants must do it on their own.

The American justice system takes into account this disparity, however, by providing the defendant with certain procedural rights and advantages that are intended to equalize the courtroom battle in criminal cases. This system assumes that when a powerful litigant, the state, faces a weaker litigant, the defendant, there is a high probability of a wrongful conviction of an innocent person unless the state follows procedures designed to make it a fair fight. And in our criminal legal tradition, there is no greater miscarriage of justice than sending innocent individuals to prison or to their death. Modern-day criminal procedure protections seek to prevent such an outcome.

Among the equalizers built into the American legal system are: the presumption of innocence; the beyond-a-reasonable-doubt standard of proof; the prohibitions against unreasonable search and seizure, forced self-incrimination, excessive bail, excessive fines, double jeopardy, and cruel and unusual punishment; the right to counsel, a trial by jury, a public and speedy trial, to speak at trial, to confront and cross-examine hostile witnesses, to present favorable witnesses, and guaranteed access to the writ of *habeas corpus.* Some of these "equalizers" have been incorporated into our system as part of formal documents, or constitutions, that act as the blueprints for our American governments, while others were added as our criminal justice system evolved and became part of our legal tradition.

For Judge Rothwax the balance between the state and the criminally accused is fundamentally flawed. Criminal defendants are not the "weak sisters" in a criminal trial; the state is. For Judge Rothwax, a "liberal" judiciary led by the U.S. Supreme Court has conspired to create new and extreme rights for the defendant. These extravagant rights, moreover, make it extremely difficult for the prosecutor and the police to do their jobs. Seemingly guilty defendants are released from custody because their defense lawyers exploited some constitutional technicality. The murder trial of O. J. Simpson is seen as a case in point. Overworked, underpaid, and inept prosecutors fumbled before a group of highly paid "dream team" defense lawyers, who exploited every procedural technicality to achieve a verdict of innocence.

Judge Rothwax offers up an alternative system of criminal justice that tips the balance in the courtroom battle toward the side of the prosecution by limiting a defendant's right to counsel, altering the presumption of innocence, increasing the power of police to search for proof of criminality and to interrogate defendants, allowing more evidence favoring the prosecution's case to be admitted in court, and altering the nature of jury deliberations in criminal trials. In short, the Rothwax system makes it easier for the prosecution to prove to a jury that a criminal defendant is guilty as charged, and deserving of punishment.

THE "SUSPECT RIGHTS" OF SUSPECTS

The Presumption of Innocence

Our legal system recognizes that a criminal dispute is more serious than a civil dispute. In criminal law, society has the capacity to publicly punish the convicted criminal, using several forms of punishment. First, the defendant faces the shame and consequences associated with being declared a convicted criminal, including the loss of certain freedoms and rights, as for example, access to a variety of licenses, or the freedom to perform certain jobs. Second, criminal conviction can bring with it the possibility of substantial monetary fines, often in the thousands of dollars. Third, criminal conviction can result in a complete loss of freedom through incarceration, with all the unintended consequences of life behind bars, a violent world often filled with physical assault, rape, and other indignities. Finally, in 38 states and at the federal level, defendants charged with capital crimes face the ultimate punishment of being put to death by the state.

Given the seriousness of being charged with a crime, the American legal system confers on the defendant an important protection: the presumption of innocence. The primary purpose of this rule is to prevent a wrongful conviction that sends an innocent person to prison or to death. There is a simple yet profound logic behind this rule. When a criminal victimizes an individual, society intervenes to find, try, and punish the criminal. The harm suffered by the victim can never be undone, but some solace comes from the fact that the state takes a direct interest in resolving the criminal dispute. On the other hand, when the state wrongfully punishes an innocent defendant, the victimization is absolute. There is no solace available to the innocent person, since the perpetrator is the state. This perspective gives rise to the old saw that it is better to let ten guilty persons go free than to send one innocent individual to prison or death. For Judge Rothwax, however, that old saw is apparently a bit rusty and should be replaced by a new motto: The criminal justice system almost never convicts the wrong person; and those guilty individuals who are set free are threatening us all.

Judge Rothwax makes a distinction between the investigative (pretrial) and trial stages of the criminal process. Rothwax argues that during the investigative stage, defendants are assumed to be guilty by the police and the prosecutor or they would not have been arrested and indicted in the first place. He concludes that when defendants appear before his bench, they are probably guilty of the charges or their cases would never have reached his court. In short, Judge Rothwax gives the state the benefit of the doubt that it only prosecutes clearly guilty people. This perspective is troubling because it ignores the basic idea behind adversarial justice: Legal conflicts are not prejudged but decided through the courtroom battle.

While it is true that the great majority of police officers and prosecutors are honest people who play by the rules and who have no desire to harm innocent people, Rothwax's position ignores a number of very real problems. The most obvious problem of the proposed system is that it fails to take into account that justice officials can and do make mistakes, and the importance of the trial process in detecting these honest errors. Second, Judge Rothwax ignores the fact that a minority of justice officials, however small, are lazy, dishonest, corrupt, racist, or some combination of these. Examples of these troubling behaviors abound in our criminal justice system. In 1997, for example, an internal U.S. Department of Justice investigation revealed that agents of the highly respected FBI crime laboratory altered evidence and skewed testimony to assist prosecutors.[4] In Texas and West Virginia false testimony given by an incompetent and dishonest medical examiner sent at least six innocent men to prison.[5] To avoid the embarrassment and political fallout of being unable to convict the perpetrators of an arson fire with multiple deaths in New York[6] and the killing of a police officer in Houston,[7] prosecutors in both cities tenaciously pursued capital murder charges against apparently innocent individuals, while ignoring or concealing exculpatory evidence in the prosecution's possession. And evidence that some police officers and prosecutors target young black and Hispanic men for questionable arrest and prosection comes to light with alarming frequency, as in the case of Carlton Brown.[8]

The case of Carlton Brown is particularly enlightening. Mr. Brown, who is black, is paralyzed from the chest down following injuries he sustained while under arrest in New York City's 63rd Precinct. Charged with driving with a suspended license, Mr. Brown contended that the arresting officers, after becoming irritated with his demands for information on his arrest, smashed his head while he was handcuffed into a bullet-proof, double-plate glass window and severely injured his spine. The two police officers involved with his arrest countered that Mr. Brown had hurt himself falling down in the police station. The police officers were charged, tried before a judge, and acquitted. In a subsequent civil proceeding, however, the city of New York agreed to pay Mr. Brown $4.5 million in civil damages, a record-setting pretrial settlement. Needless to say, such a settlement calls into question Judge Rothwax's confidence in the criminal justice system's ability to function in an unbiased manner. Our system of justice assumes that people, including law-enforcement officials, are not angels[9] or saints; nor are they infallible; and it builds in protections, like the presumption of innocence, accordingly. The Rothwax system depends on an angelic conversion among these officials, an unlikely occurrence now or ever.

Miranda and the Right to Remain Silent and the Right to Counsel

Judge Rothwax reserves some of his harshest criticism for the U.S. Supreme Court's 1966 decision in *Miranda* v. *Arizona*.[10] In that decision the Court ruled that a confession made by Ernest Miranda, who was charged with kidnapping and raping an 18-year-old woman, was unconstitutionally obtained by police interrogators.[11] Extending its ruling beyond the immediate circumstances of the arrest and interrogation of Miranda, the Court required that henceforth all police officers and prosecutors must inform defendants of their rights to remain silent and to have counsel.[12] Commenting on state law-enforcement officials, the Court observed:

> The use of physical brutality and violence is not, unfortunately, relegated to the past or to any part of the country. Only recently in Kings County [Brooklyn Borough], New York the police brutally beat, kicked and placed lighted cigarette butts on the back of a potential witness under interrogation for the purpose of securing a statement incriminating a third party.[13]

The Court added that while not using physical violence, other police interrogators use psychological abuse and lies to trick defendants into confessing to crimes.

Seen as an indictment against all police officers and prosecutors, the decision in *Miranda* was, and, as highlighted by Judge Rothwax, still is, very unpopular within the law-enforcement community. This is unfortunate because, as Chief Justice Warren argued in the opinion, the *Miranda* requirements do not prevent good law-enforcement officers from doing their job. Indeed, as pointed out by Warren, agents of the FBI had already been using the warnings and were still able to investigate and assist in the conviction of federal defendants. What the warnings were designed to do was prevent an innocent defendant from confessing in order to bring an end to an abusive interrogation. The fact of the matter is that police officers who do not abuse defendants have nothing to fear from the *Miranda* requirements.

The *Miranda* decision also sought to make effective two important equalizers in the Bill of Rights: the prohibition against self-incrimination and the right to counsel. The right against self-incrimination or the right to remain silent is based on an old common law principle that the state cannot force defendants to testify against themselves. Rather, the state makes the charges and must prove its case. Although the right to counsel came later in the Anglo-American legal tradition, it is based on the belief that it is unreasonable to expect ordinary persons to understand the legal implications of statements they might make or actions they might take in the pretrial stage, actions that might again lead to their wrongful conviction. The *Miranda* requirement was based on the reasonable assumption that illiterate or uniformed defendants probably are not aware of these protections and therefore the state has a responsibility to inform them.

Judge Rothwax argues against this necessity, contending that, because defense attorneys step in and convince their clients to do otherwise, *Miranda* prevents the police from securing confessions from cooperative defendants. Apparently Judge Rothwax is opposed to the general principle of informed consent, that is, that defendants should know what they are doing before they say anything or confess. Judge Rothwax also seems to believe that the abuse of defendants while in police custody, cited by Chief Justice Warren in *Miranda,* is no longer a problem. Unfortunately, evidence suggests that in his zeal to get tougher on crime and criminals, Judge Rothwax is ignoring the fact that abuses continue in the interrogation stage of the pretrial process. An example from Rothwax's own hometown underscores this conclusion.[14] Police officers in New York's 24th Precinct arrested a 17-year-old white male for a misdemeanor. He refused to confess. The defendant was held in a jail cell for two nights. At one point, he was placed in a van and chained in the sweltering heat. At another point a police officer waved his gun in front of the defendant and threatened to "shoot his dick off." One wonders if the cameras in the precinct, called for by Judge Rothwax to protect against such abuse, would have captured this particular "Kodak moment"! The evidence suggests that this incident is not a random occurrence, in New York or nationally. Amnesty International has cited 90 cases of police brutality allegedly perpetrated by officers of the New York Police Department alone. Similar charges by other watchdog groups have been leveled at other departments around the country.[15]

For most first-time defendants the pretrial process can be a very frightening experience. Defendants, innocent or guilty, who cannot post bail are held in jail until their trial. The pace of some criminal justice systems can be glacial, taking up to two years for a case to make it to trial. This delay, moreover, can be used to entice or coerce a defendant into making a confession, even a false one. For example, a prosecutor can offer defendants awaiting trial a plea bargain that gives them credit for time served while awaiting trial in exchange for a guilty plea. Given this offer, an innocent defendant might make a false confession, assuming that the conviction is a small price to pay for immediate release from prison.[16] The deal may be especially appealing if the defendant considers that a guilty verdict by jury at trial could yield an even stiffer sentence. Interrogations are also daunting for a defendant unfamiliar with the law. And although the great majority of questionings are conducted by professional officers observing all relevant constitutional requirements, the fact remains that police officers have substantially more experience in the process than do defendants, thereby increasing the probability that defendants will unwittingly damage their own case. In these and every other pretrial situation defendants would be at a severe disadvantage without legal representation.

In the end, the Rothwax system would punish the ignorant, the weak, and the poor. Wealthy or more highly educated defendants, who have a basic understanding of the legal system, are more likely to know they have the right to remain silent and to make informed choices about its use. Likewise, sophisticated defendants who are not intimidated by pretrial detention and rough treatment are also more likely to refuse to assist the police in developing the state's case against them. Moreover, defendants with long-standing criminal records are also likely to be especially cognizant of their right to remain silent. In addition, multiple offenders who have experienced the daily violence of the corrections system are probably less likely to be frightened into confessing as the result of a difficult interrogation.

The most troubling aspect of Rothwax's system, however, from the point of view of equal justice for all, is that it rewards wealthier criminal defendants. Individuals who can afford to hire a lawyer and post bail are able to avoid the various forms of pretrial pressure since they can await trial in the comfort of their own homes; and, with the advice of counsel, they are more likely to remain silent, thereby putting the government to its full task of convicting them without their assistance. It is quite possible, therefore, that the system proposed by Judge Rothwax will have the unintended consequence of convicting more innocent, first-time criminal defendants, while releasing those defendants with experience and/or money. These potential biases do not seem to concern Judge Rothwax. Like some American generals in Vietnam, Judge Rothwax seems to be singularly concerned only with body counts: So what if these new convictions are gained at the expense of fairness; they're convictions; and that's what counts! A justice system that operates in this manner has abandoned any pretense of being blind to a defendant's wealth or social status. It is a justice system more likely to convict an innocent defendant whose real crime is that he or she lives in the South Bronx rather than on Long Island.

The Exclusionary Rule

The exclusionary rule is an American invention, created by the U.S. Supreme Court in 1914.[17] It was designed to resolve the question of what should be done when a police officer or prosecutor violates the constitutional protections of defendants who have been the targets of illegal searches or interrogations. By making this ruling, the Supreme Court, using a classic American "free-market" approach, has ruled that such evidence is tainted and must therefore be excluded from trial. The exclusionary rule, the Court has argued, removes any incentive for law-enforcement officials to engage in unconstitutional and illegal activities, since ill-gotten gains cannot be used in court.

Since the Bill of Rights make no mention of this rule in the Fourth Amendment's prohibition against unreasonable searches and seizures, Judge Rothwax contends that the rule is an illegitimate hindrance to the criminal justice system's operation. He argues that excluded evidence prevents the court from getting the total truth surrounding a case. To accept this logic, however, one must, again, accept, as Rothwax clearly does, that in the rule's absence, police officers or prosecutors are unlikely to violate the Fourth or Fifth Amendments in their search for evidence or confessions. Given the examples of illegal police conduct cited above, it is difficult to share Justice Rothwax's views of the motives and actions of the police.

Judge Rothwax is also upset because the exclusionary rule has, in his view, been used by judges in an overly technical and picky manner, with good cases being thrown out because investigating officers forgot to "dot the i's and cross the t's." He blames the "liberal" U.S. Supreme Court for decisions that favor criminal defendants. What Judge Rothwax disingenuously ignores, however, is that the Supreme Court of 1997 is, in fact, a quite conservative one, particularly in its decisions dealing with the rights of criminal defendants. Since the mid-1970s, the U.S. Supreme Court has consistently shifted the constitutional advantage in criminal matters away from criminal defendants toward the police and prosecution. Specifically, in terms of the exclusionary rule, the Court has ruled in ways that enable prosecutors to use more questionable evidence and confessions against criminal defendants. Two examples highlight this shift. In *U.S.* v. *Havens*,[18] the Court allowed illegally obtained evidence to be used in trial to discredit testimony during cross examination. And in *Nix* v. *Williams*,[19] the Court ruled that tainted evidence can be used against the defendant if the trial court judge concludes that evidence would inevitably have been discovered.

Peremptory Challenges and Unanimous Jury Verdicts

Judge Rothwax's remaining indictments of the present criminal justice system deal with criminal juries. Responding to the controversy surrounding the O. J. Simpson murder trial, he criticizes the defense team's use of peremptory challenges to eliminate prospective jurors.[20] He argues that the Simpson defense team used such challenges to seat a jury that could be easily fooled by courtroom pyrotechnics. Whether this is true or not is a matter of conjecture, but it should be noted that Judge Rothwax ignores the fact that the prosecution had the same opportunity to affect the makeup of the jury. In reality, peremptory challenges help both sides in the courtroom battle, and thus we can assume that their removal would potentially hurt both sides as well. Rothwax, however, clearly presumes that these challenges only help the defendant; in fact, this presumption is not warranted. In 1997, for example, a videotape surfaced that was used as a training device for assistant prosecutors in Philadelphia.[21] The tape shows a senior prosecutor counseling his trainees to exclude black citizens from serving on criminal juries because they are distrustful of the police, and therefore less likely to convict. The tape tells the trainees they should especially avoid placing young black women on their juries, because they are very bad for the prosecution's case. Although this episode remains to be investigated, and the attorney featured in the video vehemently denies having done anything illegal or morally wrong, the advice presented on this tape would appear to violate a Supreme Court ruling prohibiting race from being used as a factor in selecting jurors. More fundamentally, this example calls into question Judge Rothwax's contention that the justice system has solved the problem of systemic racism.

Judge Rothwax also opposes the requirement that a criminal jury reach a verdict of guilt unanimously, suggesting instead that we should allow a jury to convict a defendant with a substantial majority, for example, a vote of 11–1 or 10–2. In fact, the practice of jury unanimity[22] is merely a legal custom and not an explicit constitutional right, and the U.S. Supreme Court has established that if states choose, they can allow juries to reach their decision with a clear, nonunanimous verdict.[23] Given the Supreme Court's view on this issue, Judge Rothwax's gripe, then, is with the legal system of the state of New York, which apparently has decided to continue the practice of jury unanimity, and not with the rulings of the so-called liberal U.S. Supreme Court in Washington.

WE FACE THE CHOICE OF OUR LIVES

The late Senator Sam Ervin once said: "In a free society you have to take some risks. If you lock everybody up, or even if you lock up everybody you think might commit a crime, you'll be pretty safe, but you won't be free."[24] To this one might add, and you might end up getting locked up yourself!

This country was shaped in part by a healthy concern for the potential abuses of governments. The U.S. Bill of Rights and the civil liberty protections of the state constitutions were created to ensure certain fundamental protections to all citizens. These guarantees were designed to withstand the shifting winds created by agitated majorities. Judge Rothwax is not the first American, nor will he likely be the last, to tell his fellow citizens that we live in a particularly dangerous time and that to survive we must forego the "luxury" of our civil liberties.

Judge Rothwax is wrong. The guarantees created by James Madison and the Constitution are not luxuries. Rather, they make up a very battered constitutional firewall that barely protects us from the police state that he, cynical politicians, and a very conservative U.S. Supreme Court seem to be inching towards. These civil liberties are not excessive; if anything, they provide too little protection for the realities of daily life in an increasingly urban, multicultural society facing the 21st century.

Of course, many Americans share Judge Rothwax's concern over criminal predators, like Leonardo Turriago, who prey on their fellow citizens. These violent criminals should be punished severely. But the same level of concern ought to be expressed in regard to how today's criminal justice system treats black, Hispanic, American Indian, poor, and uneducated Americans. Americans ought to be concerned about the rights of innocent, hardworking Americans who are harassed, injured, maimed, or killed every day by abusive police officers for being in the "wrong" neighborhood or driving too "nice" a car. Judge Rothwax's system will not win the war against the Leonardo Turriagos of the world; it will likely create more Carlton Browns.

NOTES

1. Bernard Gavzer, "We're in the Fight of Our Lives." *Parade,* July 28, 1996, 4–6.
2. Haya El Nasser, "Historic Crime Drop," *USA Today,* April 14, 1997, 1A.
3. In other countries, for example, most of the nations of continental Europe, an inquisitorial system of justice is used. In this system, it is the judge who determines the direction of the trial by calling witnesses, examining evidence, and drawing final conclusions of fact. When compared to an adversarial justice system, inquisitorial disputants and, more importantly, their lawyers play a much less active role in affecting the composition of the case. Instead of a courtroom battle, the inquisitorial trial might be likened to a trip to the principal's office to determine who did what to whom and what should be done about it.
4. David Johnston, "Report Criticizes Scientific Testing at FBI Crime Lab," *New York Times,* April 16, 1997, A1.
5. Mark S. Warnick, "A Matter of Conviction," *Pittsburgh Post-Gazette,* September 24, 1995, A1.
6. Bob Herbert, "Brooklyn's Obsessive Pursuit," *New York Times,* August 21, 1994, E15.
7. "Mexican Once Nearly Executed Wins Freedom in Texas," *New York Times,* April 17, 1997, A8.
8. Bob Herbert, "Savagery Beyond Sense," *New York Times,* October 18, 1996, A12.
9. James Madison, the leading figure in the development of the U.S. Constitution and Bill of Rights, commented on the need for checks on human behavior associated

with the affairs of the state in *Federalist* No. 51: "If men were angels, no government would be necessary. If angels were to govern men, neither external nor internal controls on government would be necessary."

10. 384 U.S. 436.
11. Both sides conceded that during the interrogation, the police did not use any force, threats, or promises of leniency if Miranda would confess. Both sides also conceded that at no point did the police inform Miranda that he had a constitutional right to refuse to talk to the police and that he could have counsel if he so desired.
12. Thus yielding the famous *Miranda* warnings:

   You have the right to remain silent.

   Anything you say can and will be used against you in a court of law.

   You have a right to a lawyer.

   If you can't afford a lawyer one will be provided to you.

   If you say at any point that you do not want to talk to the police the interrogation must cease.

13. 384 U.S. 446.
14. *Economist,* July 13, 1996, 29.
15. *Ibid.*
16. It is important to note that only about 10 percent of criminal cases are resolved through the formal trial process. Most criminal convictions in this country are the result of plea bargaining between the defendant and the prosecutor.
17. *Weeks* v. *U.S.,* 232 U.S. 383 (1914).
18. 446 U.S. 620 (1980).
19. 467 U.S. 431 (1984).
20. When a jury is used as the fact finder in a criminal case the defense and prosecution have a significant role in determining who will sit on the jury. In the jury selection process both sides can challenge a prospective juror in two ways. A challenge for cause is used when an attorney can show the court that there are tangible characteristics of the prospective jurors that make them biased and warrant their removal from consideration; lawyers have an unlimited ability to challenge for cause. A peremptory challenge allows a lawyer to remove a potential juror without giving a reason; each lawyer in a case gets a limited number of these. But peremptory challenges are not as peremptory as their name implies. The Supreme Court has ruled that lawyers cannot use them to systematically exclude all blacks or women from consideration for jury service.
21. Michael Janofsky, "Under Siege, Philadelphia's Criminal Justice System Suffers Another Blow," *New York Times,* April 10, 1997, A9.
22. Jury unanimity is another balancer, and is based on the notion that the prosecutor should be required to present a case that convinces all jurors that the defendant is guilty beyond a reasonable doubt.
23. *Johnson* v. *Louisiana,* 406 U.S. 356 (1972), and *Apodaco* v. *Oregon,* 406 U.S. 404 (1972).
24. Quoted in Richard Harris, *Justice* (New York: Avon 1969), p. 162.

15

CIVIL LIBERTIES

Free Speech

*I*ntolerance of one kind or another, long a feature of American society, has nevertheless been more in evidence during some periods of our history than others. Events of the last several years suggest that we have once again entered a cycle in which bigotry is being expressed more publicly. Regrettably, this phenomenon has also manifested itself on our campuses, where university property has been defiled by racial epithets and African-American students have been subject to verbal and physical abuse. Alarmed by the growing number of such incidents, several universities have instituted regulations prohibiting discriminatory behavior, with violators thereof subject to disciplinary action.

Some observers, however, believe that these regulations are just as distasteful as the behavior they are designed to discourage. Thus, in the first essay which follows, Professor Chester Finn contends that a university—of all places—should be characterized by unfettered freedom of expression. In his judgment, there were disturbing signs that "unpopular" views were being stifled on many campuses even before these regulations were adopted. The presence of such regulations—often vaguely worded—can only have the effect of further dampening the robust expression of opinions and ideas in and outside the classroom.

Charles Lawrence, in the second essay, readily admits that under some circumstances even the most offensive speech must be tolerated on campus and believes that university regulations should be carefully crafted to allow for it. At the same time, however, he also insists that neither the First Amendment nor Supreme Court rulings require a university to tolerate racist expression within its walls under any and all circumstances.

The Campus:
"An Island of Repression in a Sea of Freedom"

Chester E. Finn, Jr.

Two weeks before the Supreme Court held that the First Amendment protects one's right to burn the flag, the regents of the University of Wisconsin decreed that students on their 12 campuses no longer possess the right to say anything ugly to or about one another. Though depicted as an antidiscrimination measure, this revision of the student-conduct code declares that "certain types of expressive behavior directed at individuals and intended to demean and to create a hostile environment for education or other university-authorized activities would be prohibited and made subject to disciplinary sanctions." Penalties range from written warnings to expulsion.

Several months earlier, the University of Michigan adopted a six-page "antibias code" that provides for punishment of students who engage in conduct that "stigmatizes or victimizes an individual on the basis of race, ethnicity, religion, sex, sexual orientation, creed, national origin, ancestry, age, marital status, handicap, or Vietnam-era veteran status." (Presumably this last bizarre provision applies whether the "victim" is labeled a war hero or a draft dodger.)

Nor are Wisconsin and Michigan the only state universities to have gone this route. In June [1989], the higher-education regents of Massachusetts prohibited "racism, anti-Semitism, ethnic, cultural, and religious intolerance" on their 27 campuses. A kindred regulation took effect on July 1 at the Chapel Hill campus of the University of North Carolina. And in place for some time at the law school of the State University of New York at Buffalo has been the practice of noting a student's use of racist language on his academic record and alerting prospective employers and the bar association.

Not to be outdone by the huge state schools, a number of private universities, like Emory in Atlanta and Stanford in California, have also made efforts to regulate unpleasant discourse and what the National Education Association terms "ethnoviolence," a comprehensive neologism that includes "acts of insensitivity."

Proponents of such measures are straightforward about their intentions. Says University of Wisconsin President Kenneth Shaw of the new rule: "It can particularly send a message to minority students that the board and its administration do care." Comments Emory's director of equal opportunity: "We just wanted to ensure that at a time when other universities were having problems that we made it clear that we wouldn't tolerate graffiti on walls or comments in classes." And in Massachusetts, the regents concluded that "There must be a unity and cohesion in the diversity which we seek to achieve, thereby creating an atmosphere of pluralism."

This "pluralism" is not to be confused with the version endorsed by the First Amendment. Elsewhere we are expected, like it or not, to attend to what Justice

Chester E. Finn, Jr., is professor of education and public policy at Vanderbilt University and former Assistant Secretary, U.S. Department of Education (1985–88). From Chester E. Finn Jr., "The Campus: An Island of Repression in a Sea of Freedom." Reprinted from Commentary, *September 1989, by permission; all rights reserved.*

Brennan calls the "bedrock principles . . . that the government may not prohibit the expression of an idea simply because society finds the idea itself offensive or disagreeable." Not so for those running universities. "What we are proposing is not completely in line with the First Amendment," a leader of Stanford's student government has acknowledged to a reporter, but "I'm not sure it should be. We . . . are trying to set a standard different from what society at large is trying to accomplish." Explains the Emory official: "I don't believe freedom of speech on campus was designed to allow people to demean others on campus." And a Stanford law professor contends that "racial epithets and sexually haranguing speech silences rather than furthers discussion."

Disregard the hubris and the sanctimony. Academics and their youthful apprentices have long viewed their own institutions and causes as nobler than the workaday world and humdrum pursuits of ordinary mortals. Forget, too, the manifest evidence of what some of the nation's most esteemed universities are teaching their students about basic civics. Consider only the two large issues that these developments pose, each freighted with a hefty burden of irony.

The first can still evoke a wry smile. We are, after all, seeing students pleading for controls to be imposed on campus behavior in the name of decency and morality. Yet these same students would be outraged if their colleges and universities were once again to function *in loco parentis* by constraining personal liberty in any other way. What is more, faculties, administrators, and trustees are complying with the student demands; they are adopting and—one must assume—enforcing these behavior codes. By and large, these are the same campuses that have long since shrugged off any serious responsibility for student conduct with respect to alcohol, drugs, and promiscuity (indeed, have cheerily collaborated in making the last of these behaviors more heedless by installing condom dispensers in the dorms). These are colleges that do not oblige anyone to attend class regularly, to exercise in the gym, to drive safely, or to eat a balanced diet. A student may do anything he likes with or to his fellow students, it appears, including things that are indisputably illegal, unhealthy, and dangerous for everyone concerned, and the university turns a blind eye. But a student may not, under any circumstances, speak ill of another student's origins, inclinations, or appearance.

The larger—and not the least bit amusing—issue is, of course, the matter of freedom of expression and efforts to limit it. That the emotionally charged flag-burning decision emerged from the Supreme Court the same month as authorities in China shot hundreds of students (and others) demonstrating for democracy in the streets of Beijing is as stark an illustration as one will ever see of the gravity and passion embedded in every aspect of this question.

In the Western world, the university has historically been the locus of the freest expression to be found anywhere. One might say that the precepts embodied in the First Amendment have applied there with exceptional clarity, and long before they were vouchsafed in other areas of society. For while private colleges are not formally bound by the Bill of Rights, they, like their public-sector counterparts, are heirs to an even older tradition. The campus was a sanctuary in which knowledge and truth might be pursued—and imparted—with impunity, no matter how unpopular, distasteful, or politically heterodox the process might sometimes be. That is the essence of academic freedom and it is the only truly significant distinction between the universities of the democracies and those operating under totalitarian regimes. Wretched though the food and lodging are for students on Chinese campuses, these were not the provocations that made martyrs in Tiananmen Square. It was the idea of freedom that stirred China's students and professors (and millions of others, as well). And it was the fear of allowing such ideas to take root that prompted the government's brutal response.

Having enjoyed almost untrammeled freedom of thought and expression for three and a half centuries, and having vigorously and, for the most part, successfully fended off efforts by outsiders (state legislators and congressional subcommittees, big donors, influential alumni, etc.) to constrain that freedom, American colleges and universities are now muzzling themselves. The antidiscrimination and antiharassment rules being adopted will delimit what can be said and done on campus. Inevitably, this must govern what can be taught and written in lab, library, and lecture hall, as well as the sordid antics of fraternity houses and the crude nastiness of inebriated teenagers. ("The calls for a ban on 'harassment by vilification' reached a peak last fall" at Stanford, explained the *New York Times,* "after two drunken freshmen turned a symphony recruiting poster into a black-face caricature of Beethoven and posted it near a black student's room.")

Constraints on free expression and open inquiry do not, of course, depend on the adoption of a formal code of conduct. Guest speakers with controversial views have for some years now risked being harassed, heckled, even shouted down by hostile campus audiences, just as scholars engaging in certain forms of research, treading into sensitive topics, or reaching unwelcome conclusions have risked calumny from academic "colleagues." More recently, students have begun to monitor their professors and to take action if what is said in class irks or offends them.

Thus, at Harvard Law School this past spring, Bonnie Savage, the aptly-named leader of the Harvard Women's Law Association (HWLA), sent professor Ian Macneil a multicount allegation of sexism in his course on contracts. The first offense cited was Macneil's quoting (on page 963 of his textbook) Byron's well-known line, "And whispering, 'I will ne'er consent,'—consented." This, and much else that he had said and written, the HWLA found objectionable. "A professor in any position at any school," Savage pronounced, "has no right or privilege to use the classroom in such a way as to offend, at the very least, 40 percent of the students. . . ."

This was no private communication. Savage dispatched copies to sundry deans and the chairman of the faculty-appointments committee because, she later explained, "We thought he might be considered for tenure." The whole affair, Macneil responded in the *Harvard Law Record,* was "shoddy, unlawyerlike, reminiscent of Senator McCarthy, and entirely consistent with HWLA's prior conduct." As for the Byron passage, it "is in fact a perfect summary of what happens in the Battle of Forms" (a part of the contract-making process).

Macneil is not the only Harvard professor to have been given a hard time in recent years for writing or uttering words that upset students, however well-suited they might be to the lesson at hand. Not long ago, the historian Stephan Thernstrom was accused by a student vigilante of such classroom errors as "read[ing] aloud from white plantation owners' journals 'without also giving the slaves' point of view.'" Episodes of this kind, says Thernstrom, serve to discourage him and other scholars from even teaching courses on topics that bear on race and ethnicity.[1]

Nor is Harvard the only major university where student allegations, unremonstrated by the administration, have produced such a result. At Michigan last fall, the distinguished demographer, Reynolds Farley, was teaching an undergraduate course in "race and cultural contact," as he had done for the previous ten years, when a column appeared in the Michigan *Daily* alleging racial insensitivity on his part, citing—wholly out of context, of course—half a dozen so-called examples, and demanding that the sociology department make amends. Farley was not amused and, rather than invite more unjust attacks, is discontinuing the course. Consequently 50 to 125 Michigan students a year will be deprived of the opportunity to examine issues of ethnicity and the history of race relations in America under the tutelage of this world-class scholar. And to make matters even worse, Farley notes that several faculty colleagues have mentioned that they are dropping any discussion of various important race-related issues from their courses, lest similar treatment befall them.

This might seem perverse, not least from the standpoint of "aggrieved" students and their faculty mentors, because another of their major goals is to oblige everyone to take more courses on precisely these topics. "I would like to see colleges engage all incoming students in mandatory racial-education programs," writes William Damon, professor of psychology and chairman of the education department at Clark University, in the *Chronicle of Higher Education.* And his call is being answered on a growing number of campuses, including the state colleges of Massachusetts, the University of Wisconsin, and the University of California at Berkeley.

Ironies abound here, too, since the faculties and governing boards adopting these course requirements are generally the very bodies that resist any suggestion of a "core curriculum" or tight "distribution requirements" on the ground that diverse student preferences should be accommodated and that, in any case, there are no disciplines, writings, or ideas of such general importance that everyone should be obliged to study them. Curricular relativism can be suspended, though, when "pluralism" is itself the subject to be studied. "It is important to make such programs mandatory," Professor Damon explains, "so that they can reach students who otherwise might not be inclined to participate."

. . . Diversity and tolerance, evenhandedly applied, are estimable precepts. But that is not how they are construed in the academy today. Nor do the narrowing limits on free expression lead only to penalties for individuals who engage in "biased" talk or "hostile" behavior. They also leave little room for opinion that deviates from campus political norms or for grievances from unexpected directions. During Harvard's race-awareness week last spring, when a white student dared to complain that she had experienced "minority ethnocentrism" on campus—African-American and Hispanic students, it seems, often ignored her—she was given short shrift and no sympathy by the speaker (who had already suggested that Harvard and Dartmouth were "genocidal" institutions).

More commonly, however, it is rambunctious student newspapers and magazines that get into trouble with academic authorities for printing something that contravenes the conventional wisdom. Given the predominant campus climate, it is not surprising that these are often publications with a moderate or right-of-center orientation. Sometimes, clearly, they do mischievous, stupid, and offensive things, but for such things the degree of toleration in higher education seems to vary with the ideology of the perpetrator. (Acts of discrimination and oppression based on political views, it should be observed, are *not* among the categories proscribed in the new codes of behavior.) In addition to a much-reported sequence of events at Dartmouth, there have been recent efforts to censor or suppress student publications, and sometimes to discipline their staff members, at Brown, Berkeley, UCLA, Vassar, and California State University at Northridge.

The last of these prompted one of the most extraordinary media events of 1989, a joint press conference on May 16 featuring—no one could have made this up—former Attorney General Edwin Meese III and the director of the Washington office of the American Civil Liberties Union (ACLU), Morton Halperin. What brought them together was shared outrage over what Halperin termed the "double standard" on campus. "Our position," he reminded the attending journalists, "is that there is an absolute right to express views even if others find those views repugnant." He could cite numerous instances, he said, where campus authorities were making life difficult for outspoken conservative students, yet could find "no cases where universities discipline students for views or opinions on the Left, or for racist comments against non-minorities."

Meese, not surprisingly, concurred, as did James Taranto, the former Northridge student journalist whose lawsuit settlement afforded the specific occasion for the press conference. In 1987, Taranto, then news editor of his campus paper, had written a column faulting UCLA officials for suspending a student editor who had published a cartoon mocking affirmative action. Taranto reproduced the offending cartoon in the Northridge paper, whereupon its faculty adviser suspended *him* from his position for two weeks because he had printed "controversial" material without her permission. The ACLU agreed to represent him in a First Amendment suit—"We were as outraged as he was by the attempt to censor the press," Halperin recalled—and two years later a settlement was reached.

While we are accumulating ironies, let it be noted that the ACLU, the selfsame organization in which Michael Dukakis's "card-carrying membership" yielded George Bush considerable mileage in the 1988 election campaign, has been conspicuously more vigilant and outspoken about campus assaults on free expression in 1989 than has the Bush administration. The Secretary of Education, Lauro Cavazos (himself a former university president), has been silent. The White House has been mute. During an incident at Brown in May, when an art professor canceled a long-planned screening of the classic film, *Birth of a Nation,* because the Providence branch of the NAACP had denounced it, the local ACLU affiliate was the only voice raised in dismay. "University officials," declared its executive director, "have now opened the door to numerous pressure groups who may wish to ban from the campus other films that they too deem 'offensive.'" Indeed, a colleague of mine recently revived a long-lapsed membership in the ACLU on the straightforward ground that no other national entity is resisting the spread of attitude-adjustment, censorship, and behavior codes in higher education.

. . . Meanwhile, in the realms of intellectual inquiry and expression, [colleges] permit ever less diversity, turning the campus (in the memorable phrase of civil-rights scholar Abigail Thernstrom) into "an island of repression in a sea of freedom."

NOTE

1. See "A New Racism on Campus?" by Thomas Short, *Commentary,* August 1988.

The Justification for Curbing Racist Speech on Campus

Charles R. Lawrence III

I have spent the better part of my life as a dissenter. As a high-school student, I was threatened with suspension for my refusal to participate in a civil-defense drill, and I have been a conspicuous consumer of my First Amendment liberties ever since. There are very strong reasons for protecting even racist speech. Perhaps the most important of these is that such protection reinforces our society's commitment to tolerance as a value, and that by protecting bad speech from government regulation, we will be forced to combat it as a community.

But I also have a deeply felt apprehension about the resurgence of racial violence and the corresponding rise in the incidence of verbal and symbolic assault and harassment to which African-Americans and other traditionally subjugated and excluded groups are subjected. I am troubled by the way the debate has been framed in response to the recent surge of racist incidents on college and university campuses and in response to some universities' attempts to regulate harassing speech. The problem has been framed as one in which the liberty of free speech is in conflict with the elimination of racism. I believe this has placed the bigot on the moral high ground and fanned the rising flames of racism.

Above all, I am troubled that we have not listened to the real victims, that we have shown so little understanding of their injury, and that we have abandoned those whose race, gender, or sexual preference continues to make them second-class citizens. It seems to me a very sad irony that the first instinct of civil libertarians has been to challenge even the smallest, most narrowly framed efforts by universities to provide African-American and other minority students with the protection the Constitution guarantees them.

The landmark case of *Brown* v. *Board of Education* is not a case that we normally think of as a case about speech. But *Brown* can be broadly read as articulating the principle of equal citizenship. *Brown* held that segregated schools were inherently unequal because of the *message* that segregation conveyed—that black children were an untouchable caste, unfit to go to school with white children. If we understand the necessity of eliminating the system of signs and symbols that signal the inferiority of African-Americans, then we should hesitate before proclaiming that all racist speech that stops short of physical violence must be defended.

University officials who have formulated policies to respond to incidents of racial harassment have been characterized in the press as "thought police," but such

Professor Charles R. Lawrence III is professor of law at Georgetown University. This article is reprinted by permission of the author from The Chronicle of Higher Education, *October 25, 1989, B1–B3. The article is adapted from a longer article, "If He Hollers Let Him Go: Regulating Racist Speech on Campus" by Charles R. Lawrence III,* Duke Law Journal *(1990), pp. 431–83.*

policies generally do nothing more than impose sanctions against intentional face-to-face insults. When racist speech takes the form of face-to-face insults, catcalls, or other assaultive speech aimed at an individual or small group of persons, it falls directly within the "fighting words" exception to First Amendment protection. The Supreme Court has held that words which "by their very utterance inflict injury or tend to incite an immediate breach of the peace" are not protected by the First Amendment.

If the purpose of the First Amendment is to foster the greatest amount of speech, racial insults disserve that purpose. Assaultive racist speech functions as a preemptive strike. The invective is experienced as a blow, not as a proffered idea, and once the blow is struck, it is unlikely that a dialogue will follow. Racial insults are particularly undeserving of First Amendment protection because the perpetrator's intention is not to discover truth or initiate dialogue but to injure the victim. In most situations, members of minority groups realize that they are likely to lose if they respond to epithets by fighting and are forced to remain silent and submissive.

Courts have held that offensive speech may not be regulated in public forums such as streets where the listener may avoid the speech by moving on, but the regulation of otherwise protected speech has been permitted when the speech invades the privacy of the unwilling listener's home or when the unwilling listener cannot avoid the speech. Racist posters, fliers, and graffiti in dormitories, bathrooms, and other common living spaces would seem to clearly fall within the reasoning of these cases. Minority students should not be required to remain in their rooms in order to avoid racial assault. Minimally, they should find a safe haven in their dorms and in all other common rooms that are a part of their daily routine.

I would also argue that the university's responsibility for insuring that these students receive an equal educational opportunity provides a compelling justification for regulations that insure them safe passage in all common areas. A minority student should not have to risk becoming the target of racially assaulting speech every time he or she chooses to walk across campus. Regulating vilifying speech that cannot be anticipated or avoided would not preclude announced speeches and rallies—situations that would give minority-group members and their allies the chance to organize counter-demonstrations or avoid the speech altogether.

The most commonly advanced argument against the regulation of racist speech proceeds something like this: We recognize that minority groups suffer pain and injury as the result of racist speech, but we must allow this hate mongering for the benefit of society as a whole. Freedom of speech is the lifeblood of our democratic system. It is especially important for minorities because often it is their only vehicle for rallying support for the redress of their grievances. It will be impossible to formulate a prohibition so precise that it will present the racist speech you want to suppress without catching in the same net all kinds of speech that it would be unconscionable for a democratic society to suppress.

Whenever we make such arguments, we are striking a balance on the one hand between our concern for the continued free flow of ideas and the democratic process dependent on that flow, and, on the other, our desire to further the cause of equality. There can be no meaningful discussion of how we should reconcile our commitment to equality and our commitment to free speech until it is acknowledged that there is real harm inflicted by racist speech and that this harm is far from trivial.

To engage in a debate about the First Amendment and racist speech without a full understanding of the nature and extent of that harm is to risk making the First Amendment an instrument of domination rather than a vehicle of liberation. We have not all known the experience of victimization by racist, misogynist, and homophobic speech, nor do we equally share the burden of the societal harm it inflicts. We are often quick to say that we have heard the cry of the victims when we have not.

The *Brown* case is again instructive because it speaks directly to the psychic injury inflicted by racist speech by noting that the symbolic message of segregation affected "the hearts and minds" of Negro children "in a way unlikely ever to be undone." Racial epithets and harassment often cause deep emotional scarring and feelings of anxiety and fear that pervade every aspect of a victim's life.

Brown also recognized that African-American children did not have an equal opportunity to learn and participate in the school community if they bore the additional burden of being subjected to the humiliation and psychic assault contained in the message of segregation. University students bear an analogous burden when they are forced to live and work in an environment where at any moment they may be subjected to denigrating verbal harassment and assault. The same injury was addressed by the Supreme Court when it held that sexual harassment that creates a hostile or abusive work environment violates the ban on sex discrimination in employment of Title VII of the Civil Rights Act of 1964.

Carefully drafted university regulations would bar the use of words as assault weapons and leave unregulated even the most heinous of ideas when those ideas are presented at times and places and in manners that provide an opportunity for reasoned rebuttal or escape from immediate injury. The history of the development of the right to free speech has been one of carefully evaluating the importance of free expression and its effects on other important societal interests. We have drawn the line between protected and unprotected speech before without dire results. (Courts have, for example, exempted from the protection of the First Amendment obscene speech and speech that disseminates official secrets, that defames or libels another person, or that is used to form a conspiracy or monopoly.)

African Americans and other people of color are skeptical about the argument that even the most injurious speech must remain unregulated because, in an unregulated marketplace of ideas, the best ones will rise to the top and gain acceptance. Our experience tells us quite the opposite. We have seen too many demagogues elected by appealing to America's racism. We have seen too many good liberal politicians shy away from the issues that might brand them as being too closely allied with us.

Whenever we decide that racist speech must be tolerated because of the importance of maintaining societal tolerance for all unpopular speech, we are asking African Americans and other subordinated groups to bear the burden for the good of all. We must be careful that the ease with which we strike the balance against the regulation of racist speech is in no way influenced by the fact that the cost will be borne by others. We must be certain that those who will pay that price are fairly represented in our deliberations and that they are heard.

At the core of the argument that we should resist all government regulation of speech is the ideal that the best cure for bad speech is good, that ideas that affirm equality and the worth of all individuals will ultimately prevail. This is an empty ideal unless those of us who would fight racism are vigilant and unequivocal in that fight. We must look for ways to offer assistance and support to students whose speech and political participation are chilled in a climate of racial harassment.

Civil-rights lawyers might consider suing on behalf of African Americans whose right to an equal education is denied by a university's failure to insure a non-discriminatory educational climate or conditions of employment. We must embark upon the development of a First Amendment jurisprudence grounded in the reality of our history and our contemporary experience. We must think hard about how best to launch legal attacks against the most indefensible forms of hate speech. Good lawyers can create exceptions and narrow interpretations that limit the harm of hate speech without opening the floodgates of censorship.

Everyone concerned with these issues must find ways to engage actively in actions that resist and counter the racist ideas that we would have the First Amendment protect. If we fail in this, the victims of hate speech must rightly assume that we are on the oppressors' side.

Pornography

The two previous selections highlighted the difference of opinion over what we should be free to say. Similar disagreement exists over what we should be free to see, read, and hear, when the subject matter in question is "obscene" or "pornographic" in character.

In the first of the following essays, Ernest van den Haag is concerned with two basic questions: First, is pornographic material clearly definable so that it may be distinguished from other kinds of expression we would not want to suppress? Second, even if we can define it, is there any public interest to be served by prohibiting our citizens from having access to it? Van den Haag answers both questions in the affirmative.

Geoffrey Stone does not object to laws against child pornography nor to age and zoning restrictions limiting access to pornography in general. In contrast to van den Haag, however, he wholly opposes any attempt to limit the distribution of obscene material to consenting adults. In his judgment, a careful weighing of the costs and benefits associated with censorship clearly reveals that the individual incurs very great costs, while the society derives very little benefit.

Pornography and Censorship

Ernest van den Haag

Ultramoralists want to prohibit any display of nudity while ultralibertarians feel that even the most scabrously prurient display must be tolerated. However, most people are not that extreme. They are uneasy about obscene incitements to lechery; but uncertain about what to do about them. They wonder whether distaste, even when shared by a majority, is reason enough to prohibit what a minority evidently wants. Beyond distaste, is there enough actual harm in pornography? Where will suppression end, and how harmful might it be? Can we legally distinguish the valuable from the pornographic, the erotic from the obscene? Would courts have to act as art critics? Not least, we wonder about our own disapproval of obscenity. We are aware, however dimly, of some part of us which is attracted to it. We disapprove of our own attraction—but also worry whether we may be afraid or hypocritical when we suppress what attracts us as well as many others.

Still, most people want something done about pornography. As so often in our public life, we turn to the Constitution for a rule. "Congress" it tells us "shall make no law . . . abridging the freedom of speech or of the press." Although addressed to the federal government only, the First Amendment has been echoed in many state constitutions and applied to all states by the courts. Further, its scope has been broadened, perhaps unduly so, by court decisions which hold that all expressions rather than just words are protected by the First Amendment. Yet speech—words, spoken, or printed, or otherwise reproduced—is a narrow subclass of expression and the only one protected by the First Amendment. Music, painting, dance, uniforms, or flags—expressions but not words—are not.[1] The framers wanted to protect political and intellectual discourse—they thought free verbal interchange of ideas indispensable to consensual government. But obscenity hardly qualifies as an interchange of ideas, and is no more protected than music is. Whatever their merits, neither addresses the intellect, nor is indispensable to free government. For that matter words without cognitive content, words not used as vehicles for ideas—e.g., "dirty words" or expletives—may not be constitutionally protected. And even the constitutional right to unfettered verbal communication of ideas is limited by other rights and by the rights of others. Else there could be no libel or copyright laws and no restrictions on incitements to illicit or harmful action.

The Constitution, then, gives us the right to outlaw pornography. Should we exercise it? Is there a sufficient social interest in suppression? And how can we separate pornography from things we constitutionally cannot or do not want to suppress?

Some people feel that there can be no objective standard of obscenity: "Beauty is in the eye of the beholder—and so is obscenity," they argue. This notion is popular among pseudo-sophisticates; but it seems wildly exaggerated. Is the difference between

Ernest van den Haag was John M. Olin Professor of Jurisprudence and Public Policy at Fordham University before joining the Heritage Foundation as distinguished scholar in 1981. From Ernest van den Haag, "Pornography and Censorship," Policy Review, *13 (Summer 1980), pp. 73–81. Reprinted with permission of* Policy Review. *Published by the Heritage Foundation.*

your mother-in-law and the current Miss America merely in the eye of the beholder (yours)? How come everyone sees the difference you see? Is the distinction between pictures which focus on exposed human genitals or on sexual intercourse, and other pictures only in the eye of the beholder? To be sure, judgments of beauty, or of obscenity, do have subjective components—as most judgments do. But they are not altogether subjective. Why else do even my best friends not rate me a competitor to Apollo? For that matter judgments of art are not altogether subjective either. Museums persistently prefer Rembrandt's paintings to mine. Do they all have a subjective bias against me?

Pornography seems a reasonably objective matter which can be separated from other things. Laws, if drawn sensibly, might effectively prohibit its display or sale. An in-between zone between the obscene and the nonobscene may well remain, just as there is such a twilight zone between brightly lit and dark areas. But we still can tell which is which; and where necessary we can draw an arbitrary, but consistent (i.e., non-capricious), line. The law often draws such a line: to enable the courts to deal with them the law treats as discontinuous things that in nature may be continuous. The law quite often leaves things to the judgment of the courts: just how much spanking is cruelty to children? Just when does behavior become reckless?—courts always have to decide cases near the dividing line. But courts would have to decide only the few cases near the line which divides obscene from nonobscene matters. Most of the obscene stuff now displayed is not even near that line. With sensible laws it will no longer be displayed or offered for sale. The doubtful cases will be decided by juries applying prevailing standards. Such standards vary greatly over time and space, but at any given time, in any place, they are fairly definite and knowable. Lawyers who argue otherwise never appear in court, or for that matter in public places, without pants (or skirts, as the case may be). They seem to know what is contrary to the standards prevailing in the community in which they practice—however much they pretend otherwise.

A word on the current legal situation may not be amiss. The courts have not covered themselves with glory in clarifying the notion of obscenity. At present they regard the portrayal of sex acts, or of genitalia, or of excretion, as obscene if (a) patently offensive by contemporary community standards and if (b) taken as a whole[2] it appeals dominantly to a prurient (morbid or shameful) interest in sex and if (c) it lacks serious scientific, literary or artistic merit. The courts imply that not all appeals to sexual interest are wrong—only prurient ones are. They have not said directly which appeals are prurient. The courts might have been more explicit but they are not unintelligible.

An appeal to sexual interest need not be obscene per se; only attempts to arouse sexual interest by patently offensive, morbid, shameful means are. By contemporary standards a nude is not obscene. But an appeal to sexual interest is, when carried out by focusing on exposed genitalia, or on the explicit, detailed portrayal of sex acts. Detailed portrayals of excretion may be patently offensive too, but since they scarcely appeal to the sexual interest of most people they may pass under present law unless specifically listed as unlawful; so may portrayals of sexual relations with animals for the same reason—if the jury is as confused as the law is. The courts never quite made up their minds on the relative weight to be given to "offensive," to "prurient," and to "sexual." Thus intercourse with animals may be offensive to most people and prurient, i.e., morbid and shameful, but not necessarily sexual in its appeal to the average person. Therefore some exhibitors of such spectacles have been let off. But should the fact that some sexual acts are so disgusting to the majority as to extinguish any sexual appeal they might otherwise have legitimize these acts? Offensiveness, since in effect it is also a criterion for the prurience of a sexual appeal, is a decisive element of obscenity; yet the other two elements must be present.

If more clearly drawn laws would leave few doubtful cases for juries to decide, why do many literary, sociological, or psychological experts find it so hard to determine what is obscene? Why do they deny that such laws can be fashioned? Most people who protest that they cannot draw the line dividing the pornographic from the nonpornographic are deliberately unhelpful. "None so blind as they that won't see." They don't want to see because they oppose any pornography laws. They certainly have a right to oppose them. But this right does not entitle anyone to pretend that he cannot see what he does see. Critics who testify in court that they cannot distinguish pornography from literature, or that merely pornographic stuff has great literary or educational merit, usually know better. If they didn't they would have no business being critics or experts. To oppose pornography laws is one thing. It is quite another thing to attempt to sabotage them by testifying that hardcore stuff cannot be separated from literature or art, pornographic from aesthetic experience. Such testimony is either muddleheaded beyond belief or dishonest.

Once we have decided that the obscene is not inseparable from the nonobscene, we can address the real issue: are there compelling grounds for legally restraining public obscenity?

Some argue that pornography has no actual influence. This seems unpersuasive. Even before print had been invented Francesca blamed a book for her sin: "Galeotto fu il libro" (the book was the panderer) she told Dante in the *Divine Comedy.* Did she imagine the book's influence? Literature—from the Bible to Karl Marx or to Hitler's *Mein Kampf*—does influence people's attitudes and actions, as do all communications, words or pictures. That is why people write, or, for that matter, advertise. The influence of communications varies, depending on their own character, the character of the person exposed to them, and on many other circumstances. Some persons are much influenced by the Bible—or by pornography—others not. Nor is the direction of the influence, and the action to which it may lead altogether predictable in each case. But there is little doubt that for the average person the Bible fosters a religious disposition in some degree and pornography a lecherous one.

Granted that it has some influence, does pornography harm nonconsenting persons? Does it lead to crime? Almost anything—beer, books, poverty, wealth, or existentialism—can "lead" to crime in some cases. So can pornography. We cannot remove all possible causes of crime—even though we might remove those that can be removed without much difficulty or loss. But crime scarcely seems the major issue. We legally prohibit many things that do not lead to crime, such as polygamy, cocaine, or dueling. Many of these things can easily be avoided by those who do not wish to participate; others cannot be shown to be actually harmful to anyone. We prohibit whatever is *perceived* as socially harmful, even if merely contrary to our customs, as polygamy is.

When we prohibit cartels, or the sale of marijuana, when we impose specific taxes, or prohibit unlicensed taxis from taking fares, we believe our laws to be useful, or to prevent harm. That belief may be wrong. Perhaps the tax is actually harmful or unjust, perhaps we would all be better off without licensing any taxis, perhaps cartels are economically useful, perhaps marijuana smoking is harmless or beneficial. All that is needed to justify legislation is a rational social interest in accomplishing the goals of the legislation. Thus, an activity (such as marijuana smoking) can be prohibited because it is *perceived* to be socially harmful, or even merely distasteful. Pornography is. The harm it actually may do cannot be shown the way a man can be shown to be guilty of a crime. But such a demonstration of harm or guilt is not required for making laws—it is required only if someone is to be convicted of breaking them.

Still, unless we are convinced that pornography is harmful the whole exercise makes little sense. Wherein then is pornography harmful? The basic aim of pornographic communication is to arouse impersonal lust, by, in the words of Susan Sontag (incidentally a defender of pornography), driving "a wedge between one's existence as a full human being and one's sexual being . . . a healthy person prevents such a gap from opening up. . . ." A healthy society too must help "prevent such gaps from opening up," for, to be healthy, a society needs "full human beings," "healthy persons" who integrate their libidinal impulses with the rest of their personality, with love and with personal relationships.

We all have had pre-adolescent fantasies which ignore the burdens of reality, of commitment, concern, conflict, thought, consideration and love as they become heavier. In these fantasies others are mere objects, puppets for our pleasure, means to our gratification, not ends in themselves. The Marquis de Sade explored such fantasies most radically; but all pornographers cater to them: they invite us to treat others merely as means to our gratification. Sometimes they suggest that these others enjoy being so treated; sometimes they suggest, as the Marquis de Sade did, that pleasure lies in compelling unwilling others to suffer. Either way pornography invites us to reduce fellow humans to mere means. The cravings pornography appeals to—the craving for contextless, impersonal, anonymous, totally deindividualized, as it were abstract, sex—are not easy to control and are, therefore, felt as threats by many persons, threats to their own impulse-control and integration. The fear is real and enough sex crimes certainly occur . . . to give plausibility to it. People wish to suppress pornography, as they suppress within themselves impulses that they feel threaten them. Suppression may not be an ideal solution to the problem of anxiety arousing stimuli, external or internal. Ideally we should get rid of anxiety, and of unwelcome stimuli, by confrontation and sublimation. But we are not ideal and we do not live in an ideal world. Real as distinguished from ideal persons must avoid what threatens and upsets them. And real as distinguished from utopian societies must help them to do so.

However, there are stronger grounds for suppressing pornography. Unlike the 18th-century rationalists from whom the ultralibertarians descend, I do not believe that society is but an aggregation of individuals banded together for their mutual convenience. Although society does have utilitarian functions, it is held together by emotional bonds, prior to any rational calculations. Societies survive by feelings of identification and solidarity among the members, which lead them to make sacrifices for one another, to be considerate and to observe rules, even when they individually would gain by not doing so. In animal societies (e.g., among social insects) the members identify one another instinctively, for example, by smell. The identification leads them not to attack or eat one another and it makes possible many manifestations of solidarity. It makes the insect society possible. Human societies, too, would be impossible without such identification and solidarity among the members. Else we would treat one another as we now treat insects or chickens—or as the Nazis treated Jews. It is to preserve and strengthen traditional emotional bonds, and the symbols that stand for them, that the government of Israel prohibits the raising of pigs, that of India the slaughtering of cows.

Solidarity is as indispensable to the United States as it is to Israel. It is cultivated by institutions which help each of us to think of others not merely as means to his own gratification, but as ends in themselves. These institutions cultivate shared customs, expectations, traditions, values, ideals and symbols. The values we cultivate differ from those of an aboriginal tribe; and the range left to individual choice is broader. Social solidarity is less stringent than it is in most primitive tribes. But neither our society nor an aboriginal tribe could survive without shared values which make it possible for us to identify with one another.

One of our shared values is the linkage of sexual to individual affectional relations—to love and stability. As our society has developed, the affectional bonds associated with sexual love have become one of its main values. Indeed with the weakening of religious institutions these bonds have acquired steadily more importance. Love is worshiped in numerous forms. There is, to be sure, a gap between the reality and the ideal, just as there is a gap between the reality of patriotism—or nationalism—and the ideal. But it would be silly to deny that patriotism plays an important role in our society—or that love, affection, and compassion do.

Pornography tends to erode these bonds, indeed, all bonds. By inviting us to reduce others and ourselves to purely physical beings, by inviting each of us to regard the other only as a means to physical gratification, with sensations, but without emotions, with contacts but without relations, pornography not only degrades us (and incidentally reduces sex to a valueless mechanical exercise),[3] but also erodes all human solidarity and tends to destroy all affectional bonds. This is a good enough reason to outlaw it.

There are additional reasons. One is very simply that the majority has a right to protect its tradition. The minority is entitled to argue for change. But not to impose it. Our tradition has been that sexual acts, sexual organs, and excretion are private rather than public. The majority is entitled to preserve this tradition by law where necessary just as the majority in India, offended by the slaughtering of cows which is contrary to Hindu tradition, can (and does) prohibit it.

Nobody is forced to see the dirty movie or to buy the pornographic magazine. Why then should the minority not be allowed to have them? But a public matter—anything for sale—can never be a wholly private matter. And once it is around legally one cannot really avoid the impact of pornography. One cannot avoid the display and the advertising which affect and pollute the atmosphere even if one does not enter or buy. Nor is it enough to prohibit the movie marquee or the display of the magazine. Anything legally for sale is the more profitable the more customers it attracts. Hence the purveyors of pornography have a strong interest in advertising and in spreading it, in persuading and in tempting the public. Prohibitions of advertising will be circumvented as long as the sale of pornography is lawful. Moreover, if the viewer of the pornographic movie is not warned by the marquee that he is about to see a dirty movie, he might very likely complain that he has been trapped into something that upsets him without being warned.

I should not prohibit anyone from reading or seeing whatever he wishes in his own home. He may be ill advised. But interfering with his home habits surely would be more ill advised. Of course if the stuff is not legally available the pornography fan will have difficulty getting it. But society has no obligation to make it easy. On the contrary, we can and should prohibit the marketing, the public sale of what we perceive as harmful to society even if we do not wish to invade homes to punish those who consume it.

NOTES

1. The First Amendment right to peacefully assemble may protect whatever is part of, or required for, peaceful assembly. It is hard to see that either nudity or swastikas are needed for that purpose.
2. Thus a prurient passage does not make a magazine or a book offensive unless, taken as a whole, the magazine or book dominantly appeals to the prurient interest.
3. As feminists have pointed out, pornography often degrades females more directly than males. But, in reducing themselves to a mere craving for physical gratification males degrade themselves as well.

Repeating Past Mistakes:
The Commission on Obscenity and Pornography

Geoffrey R. Stone

[In 1986] the Attorney General's Commission on Pornography had a unique opportunity to redirect society's regulation of obscene expression. The current state of the law is marred by overly broad, ineffective, and wasteful regulation. This was an appropriate opportunity to take a fresh look at the problem and to strike a new balance—a balance that more precisely accommodates society's interests in regulation with the individual's often competing interests in privacy, autonomy, and free expression. The commission squandered this opportunity. Instead of taking a fresh look, it blindly performed its appointed task of renewing and reaffirming past mistakes.

The United States Supreme Court has held that federal, state, and local government officials have the power, consonant with the First Amendment, to prohibit all distribution of obscene expression. The mere existence of power, however, does not mean that its exercise is sound. The commission should have recommended that government officials exercise restraint. Specifically, the commission should have recommended the repeal of laws that criminalize the distribution of obscene expression to consenting adults.

The Supreme Court itself is sharply divided over the constitutional power of government officials to prohibit the distribution of obscene expression to consenting adults. In its 1973 decisions in *Miller* v. *California* and *Paris Adult Theatre* v. *Slaton,* the Court divided five-to-four on this issue. Justices Douglas, Brennan, Stewart, and Marshall concluded that the First Amendment strips government officials of any power to deny consenting adults the right to obtain obscene expression.

Even apart from the division of opinion in these cases, the Court's analysis of obscene expression is anomalous in terms of its overall First Amendment jurisprudence. At one time, obscene expression was merely one of several categories of expression held by the Supreme Court to be "of such slight social value as a step to truth that any benefit that may be derived from them is clearly outweighed by the social interest in order and morality." In the past quarter-century, the Court has increasingly recognized that such previously unprotected categories of expression as profanity, commercial advertising, incitement, and libel can no longer be regarded as wholly unprotected by the First Amendment. The Court has held that, although such categories of expression have only a "subordinate position in the scale of First Amendment values," they can nonetheless be restricted only if government has at least a substantial justification for the restriction. The Court has thus recognized that even low-value expression may have some First Amendment value, that government efforts to restrict low-value expression

Geoffrey R. Stone is Harry Kalven, Jr., Professor of Law and Provost, University of Chicago. Reprinted by permission of Transaction Publishers. "Repeating Past Mistakes," by Geoffrey R. Stone, Society, *24, July/August 1987, pp. 30–32. Copyright © 1987 by Transaction Publishers, Inc.; all rights reserved.*

will often chill more valuable expression, and that the constitutional and institutional risks of restricting low-value expression are worth taking only if the restriction furthers at least a substantial governmental interest.

Obscene expression now stands alone. No other category of expression is currently regarded as wholly outside the protection of the First Amendment. No other category of expression may be suppressed merely because it has only "slight social value." No other category of expression may be censored without a showing that the restriction serves at least a substantial governmental interest. The current analysis of obscene expression is thus the sole remaining artifact of a now discarded jurisprudence.

The current analysis of obscenity is not necessarily wrong as a matter of constitutional law. Nevertheless, the constitutional authority to act in this context hangs by the slender thread of a single vote and is very much in doubt as a matter of constitutional principle. In such circumstances, government must exercise special care in deciding whether and how to exercise its power. We should not simply assume that because it is constitutional to act it is wise to do so. The very closeness of the constitutional question is itself a compelling reason for caution.

In deciding on the appropriate regulation of obscene expression, we must consider both the costs and benefits of regulation. Laws prohibiting the distribution of obscene expression to consenting adults impose at least three types of costs. First, although the Court has held that such expression has only low First Amendment value, it may nonetheless serve a useful function both for society and the individual. That the demand for sexually explicit expression is as great as it is, suggests that such expression serves an important psychological or emotional function for many individuals. It may satisfy a need for fantasy, escape, entertainment, stimulation, or whatever. Thus, whether or not obscene expression has significant First Amendment value, it may have important value to the individual. Laws prohibiting its distribution to consenting adults may frustrate significant interests in individual privacy, dignity, autonomy, and self-fulfillment.

The suppression of obscene expression may also have a severe chilling effect on more valuable expression. The legal concept of obscenity is vague in the extreme. As a consequence, individuals who wish to purchase or distribute sexually explicit expression will invariably censor themselves in order to avoid being ensnared in the ill-defined net of our obscenity laws. Laws prohibiting the distribution of obscene expression spill over and significantly limit the distribution of constitutionally protected expression as well.

Any serious effort to enforce laws prohibiting the distribution of obscene expression to consenting adults necessarily draws valuable police and prosecutorial resources away from other areas of law enforcement. In a world of limited resources, we must recognize that the decision to criminalize one form of behavior renders more difficult and less effective the enforcement of laws directed at other forms of behavior. It is necessary to set priorities, for the failure to enforce our laws vigorously can serve only to generate disrespect for law enforcement and bring the legal system into disrepute.

Two interests are most commonly asserted in support of laws prohibiting the distribution of obscene expression to consenting adults. First, it is said that government must suppress the distribution of such expression to consenting adults in order to prevent the erosion of moral standards. The moral fabric of a society undoubtedly affects the tone and quality of life. It is thus a legitimate subject of government concern; but as Justice Brennan recognized in his opinion in *Paris Adult Theatre,* "the State's interest in regulating morality by suppressing obscenity, while often asserted, remains essentially ill-focused and ill-defined." It rests ultimately on "unprovable . . . assumptions about human behavior, morality, sex, and religion." Perhaps more importantly, the notion that government may censor expression because it may alter accepted moral standards flies in the face of the guarantee of free expression. A democratic society must be free to determine its own moral standards through robust and wide-open debate and expression. Although government may legitimately inculcate moral values through education and related activities, it may not suppress expression that reflects or encourages an opposing morality. Such paternalism is incompatible with the most basic premises of the First Amendment.

Second, it is said that government must suppress the distribution of obscene expression to consenting adults because exposure to such expression may "cause" individuals to engage in unlawful conduct. The prevention of unlawful conduct is a legitimate governmental interest, but the correlation between exposure to obscene expression and unlawful conduct is doubtful, at best. As the President's Commission on Obscenity and Pornography found in 1970, there is "no evidence to date that exposure to explicit sexual materials plays a significant role in the causation of delinquent or criminal behavior." The Attorney General's Commission's contrary conclusion in 1986 is based more on preconception than on evidence. An issue that has long divided social scientists and other experts in the field can hardly be definitively resolved by a commission of nonexperts, most of whom were appointed because of their preexisting commitment to the suppression of obscene expression. In any event, even those who claim a connection between exposure to obscene expression and unlawful conduct claim no more than an indirect and attenuated "bad tendency." Thus, although some individuals may on some occasions commit some unlawful acts "because of" their exposure to obscene expression, the connection is indirect, speculative, and unpredictable. It is not even remotely comparable to the much more direct harm caused by such products as firearms, alcohol, and automobiles. The suppression of obscene expression is also a stunningly inefficient and overly broad way to deal with this problem, for even a modest change in law enforcement or sentencing practices would have a much more direct and substantial impact on the rate of unlawful conduct than the legalization or criminalization of obscene expression.

Laws prohibiting the distribution of obscene expression to consenting adults impose significant costs on society and frustrate potentially important privacy and autonomy interests of the individual for only marginal benefits. It is time to bring our regulation of such expression into line with our constitutional traditions, our law enforcement priorities, and our own self-interest and common sense.

The course I propose, and which the commission emphatically rejected, would leave government free to direct its enforcement energies at the more important concerns generated by obscene expression. These fall into three related categories: the protection of juveniles, the protection of captive viewers, and the regulation of the secondary effects of obscene expression. The Court has long recognized government's interest in sheltering children from exposure to obscene expression. What I propose does not undermine this interest. Nor does it interfere with society's substantial interest in restricting child pornography, which poses significantly different issues. My proposal would not in any way prevent government from protecting individuals against the shock effect of unwanted exposure to obscene expression. Government would remain free to prohibit children from viewing movies or buying books found "obscene," and it would remain free to prohibit or otherwise regulate the exhibition of obscene expression over the airwaves. Sensible accommodations can also be devised for other media, such as cable television. Also, my proposal would not prevent government from using zoning and other regulatory devices to control the distribution of obscene expression in order to prevent the decay of neighborhoods or other secondary effects associated with the availability of obscene expression.

By leaving consenting adults free to obtain obscene expression at their discretion, and by protecting our important interests through narrowly defined regulations, we can strike a sensible balance, protecting important societal interests while at the same time preserving our traditional respect for free expression and for the privacy and autonomy of the individual.

The commission has opted to do otherwise and repeat past mistakes—with a vengeance. It has recommended, among other things, significant changes in state and federal legislation to enable more vigorous enforcement of antiobscenity laws; creation of a special Obscenity Task Force in the office of the attorney general to coordinate the prosecution of obscenity cases at the national level; allocation of additional resources at the federal, state, and local levels for the prosecution of obscenity cases; "aggressive" Internal Revenue Service investigation of the "producers and distributors of obscene materials"; and imposition of "substantial periods of incarceration" for violators of anti-obscenity laws. This draconian approach is wasteful, misguided, and inconsistent with the real concerns of most of our citizens.

16

CIVIL RIGHTS

Affirmative Action

*F*or more than three decades, the federal government and many state governments have pursued a policy of "affirmative action," which requires government agencies and many public and private groups to take positive steps to guarantee nondiscrimination and a fair share of jobs, contracts, and college admissions for racial minorities and women. The underlying assumption of these requirements has been that since racial minorities, particularly African Americans, have been historically discriminated against, special efforts must be made to correct past discriminatory policies and practices and to assure greater opportunities in the future.

In recent years, "affirmative action" has become a "hot-button" issue, often generating heated debate between proponents and opponents. The debate revolves around these fundamental questions: Should minorities and women, because of past discrimination, be given special consideration in employment, admission to colleges and universities, government contracts, and the like; or, should race and gender be totally ignored, even if the result leads to a lack of diversity and opportunity in many fields?

The two selections in this chapter speak to these and other questions in the affirmative action debate. In the first article, Terry Eastland presents the case for ending affirmative action, arguing that government should never use race either "to confer or deny a benefit" in society. To do otherwise is to act at odds with the "best principles" of our nation, including the principle of equal protection of the law without regard to race, color, or gender. The response to Eastland is provided by Barbara R. Bergmann, who argues that the abandonment of affirmative action is neither warranted by present-day conditions nor contrary to historic principles, including principles of racial and cultural diversity and a fair and just society.

Ending Affirmative Action:

The Case for Colorblind Justice

Terry Eastland

BY ANY OTHER NAME

When he joined the police department in Memphis, Tennessee, in 1975, Danny O'Connor wanted someday to make sergeant. In 1988, he took a shot at it. Like the other 209 officers competing for 75 promotions, O'Connor completed the written exam and sat for his interview. When his scores on both parts were added to points awarded for seniority and on-the-job performance over the past year, he placed fifty-sixth on the Composite Scores List. The department had indicated that the 75 top-ranked officers on this list would be the ones promoted. O'Connor knew his ranking and thought he had realized his dream. But then affirmative action struck.

When the candidates took the written exam, they were required on the answer sheets to indicate their race and sex. On the basis of this information, the department created a second set of rankings—the Promotional Eligibility List. This new list, created to satisfy the department's affirmative action plan, modified the Composite Scores List by bumping blacks up into every third position. Necessarily, whoever had been there originally was bumped down. Some 26 blacks were on the eligibility list; 7 had been on the composite list. So 19 blacks (originally ranked between 76 and 132) had been bumped up the list—in some cases way up—and were promoted. Whites were bumped down, and those who had been ranked in the lower regions of the composite list were bumped below the 75th spot—and thus out of a promotion, Danny O'Connor, who is white, was one of these.

Undaunted, O'Connor tried again the next year. The department proceeded much as it had in 1988, using the same four-part process (though it changed the basis for awarding seniority points). Of 177 candidates, 94 would be promoted. They received their composite scores and on the basis of those scores were ranked. Affirmative action stepped in again, however, as the department used race to rerank the candidates. Where 15 blacks had made the top 94 on the composite list, 33 blacks were among the top 94 on the new list. Eighteen blacks had been bumped up into the top 94 and 18 whites previously in the top 94 had been bumped down. One of these was O'Connor, 75th on the original list.

Over the two years, while Danny O'Connor remained a patrol officer, 43 candidates with lower composite scores were bumped ahead of him and promoted to sergeant in the name of affirmative action.

Terry Eastland is former Director of Public Affairs in the U.S. Department of Justice (1985–1988) and currently a resident fellow at the Ethics and Public Policy Center in Washington, D.C. Excerpted from pp. 1–20, 219–20 from Ending Affirmative Action *by Terry Eastland. Copyright © 1996 by Terry Eastland. Reprinted by permission of Basic Books, a division of HarperCollins Publishers, Inc. Notes have been renumbered to correspond to edited text—Editors.*

Affirmative action was begun in the late 1960s to benefit blacks and over time has come to embrace certain other minority groups, as well as women (in the areas of employment and public contracting). There are, of course, forms of affirmative action that do not bump people out of an opportunity on account of race or sex. In employment, these forms of affirmative action can include outreach, recruitment, and training programs that are open to all, regardless of race or sex. But the affirmative action Danny O'Connor experienced is the kind that for years has been unsettling America. While it takes different guises and has different justifications, this type of affirmative action makes a virtue of race, ethnicity, and sex in order to determine who gets an opportunity and who does not. To call it by its proper name, it is discrimination.

Cheryl Hopwood had an experience like Danny O'Connor's. In 1992 she applied for admission to the University of Texas School of Law. She had earned a degree in accounting from California State University in 1988, achieving a 3.8 grade point average and scoring 39 (the highest score being 48) on the Law School Admissions Test (LSAT). She was, in addition, a certified public accountant. In the four years since finishing at Cal State, Hopwood had married and moved close to San Antonio, where her husband, an air force captain, was stationed. A Texas resident, she had just given birth to her first child when she applied for admission to the prestigious University of Texas law school.

Hopwood thought her credentials were excellent, but the law school turned her down. "The only thing I could think of," she says of her initial response to the news, "was that the class the school admitted must have been very, very good." Wanting to find out just how good, she discovered instead that because she is white she had not been able to compete with all other applicants for admission. Under the school's affirmative action plan, 15 percent of the approximately 500 seats in the class had been set aside for blacks and Mexican-Americans, who were admitted under academic standards different from—in fact, lower than—those for all other students. Hopwood's admissions score—a composite number based on her undergraduate grade point average and her LSAT score—was 199. Eleven resident Mexican-American applicants had scores this high or higher, and only one resident black had a score of 199. The school admitted all 12 of these applicants but not Hopwood, and then, in pursuit of its 15 percent affirmative action goal, admitted 84 additional resident Mexican-American and black applicants. Their scores were lower—in some cases substantially lower—than Hopwood's. Indeed, the school admitted every resident black with a score of 185 or higher. If Hopwood were black or Mexican American, she would have been admitted.

Hopwood's experience differs from O'Connor's only in terms of the opportunity she sought, an educational one. Like O'Connor, she was bumped down and out by affirmative action that bumped others below her up and in. "I can't change my race," she says.

Neither can Randy Pech. The owner of Adarand Constructors, Inc., in Colorado Springs, Colorado, Pech, who is white, submitted the low bid for the guardrail portion on a federal highway construction project. But the business went to Gonzales Construction Company, which submitted a higher bid but is Hispanic-owned. That happens to be a virtue in the eyes of the U.S. Department of Transportation, which enforces a law that "sets aside" a portion of federal construction funds for businesses owned by minorities and women. Pech says he competes with four other companies in Colorado that build guardrails. Two are owned by Hispanics. Two are owned by women. Set-aside laws, he says, work solely against him. "If I weren't here, they'd have no impact.". . .

Danny O'Connor, Cheryl Hopwood, [and] Randy Pech, decided to challenge in court the discrimination that goes by the name of affirmative action.[1] They are gallant foot soldiers in the fight against a policy that by allocating opportunity on the basis of race and sex is dividing and damaging the nation. The time has come for us to end it.

A BARGAIN WITH THE DEVIL

. . . The original purpose of affirmative action was to remedy the ill effects of past discrimination against blacks. "To get beyond racism," as Justice Harry Blackmun famously put it in his opinion in the 1978 case *Regents of the University of California v. Bakke,* "we must first take account of race.[2] "Taking account of race" meant distinguishing on the basis of race and treating blacks differently. In the old days, this would have looked like racial discrimination. But the first advocates of affirmative action assured us that affirmative action was well intentioned. Race could be regulated to good effect, we were told, and affirmative action would end soon enough, with the nation the better for it. As one of the early architects of affirmative action put it, "We are in control of our own history."[3]

By the early 1970s, affirmative action was extended to cover additional minority groups and in some contexts women, and over the years its backers have offered additional justifications, such as overcoming "underrepresentation" and achieving "diversity." But the nation has paid a steep price for departing from colorblind principle, for affirmative action has turned out to be a bargain with the devil. Not only has the policy worked discrimination against those it does not favor—a Danny O'Connor or a Cheryl Hopwood, for example—but it also has guaranteed the salience of race and ethnicity in the life of the nation, thus making it harder to overcome the very tendency the civil rights movement once condemned; that of regarding and judging people in terms of their racial and ethnic groups. . . .

By formally drawing racial and ethnic lines, affirmative action invites judgments about the abilities and achievements of those who are members of the targeted groups. One persistent judgment is that those who received a benefit through affirmative action could not have secured it on their own. In many cases, this happens to be true. Indeed, the whole point of many affirmative action programs is to help those who otherwise could not have landed the opportunity in open competition. The program Cheryl Hopwood encountered at the Texas law school lowered the school's academic standards in order to admit blacks and Mexican Americans. The school also segregated the applications of blacks and Mexican Americans, assigning them to a separate admissions committee while a different committee reviewed the merits of the "white and other" applicants. Thus treated differently, the members of the two minority groups competed only among themselves. Had they competed among all applicants under the same standards, many fewer blacks and Mexican Americans would have gained admission to the Texas law school.

This is not, however, the whole story. The black and Mexican-American applicants admitted under affirmative action were not *un*qualified to study law; their academic qualifications were good enough to win admission under nonaffirmative action standards at fully two-thirds of the nation's law schools.[4] Affirmative action thus stigmatizes beneficiaries who could succeed—and be seen to succeed—without it. At the same time, it stigmatizes those eligible for it who are not its beneficiaries. At the Texas law school, one Hispanic student who had a composite score good enough to warrant admission under the standards applicable to "whites and others" said that he felt he needed a shirt indicating he got in on his own, just to let people know the genuine nature of his accomplishment.[5] It is sadly ironic that affirmative action can put a non–affirmative action minority student in this situation, but the student's response is hardly irrational. He knows that the mere existence of the law school's program invites people to think, in his case: "You're Hispanic, so you got in through affirmative action."

An abiding truth about much affirmative action is that those who are its ostensible beneficiaries are burdened with the task of overcoming it—if, that is, they wish to be treated as individuals, without regard to race. It is possible, of course, for someone extended an opportunity through affirmative action to overcome it by doing extraordinarily well, meeting the highest standards. But some minorities have concluded that the best way to escape the public implications of affirmative action is to say "no" when they know it is being offered. In 1983, Freddie Hernandez, a Hispanic who serves in the Miami fire department, rejected an affirmative action promotion to lieutenant. Instead, he waited three years until he had the necessary seniority and had scored high enough to qualify for the promotion under procedures that applied to nonminorities. This decision cost Hernandez $4,500 a year in extra pay and forced him to study 900 additional hours to attain the required test results. But, as he proudly told the *Wall Street Journal,* "I knew I could make it on my own."[6]

Hernandez rejected the affirmative action bargain. He wanted to be judged as an individual, on his own merits, without regard to his ethnic background—just the way the old civil rights pioneers said he had a right to be judged.

THE LANGUAGE OF AFFIRMATIVE ACTION

Affirmative action has taken a toll on public discourse. Through the years its supporters have said, for example, that they do not support quotas. But . . . there was a reason police officer Danny O'Connor was bumped down and out of a promotion. There was a reason black officers were bumped up into every third position. The Memphis police department was trying to fill a quota that reserved one-third of the promotions for blacks. Bumping blacks up into every third position on the list of 75 may have been a crude way of making the quota, but it got the job done. Faced with evidence of a quota, supporters of affirmative action backtrack, saying that they are against "hard and fast" or "rigid" quotas and for "flexible" goals. The distinction in practice may mean that a slightly lesser number of the preferred minority group or women is hired or admitted. This happened at the University of Texas School of Law, which in 1992 fell a bit short of its 15 percent goal for black and Mexican-American admittees. But whatever term is used to describe what the law school was doing, race was determining the bulk of these admissions decisions.

Affirmative action supporters may concede that race is the determining factor but insist that the practice benefits only qualified people. Yet what matters to those competing for a limited number of openings or opportunities is not whether they are qualified in the abstract, but whether they are *more* qualified than the others seeking that position. The rankings Danny O'Connor earned showed that he was more qualified than officers bumped above him and promoted to sergeant on account of race. And Cheryl Hopwood's composite score showed she was more qualified than many of those with lower scores who were admitted under the Texas law school's affirmative action plan. Some supporters of affirmative action respond by claiming that differences in qualifications—above a certain minimum—are negligible. They will not say, however, that differences in qualifications are unimportant in the case of those who are *not* eligible for affirmative action. And judgments about who is better are routinely made by all of us when we seek the services of, say, a doctor or lawyer. Not surprisingly, though most unfortunately, some affirmative action programs have dispensed with even minimal qualifications. In 1993, in an effort to increase the "diversity" of its workforce, the U.S. Forest Service's Pacific Southwest Region established "upward mobility positions" that it set aside for applicants who do not meet the service's usual employment requirements. The dictionary of affirmative action does not appear to include words like "excellence" and "outstanding" and "best.". . .

THE MYTH OF "TEMPORARY" AFFIRMATIVE ACTION

In the late 1960s and during the 1970s, advocates of affirmative action often said that it was only a temporary measure whose success would render it unnecessary in the future. But these temporary measures often seem to go on and on and on—well beyond the point at which they were supposed to end.

Let us return to Danny O'Connor's story. It actually began back in 1974, when the Justice Department sued the city of Memphis under Title VII of the Civil Rights Act of 1964, alleging that it had engaged in unlawful employment discrimination against blacks and women. Quickly, the city and the federal government settled the suit through a consent decree that won federal court approval. Other lawsuits followed: black police officers sued the city in 1975, charging racially discriminatory promotion practices, and a black firefighter filed a similar suit in 1977. Judicially approved consent decrees also concluded these cases. And then, in 1981, the city and the federal government amended their 1974 agreement. Though the city never admitted to past discrimination, it did agree to hire and promote blacks and females in proportions, as the 1981 decree put it, "approximating their respective proportions in the relevant Shelby County civilian labor force."

Now, we may regard the lawsuits of the 1970s as necessary in forcing change upon an Old South city. And for the sake of argument, let us concede that proportional hiring and promoting were needed to effect change in the 1970s and early 1980s. But having achieved proportional representation in the fire and police workforces by the mid-1980s, the city did not end its attachment to proportionalism, as Danny O'Connor's case shows. City officials claim that the 1981 decree tied their hands, but it did not *require* race-based employment decisions. In fact, the decree provided that the city was not obligated to hire or promote a less-qualified person over a better-qualified person. The inconvenient truth appears to be that proportional hiring and promoting proved administratively a lot easier for the city than trying to treat applicants and employees fairly without regard to race. In 1994, a federal appeals court rejected the city's motion to dismiss the complaint brought by Danny O'Connor and other white employees. In its opinion the court expressed concern that the city "has made no effort to limit the duration of the [race-based promotional] remedies."[7]

The federal executive branch has made no effort in this regard, either. The 1981 consent decree governing the city of Memphis could have been dissolved by agreement of the parties as early as March 1984, but the Justice Department under Ronald Reagan did not ask the city to end its hiring and promotional remedies. Nor, for that matter, did the Justice Department under George Bush. And when the city found itself in 1994 in the court of appeals trying to fend off Danny O'Connor's lawsuit, the Justice Department under Bill Clinton filed a brief in support of the city's never-ending affirmative action. . . .

THE CHOICE

Failing to make good on its promise to be only temporary, affirmative action has entrenched itself more deeply in our institutions, attracting political constituencies that demand its retention. Surveys of public opinion show, however, that preferences have never enjoyed the majority support of the American people. Moreover, the substantial immigration the nation has experienced since, coincidentally, the advent of affirmative action is rendering the policy increasingly incoherent.

Roughly three-quarters of those who come to the United States each year are of a race or ethnic background that makes them eligible for affirmative action, and most affirmative action programs are indifferent as to whether their beneficiaries are U.S. citizens or not, or whether, if they are U.S. citizens, they recently arrived here or not. We thus have a policy originally designed to remedy the ill effects of past discrimination that is open to immigrants with no past in the United States during which they could have experienced discrimination. . . .

. . . [I]mmigration since the late 1960s has swollen the ranks of Hispanics and Asians, making them, combined, more numerous than blacks. As a result, we now face the prospect (especially in our largest cities, where the Hispanic and Asian populations are most concentrated) of increasing conflict among affirmative action groups.

Los Angeles, a city being dramatically reshaped by Hispanic immigration, is a case in point. In 1988 the Los Angeles County Office of Affirmative Action Compliance issued a report showing that while Hispanics made up 27.6 percent of the county population and held 18.3 percent of county jobs, blacks constituted 12.6 percent of the population and 30 percent of the workforce. The county board of supervisors accepted the affirmative action office's recommendation to hire minorities in accordance with a scheme of "population parity."[8] This meant members of the "underrepresented" group that is, Hispanics—would be preferred over those belonging to the "overrepresented" group—blacks. Black county employees quickly protested, declaring their opposition to preferential treatment based on race and ethnicity. Over the years the struggle has continued, and now the county is thinking about dropping population parity in favor of an affirmative action approach that would result in fewer preferences for Hispanics, whose portion of the county population has risen to 38 percent. To prevent this change, Hispanic county employees have filed a lawsuit.[9]

The impact of immigration is another reason to reevaluate affirmative action. We can choose to stick with the status quo, perhaps mending it a bit here and there, or we can end affirmative action once and for all. The choice was clarified politically in the months following the 1994 midterm elections in which the Republicans, for the first time in 40 years, captured both houses of Congress. Though the campaign was not explicitly about affirmative action, the election results necessarily altered the nation's political agenda, pushing it in a more conservative direction. . . . [T]he new Congress voted to terminate a 17-year-old program under which corporations selling their broadcast outlets at a discounted price to minorities may defer sales taxes indefinitely. President Clinton, sensing the shift in political sentiment, signed the bill into law. Senator Robert Dole, preparing to draft legislation on affirmative action, asked the Congressional Research Service (CRS) to supply him with a list of programs containing preferences for minorities or women, whereupon President Clinton ordered his own review of government programs. Both branches of government had a lot to digest—the CRS reported to Dole more than 160 federal programs that might be construed as requiring or authorizing or encouraging preferences.

And then on June 12, 1995, the Supreme Court handed down its decision in the case involving Randy Pech. In *Adarand Constructors* v. *Pena,* the Court held that federal affirmative action programs must be held to a standard of "strict scrutiny," the most demanding level of justification, whose application routinely has led to the invalidation of governmental measures that classify on the basis of race and ethnicity.[10] Sending Randy Pech's case back to the lower courts for review under the tougher standard, the Court signaled that preferential treatment deserves not only strict judicial scrutiny but also strict political scrutiny, since the very idea that government should distinguish on the basis of race to confer or deny a benefit is at odds with our best principles as a nation. No fewer than four times did Justice Sandra Day O'Connor, who wrote the Court's opinion, refer to the luminous passage in the 1943 *Hirabayashi* decision: "Distinctions between citizens solely because of their ancestry are by their very nature odious to a free people whose institutions arc foundcd upon thc doctrinc of cquality." O'Connor emphasized that the Constitution protects "*persons,* not *groups,*" and that "all governmental action based on race" is a "*group* classification" that should be examined to make sure that "personal" rights have been protected.

Affirmative action broke with the colorblind tradition, one acknowledged in the Japanese Relocation Cases. Indeed, this tradition stretches back to the American founding. In making the choice before us about the future of affirmative action, it is imperative that we as a nation return to the place from which we began, and understand afresh the compelling and true case for colorblind justice.

NOTES

Note: Quotes besides those cited in the text itself or in the following endnotes are from interviews with the author.

1. In December 1995, all . . . cases were still in litigation.
2. 438 U.S. 265 (1978).
3. Alfred W. Blumrosen, *Black Employment and the Law* (New Brunswick, N.J.: Rutgers University Press, 1971), p. viii.
4. Lino A. Graglia, "*Hopwood* v. *Texas:* Racial Preferences in Higher Education Upheld and Endorsed," *Journal of Legal Education* 45, no. 1 (March 1995): 82.
5. "Suit Against U. of Texas Challenges Law School's Affirmative-Action Effort." *Chronicle of Higher Education,* February 9, 1994. Hopwood and three other applicants rejected by the law school filed the lawsuit. . . .
6. Sonia L. Nazario, "Many Minorities Feel Torn by Experience of Affirmative Action," *Wall Street Journal,* June 27, 1989.
7. *Aiken* v. *City of Memphis,* 37 F. 3d. 1155 (6th Cir. 1994).
8. Peter Skerry, "Borders and Quotas: Immigration and the Affirmative-Action State," *The Public Interest,* no. 96 (summer 1989): 93.
9. Jonathan Tilove, "Affirmative Action Has Drawbacks for Blacks," *Cleveland Plain Dealer;* July 20, 1995.
10. 115 S. Ct. 2097 (1995). . .

In Defense of Affirmative Action

Barbara R. Bergmann

IS DISCRIMINATION A THING OF THE PAST?

Pollsters surveying people about their attitudes toward affirmative action frequently ask, "Do you think blacks or women should receive preference in hiring and promotion to make up for past discrimination?" This wording encourages respondents to assume that discrimination has ended and is no longer an important problem. Respondents to one such poll, when asked to comment on their answers, spoke of discrimination that had occurred "100 years ago" and said that such ancient history did not justify "preferences" in the present.[1]

As we shall see . . . there are good reasons to believe that discrimination by race and sex is not a thing of the past. Those under the impression that discrimination ended a long time ago are simply mistaken. However, they are right about one thing: our need for affirmative action depends not on what happened 100 years ago but on the situation in the labor market today. . . .

THE EVIDENCE ON WAGES

In judging the conflicting claims about the state of the labor market, it is useful to start by looking at how much change has actually occurred. Chart 1 shows the weekly wages of those who worked full-time in the years 1967–95, corrected to eliminate the effect of inflation.[2] The inflation-corrected wages of white men have been on a downtrend since the mid-1970s. However, white men have not lost their superior position in the labor market: a substantial gap remains between their wages and those of white women and black men and women. Given the slowness of change in the labor market, as shown in Chart 1, that gap will not close anytime soon.

Modest reductions have been made in that gap since 1967. Black men's wages were 69 percent of white men's in 1967. By 1976 their wages had risen to 79 percent of white men's. Since then, they have been losing rather than gaining ground on white men. The loss of manufacturing jobs, some of them unionized and thus relatively well-paying, has hit both white and black men, but the latter have been particularly hard hit.[3] White women gained no ground on white men until the early 1980s; they have been gaining in the years since. In 1995 their wages were 73 percent of white men's, compared with 61 percent in 1967. Black women have made gains throughout the period,

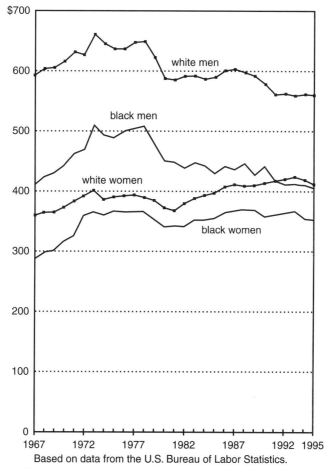

CHART 1 Weekly Wages by Sex and Race in 1995 Dollars

Based on data from the U.S. Bureau of Labor Statistics.

but recently their gains have not matched those of white women. In 1995, black women's wages were 63 percent of white men's.

The fall in black men's wages relative to white men's over the last twenty years suggests that whatever help they have received from affirmative action has been modest at best, and has not been enough to counterbalance the effects of their buffeting from market forces. The globalization of the labor market has reduced the demand by U.S. employers for the labor of the less skilled—both black and white—and black men have suffered disproportionately. While affirmative action has allowed some college-educated black men to enter the middle class, the deterioration of the labor market for non-college-educated black men has been disastrous. It has made their lives increasingly precarious; their decreased chances for decently paid work have contributed to the fall in the black marriage rate, the increase in single parenthood, and the recruitment of black men into crime and the drug trade in the inner city. . . .

THE EVIDENCE FROM LAWSUITS

Lucky Stores, Inc., a West Coast grocery chain, agreed in 1993 to pay nearly $75 million in damages to women who had been denied promotion opportunities and another $20 million to set up and run affirmative action programs.[4] The women had been denied full-time slots, and the relatively small group of women in management jobs had been segregated into certain departments (bakery and delicatessen) marked off as dead end. The managers of these departments received lower pay than other managers. One of the women whose complaint sparked the suit had worked at the cash register for 21 years. When her teenage son came to Lucky and worked beside her, he was offered training opportunities that had been denied to her. Suits alleging similar employment practices have been filed against Safeway Stores and several other grocery chains.

The facts of the Lucky Stores case were strikingly similar to the facts in a 1972 suit against Giant Foods, a Washington, D.C.-area grocery chain. That suit was settled, with the company under order until the late 1980s to remedy the problems. However, a 1994 telephone survey to ascertain the sex of managers by department revealed that in the 20 years since the suit, very little integration of managerial positions had been accomplished.[5] Meat cutting, a skilled trade requiring apprenticeship, had been maintained as an all-male specialty. Bakery managers, still overwhelmingly female, continued to receive lower salaries than other department managers, almost all male. The cost of remedying the bakery managers' relatively low pay would have amounted to a few dollars an hour per store; the fact that their pay had not been increased raises questions about the symbolic significance of low pay to those in control. Giant's history illustrates the stubbornness of discrimination problems and the difficulty of fixing them when management is indifferent or opposed to change. A successful lawsuit may give the particular complainants some recompense but leave the underlying situation unchanged. The supermarket cases also show the complicity of some unions in maintaining segregation by sex and women's lower pay.

A recent claim of racial discrimination against the Shoney restaurant chain listed 211 Shoney officials against whom there was direct evidence of discriminatory behavior. Employment applications were color-coded by race, Blacks were tracked to kitchen jobs so that all employees in the dining area would be white. The case began when two white managers complained that they had been pressured by their supervisors to limit the number of black employees, and that they had been terminated when they resisted the pressure. The case was settled out of court for $65 million. Kerry Scanlon, an attorney for the black plaintiffs, said, "This was going on while the Bush Administration and others were telling the country that in the area of civil rights, the major problem was quotas and unfair protection for blacks. The quota that African Americans are most familiar with in employment is zero.[6]

EVIDENCE BASED ON "TESTING" THE JOB MARKET

So far, in reviewing the labor market situation for women and blacks, we have been looking at their treatment on the job, that is, where they are placed and what they are paid. We need also to look at their ability to land jobs. An important aspect of the labor market disadvantage suffered by African Americans is their high unemployment rate. People are counted as "unemployed" in government statistics only if they are actively looking for work. In good times and bad, unemployment rates for African Americans are twice as high as those for whites. The problem is particularly acute for 18- to 19-year-old black people, who suffer unemployment rates above 30 percent.[7] When they leave school, it is very hard for them to find jobs, and when they lose a job, they are typically in for a long spell of unemployment before landing the next one.

The results of a recent research project reveal the extent of discrimination against young black men in hiring and give an insight into the connection between that discrimination and their high rate of unemployment.[8] The Urban Institute assembled pairs of young men to serve as "testers." In each pair, one tester was black, the other white. Entry-level job openings were chosen at random from the newspaper, and a pair of testers was assigned to apply for each opening.

The researchers made the pairs of testers as similar as possible, except with regard to race. Testers were matched in physical size and in the education and experience they claimed to have. An attempt was also made to match each pair in openness, energy level, and articulateness. The testers were actually college students, but most of them posed as recent high school graduates and were supplied with fictional biographies that gave them similar job experience. They were put through mock interviews and coached to act like the person they were paired with to the greatest possible extent. The testers were then sent to apply for low-skill, entry-level jobs usually filled by young high-school graduates in manufacturing, hotels, restaurants, retail sales, and office work. The job titles ranged from general laborer to management trainee. The testers were instructed to refuse any job offered them so that the other member of the pair could have a chance at it.

The black testers posing as job seekers were carefully coached to present qualifications apparently equal to those of their white counterparts. In reality they were all, black and white, excellently qualified for the jobs they applied for. The Urban Institute researchers found that the young white men were offered jobs 45 percent more than the young black men. This result clearly reveals that some employers were not treating male minority job seekers equally with white males of similar qualifications.

The same researchers paired white Anglo testers and Hispanic testers who were fluent in English.[9] Again, the pairs of young men were matched to minimize the differences between them; the only apparent differences were the slight accents, somewhat darker complexions, and Spanish names of the Hispanic testers. The Anglos received 52 percent more job offers than the Hispanics.

THE DIFFICULTY OF CHANGING HIRING HABITS

Patterns of occupational segregation by race and sex tend to persist in part because people have good reason to be cautious in making hiring and promotion decisions. These decisions are the most crucial to any organization's success. A bad mistake in hiring or promotion can result in large monetary losses and a lot of misery. When an unsuitable person has been chosen for a job, there may be painful weeks or months during which work is botched, tempers flare, feelings are bruised, and customers are alienated. Employers have an understandable tendency to move cautiously and to continue doing what has worked well previously. Hiring candidates of a different race or sex is likely to be seen as risky, as asking for trouble. . . .

If the people involved in the selection process want to do nothing more than select the candidate who will perform the best, regardless of sex, race, or ethnicity, they are not likely to select a candidate of a nontraditional race or gender, even if very promising candidates of this kind are available. People use minimal clues of manner and appearance and way of talking to make snap judgments about candidates of a familiar type. A white person who has little experience with the performance of blacks on the job may not feel capable of making good judgments about their abilities based on such clues, and he or she may find it safer to stick with candidates of a familiar kind.

One way employers stick with the kinds of workers they are used to is by filling their vacancies with people recommended by those already working there in the kind of job they are filling. There is a considerable incentive for employers to fill jobs this way, and the practice is apparently widespread.[10] It saves recruiting expenses and may make for congenial work groups. A worker who recommends someone vouches for that person as someone likely to do well. Unfortunately, this seemingly innocent recruiting practice makes it particularly hard for African Americans to improve their status. Relying on employee recommendations effectively excludes from good jobs those who do not have relatives and friends with good jobs.

Women candidates may be particularly disadvantaged by sexual conventions. A woman who wears a standard amount of makeup and jewelry may be judged to be unbusinesslike, since the standard businessperson—a man—wears none. On the other hand, a woman who wears less than the standard amount of makeup and jewelry risks being considered not feminine enough to be a normal woman and is therefore judged to be peculiar. People making hiring decisions tend to shy away from people who seem peculiar.

PROBLEMS OF ACCEPTANCE BY COWORKERS

Production on the job has its social aspects. Each worker has to learn from and teach others, engage in cooperative endeavors, transmit and receive information, help provide a friendly environment, cover occasionally for another's mistakes, and at least appear to be amused by the jokes that go around. The people doing the hiring customarily consider not only a candidate's technical abilities and general pleasantness but also the chances of the candidate being accepted by coworkers so that they will interact well. . . .

Some of the hostility to the worker of untraditional race or sex may be motivated by self-defense. Men know that jobs in which white males predominate tend to be compensated with high status and pay; feeling those benefits threatened, they may not welcome a coworker who dilutes the maleness or whiteness of their job. They may fear that future vacancies will be filled with lower-status people or that they will have to leave the occupation or risk being trapped in a devalued job. As a result of such worries, there may be difficulties in convincing the old hands to introduce the newcomer of untraditional race or gender to the tricks of the trade.

Donald Tomaskovic-Devey reports an instance of this problem:

> A pilot told me a story about the first woman pilot at the busy corporate airport where he worked. The other pilots knew from the start that she would not be able to cut it. To give her a "fair" chance to prove herself, they had decided not to show her the ropes, to allow her to figure out on her own the controls on planes she had not flown before, and not to introduce her to the control tower and maintenance staffs, although this information was routinely shared with new male pilots. After all, they knew from the start that a woman could not be a pilot. Of course, what they knew did not matter; it was what they did that was decisive. By refusing to share their knowledge, they insured her failure. . . .[11]

GOALS AS ENERGIZING DEVICES

When critics of affirmative action say that goals are the same as quotas, and that quotas are bad, they presumably are saying, "Get rid of discrimination if there is any; give everyone a fair chance. But make sure you don't measure success or failure in numbers. If you do, you may be tempted to do some unfair and stupid things to make the numbers look good." The problem is that the directive "Be fair from now on" is far less energizing, and far more easily evaded, than "There are some good black people out there. Have one of them aboard by a month from next Thursday, or at least show that you've tried." Recruitment methods are highly resistant to change. And as our review of labor market realities has shown, there are many workplaces where these methods need changing if we are to make significant progress toward fairness.

The use of numerical goals to spur managers into action and to direct their behavior has been useful in all aspects of modern management; indeed, its use in affirmative action follows from its success in other areas. Modern businesses use numerical goals to manage production, productivity, sales, investments, and costs. The announcement of goals helps to specify explicit standards for performance of managers. In the absence of numerical goals and timetables for meeting them, it is difficult to determine whether managers have done a good job or to hold anyone responsible for failures. When people know they will not be held responsible, they are less likely to make significant efforts. . . .

If we were to establish goals for both sexes and for each of the ethnic groups represented in the United States, the labor market would become a balkanized nightmare: each slot would be earmarked for a person of a particular extraction and gender. Moreover, an expansion of the share of the population for whom goals are set might have an adverse impact on groups for which no goals are set, groups that contain relatively large numbers of high achievers—Jews and Asians, for example. A severe shrinking of the proportion of the population not included in affirmative action goals might reduce tolerance of the high success rates of such groups. In short, there are good reasons to have fewer goals rather than more. Establishing goals for a particular group should not be done without substantial reason. There is no sign that we are tending in the direction of an overproliferation of groups covered by affirmative action goals.

Common sense suggests that employment goals should be set for a group only if all of the following conditions are met:

1. The group is seriously underrepresented in an occupation or at a hierarchical level in the workplace.
2. The underrepresentation continues because of present discrimination, or because of current employer practices or habits that effectively exclude members of the group.
3. The pattern of exclusion is unlikely to change in the absence of special efforts.

For jobs in which discriminated-against groups are overrepresented, goals should be set for integrating whites and males into them. This effort will fail if the salaries for such jobs are significantly lower than what white males with the required skills can earn in other jobs. Nor will it be possible to recruit white males into jobs that have obviously been set up as dead ends, jobs whose duties are overly repetitive, or jobs over which the supervision is more rigid than white males of that skill level are used to. Integrating the all-female jobs with males, or the all-black jobs with whites, will force employers to rethink wage levels and working conditions—to the benefit of those members of disadvantaged groups who stay in traditionally sex- or race-specific occupations.

Different areas of the country, occupations, industries, and hierarchical levels call for different sets of goals. The evidence suggests that goals are needed almost everywhere for black men and women and white women, and in many places for Hispanics of both sexes. The Civil Rights Act would forbid discrimination against people of Hungarian extraction on account of their origin. However, if there is no reason to think that Hungarians are being excluded, we should not have goals for them.

Consider, however, the situation of a New England law firm that employs 40 lawyers and has no partners or associates of Irish or Jewish extraction. There are many people of Irish extraction in New England, and a considerable number of Jews as well. In the past these groups were commonly denied access to jobs reserved for upper-crust males of British extraction. Many lawyers of Irish and Jewish extraction now have elite legal credentials, and if a firm of that size has no such lawyers on its staff, it is likely that some aspects of the recruitment process are keeping them from being hired. Our guidelines suggest that having a goal for hiring lawyers of Irish and Jewish ancestry would be desirable for this firm. On the other hand, in other parts of the country, and in some occupations in which being of Irish or Jewish ancestry has not recently been a substantial disadvantage, goals for such people, even when they are underrepresented, would be unnecessary and undesirable. . . .

THE FUZZINESS OF MERIT

We frequently think and act as though there were only one correct way to define merit, one right and infallibly accurate way to measure it, and one right way to use measurements of merit in making hiring or school admission decisions. We also tend to assume that these obviously right ways are everywhere in current use. They are not, of course.

The rankings of candidates as to merit will depend on which of the candidates' characteristics are taken into consideration, how much weight is given to each characteristic, and how the judging is done—formally, objectively, and consistently for all candidates, or informally and inconsistently. Faye Crosby's research . . . shows that people do unconsciously give more weight to the good points of the person they consider appropriate for the job (for instance, a white man for a management job) and tend to ignore the good points of a person they think is less appropriate.

In thinking about affirmative action erroneous assumptions are frequently made:

1. That for each job opening there is one person who is unambiguously the best among the candidates.
2. That the identity of that candidate is unerringly revealed by the employer's selection process.
3. That the evaluation process is uninfluenced by the sex, race, ethnicity, age, or disability status of the candidates.
4. That the "best" candidate is head and shoulders above all the others, so that the substitution of the one judged third- or fourth-best instead of the one judged best would make a great difference to productivity.

These assumptions are unrealistic in many, even most cases. The American Society for Personnel Administration, in a brief supporting affirmative action in a case before the Supreme Court, said:

> It is a standard tenet of personnel administration that there is rarely a single, "best qualified" person for a job. An effective personnel system will bring before the selecting official several fully-qualified candidates who each may possess different attributes which recommend them for selection. Especially where the job is an unexceptional, middle-level craft position, without the need for unique work experience or educational attainment and for which several well-qualified candidates are available, final determinations as to which candidate is "best qualified" are at best subjective.[12] . . .

Measurements of merit for a job or for school admission, then, are dependent on the methods used and subject to error and subversion; moreover, they may not differentiate among candidates with any great accuracy. A process of assessing merit that cuts out all but white males may mask purposeful discrimination or set up hurdles that female and black candidates, for no job-related reason, have particular difficulty in getting over. An interviewer whose method of measuring congeniality is to chat with candidates about golf is not going to be giving very many black or female candidates high grades for that quality. . . .

THE ILLUSION THAT BLACKS ALWAYS WIN

In their talk of fairness, the foes of affirmative action focus on two individuals—a black person and a white person—competing for a job. The black person in their story is poorly qualified for the job. The white person is highly qualified, has worked very hard to get himself qualified, and is innocent of any wrongdoing toward this black person or any other. Most likely, the white person is from a poor family and the black person grew up in comfortable circumstances. Affirmative action, its foes would have you believe, has turned the labor market into a succession of contests between pairs of individuals like these. In each contest, the undeserving black person is declared the winner and gets 100 percent of the prize, while the deserving white person is left with nothing. With this perennial outcome, the situation has become pretty hopeless if you are a white man. With white males depicted as losing in each of these matchups, one may get the impression that the white male group has suffered severely from affirmative action.

The evidence of how the labor market "contests" actually come out—who is getting seats on the "good jobs bus"—shows, of course, a quite different picture. There has been some desegregation since the 1960s, but as we have seen, many jobs in many workplaces remain segregated. In the wages they earn, black people and white women are still far behind white males of similar education and experience. Members of the white male group continue to win almost all of the contests for the best jobs in each of the major occupational groups in most workplaces.

Affirmative action's removal of white men's privilege of exclusive access to high-paying jobs does inflict losses on white men. The foes of affirmative action fixate on those losses and ignore the reasons they are necessary, desirable, and fair. Foes pay no attention to the losses of those individuals who, in the absence of affirmative action, have been excluded because they are black or female.

The press has spotlighted the loss of privilege of certain white men and rendered invisible those black individuals who are cut out when white privilege is allowed to persist. One suburban county adopted an affirmative action program to desegregate its fire department, which had a history of total segregation by race. Some of the rejected white applicants organized a demonstration and invited the press. The local newspaper ran a photograph of the group of rejected white candidates across the street from the headquarters of the fire department, gazing at it mournfully and reproachfully. No pictures ever appeared in that newspaper showing the far larger group of blacks who for years had been rejected from firefighter jobs by a selection system rigged to exclude them. Able blacks had been excluded in favor of less qualified or equally qualified whites. The invisibility of the blacks who have been excluded by discrimination promotes the topsy-turvy view that whites are victims and blacks are in a privileged position in our society—that blacks have been "given too much."

IS AFFIRMATIVE ACTION A ZERO-SUM GAME?

Would every gain for blacks and other minorities under affirmative action spell an equal loss for whites? Will men lose to the extent that women gain? If there were a rigidly fixed number of "good" jobs and "bad" jobs, then every time a "good" job was assigned through affirmative action to a black or a woman, a white man would be forced into a "bad" job. . . .

. . . Affirmative action, which breaks up the labor market monopolies that have been held by favored groups and makes blacks and women eligible for a greater variety of jobs, should have the effect of reducing the gap in pay and conditions between jobs that whites and blacks with a given education typically get. If affirmative action is successful, some whites will find themselves applying for jobs that hitherto only blacks have applied for, and some men will be applying for jobs that only women have previously held. But these jobs are likely to be better jobs than they would have been in the absence of affirmative action.

Finally, if we can reduce discrimination and segregation in the labor market, there will be gains outside of the labor market as well. All of us will benefit from revitalized central cities, lower crime rates, and fewer panhandlers, fewer homeless. It will be easier, more pleasurable, less guilt-inducing, and safer to live in a more just society.

NOTES

1. Richard Morin and Sharon Warden. "Americans Vent Anger at Affirmative Action." *Washington Post,* March 24, 1995, pp. 1, 4.
2. Weekly wages of full-time workers by race and sex are published by the U.S. Bureau of Labor Statistics in the periodical *Employment and Earnings.*
3. See Francine D. Blau and Lawrence M. Kahn, "Gender and Pay Differentials," in *Research Frontiers in Industrial Relations and Human Resources,* ed. David Lewin, Olivia S. Mitchell, and Peter D. Sherer (Madison, Wisc.: IRRA, 1992), p. 389.
4. Jane Gross, "Big Grocery Chain Reaches Landmark Sex-Bias Accord," *New York Times,* December 17, 1993, pp. A1, B10.
5. Unpublished papers by Akiko Naono (1993) and Jacqueline Chu (1994), Economics Department, American University, Washington, D.C.
6. Lynne Duke, "Shoney's Bias Settlement Sends $105 Million Signal," *Washington Post,* February 5, 1993, pp. A1, A20.
7. *Employment and Earnings* (January 1995): table A-13.
8. Michael Fix and Raymond J. Struyk, eds., *Clear and Convincing Evidence: Measurement of Discrimination in America* (Washington, D.C.: Urban Institute Press, 1993).
9. *Ibid.*
10. Arthur Stinchcombe, *Information and Organizations* (Berkeley: University of California Press, 1990), pp. 243–44.
11. Donald Tomaskovic-Devey, *Gender and Racial Inequality at Work: The Sources and Consequences of Job Segregation* (Ithaca, N.Y.: ILR Press, 1993), pp. 161–62.
12. American Society for Personnel Administration, amicus curiae brief submitted to the Supreme Court, quoted in Justice William J. Brennan's majority opinion in *Johnson* v. *Transportation Agency of Santa Clara County, Calif.,* 107 Sup. Ct. 1442 (1987), p. 1457.

Abortion

Probably no domestic issue has polarized the nation more during the last 30 years than abortion. It has proved to be a hotly contested subject in state and national elections and has been the occasion for repeated mass demonstrations in our nation's capital. That abortion has aroused such strong feelings is not surprising, for some see the right to privacy at stake even as others insist that the real issue is the taking of human life.

In the first selection, Susan Estrich and Kathleen Sullivan argue that if the decision on abortion is taken out of the hands of the mother, then she will necessarily be forced to surrender autonomy over both her body and family decisions. Government intrusion into these spheres would constitute an intolerable infringement on the fundamental right to privacy—a view shared by the Supreme Court when it upheld a woman's right to an abortion in Roe v. Wade *(1973).*

In the second essay James Bopp and Richard Coleson contend that the Roe v. Wade *decision was a glaring example of judicial power gone wild, with the justices manufacturing a right to privacy in the Constitution where it was nowhere to be found. In doing so, the Court not only violated its own stated criteria for determining what qualifies as a fundamental right, but also arrogated to itself a power which the people alone may exercise. Bopp and Coleson further argue that the right to abortion should be rejected on moral as well as legal grounds, and they also challenge pro-choice claims that the outlawing of abortions would have harmful social consequences for women.*

Abortion Politics:
The Case for the Right to Privacy

Susan R. Estrich and Kathleen M. Sullivan

I. THE EXISTENCE OF A LIBERTY INTEREST

A. Reproductive Choice Is Essential to Woman's Control of Her Destiny and Family Life

Notwithstanding the abortion controversy, the Supreme Court has long acknowledged an unenumerated right to privacy as a species of "liberty" that the due process clauses protect.[1] The principle is as ancient as *Meyer* v. *Nebraska*[2] and *Pierce* v. *Society of Sisters*,[3] which protected parents' freedom to educate their children free of the state's controlling hand. In its modern elaboration, this right continues to protect child rearing and family life from the overly intrusive reach of government.[4] The modern privacy cases have also plainly established that decisions whether to bear children are no less fundamental than decisions about how to raise them. The Court has consistently held since *Griswold* v. *Connecticut*[5] that the Constitution accords special protection to "matters so fundamentally affecting a person as the decision whether to bear or beget a child," and has therefore strictly scrutinized laws restricting contraception.[6] *Roe* held that these principles extend no less to abortion than to contraception.

The privacy cases rest, as Justice Stevens recognized in *Thornburgh,* centrally on "'the moral fact that a person belongs to himself [or herself] and not others nor to society as a whole.'"[7] Extending this principle to the abortion decision follows from the fact that "[f]ew decisions are . . . more basic to individual dignity and autonomy" or more appropriate to the "private sphere of individual liberty" than the uniquely personal, intimate, and self-defining decision whether or not to continue a pregnancy.[8]

In two senses, abortion restrictions keep a woman from "belonging to herself." First and most obviously, they deprive her of bodily self-possession. As Chief Justice Rehnquist observed in another context, pregnancy entails "profound physical, emotional, and psychological consequences."[9] To name a few, pregnancy increases a woman's uterine size 500–1,000 times, her pulse rate by 10 to 15 beats a minute, and her body weight by 25 pounds or more.[10] Even the healthiest pregnancy can entail nausea, vomiting, more frequent urination, fatigue, back pain, labored breathing, or water retention.[11] There are also numerous medical risks involved in carrying pregnancy to term: of every 10 women who experience pregnancy and childbirth, 6 need treatment

Susan R. Estrich is Robert Kingsley Professor of Law at the University of Southern California, and Kathleen M. Sullivan is professor of law at Stanford University. This selection is from Susan R. Estrich and Kathleen M. Sullivan, "Abortion Politics: Writing for an Audience of One," University of Pennsylvania Law Review, *138:125–32, pp. 150–55 (1989). Copyright © 1989 by the University of Pennsylvania. Reprinted by permission. Notes have been renumbered to correspond with edited text—Editors.*

for some medical complication, and 3 need treatment for major complications.[12] In addition, labor and delivery impose extraordinary physical demands, whether over the 6-to-12 hour or longer course of vaginal delivery, or during the highly invasive surgery involved in a cesarean section, which accounts for one out of four deliveries.[13]

By compelling pregnancy to term and delivery even where they are unwanted, abortion restrictions thus exert far more profound intrusions into bodily integrity than the stomach-pumping the Court invalidated in *Rochin* v. *California*,[14] or the surgical removal of a bullet from a shoulder that the Court invalidated in *Winston* v. *Lee*.[15] "The integrity of an individual's person is a cherished value of our society"[16] because it is so essential to identity: as former Solicitor General Charles Fried, who argued for the United States in *Webster,* recognized in another context: "[to say] that my body can be used is [to say] that I can be used."[17]

These points would be too obvious to require restatement if the state attempted to compel abortions rather than to restrict them. Indeed, in colloquy with Justice O'Connor during the *Webster* oral argument, former Solicitor General Fried conceded that in such a case, liberty principles, although unenumerated, would compel the strictest view. To be sure, as Mr. Fried suggested, restrictive abortion laws do not literally involve "laying hands on a woman."[18] But this distinction should make no difference: the state would plainly infringe its citizens' bodily integrity whether its agents inflicted knife wounds or its laws forbade surgery or restricted blood transfusions in cases of private knifings.[19]

Apart from this impact on bodily integrity, abortion restrictions infringe a woman's autonomy in a second sense as well; they invade the autonomy in family affairs that the Supreme Court has long deemed central to the right of privacy. Liberty requires independence in making the most important decisions in life.[20] "The decision whether or not to beget or bear a child" lies at "the very heart of this cluster of constitutionally protected choices,"[21] because few decisions can more importantly alter the course of one's life than the decision to bring a child into the world. Bearing a child dramatically affects " 'what a person is, what [s]he wants, the determination of [her] life plan, of [her] concept of the good' " and every other aspect of the " 'self-determination . . . [that] give[s] substance to the concept of liberty.' "[22] Becoming a parent dramatically alters a woman's educational prospects,[23] employment opportunities,[24] and sense of self.[25] In light of these elemental facts, it is no surprise that the freedom to choose one's own family formation is "deeply rooted in this Nation's history and tradition."[26]

Today, virtually no one disputes that these principles require heightened scrutiny of laws restricting access to contraception.[27] But critics of *Roe* sometimes argue that abortion is "different in kind from the decision not to conceive in the first place."[28] Justice White, for example, has asserted that, while the liberty interest is fundamental in the contraception context,[29] that interest falls to minimal after conception.[30]

Such a distinction cannot stand, however, because no bright line can be drawn between contraception and abortion in light of modern scientific and medical advances. Contraception and abortion are points on a continuum. Even "conception" itself is a complex process of which fertilization is simply the first stage. According to contemporary medical authorities, conception begins not with fertilization, but rather six to seven days later when the fertilized egg becomes implanted in the uterine wall, itself a complex process.[31] Many medically accepted contraceptives operate after fertilization. For example, both oral contraceptives and the intra-uterine device (IUD) not only prevent fertilization but in some instances prevent implantation.[32] Moreover, the most significant new developments in contraceptive technology, such as RU486, act by foiling implantation.[33] All such contraceptives blur the line between contraception and abortion.

In the absence of a bright physiological line, there can be no bright constitutional line between the moments before and after conception. A woman's fundamental liberty does not simply evaporate when sperm meets ovum. Indeed, as Justice Stevens has recognized, "if one decision is more 'fundamental' to the individual's freedom than the other, surely it is the postconception decision that is the more serious."[34] Saying this much does not deny that profound evolutionary changes occur between fertilization and birth. Clearly, there is some difference between "the freshly fertilized egg and . . . the 9-month-gestated . . . fetus on the eve of birth."[35] But as *Roe* v. *Wade* fully recognized, such differences go at most to the weight of the state's justification for interfering with a pregnancy; they do not extinguish the underlying fundamental liberty.

Thus *Roe* is not a mere "thread" that the Court could pull without "unravel[ing]" the now elaborately woven "fabric" of the privacy decisions.[36] Rather, *Roe* is integral to the principle that childbearing decisions come to "th[e] Court with a momentum for respect that is lacking when appeal is made to liberties which derive merely from shifting economic arrangements.[37] The decision to become a mother is too fundamental to be equated with the decision to buy a car, choose optometry over ophthalmology, take early retirement, or any other merely economic decision that the government may regulate by showing only a minimally rational basis.

B. Keeping Reproductive Choice in Private Hands Is Essential to a Free Society

Even if there were any disagreement about the degree of bodily or decisional autonomy that is essential to personhood, there is a separate, alternative rationale for the privacy cases: keeping the state out of the business of reproductive decision-making. Regimentation of reproduction is a hallmark of the totalitarian state, from Plato's Republic to Hitler's Germany, from Huxley's *Brave New World* to Atwood's *Handmaid's Tale.* Whether the state compels reproduction or prevents it, "totalitarian limitation of family size . . . is at complete variance with our constitutional concepts."[38] The state's monopoly of force cautions against *any* official reproductive orthodoxy.

For these reasons, the Supreme Court has long recognized that the privacy right protects not only the individual but also our society. As early as *Meyer*[39] and *Pierce,*[40] the Court acknowledged that "[t]he fundamental theory of liberty" on which a free society rests "excludes any general power of the State to standardize" its citizens.[41] As Justice Powell likewise recognized for the *Moore* plurality, "a free society" is one that avoids the homogenization of family life.[42]

The right of privacy, like freedoms of speech and religion, protects conscience and spirit from the encroachment of overbearing government. "Struggles to coerce uniformity of sentiment," Justice Jackson recognized in *West Virginia State Board of Education* v. *Barnett*,[43] are the inevitably futile province of "our totalitarian enemies."[44] Preserving a private sphere for childbearing and childrearing decisions not only liberates the individual; it desirably constrains the state.[45]

Those who would relegate all control over abortion to the state legislatures ignore these fundamental, systematic values. It is a red herring to focus on the question of judicial versus legislative control of reproductive decisions, as so many of *Roe's* critics do. The real distinction is that between private and public control of the decision: the private control that the courts protect through *Griswold* and *Roe,* and the public control that the popular branches could well usurp in a world without those decisions.

Precisely because of the importance of a private sphere for family, spirit, and conscience, the framers never intended to commit all moral disagreements to the political arena. Quite the contrary:

> The very purpose of a Bill of Rights was to withdraw certain subjects from the vicissitudes of political controversy, to place them beyond the reach of majorities and officials and to establish them as legal principles to be applied by the courts. One's right to life, liberty, and property, to free speech, a free press, freedom of worship and assembly, and other fundamental rights may not be submitted to vote; they depend on the outcome of no elections.[46]

Such "withdrawal" of fundamental liberties from the political arena is basic to constitutional democracy as opposed to rank majoritarianism, and nowhere is such "withdrawal" more important than in controversies where moral convictions and passions run deepest. The inclusion of the free exercise clause attests to this point.[47]

The framers also never intended that toleration on matters of family, conscience, and spirit would vary from state to state. The value of the states and localities as "laborator[ies for] . . . social and economic experiments"[48] has never extended to "'experiments at the expense of the dignity and personality of the individual.'"[49] Rather as Madison once warned, "' it is proper to take alarm at the first experiment on our liberties. We hold this prudent jealousy to be the first duty of citizens, and one of [the] noblest characteristics of the late Revolution.'"[50]

Roe v. *Wade* thus properly withdrew the abortion decision, like other decisions on matters of conscience, "from the vicissitudes of political controversy." It did not withdraw that decision from the vicissitudes of moral argument or social suasion by persuasive rather than coercive means.[51] In withdrawing the abortion decision from the hot lights of politics, *Roe* protected not only persons but the processes of constitutional democracy. . . .

II. THE POLITICAL PROCESS: NOT TO BE TRUSTED

On October 13, 1989, the *New York Times* declared that the tide had turned in the political process on abortion.[52] The Florida legislature, in special session, rejected a series of proposals to restrict abortion, and Congress voted to expand abortion funding for poor women to cases of rape and incest. And most stunningly of all, the Attorney

General of Illinois on November 2, 1989, settled a pending challenge to Illinois' abortion clinic regulation rather than risk winning his case in the United States Supreme Court. These events have triggered the assessment that the post-*Webster* pro-choice mobilization has succeeded. Which raises the question: why not leave these matters to the political process?

The short answer, of course, is that we don't leave freedom of speech or religion or association to the political process, even on good days when the polls suggest they might stand a chance, at least in some states. The very essence of a fundamental right is that it "depend[s] on the outcome of no elections."[53]

The long answer is, as always, that fundamental liberties are not occasions for the experimentation that federalism invites. The right to abortion should not depend on where you live and how much money you have for travel.[54] And, regardless of our recent, at long-last successes, the reality remains that the political process is to be trusted the least where, as here, it imposes burdens unequally.

The direct impact of abortion restrictions falls exclusively on a class of people that consists entirely of women. Only women get pregnant. Only women have abortions. Only women will endure unwanted pregnancies and adverse health consequences if states restrict abortions. Only women will suffer dangerous, illegal abortions where legal ones are unavailable. And only women will bear children if they cannot obtain abortions.[55] Yet every restrictive abortion law has been passed by a legislature in which men constitute a numerical majority. And every restrictive abortion law, by definition, contains an unwritten clause exempting all men from its strictures.

As Justice Jackson wrote, legislators threaten liberty when they pass laws that exempt themselves or people like them: "The framers of the Constitution knew, and we should not forget today, that there is no more effective practical guaranty against arbitrary and unreasonable government than to require that the principles of law which officials would impose upon a minority must be imposed generally."[56] The Supreme Court has long interpreted the equal protection clause to require even-handedness in legislation, lest the powerful few too casually trade away for others key liberties that they are careful to reserve for themselves.

For example, in striking down a law permitting castration of recidivist chicken thieves but sparing white collar embezzlers the knife, the Court implied that, put to an all-or-nothing choice, legislators would rather sterilize no one than jeopardize a politically potent class.[57] In the words of Justice Jackson: "There are limits to the extent to which a legislatively represented majority may conduct biological experiments at the expense of the dignity and personality and natural powers of a minority—even those who are guilty of what the majority defines as crimes."[58]

At least there should be. Relying on state legislatures, as Chief Justice Rehnquist would, to protect women against "abortion regulation reminiscent of the dark ages,"[59] ignores the fact that the overwhelming majority of "those who serve in such bodies"[60] are biologically exempt from the penalties they are imposing.

The danger is greater still when the subject is abortion. The lessons of history are disquieting. Abortion restrictions, like the most classic restrictions on women seeking to participate in the worlds of work and ideas, have historically rested on archaic stereotypes portraying women as persons whose "paramount destiny and mission . . . [is] to fulfill the noble and benign office of wife and mother."[61] Legislation prohibiting abortion, largely a product of the years between 1860 and 1880, reflected *precisely* the same ideas about women's natural and proper roles as other legislation from the same period, long since discredited, that prohibited women from serving on juries or participating in the professions, including the practice of law.[62] And modern studies have found that support for laws banning abortion continues to be an outgrowth of the same stereotypical notions that women's only appropriate roles are those of mother and housewife. In many cases, abortion laws are a direct reaction to the increasing number of women who work outside of the home.[63] Those involved in anti-abortion activities tend to echo the well-known views of Justice Bradley in *Bradwell:*

> Men and women, as a result of . . . intrinsic differences, have different roles to play. Men are best suited to the public world of work, whereas women are best suited to rearing children, managing homes, and loving and caring for husbands. . . . Mothering, in their view, is itself a full-time job, and any woman who cannot commit herself fully to mothering should eschew it entirely.[64]

But the lessons of history are not limited to the powers of enduring stereotypes. History also makes clear that a world without *Roe* will not be a world without abortion but a world in which abortion is accessible according to one's constitutional case. While affluent women will travel to jurisdictions where safe and legal abortions are available, paying whatever is necessary, restrictive abortion laws and with them, the life-threatening prospect of back-alley abortion, will disproportionately descend upon "those without . . . adequate resources" to avoid them.[65] Those for whom the burdens of an unwanted pregnancy may be the most crushing—the young, the poor, women whose color already renders them victims of discrimination—will be the ones least able to secure a safe abortion.

In the years before *Roe*, "[p]oor and minority women were virtually precluded from obtaining safe, legal procedures, the overwhelming majority of which were obtained by white women in the private hospital services on psychiatric indications."[66] Women without access to safe and legal abortions often had dangerous and illegal ones. According to one study, mishandled criminal abortions were the leading cause of maternal deaths in the 1960s,[67] and mortality rates for African-American women were as much as nine times the rate for white women.[68] To trust the political process to protect these women is to ignore the lessons of history and the realities of power and powerlessness in America today.

In the face of such lessons, those who would have us put our faith in the political process might first want to look a little more closely at the victories which are said to support such a choice. The Florida legislature's rejection of proposed abortion restrictions came days *after* the state's highest court held that the State Constitution protects the right to choose abortion, rendering the entire session, by the press's verdict before it began, symbolic at best. The session was still a triumph, but hardly one in which the courts were beside the point. And while extending funding to cases of rape and incest would have been a step forward, the narrowness of the victory and the veto of the resulting legislation should give pause, at least.[69]

We believe that energizing and mobilizing pro-choice voters, and women in particular, is vitally important on its own terms. We hope, frankly, that with apportionment approaching in 1990, that mobilization will affect issues well beyond abortion. We hope more women will find themselves running for office and winning. We hope pro-choice voters and the legislators they elect will attack a range of issues of particular importance to women, including the attention that children receive after they are born.

But we have no illusions. We will lose some along the way. Young and poor and minority women will pay most dearly when we do. That's the way it is in politics. That's why politics should not dictate constitutional rights. . . .

NOTES

1. The right of privacy is only one among many instances in which the Court has recognized rights that are not expressly named in the Constitution's text. To name just a few other examples, the Court has recognized unenumerated rights to freedom of association, see *National Association for the Advancement of Colored People* v. *Alabama,* 357 U.S. 449, 466 (1958); to equal protection under the Fifth Amendment due process clause, see *Bolling* v. *Sharpe,* 347 U.S. 497, 500 (1954); to travel between the states, see *Shapiro* v. *Thompson,* 394 U.S. 618, 638 (1966); to vote, see *Harper* v. *Virginia Bd. of Elections,* 383 U.S. 663, 665-66 (1966); *Reynolds* v. *Sims,* 377 U.S. 533, 554 (1964); and to attend criminal trials, see *Richmond Newspapers Inc.* v. *Virginia,* 448 U.S. 555, 579–80 (1980).
2. 262 U.S. 390 (1923).
3. 268 U.S. 510 (1925).
4. See, e.g., *Moore* v. *City of East Cleveland,* 431 U.S. 494, 503–06 (1977) (plurality opinion) (noting a constitutional right to live with one's grandchildren); *Loving* v. *Virginia,* 388 U.S. 1, 12 (1967) (affirming a right to interracial marriage).
5. 381 U.S. 479 (1965).
6. *Eisenstadt* v. *Baird,* 405 U.S. 438, 453 (1972).
7. *Thornburgh* v. *American College of Obstetricians & Gynecologists,* 476 U.S. 747, 777 n.5 (1985) (Stevens, J., concurring) (quoting former Solicitor General Fried, "Correspondence," 6 *Phil. & Pub. Aff.* 288-89 (1977)).
8. *Thornburgh,* 476 U.S. at 772.
9. *Michael M.* v. *Sonoma County Superior Court,* 480 U.S. 464, 471 (1981).
10. See J. Pritchard, P. McDonald & N. Gant, *Williams Obstetrics,* 181–210, 260–63 (17th ed. 1985) [hereinafter *Williams Obstetrics*].
11. See *Id.*
12. See R. Gold, A. Kenney & S. Singh, *Blessed Events and the Bottom Line: Financing Maternity Care in the United States,* 10 (1987).
13. See D. Danforth, M. Hughey & A. Wagner, *The Complete Guide to Pregnancy,* 228–31 (1983); S. Romney, M. J. Gray, A. B. Little, J. Merrill, E. J. Quilligan & R. Stander, *Gynecology and Obstetrics: The Health Care of Women,* 626–37 (2d ed. 1981).

14. 342 U.S. 165 (1952).
15. 470 U.S. 753 (1985).
16. *Id.* at 760.
17. C. Fried, *Right and Wrong,* 121 n.* (1978).
18. "Transcript of Oral Argument in Abortion Case," *N.Y. Times,* Apr. 27, 1989, at B12, col. 5.
19. Likewise, a state would surely infringe reproductive freedom by compelling abortions even if it became technologically possible to do so without "laying hands on a woman."
20. See *Whalen* v. *Roe,* 429 U.S. 589, 599–600 (1977).
21. *Carey* v. *Population Serv. Int'l,* 431 U.S. 678, 685 (1977).
22. *Thornburgh* v. *American College of Obstetricians & Gynecologists,* 476 U.S. 747, 777 n.5 (1985) (Stevens, J., concurring) (quoting C. Fried, *Right and Wrong,* 146–47 (1978)).
23. Teenage mothers have high dropout rates: 8 out of 10 who become mothers at age 17 or younger do not finish high school. See Fielding, *Adolescent Pregnancy Revisited,* 299 Mass. Dep't Pub. Health, 893, 894 (1978).
24. Control over the rate of childbirth is a key factor in explaining recent gains in women's wages relative to men's. See Fuchs, "Women's Quest for Economic Equality," 3 *J. Econ. Persp.* 25, 33–37 (1989).
25. This fact is evident even if the biological mother does not raise her child. Relinquishing a child for adoption may alleviate material hardship, but it is psychologically traumatic. See Winkler & VanKeppel, *Relinquishing Mothers in Adoption: Their Long-Term Adjustment,* Monograph No. 3, Institute of Family Studies (1984).
26. *Moore* v. *City of East Cleveland,* 431 U.S. 494, 503 (1977) (plurality opinion).
27. The United States has conceded before the Supreme Court that the *Griswold* line of cases was correctly decided. See *Brief for the United States as Amicus Curiae Supporting Appellants,* 11–13; *Webster* v. *Reproductive Health Serv.,* 1109 S.Ct. 3040 (1989) (No. 88-605); "Transcript of Oral Argument in Abortion Case," *N.Y. Times,* Apr. 27, 1989, at B13, col. 1 (Argument of former Solicitor General Fried on behalf of the United States).
28. *Thornburgh,* 476 U.S. at 792 n.2 (White, J., dissenting).
29. See *Eisenstadt* v. *Baird,* 405 U.S. 438, 463–64 (1972) (White, J., concurring in result); *Griswold* v. *Connecticut,* 381 U.S. 479, 502–03 (1965) (White, J., concurring in judgment).
30. See *Thornburgh,* 476 U.S. at 792 n.2 (White, J., dissenting) (arguing that the fetus's presence after conception changes not merely the state justification but "the characterization of the liberty interest itself").
31. See *Williams Obstetrics, supra* note 10, at 88-91; Milby, "The New Biology and the Question of Personhood: Implications for Abortion," 9 *Am. J.L. & Med.* 31, 39–41 (1983). Indeed, the American College of Obstetricians & Gynecologists, the preeminent authority on such matters, has adopted the following official definition of conception: conception consists of "the implantation of the blastocyst [fertilized ovum]" in the uterus, and thus is "not synonymous with fertilization." *Obstetric-Gynecologic*

Terminology 229, 327 (E. Hughes ed. 1972). Such a definition is not surprising in view of the fact that less than half of fertilized ova ever successfully become implanted. See "Post-Coital Contraception," 1 *The Lancet* 855, 856 (1983).

32. See R. Hatcher, E. Guest, F. Stewart, G. Stewart, J. Trussell, S. Bowen & W. Gates, *Contraceptive Technology,* 252–53, 377 (14th rev. ed. 1988) [hereinafter *Contraceptive Technology*]; *United States Department of Health and Human Services, IUDs: Guidelines for Informed Decision-Making and Use* (1987).

33. See *Contraceptive Technology, supra* note 32, at 378; Nieman, Choate, Chrousas, Healy, Morin, Renquist, Merriam, Spitz, Bardin, Balieu & Loriaux, "The Progesterone Antagonist RU486: A Potential New Contraceptive Agent," 316 *N. Eng. J. Med.* 187 (1987). RU486 is approved for use in France but not in the United States.

34. *Thornburgh,* 476 U.S. at 776 (Stevens, J., concurring).

35. *Id.* at 779.

36. "Transcript of Oral Argument in Abortion Case," *N.Y. Times,* April 27, 1989, at B12, col. 5 (former Solicitor General Fried, arguing on behalf of the United States). Counsel for Appellees gave the following complete reply: "It has always been my personal experience that when I pull a thread, my sleeve falls off." *Id.* at B13, col. 1 (argument of Mr. Susman).

37. *Thornburgh,* 476 U.S. at 775 (Stevens, J., concurring) (citing *Griswold* v. *Connecticut,* 381 U.S. 479, 502–03 (1965) (White, J., dissenting)).

38. *Griswold,* 381 U.S. at 497 (Goldberg, J., concurring).

39. *Meyer* v. *Nebraska,* 262 U.S. 390 (1923).

40. *Pierce* v. *Society of Sisters,* 268 U.S. 510 (1925).

41. *Id.* at 535.

42. See *Moore* v. *City of East Cleveland,* 431 U.S. 494, 503 n.11 (1977) (quoting from a discussion of *Griswold* in Pollak, "Thomas I. Emerson, Lawyer and Scholar: *Ipse Custodiet Custodes,*" 84 *Yale L.J.* 638, 653 (1975)).

43. 319 U.S. 624 (1943).

44. *Id.* at 640–41.

45. See generally Rubenfeld, "The Right of Privacy," 102 *Harv. L. Rev.* 737, 804–07 (1989) (arguing that the constitutional right of privacy protects individuals from being turned into instrumentalities of the regimenting state, or being forced into a state-chosen identity).

46. *Barnette,* 319 U.S. at 638.

47. Justice Douglas wrote:

> The Fathers of the Constitution were not unaware of the varied and extreme views of religious sects, of the violence of disagreement among them, and of the lack of any one religious creed on which all men would agree. They fashioned a charter of government which envisaged the widest possible toleration of conflicting views.

> *United States* v. *Ballard,* 322 U.S. 78, 87 (1944). See also *Webster,* 109 S. Ct. at 3085 & n.16 (Stevens, J., concurring in part and dissenting in part) (noting that "the intensely divisive character of much of the national debate over the abortion issue reflects the deeply held religious convictions of many participants in the debate").

48. *New State Ice Co.* v. *Liebmann,* 285 U.S. 262, 311 (1932) (Brandeis, J., dissenting).

49. *Poe* v. *Ullman,* 367 U.S. 497, 555 (1961) (Harlan, J., dissenting) (quoting *Skinner* v. *Oklahoma,* 316 U.S. 535, 546 (1942) (Jackson, J., concurring)).

50. *Everson* v. *Board of Educ.,* 330 U.S. 1, 65 (1947) (Appendix, Rutledge, J., dissenting) (quoting Madison, *Memorial and Remonstrance Against Religious Assessments).*

51. Nor, of course, did it bar political efforts to reduce the abortion rate through non-coercive means, such as funding sex education and contraception, or providing economic security to indigent mothers.

52. See Apple, "An Altered Political Climate Suddenly Surrounds Abortion," *N.Y. Times,* Oct. 13, 1989, at A1, col. 4; see also Berke, "The Abortion-Rights Movement Has Its Day," *N.Y. Times,* Oct. 15, 1989, § 4 at 1, col. 1.

53. *West Virginia Bd. of Educ.* v. *Barnette,* 319 U.S. 624, 638 (1943).

54. Even if only 10 or 11 states were to preclude abortion within their borders, many women would be held hostage there by the combination of geography, poverty, and youth. This situation would be no more tolerable than the enforcement of racial segregation in a "mere" ten or eleven states in the 1950s.

55. See *Michael M.* v. *Sonoma County Superior Court,* 450 U.S. 464, 473 (1981) ("[V]irtually all of the significant harmful and inescapably identifiable consequences of teenage pregnancy fall on the young female").

56. *Railway Express Agency* v. *New York,* 336 U.S. 106, 112 (1949) (Jackson, J., concurring).

57. See *Skinner* v. *Oklahoma,* 316 U.S. 535 (1942). *Cf.* Epstein, "The Supreme Court, 1987 Term: Foreword: Unconstitutional Conditions, State Power, and the Limits of Consent," 102 *Harv. L. Rev.* 4 (1988) (arguing that enforcement of unconstitutional conditions doctrine similarly functions to put legislatures to an all-or-nothing choice).

58. *Skinner,* 316 U.S. at 546 (Jackson, J., concurring).

59. *Webster,* 109 S. Ct. at 3045.

60. *Id.*

61. *Bradwell* v. *Illinois,* 83 U.S. (16 Wall.) 130, 142 (1873) (Bradley, J., concurring).

62. See J. Mohr, *Abortion in America: The Origins and Evolution of National Policy. 1800–1900,* at 168–72 (1978). To many of the doctors who were largely responsible for abortion restrictions, "the chief purpose of women was to produce children; anything that interfered with that purpose, or allowed women to 'indulge' themselves in less important activities, threatened . . . the future of society itself." *Id.* at 169. The view of one such 19th-century doctor drew the parallel even more explicitly: he complained that "the tendency to force women into men's places" was creating the insidious new idea that a woman's "ministrations . . . as a mother should be abandoned for the sterner rights of voting and law making." *Id.* at 105; see also L. Gordon, *Woman's Body, Woman's Right: A Social History of Birth Control in America* (1976) (chronicling the social and political history of reproductive rights in the United States).

63. See generally K. Luker, *Abortion and the Politics of Motherhood,* 192–215 (1984) (describing how the abortion debate, among women, represents a "war" between

the feminist vision of women in society and the homemaker's world view); Luker, "Abortion and the Meaning of Life," in *Abortion: Understanding Differences* 25, 31–33 (S. Callahan & D. Callahan eds. 1984) (concluding that "[b]ecause many prolife people see sex as literally sacred, *and because, for women, procreative sex is a fundamental part of their "career* . . . abortion is, from their [the prolife] point of view, to turn the world upside down").

64. Luker, *supra* note 63, at 31. It is, of course, precisely such stereotypes, as they are reflected in legislation, which have over and over again been the focus of this Court's modern equal protection cases. See, e.g., *Califano* v. *Goldfarb,* 430 U.S. 199, 206–07 (1977) ("Gender-based differentiation . . . is forbidden by the Constitution, at least when supported by no more substantial justification than 'archaic and overbroad' generalizations."); *Weinberger* v. *Wiesenfeld,* 420 U.S. 636, 645 (1975) ("Gender-based generalizations" that men are more likely than women to support their families "cannot suffice to justify the denigration of the effects of women who do work. . . ."): *Stanton* v. *Stanton,* 421 U.S. 7, 14 (1975) (A child, male or female, is still a child. No longer is the female destined solely for the home and the rearing of the family, and only the male for the marketplace and the world of ideas."); *Frontiero* v. *Richardson,* 441 U.S. 677, 684 (1973) ("[O]ur Nation has had a long and unfortunate history of sex discrimination . . . which in practical effect put women, not on a pedestal, but in a cage.").

65. *Griswold* v. *Connecticut,* 318 U.S. 479, 503 (1965) (White, J., concurring).

66. *Polgar & Fried,* "The Bad Old Days: Clandestine Abortions Among the Poor in New York City Before Liberalization of the Abortion Law," 8 *Fam. Plan. Persp.* 125 (1976); see also Gold, "Therapeutic Abortions in New York: A 20-Year Review," 55 *Am J. Pub. Health* 964, 66 (1965) (noting that the ratio of legal hospital abortions per live birth was 5 times more for white women than for women of color, and 26 times more for white women than for Puerto Rican women in New York City from 1951–62); Pilpel, "The Abortion Crisis," in *The Case for Legalized Abortion Now* 97, 101 (Guttmacher ed. 1967) (noting that 93% of in-hospital abortions in New York State were performed on white women who were able to afford private rooms).

67. See Niswander, "Medical Abortion Practice in the United States," in *Abortion and the Law,* 37, 37 (D. Smith ed. 1967).

68. See Gold, *supra* note 66, at 964–65.

69. Requiring prompt reporting of cases of rape and incest to criminal authorities, measured in terms of days if not hours, as the White House has suggested, is to ignore study after study that has found precisely such cases among the least often reported to the police. Yet late reporting, which should be encouraged, becomes grounds to deny funding, and excludes altogether those who fear, often with reasons, to report at all. The pain and suffering of brutal victimization and of an unwanted pregnancy are in no way affected by the speed of the initial criminal report. A small victory, indeed.

President Bush vetoed the legislation on October 21, 1989. The House vote to override was 231–191, short of the necessary two-thirds majority. See 135 *Cong. Rec.* H7482-95 (daily ed. Oct. 25, 1989).

Abortion on Demand Has No
Constitutional or Moral Justification

James Bopp, Jr., and Richard E. Coleson

I. THE ABSENCE OF A CONSTITUTIONAL RIGHT
TO ABORTION

Abortion is not mentioned in the United States Constitution. Yet, in *Roe* v. *Wade*,[1] the United States Supreme Court held that there is a constitutional right to abortion.

How could the Court justify such a decision? Actually, it never did. The Court simply *asserted* that the "right of privacy . . . is broad enough to encompass a woman's decision whether or not to terminate her pregnancy."[2] Leading constitutional scholars were outraged at the Court's action in *Roe* and vigorously argued that the Court had no constitutional power to create new constitutional rights in this fashion.[3] And, of course, many people were incensed that a whole class of innocent human beings—those awaiting birth—was stripped of all rights, including the right to life itself.

Why does it matter whether abortion is found in the Constitution? Why shouldn't the United States Supreme Court be free to create new constitutional rights whenever it chooses? The answers lie in the carefully designed structure of our democracy, whose blueprints were drawn over two centuries ago by the framers of the Constitution and ratified by the People. This design is explained below as the foundation for rejecting abortion on demand on a constitutional basis.

But what of abortion on demand as a legislative issue? Even if there is no constitutional right to abortion, how much should state legislatures restrict abortion? The answer lies in the states' compelling interest in protecting innocent human life, born or preborn. This interest is given scant attention by abortion rights advocates. Rather, they envision an extreme abortion-on-demand regime; but their societal vision is overwhelmingly rejected by public opinion. As shown below, the states constitutionally may and morally should limit abortion on demand.

A. The People Have Created a Constitutional Democracy With
Certain Matters Reserved to Democratic Control and Other
Matters Constitutionally Protected

The United States Constitution begins with the words "We the People of the United States . . . do ordain and establish this Constitution for the United States of America."[4] Thus, our Republic is founded on the cornerstone of democratic self-governance—all

James Bopp, Jr. is an attorney in the law firm of Bopp, Coleson, & Bostrom, Terre Haute, Indiana, and general counsel to the National Right to Life Committee, Inc. Richard E. Coleson is an associate with Bopp, Coleson, & Bostrom and general counsel, Indiana Citizens for Life, Inc. This article was written especially for Points of View *in 1992.*

authority to govern is granted by the People.[5] The only legitimate form of government is that authorized by the People; the only rightful authority is that which the People have granted to the institutions of government.[6]

The People have chosen to authorize a regime governed by the rule of law, rather than rule by persons.[7] The supreme law of the land is the Constitution,[8] the charter by which the People conferred authority to govern and created the governing institutions. Thus, the only legitimate form and authority for governance are found in the Constitution.

The constitutional grant of governing authority was not a general grant but one carefully measured, balanced, and limited. Three fundamental principles underlie the Constitution: (1) the People have removed certain matters from simple majority rule by making them constitutional rights but have retained other matters to be democratically controlled through their elected representatives;[9] (2) the People have distributed governmental powers among three branches of government, with each limited to its own sphere of power;[10] and (3) the People have established a federal system in which the power to regulate certain matters is granted to the national government and all remaining power is retained by the states or by the People themselves.[11]

Because these fundamental principles were violated by the Supreme Court in *Roe* v. *Wade,*[12] leading constitutional scholars condemned the decision. Law professors and dissenting Supreme Court Justices declared that the Court had seized power not granted to it in the Constitution, because (1) it had created new constitutional rights, which power only the People have,[13] (2) it had acted as a legislature rather than as a court,[14] and (3) it had trespassed into an area governed by the states for over two centuries.[15] The scholarly rejection of *Roe* v. *Wade* continues to the present.[16]

Although the Court's power grab in *Roe* was a seizure less obvious to the public than tanks in the street, it has nevertheless been rightly characterized as a "limited *coup d'état.*"[17] The Court seized from the People a matter they had left to their own democratic governance by declaring a constitutional right to abortion without establishing any connection between the Constitution and a right to abortion. Richard Epstein attacked the Court's *Roe* decision thus, "*Roe* . . . is symptomatic of the analytical poverty possible in constitutional litigation."[18] He concluded: "[W]e must criticize both Mr. Justice Blackmun in *Roe* v. *Wade* . . . and the entire method of constitutional interpretation that allows the Supreme Court . . . both to 'define' and to 'balance' interests on the major social and political issues of our time."[19]

B. To Determine Which Matters Are Constitutionally Removed from Democratic Control, the Supreme Court Has Developed Tests to Determine Fundamental Rights

The Court did not violate the Constitution in *Roe* simply because there is no *express* mention of abortion in the Constitution. There are matters which the Constitution does not *expressly* mention which the Supreme Court has legitimately found to be within some express constitutional protection. But where the Court employs such constitutional analysis, it must clearly demonstrate that the newly recognized constitutional right properly falls within the scope of an express right. This requires a careful examination and explanation of what the People intended when they ratified the particular constitutional provision in question. It was the *Roe* Court's failure to provide this logical connection between the Constitution and a claimed right to abortion which elicited scholarly outrage.

Under the Supreme Court's own tests, the Court had to find that the claimed right to abortion was a "fundamental" right in order to extend constitutional protection to it under the Fourteenth Amendment, the constitutional provision in which the Court claimed to have found a right to abortion.[20] The Fourteenth Amendment guarantees that no "State [shall] deprive any person of life, liberty, or property, without due process of law."[21] While the provision on its face seems to guarantee only proper legal proceedings before a state may impose capital punishment, imprisonment, or a fine, the Court has assumed the authority to examine activities asserted as constitutional rights to determine whether—in the Court's opinion—they fall within the concept of "liberty."[22] The notion that the Court may create new constitutional rights at will by reading them into the "liberty" clause of the Fourteenth Amendment could readily lead to a rejection of the foundational constitutional premise of the rule of law, not of persons. If a handful of Justices can place whatever matters they wish under the umbrella of the Constitution—totally bypassing the People and their elected representatives—then these Justices have constituted themselves as Platonic guardians,[23] thereby rejecting the rule of law for the rule of persons. What would prevent a majority of the Supreme Court from declaring that there is a constitutional right to practice, e.g., infanticide or polygamy (matters which the states have historically governed)?

This danger has caused many scholars to reject the sort of analysis which allows five Justices (a majority of the Court) to read new constitutional rights into the "liberty" clause.[24] It led the Court in earlier years to forcefully repudiate the sort of analysis the Court used in *Roe* v. *Wade*.[25] This danger has caused the current Court to establish more rigorous tests for what constitutes a constitutional right to prevent the Supreme Court from "roaming at large in the constitutional field."[26] These tests had been established at the time of *Roe,* but were ignored in that case.[27]

The Court has developed two tests for determining whether a new constitutional right should be recognized. The first test asks whether an asserted fundamental right is "implicit in the concept of ordered liberty."[28] The second test—a historical test—is whether the right asserted as "fundamental" is "so rooted in the traditions and conscience of our people as to be ranked as fundamental."[29] The historical test is the one now primarily relied upon by the Court.

C. Applying the Proper Test for Determining Constitutional Rights Reveals That Abortion Is Not a Constitutional Right

In *Roe,* the Court should have determined whether or not there is a constitutional right to abortion by asking whether it has historically been treated as "implicit in the concept of ordered liberty" in this nation or whether it has been "deeply rooted [as a right] in this Nation's history and tradition."

The *Roe* opinion itself recounted how abortion had been regulated by the states by statutory law for over a century and before that it had been regulated by the judge-made common law inherited from England.[30] In fact, the period from 1860 to 1880—the Fourteenth Amendment was ratified in 1868[31]—saw "the most important burst of anti-abortion legislation in the nation's history."[32] Therefore, the framers of the Fourteenth Amendment and the People who ratified it clearly did not intend for the Amendment to protect the right to abortion, which was considered a crime at the time.

Now Chief Justice Rehnquist stated well the case against *Roe*'s right to abortion in his 1973 dissent to that decision:

> To reach its result, the Court necessarily has had to find within the scope of the Fourteenth Amendment a right that was apparently completely unknown to the drafters of the Amendment. As early as 1821, the first state law dealing directly with abortion was enacted by the Connecticut Legislature. By the time of the adoption of the Fourteenth Amendment in 1868, there were at least 36 laws enacted by state or territorial legislatures limiting abortion. While many states have amended or updated their laws, 21 of the laws on the books in 1968 remain in effect today. Indeed, the Texas statute struck down today was, as the majority notes, first enacted in 1857 and has remained substantially unchanged to the present time.
>
> There apparently was no question concerning the validity of this provision or of any of the other state statutes when the Fourteenth Amendment was adopted. The only conclusion possible from this history is that the drafters did not intend to have the Fourteenth Amendment withdraw from the states the power to legislate with respect to this matter.[33]

Thus, applying the Court's own tests, it is clear that there is no constitutional right to abortion. As a result, the Supreme Court has simply arbitrarily declared one by saying that the right of privacy—previously found by the Court in the "liberty" clause—"is broad enough to encompass a woman's decision whether or not to terminate her pregnancy."[34] In so doing, the Court brushed aside the restraints placed on it by the Constitution, seized power from the People, and placed within the protections of the Constitution an abortion right that does not properly belong there.

One thing is clear from this nation's abortion debate: abortion advocates do not trust the People to decide how abortion should be regulated.[35] However, in rejecting the voice of the People, abortion partisans also reject the very foundation of our democratic Republic and seek to install an oligarchy—with the Court governing the nation—a system of government rejected by our Constitution.

II. THE INTEREST IN PROTECTING INNOCENT HUMAN LIFE

Abortion rights advocates generally ignore one key fact about abortion: abortion requires the willful taking of innocent human life. Abortion involves not merely the issue of what a woman may do with her body. Rather, abortion also involves the question of what may the woman do with the body of another, the unborn child.

A. The People Have an Interest in Protecting Preborn Human Life

The fact that human life begins at conception was well-known at the time the Fourteenth Amendment was ratified in 1868. In fact it was precisely during the time when this Amendment was adopted that the medical profession was carrying the news of the discovery of cell biology and its implications into the legislatures of the states and territories. Prior to that time, science had followed the view of Aristotle that the unborn child became a human being (i.e., received a human soul) at some point after conception (40 days for males and 80–90 days for females).[36] This flawed scientific view became the basis for the "quickening" (greater legal protection was provided to the unborn from abortion after the mother felt movement in the womb than before) distinction in the common law received from England, which imposed lesser penalties for abortions performed prior to "quickening." With the scientific discovery of cell biology, however, the legislatures acted promptly to alter abortion laws to reflect the newly established scientific fact that individual human life begins at conception.

Victor Rosenblum summarized the history well:

> Only in the second quarter of the nineteenth century did biological research advance to the extent of understanding the actual mechanism of human reproduction and of what truly comprised the onset of gestational development. The nineteenth century saw a gradual but profoundly influential revolution in the scientific understanding of the beginning of individual mammalian life. Although sperm had been discovered in 1677, the mammalian egg was not identified until 1827. The cell was first recognized as the structural unit of organisms in 1839, and the egg and sperm were recognized as cells in the next two decades. These developments were brought to the attention of the American state legislatures and public by those professionals most familiar with their unfolding import—physicians. It was the new research findings which persuaded doctors that the old "quickening" distinction embodied in the common and some statutory law was unscientific and indefensible.[37]

About 1857, the American Medical Association led the "physicians' crusade," a successful campaign to push the legal protection provided for the unborn by abortion laws from quickening to conception.[38]

What science discovered over a century before *Roe* v. *Wade* was true in 1973 (when *Roe* was decided) and still holds true today. For example, a recent textbook on human embryology declared:

> It is the penetration of the ovum by a spermatozoon and the resultant mingling of the nuclear material each brings to the union that constitutes the culmination of the process of *fertilization* and *marks the initiation of the life of a new individual.*[39]

However, abortion rights advocates attempt to obscure the scientific evidence that individual human life begins at conception by the claiming that conception is a "complex" process and by confusing contraception with abortion.[40]

The complexity of the process of conception does not change the fact that it marks the certain beginning of individual human life.[41] Moreover, the complex process of conception occurs in a very brief time at the beginning of pregnancy.[42]

Furthermore, the fact that some so-called "contraceptives" actually act after conception and would be more correctly termed "abortifacients" (substances or devices causing abortion, i.e., acting to abort a pregnancy already begun at conception) does nothing to blur the line at which individual human life begins. It only indicates that some so-called "contraceptives" have been mislabelled.[43] Such mislabelling misleads women, who have a right to know whether they are receiving a contraceptive or are having an abortion.

The "spin"[44] which abortion advocates place on the redefinition of "contraception" is deceptive in two respects. First, there is a clear distinction between devices and substances which act before conception and those which act after conception. This was admitted by Planned Parenthood itself (before it became involved in advocating, referring for, and performing abortions) in a 1963 pamphlet entitled *Plan Your Children*: "An abortion kills the life of a baby after it has begun. . . . Birth control merely postpones the beginning of life."[45]

Second, even if there were no "bright physiological line . . . between the moments before and after conception"[46] this does not mean there can be no constitutional line.[47] At *some point* early in pregnancy, scientific truth compels the conclusion that individual human life has begun. If the indistinction is the real problem, then abortion advocates should be joining prolife supporters in protecting unborn life from a time when there is certitude.[48] However, abortion partisans are not really interested in protecting unborn human life from the time when it may be certain that it exists. They are seeking to justify absolute, on-demand abortion throughout pregnancy.

B. Abortion Rights Advocates Envision an Abortion-on-Demand Regime Unsupported by the People

Abortion rights proponents often argue that our democratic Republic must sanction abortion on demand lest women resort to dangerous "back-alley" abortions. The claims of abortion advocates that thousands of women died each year when abortion was illegal are groundless fabrications created for polemical purposes.[49] In reality, the Surgeon General of the United States has estimated that only a handful of deaths occurred each year in the United States due to illegal abortions.[50] Even since *Roe,* there are still maternal deaths from legal abortions.[51] As tragic as the death of any person is, it must be acknowledged that women who obtain illegal abortions do so by choice and most women will choose to abide by the law. In contrast, preborn human beings are destroyed—without having a choice—at the rate of about 1.5 million per year in the United States alone.[52]

Abortion supporters also resort to the practice of personally attacking prolifers and making false charges about them.[53] A founding member of what is now called the National Abortion Rights Action League (NARAL) chronicles how prolifers were purposely portrayed as Catholics whenever possible, in an attempt to appeal to latent (and sometimes overt) anti-Catholic sentiment in certain communities.[54] It is also routinely claimed that opposition to abortion is really an attempt to "keep women in their place"[55]—to subjugate them—as if requiring fathers to support their children subjugates them. And prolifers are depicted as forcing what are merely their religious views upon society,[56] despite the fact that the United States Supreme Court has held that opposition to abortion "is as much a reflection of 'traditionalist' values towards abortion, as it is an embodiment of the views of any particular religion."[57] Those attempting so to "poison the well," by attacking prolife supporters with untruthful allegations, ignore the fact that polls consistently show that abortion opinion is rather evenly divided in our country within all major demographic groups. For example, women are roughly equally divided on the subject, as are whites, non-whites, Republicans and Democrats.[58] Abortion advocates also ignore the fact that most prolifers simply are opposed to the taking of what they consider (and science demonstrates) to be innocent human life.

Of even greater risk than the risk to a few women who might choose to obtain illegal abortions is the effect of abortion on demand—for any or no reason—on society. Abortion cheapens the value of human life, promotes the idea that it is permissible to solve one's problems at the expense of another, even to the taking of the other's life, legitimizes violence (which abortion is against the unborn) as an appropriate solution for problems, and exposes a whole class of human beings (those preborn) to discrimination on the basis of their age or place of residence (or sometimes their race, gender, or disability).

The regime which abortion-on-demand advocates envision for our society is a radical one. Their ideal society is one where abortions may be obtained for any reason, including simply because the child is the wrong sex; where a husband need not be given any consideration in (or even notice of) an abortion decision involving a child which he fathered; where fathers are shut out even when the child to be aborted might be the only one a man could ever have; where parents could remain ignorant of their daughter's abortion, even when she is persuaded to abort by counselors at an abortion mill whose practitioners care only about financial gain, practice their trade dangerously, and never bother to follow up with their patients; where abortion may be used as a means of birth control; where abortionists do not offer neutral, scientific information about fetal development (and about resources for choosing alternatives to abortion) to women considering abortion; where women are not given adequate time to consider whether they really want an abortion; where abortion is available right up to the time of birth; and where our taxes are used to pay for abortion on demand.[59]

The American People reject such a regime. In fact, polls show that an overwhelming majority would ban well over 90 percent of all abortions that are performed.[60] For example a *Boston Globe* national poll . . . revealed that:

> Most Americans would ban the vast majority of abortions performed in this country.
>
> . . .
>
> While 78 percent of the nation would keep abortion legal in limited circumstances, according to the poll, those circumstances account for a tiny percentage of the reasons cited by women having abortions.
>
> When pregnancy results from rape or incest, when the mother's physical health is endangered and when there is likely to be a genetic deformity in the fetus, those queried strongly approve of legal abortion.

But when pregnancy poses financial or emotional strain, or when the woman is alone or a teen-ager—the reasons given by most women seeking abortions—an overwhelming majority of Americans believes abortion should be illegal, the poll shows.[61]

Yet *Family Planning Perspectives,* a publication of the Alan Guttmacher Institute, which is a research arm of the Planned Parenthood Federation, reveals that these are precisely the reasons why over 90 percent of abortions are performed.[62]

Thus, it is little wonder that the Supreme Court's effort to settle the abortion question with its decision in *Roe* v. *Wade* has utterly failed. That there is not an even greater groundswell of public opposition to abortion must be attributed to the fact that many Americans are not aware that *Roe* requires virtual abortion on demand for the full nine months of pregnancy.[63] Many people still believe that abortion is only available in the earliest weeks of pregnancy and that abortions are usually obtained for grave reasons, such as rape and incest, which abortion rights advocates always talk about in abortion debates. Of course, such "hard" cases make up only a tiny fraction of all abortions, and many state abortion laws, even before *Roe,* allowed abortions for such grave reasons. It is clear, therefore, that the People reject the radical abortion-on-demand regime promoted by abortion rights advocates.

III. CONCLUSION: STATES CONSTITUTIONALLY MAY AND MORALLY SHOULD LIMIT ABORTION ON DEMAND

One of the principles underlying our liberal democratic Republic is that we as a People choose to give the maximum freedom possible to members of our society. John Stuart Mill's essay *On Liberty,*[64] a ubiquitous source on the subject, is often cited for the principle that people ought to be granted maximum liberty—almost to the degree of license. Yet, Mill himself set limits on liberty relevant to the abortion debate. Mill wrote his essay *On Liberty* to assert "one very simple principle," namely, "[t]hat the only purpose for which power can be rightfully exercised over any member of a civilized community, against his will, is to prevent harm to others."[65] Thus, under Mill's principles, abortion should go unrestricted only if it does no harm to another. But that, of course, is precisely the core of the abortion debate. If a fetus is not really an individual human being until he or she is born, then the moral issue is reduced to what duty is owed to potential life (which is still a significant moral issue). If however, a fetus is an individual human being from the moment of conception (or at least some time shortly thereafter), then the unborn are entitled to legal protection. Ironically, the United States Supreme Court neglected this key determination—when human life begins—in its *Roe* decision.[66]

Science, of course, has provided the answer to us for well over a hundred years. Indeed, modern science and technological advances have impressed upon us more fully the humanity and individuality of each unborn person. As Dr. Liley has said:

> Another fallacy that modern obstetrics discards is the idea that the pregnant woman can be treated as a patient alone. No problem in fetal health or disease can any longer be

considered in isolation. At the very least two people are involved, the mother and her child.[67]

In fact, since *Roe,* the technology for improving fetal therapy is advancing exponentially.[68] In sum, modern science has shown us that:

> The fetus as patient is becoming more of a reality each year. New medical therapies and surgical technology increasingly offer parents a new choice when a fetus has a particular disorder. Recently, the only choices were abortion, early delivery, vaginal versus a cesarean delivery, or no intervention. We are now able to offer medical and/or surgical intervention as a viable alternative to a number of infants. With advancing technologies, it is clearly evident that many new and exciting therapies lie just ahead for the fetus.[69]

Because all civilized moral codes limit the liberty of individuals where the exercise of liberty would result in the taking of innocent human life, arguments that abortion is necessary to prevent the subjugation of women must also be rejected.[70] It cannot logically be considered the subjugation of anyone to prevent him or her from taking innocent human life; otherwise, society could not prevent infanticide, homicide, or involuntary euthanasia. No civilized society could exist if the unjustified killing of one citizen by another could not be prosecuted.

Nor do abortion restrictions deny women equality by denying them the same freedom which men have. Men do not have the right to kill their children, nor may they force women to do so. Thus, abortion rights advocates are really arguing for a right that men don't have, and, indeed, no one should have—the right to take innocent human life.

Society has recognized that in some situations men and women should be treated differently, because they are biologically different and are, therefore, not similarly situated for constitutional purposes. For example, the Supreme Court decided in 1981 that a statute that permitted only men to be drafted was not unconstitutional because "[m]en and women . . . are simply not similarly situated for purposes of a draft or registration for a draft."[71] The same principle, however, made constitutional a Navy policy which allowed women a longer period of time for promotion prior to mandatory discharge than was allowed for men.[72] The Supreme Court in this case found that "the different treatment of men and women naval officers . . . reflects, not archaic and overbroad generalizations, but, instead, the demonstrable fact that male and female line officers . . . are not similarly situated."[73] Because men and women are not similarly situated—by the dictates of nature rather than by society or the law—with respect to pregnancy, it is neither a denial of equality to women nor the subjugation of women to provide legal protection for unborn human beings.[74]

It is essential to a civilized society to limit liberties where reasonably necessary to protect others. Thus, government has required involuntary vaccination to prevent a plague from decimating the community,[75] military conscription to prevent annihilation of the populace by enemies,[76] and the imposition of child support—for 18 years—upon fathers unwilling to support their children.[77] These and other limits on freedom are not the subjugation of citizens, but are the essence of life in a community.

In sum, the states constitutionally may and morally should limit abortion on demand.

NOTES

1. 410 U.S. 113 (1973).
2. *Id.* at 153.
3. See *infra,* notes 13–19 and accompanying text.
4. U.S. Const., preamble.
5. In the landmark case of *Marbury* v. *Madison,* 1 Cranch 137, 176 (1803), the United States Supreme Court explained, "That the people have an original right to establish, for their future government, such principles, as, in their own opinion, shall most conduce to their own happiness is the basis on which the whole American fabric has been erected. See also The Declaration of Independence, para. 2 (U.S. 1776); *The Federalist,* No. 49 (J. Madison).
6. *Marbury,* 1 Cranch at 176 ("The original and supreme will [of the People] organizes the government, and assigns to different departments their respective powers. It may either stop here, or establish certain limits not to be transcended by those departments. The government of the United States is of the latter description.").
7. See, e.g., *id.* at 163 ("The government of the United States has been emphatically termed a government of laws, and not of men."); *Akron* v. *Akron Center for Reproductive Health,* 462 U.S. 416, 419–20 (1983) (We are a "society governed by the rule of law.").
8. *Marbury,* 1 Cranch at 177 ("Certainly all those who have framed written constitutions contemplate them as forming the fundamental and paramount law of the nation. . . ."); *id.* at 179 ("[T]he constitution of the United States confirms and strengthens the principle, supposed to be essential to all written constitutions, that a law repugnant to the constitution is void; and that courts, as well as other departments, are bound by that instrument.").
9. The Constitution enumerates certain rights; the creation of additional constitutionally protected rights is through amending the Constitution, which depends upon establishing public support for such a right by a supermajority of the People acting through their elected representatives. U.S. Const., art. V. *Cf.* Bork, "Neutral Principles and Some First Amendment Problems," 47 *Ind. L.J.* 1, 3 (1971).
10. U.S. Const., art. I, § 1, art. II, § 1, art. III, § 1.
11. U.S. Const., amend. IX ("The enumeration in the Constitution, of certain rights, shall not be construed to deny or disparage others retained by the people."), amend. X ("The powers not delegated to the United States by the Constitution, nor prohibited by it to the States, are reserved to the States respectively, or to the people.").
12. 410 U.S. 113.
13. Ely, "The Wages of Crying Wolf: A Comment on *Roe* v. *Wade,*" 82 *Yale L.J.* 920, 947 (1973) (*Roe* was "a very bad decision. Not because it [would] perceptibly weaken the Court . . . and not because it conflict[ed] with [his] idea of progress. . . . It [was] bad because it [was] bad constitutional law, or rather because it [was] *not* constitutional law and [gave] almost no sense of an obligation to try to be.") (emphasis in the original). *Doe* v. *Bolton,* 410 U.S. 179, 222 (1973) (White, J., dissenting in this companion case to *Roe*) (The Court's action is "an exercise of raw

judicial power. . . . This issue, for the most part, should be left with the people and to the political processes the people have devised to govern their affairs.").

14. The *Michigan Law Review,* in an edition devoted to abortion jurisprudence, contained two passages which summarize the scholarly critiques well. In the first, Richard Morgan wrote:

> Rarely does the Supreme Court invite critical outrage as it did in *Roe* by offering so little explanation for a decision that requires so much. The stark inadequacy of the Court's attempt to justify its conclusions . . . suggests to some scholars that the Court, finding no justification at all in the Constitution, unabashedly usurped the legislative function.

Morgan, "*Roe* v. *Wade* and the Lesson of the Pre-*Roe* Case Law." 77 *Mich. L. Rev.* 1724, 1724 (1979). The editors of the journal concluded from their survey of the literature on *Roe,* "[T]he consensus among legal academics seems to be that, whatever one thinks of the holding, the opinion is unsatisfying." "Editor's Preface," 77 *Mich. L. Rev.* (no number) (1979).

15. *Roe,* 400 U.S. at 174–77 (Rehnquist, J., dissenting).

16. See, e.g., Wardle, " 'Time Enough': *Webster* v. *Reproductive Health Services* and the Prudent Pace of Justice," 41 *Fla. L. Rev.* 881, 927–49 (1989); Bopp & Coleson, "The Right to Abortion: Anomalous, Absolute, and Ripe for Reversal," 3 *B.Y.U. J. Pub. L.* 181, 185–92 (1989) (cataloging critiques of *Roe* in yet another critique of *Roe*).

17. Bork, *supra* note 9, at 6.

18. Epstein, "Substantive Due Process by Any Other Name: The Abortion Cases," 1973 *Sup. Ct. Rv.* 159, 184.

19. *Id.* at 185.

20. The Court acknowledged this duty in *Roe* itself, but failed to apply the usual tests for determining what rights are rightfully deemed "fundamental." *Roe,* 410 U.S. at 152.

21. U.S. Const., amend. XIV, § 1, cl. 3.

22. *Roe* v. *Wade,* 410 U.S. 113, revived this sort of "substantive due process" analysis in recent years.

23. The Greek philosopher Plato advocated rule by a class of philosopher-guardians as the ideal form of government. A. Bloom, *The Republic of Plato,* 376c, lines 4–5, 412b–427d (1968).

24. See, e.g., Ely, *supra* note 13; Bork, *supra* note 9.

25. In repudiating an earlier line of "substantive due process" (i.e., finding new rights in the "liberty" clause of the Fourteenth Amendment) cases symbolized by *Lochner* v. *New York,* 198 U.S. 45 (1905), the Supreme Court declared that the doctrine "that due process authorizes courts to hold laws unconstitutional when they believe the legislature has acted unwisely, has been discarded." *Ferguson* v. *Skrupa,* 372 U.S. 726, 730 (1963). The Court concluded in *Ferguson,* "We have returned to the original constitutional proposition that courts do not substitute their social and economic beliefs for the judgment of legislative bodies, who are elected to pass laws." *Id.*

26. *Griswold* v. *Connecticut,* 381 U.S. 479, 502 (1965) (Harlan, J., concurring.)

27. *Cf. Duncan* v. *Louisiana,* 391 U.S. 145, 149–50 n.14 (1968), with *Roe* v. *Wade,* 410 U.S. at 152, and *Moore* v. *City of East Cleveland,* 431 U.S. 494, 503–04 n.12 (1977). See also Ely, *supra* note 13, at 931 n.79 (The *Palko* test was of "questionable contemporary vitality" when *Roe* was decided).

28. *Roe,* 410 U.S. at 152 (quoting *Palko* v. *Connecticut,* 302 U.S. 319, 325 (1937)) (quotation marks omitted).

29. *Palko,* 302 U.S., at 325 (quoting *Snyder* v. *Massachusetts,* 291 U.S. 97, 105 (1934)) (quotation marks omitted).

30. *Roe,* 410 U.S. at 139.

31. *Black's Law Dictionary,* 1500 (5th ed. 1979).

32. J. Mohr, *Abortion in America: The Origins and Evolution of National Policy 1800–1900,* 200 (1978). These laws were clearly aimed at protecting preborn human beings and not just maternal health, *id.* at 35–36, so that medical improvements bringing more maternal safety to abortions do not undercut the foundations of these laws, as *Roe* alleged. *Roe,* 410 U.S. at 151–52.

33. *Roe,* 410 U.S. at 174–77 (Rehnquist, J., dissenting) (citations and quotation marks omitted).

34. *Id.* at 153.

35. *Cf.* Estrich & Sullivan, "Abortion Politics: Writing for an Audience of One," 138 *U. Pa. L. Rev.* 119, 150–55 (1989), with *Webster* v. *Reproductive Health Services,* 109 S. Ct. 3040, 3058 (1989) (plurality opinion). In *Webster,* the plurality opinion declared:

> The goal of constitutional adjudication is to hold true the balance between that which the Constitution puts beyond the reach of the democratic process and that which it does not. We think we have done that today. The dissent's suggestion that legislative bodies, in a Nation where more than half of our population is women, will treat our decision today as an invitation to enact abortion regulation reminiscent of the dark ages not only misreads our views but does scant justice to those who serve in such bodies and the people who elect them.

Id. (citation omitted).

36. *Roe,* 410 U.S. at 133 n.22.

37. *The Human Life Bill: Hearings on S. 158 Before the Subcomm. on Separation of Powers of the Senate Comm. on the Judiciary,* 97th Cong., 1st Sess. 474 (statement of Victor Rosenblum). See also Dellapenna, "The History of Abortion: Technology, Morality, and Law," 40 *U. Pitt. L. Rev.* 359, 402–04 (1979).

38. J. Mohr, *supra* note 32, at 147–70. This 19th-century legislation was designed to protect the unborn as stated explicitly by 11 state court decisions interpreting these statutes and implicitly by 9 others. Gorby, "The 'Right' to an Abortion, the Scope of Fourteenth Amendment 'Personhood,' and the Supreme Court's Birth Requirement," 1979 *S. Ill, U.L.J.* 1, 16–17. Twenty-six of the 36 states had laws against abortion as early as 1865, the end of the Civil War, as did six of the ten territories. Dellapenna, *supra* note 37, at 429.

39. B. Patten, *Human Embryology,* 43 (3rd ed. 1969) (emphasis added). See also L. Arey, *Developmental Anatomy,* 55 (7th ed. 1974); W. Hamilton & H. Mossman,

Human Embryology, 1, 14 (4th ed. 1972); K. Moore, *The Developing Human: Clinically Oriented Embryology,* 1, 12, 24 (2nd ed. 1977); *Human Reproduction, Conception and Contraception,* 461 (Hafez ed., 2nd ed. 1980); J. Greenhill & E. Friedman, *Biological Principles and Modern Practice of Obstetrics,* 17, 23 (1974); D. Reid, K. Ryan & K. Benirschke, *Principles and Management of Human Reproduction,* 176 (1972).

40. See, e.g., Estrich & Sullivan, *supra* note 35, at 128–29. While a complete discussion of cell biology, genetics and fetology is beyond the scope of this brief writing, the standard reference works cited by Estrich & Sullivan verify the fact that individual human life begins at conception.

41. *Supra,* note 39.

42. *Id.*

43. By its etymology (*contra + conception,* i.e., against conception) and traditional and common usage, the term *"contraception"* properly refers to "[t]he prevention of conception or impregnation." *Dorland's Illustrated Medical Dictionary,* 339 (24th ed. 1965) or a "deliberate prevention of conception or impregnation," *Webster's Ninth New Collegiate Dictionary,* 284 (1985).

44. Estrich & Sullivan, *supra* note 35, at 1.

45. Planned Parenthood International, *Plan Your Children* (1963).

46. Estrich & Sullivan, *supra* note 35, at 129.

47. At oral arguments in *Webster* v. *Reproductive Health Services,* 109 S. Ct. 3040 (1989), Justice Antonin Scalia could see a distinction between contraception and abortion, remarking, "I don't see why a court that can draw that line [between the first, second, and third trimesters of pregnancy] cannot separate abortion from birth control quite readily."

48. For example, the West German Constitutional Court in 1975 set aside a federal abortion statute which was too permissive, for it "did not sufficiently protect unborn life." M. Glendon, *Abortion and Divorce in Western Law,* 33 (1987). The West German court began with the presumption that "at least after the fourteenth day, developing human life is at stake." *Id.* at 34.

49. B. Nathanson, *Aborting America,* 193 (1979). Nathanson, a former abortionist and early, organizing member of the National Association for the Repeal of Abortion Laws (NARAL, now known as the National Abortion Rights Action League), says:

In N.A.R.A.L. . . . . it was always "5,000 to 10,000 deaths a year [from illegal abortion]." I confess that I knew the figures were totally false. . . . In 1967, with moderate A.L.I.-type laws in three states, the federal government listed only 160 deaths from illegal abortion. In the last year before the [*Roe*] era began, 1972, the total was only 39 deaths. Christopher Tietze estimated 1,000 maternal deaths as the outside possibility in an average year before legalization; the actual total was probably closer to 500.

Id. at 193. Nathanson adds that even this limited "carnage" argument must now be dismissed "because technology has eliminated it." *Id.* at 194 (referring to the fact that even abortions made illegal by more restrictive abortion laws will generally be performed with modern techniques providing greater safety, and antibiotics now resolve most complications).

50. U.S. Dept. of Health and Human Services, *Centers for Disease Control Abortion Surveillance,* 61 (annual summary 1978, issued Nov. 1980) (finding that there were 39 maternal deaths due to illegal abortion in 1972, the last year before *Roe*).

51. Deaths from legally induced abortions were as follows: 1972 = 24, 1973 = 26, 1974 = 26, 1975 = 31, 1976 = 11, 1977 = 17, 1978 = 11. *Id.* During the same period, deaths from illegal abortions continued as follows: 1972 = 39, 1973 = 19, 1974 = 6, 1975 = 4, 1976 = 2, 1977 = 4, 1978 = 7. *Id.*

52. See, e.g., Henshaw, Forrest & Van Vort, "Abortion Services in the United States, 1984 and 1985," 19 *Fam. Plan. Persps.* 64, table 1 (1987) (at the rate of roughly 1.5 million abortions per year for the 18 years from 1973 to 1990, there have been about 27 million abortions in the U.S.A.).

53. Estrich & Sullivan, *supra* note 35, at 152–54.

54. B. Nathanson, *The Abortion Papers: Inside the Abortion Mentality,* 177–209 (1983).

55. Estrich & Sullivan, *supra* note 35, at 152–54.

56. See, e.g., *id.* at 153 n.132.

57. *Harris* v. *McRae,* 448 U.S. 297, 319 (1980).

58. See generally R. Adamek, *Abortion and Public Opinion in the United States* (1989).

59. These are some of the radical positions urged by abortion rights partisans in cases such as *Roe* v. *Wade,* 410 U.S. 113, *Planned Parenthood of Central Missouri* v. *Danforth,* 428 U.S. 52 (1976), and *Thornburgh* v. *American College of Obstetricians and Gynecologists,* 476 U.S. 747 (1986).

60. "Most in US favor ban on majority of abortions, poll finds," *Boston Globe,* March 31, 1989, at 1, col. 2–4.

61. *Id.*

62. Torres & Forrest, "Why Do Women Have Abortions?" 20 *Fam. Plan. Persps.,* 169 (1988). Table 1 of this article reveals the following reasons and percentages of women giving their most important reason for choosing abortion: 16% said they were concerned about how having a baby would change their life; 21% said they couldn't afford a baby now; 12% said they had problems with a relationship and wanted to avoid single parenthood; 21% said they were unready for responsibility; 1% said they didn't want others to know they had sex or were pregnant; 11% said they were not mature enough or were too young to have a child; 8% said they had all the children they wanted or had all grown-up children; 1% said their husband wanted them to have an abortion; 3% said the fetus had possible health problems; 3% said they had a health problem; less than .5% said their parents wanted them to have an abortion; 1% said they were a victim of rape or incest; and 3% gave another, unspecified reason. (Figures total more than 100% due to rounding off of numbers.) It is significant to note, also, that 39% of all abortions are repeat abortions. Henshaw, "Characteristics of U.S. Women Having Abortions, 1982–1983," 19 *Fam. Plan. Persps.* 1, 6 (1987).

63. *Roe* held that a state may prohibit abortion after fetal viability, but that it may not do so where the mother's "life or health" would be at risk. 410 U.S. at 165. In the companion case to *Roe, Doe* v. *Bolton,* the Supreme Court construed "health" in an

extremely broad fashion to include "all factors—physical, emotional, psychological, familial, and the woman's age—relevant to the well-being of the patient." 410 U.S. 179, 195 (1973). The breadth of these factors makes a "health" reason for an abortion extremely easy to establish, so that we have virtual abortion on demand for all nine months of pregnancy in America. Moreover, there are physicians who declare that if a woman simply seeks an abortion she *ipso facto* has a "health" reason and the abortion may be performed. *McRae* v. *Califano,* No. 76-C-1804 (E.D.N.Y. Transcript, August 3, 1977, pp. 99–101) (Testimony of Dr. Jane Hodgson) (Dr. Hodgson testified that she felt that there was a medical indication to abort a pregnancy if it "is not wanted by the patient.").

64. J. Mill, *On Liberty* (Atlantic Monthly Press edition 1921).

65. *Id.* at 13. It should be noted that Mill's contention that society should never use its power to protect the individual from the actions of himself or herself is hotly disputed. See, e.g., J. Stephen, *Liberty, Equality, Fraternity* (R. White ed. 1967) (the 1873 classic response to Mill); P. Devlin, *The Enforcement of Morals* (1974).

66. *Roe,* 410 U.S. at 159 ("We need not resolve the difficult question of when life begins.").

67. H. Liley, *Modern Motherhood* 207 (1969).

68. "Technology for Improving Fetal Therapy Advancing Exponentially," *Ob. Gyn. News,* Aug. 1–14, 1987, at 31.

69. P. Williams, "Medical and Surgical Treatment for the Unborn Child," in *Human Life and Health Care Ethics,* 77 (J. Bopp ed. 1985).

70. Estrich & Sullivan, *supra* note 35, at 152–54. In legal terms, this argument is an equal protection one. See *id.* at 124 n.10. However, equal protection of the laws is only constitutionally guaranteed to those who are equally situated, and the Supreme Court has held that treating pregnancy differently from other matters does not constitute gender-based discrimination. *Geduldig* v. *Aiello,* 417 U.S. 484, 496–97 n.20 (1974). For a further discussion of this point, see Bopp, "Will There Be a Constitutional Right to Abortion After the Reconsideration of *Roe* v. *Wade?*" 15 *J. Contemp. L.* 131, 136–41 (1989). See also Smolin, "Why Abortion Rights Are Not Justified by Reference to Gender Equality: A Response to Professor Tribe," 23 *John Marshall L. Rev.* 621 (1990).

71. *Rostker* v. *Goldberg,* 453 U.S. 57 (1981).

72. *Schlesinger* v. *Ballard,* 419 U.S. 498 (1975).

73. *Id.* at 508.

74. Bopp, "Is Equal Protection a Shelter for the Right to Abortion?" in *Abortion, Medicine and the Law* (4th ed. 1991) (in press).

75. *Jacobson* v. *Massachusetts,* 197 U.S. 11 (1905).

76. The Selective Service Draft Law Cases, 245 U.S. 366 (1918).

77. See, e.g., *Sistare* v. *Sistare,* 218 U.S. 1 (1910). All states have recognized this obligation by passage of the Uniform Reciprocal Enforcement of Support Act. See Fox, "The Uniform Reciprocal Enforcement of Support Act," 12 *Fam. L.Q.* 113, 113–14 (1978).